BHAKTI MOVEMENT IN MEDIEVAL INDIA

Bhakti Movement in Medieval India
Social and Political Perspectives

SHAHABUDDIN IRAQI

CENTRE OF ADVANCED STUDY
Department of History
Aligarh Muslim University

MANOHAR
2009

First published 2009

© Shahabuddin Iraqi, 2009

All rights reserved. No part of this publication may be reproduced or transmitted, in any form or by any means, without prior permission of the author and the publisher

ISBN 978-81-7304-800-5

Published by
Ajay Kumar Jain *for*
Manohar Publishers & Distributors
4753/23 Ansari Road, Daryaganj
New Delhi 110 002

Typeset at
Digigrafics
New Delhi 110 049

Printed at
Salasar Imaging Systems
Delhi 110 035

To
*the Sants and Sufis for their
contribution to the development of a
composite culture in India*

Contents

Preface	9
Acknowledgements	11
Introduction	13
1. Hindus Under Muslim Rule	29
2. Sufism in India	55
3. The Bhakti Movement and the Evolution of its Thought	102
4. Historical Importance of the *Sant-sahitya* or Bhakti Literature	115
5. Kabir and His Followers	144
6. Nanak and His Followers	168
7. Dadu and His Followers	189
8. Maharashtra Dharma	213
9. The Pranami Sect	225
10. The Satnami Sect of Narnaul	229
11. The Response and Reactions of Some Other Cults	237
12. Interaction between *Sant* and Sufi	241
Conclusion	258
Bibliography	271
Index	283

Preface

It is generally understood that the bhakti saints were peace loving reformers of their respective communities. The fact is, however, that the Bhakti movement that emerged in northern India in the beginning of the fifteenth century comprised two schools, *Saguna Bhakti* and *Nirguna Bhakti*. Saguna Bhakti leaders like Tulsidas were revivalist in the sense that they stood for adherence to traditional Hinduism and the varna system. In contrast, Nirguna Bhakti led by non-conformist men like Kabir, Nanak, and Dadu formed a spiritual movement outside the institutional fold of Hindusim.

Most of the Nirguna Bhakti saints who came to prominence in northern and central India in the fifteenth to seventeenth centuries and were born Hindu or Muslim, belonged to the lower strata of society. They adhered neither to Hindusim nor to Islam and rejected the whole system and all norms of institutionalized religion. They dealt with the practical aspects of human life, having certain aims and objectives in mind. Their voices of protest were, therefore, not confined to religious issues but extended to socio-economic problems and even to the political and administrative sphere. A number of such saints became political and at times even resorted to armed resistance against their rulers for the attainment of their political ends.

My study offers an analysis of different trends of bhakti thought and movement and their impact on society. This book consists of twelve chapters and a conclusion. The first chapter deals with the attitude of the Muslim rulers, nobles, and ulama towards all categories of Indian people; the second depicts the position of different Sufi orders, their institutional organization, and their practices. The third chapter is devoted to the evolution of bhakti thought and the nature and character of the movement in northern India from the fifteenth century onwards. Chapter 4 provides a detailed description of bhakti literature in historical perspective.

The three chapters that follow spell out a critical assessment of the role played by Kabir, Nanak, and Dadu and their followers in the religious life and also in political and administrative matters of the time. There is a focus on the problems of revenue administration and the commercial system of medieval times that led to the exploitation of common people.

Chapters 8 and 9 cover the spiritual and political functions of Maharashtra Dharma and the Pranami sect. Although Guru Ramdas in Maharashtra and Prannath in Bundelkhand talked about communal harmony by emphasizing the unity of religions and of human beings, in political matters they exploited the religious sentiments of the Hindus in favour of Shivaji and Chhatrasal Bundela, against the Mughals. An attempt has been made in these chapters to explain how certain religious movements turned political, infused with militant Hindu revivalism, to provide a favourable communal background to the political leaders in their wars against the Mughals. Chapter 10 deals with the militant character of the Satnamis and their rebellion against Aurangzeb. The role of the holy men of the *Pushti Marga* and of the Radha-Vallabha Sect discussed in the following chapter. While some of the men of these orders were associated with the Mughal government, there were others who disliked visiting the royal court and did not accept royal gifts. For instance, a holy person named Kumbhandas visited the court of Akbar on persuasion, but declined to accept the gifts offered by the Emperor.

In Chapter 12 the interaction between the thoughts and practices of different Sufi orders and those of the saints of different indigenous cults has been analysed showing the extent of their mutual understanding and co-existence in the country. The hitherto misunderstood and misinterpreted problem of conversion has also been discussed here. It is hoped that the book will open new vistas of research for further probe into the matter.

SHAHABUDDIN IRAQI

Acknowledgements

I feel it my pleasant duty to thank all those who helped and cooperated with me in different ways in the completion of this book. Firstly, I express my grateful thanks to the authorities and staff of the following institutions and libraries, who extended to me all necessary facilities in taping and utilizing the relevant source material in Hindi for preparation of the text of the book:

1. Kashi Nagari Pracharini Sabha, Banaras
2. Dadu Mahavidyalaya, Jaipur
3. Rajasthan Oriental Research Institute, Jodhpur
4. Saraswati Bhandar, Udaipur
5. Sahitya Sammelan, Prayag
6. Punjab University Library, Punjab

I am also indebted to the staff of Maulana Azad Library, Aligarh Muslim University, Aligarh and the staff of our Research Library, Department of History, AMU, Aligarh, who extended full co-operation to me during the collection of material and drafting of the text.

I am extremely grateful to my colleagues and the staff of our Department for their fraternal help and cooperation at various levels during the preparation of the manuscript. Prof. Iqtidar Husain Siddiqui, Prof. B.L. Bhadani, Prof. Tariq Ahmad, Dr. S.L.H. Moini, Dr. M. Afzal Khan, Dr. Ali Athar, Dr. Iqbal Sabir, Dr. Hasan Imam and Dr. S. Bashir Hasan deserve special mention in this regard.

My special obligation is due to my mother, Ms. Noor Jahan, Begum Late Mr. Zainul Abedin, and my wife Mrs. Iffat Ara Iraqi, who provided conducive atmosphere at home to enable me to complete the work with full concentration.

Last but not the least I am especially beholden to Ramesh Jain of Manohar Publishers & Distributors who took a keen interest in the production of this book.

SHAHABUDDIN IRAQI

Introduction

The tradition of religious thought in India is incredibly long, complicated and complex. The four Vedas, known as Samhitas or revealed scripture, are considered to be the primary source of religion and philosophy in Hinduism. The twelve Upanishads constitute the latest in the Vedic tradition, and the Puranas, Shastras and *Bhagavad Gita* are considered Smriti.

In the Vedic period the religious system was simple. The Vedas contained simply certain *vidhis* (commandments) as well as *nisedhas* (prohibitions) followed by stories to explain them. At that time only the nature gods and goddesses were worshipped. Different sections of Vedic people worshipped different nature gods such as the *soma* plant and fire.[1] Thus there was a conflicting trend which Max Müller termed henotheism.[2]

Subsequently, there appeared two currents of thought opposed to each other, orthodox and heterodox, which gave way to the evolution of two schools, one represented by Sankhya, Patanjala, Nyaya-Vaisheshika, and Mimamsa and the other by Jainism, Buddhism, and Charvaka. The first set of schools remained within the Vedic tradition, the others flourished outside of it. It is significant that the division was not on the basis of whether they believed in God but whether they believed in the scriptural authority of the Vedas. Thus all radical forces invariably fell outside the Vedic tradition. The basic difference in approach was that the orthodox schools held household life as the ideal and heaven as the goal, but the heterodox schools believed in asceticism and *nirvana* (salvation) as the goal, which led to belief in the theory of *avagaman* (the transmigration of the soul).

However, within the Vedic tradition itself the simplicity of religion was eclipsed by philosophical developments during the Vedanta and post-Vedic period, i.e. from about AD 400 onwards, when the Upanishads, Brahma Sutras, *Bhagavad Gita*, and the Puranas were written. The religion underwent a major change during the Puranic period. *Brahmavid apnoti param* meant that the knower of Brahma attains the highest, which stood for the unity of the threefold Vedantic system of *tattva* (philosophical apprehension of reality) *hita* (moral and spiritual methods of knowing), and *purusartha* (direct knowledge of reality).³ Consequently, there appeared different approaches and the major trends being two. The monistic concept lead to *nirguna* or the formless aspect of God, and defined God as *neti, neti* (neither this nor that) but otherwise found Him everywhere without apparent form or attributes. The second concept was to hold God as ruler, creator, and destroyer of universe, which are possible only when God has form and attributes. The different approaches led to the rise of *manan*, logical or rational thinking on the essence and attributes of God.

It is significant that about the same time in Islamic philosophy too, there emerged a similar trend of logical thinking with argumentation which was termed as *Ilam-ul Kalam* (scholasticism). In the eighth and ninth centuries the Mutazalites attempted to reconcile the *zat* (essence) and *sifat* (attributes) of God.⁴ The Quran asserts the unity of God as One, Absolute, and Eternal. But His attributes are also explicitly described as all-powerful, merciful, just, all-seeing, etc. This led to a controversy among scholars. The Mutazalites came up with two alternatives. Attributes either coexisted with the essence, or developed later. But both alternatives were un-Islamic, because the first suggested that two things were eternally living together and the second denoted that the essence was previously imperfect and became perfect later with the addition of attributes. Thus divine attributes were taken as identical with the essence. Opposed to this school there appeared the *asharism* of the tenth and eleventh centuries,⁵ a philosophy believing in both revelation and realization. The Asharites introduced the doctrine of *mukhalafa* or dissent and tried to reconcile the problem by saying that the attributes too are eternal, neither identical with nor different from the essence (لاعين ولاغيره) but co-existing in a unique form. The great philosopher Imam Ghazali (1058–1111) took this situation to be a danger to Islam and condemned all such logical or rational interpretations. He said it was sufficient to have faith in one God.

As mentioned above, logical thinking regarding the relationship between the essence and the attributes of God had already been

Introduction 15

developed by the Vedantists. This trend was experienced not only in monistic sphere but otherwise also. Ancient Indian intellectuals were advanced in religious philosophy and evolved an epistemology or theory of knowledge.[6] This was based on *janatra* (knower) and *janeya* (object), roughly corresponding to mind and matter of the Europeans. Not only this, Indians also found six sources of knowledge as against two of the West, perception and inference. The Indian sources are *pratyaksa* or perception; *anuman* or inference; *sabda* or the testimony of scripture; *upamāna* or similarity from comparison; *arthapatti* or supposition; and *anupalabdhi* or non-cognition by wisdom, a unique source of knowledge. The first source was particularly taken up by the heterodox schools, and the second and third by all except the Charvaka, a materialistic school.

Such diverse approaches led to the emergence of different schools of thought. Since all of them aimed at seeking the means of salvation, there emerged three distinct *paths* (ways), *jnana* (knowledge), *karma* (action), and *bhakti* (devotion). All three co-existed from the very beginning and it was only their importance or dominance that varied from time to time.[7] Bhakti was, however, the one that got prominence. Two schools of religious thought then developed, the Vaishnavite which was based on Vedanta Upanishads and propounded by Shankaracharya, Ramaniya, and Ramananda, and the Krishnite which was based on the *Bhagavata Purana* and was propounded by men like Nimbarka, Vallabhacharya and Chaitanya.

Shankaracharya, who flourished between AD 788 and 820 in Kerala, was the first great propounder of the Upanishads and Brahmasutra. His approach was rational and logical; he believed in both revelation and realization, and endeavoured to reconcile the two opposite currents of thought, orthodox and heterodox. The way Shankaracharya adopted for the expression of his religio-philosophical idea, was the way of *jnana* or knowledge in which the Vedic commandments were to be tested by realization and only those were to be accepted that were practically reasonable. Thus, he brought the scriptural authority of the Vedas to the realm of knowledge.[8]

Shankaracharya propounded the Advaita philosophy (monism or the unity of God) of the Upanishads, which meant God was one, without attributes, and contained everywhere. At the same time he also held that God can be realized with attributes. To reconcile this contradictory position he attributed two sets of qualities or powers to the two forms of God:

1. *Swaroop lakshana* or the essential features which are attached to the supreme being, Brahma, not as apparent but as inherent attributes of *satchitanand* or existence, consciousness and bliss (all permanent).
2. *Tatasta lakshana* or accidental features which are possessed by Ishwara as powers of creation, destruction and the maintenance of worldly affairs.

In the first form God is absolute, non-relational and beyond our senses and reason. He can be grasped only by intuition. The second form of God is relational and phenomenal. The position of the second form of God is lower than the first one who maintains the worldly affairs with the help of the second.[9] As far as the relationship between God and man is concerned, the Upanishads declared, *tat tvam asi* or 'you are that'. This vague expression has been explained differently by different thinkers. Shankaracharya took it not as the relation between God and man, but as oneness as such; he declared, *aham Brahma asmi*, 'I am Brahma' which is quite similar to Al-Mansoor's *Anal haq* or 'I am the Truth'.

In Islam and even in classical Sufism there was no concept of *ittihad* (unity) between *abad* (worshipper) and *ma'abood* (worshipped). Sheikh Mohiuddin was the first to introduce the philosophy of *Wahdat-ul Wujud* (God is everywhere). This monistic approach, which gave way to the concept of *fana* (annihilation) of Bayazid (d. AD 874), ultimately led certain Sufis to hold a pantheistic view[10] similar to that of Shankaracharya. The entire doctrine of Shankaracharya rests on the belief that 'Brahma alone is real, the world is *mithya* (false), and the individual is Brahma and nothing else'. But his speciality is to neither accept nor reject any established theory but to give a different interpretation aiming at reconciliation. For instance, he refers to world not as *maya* but as *mithya* which means it is neither real nor unreal but a dream, i.e. real within the limits of the dream.[11] It is significant that both Shankaracharya and Imam Ghazali said there are three orders of existence:

1. *Pratibhasika* ('golden mountain'   *Alam-ul Mulk*
   or dreamland)   (phenomenal world)
2. *Vyavaharika* (empirically real   *Alam-ul Malakut*
   held by Ishwara)   (angelic world)
3. *Paramarthika* (supremely real   *Alam-ul Jabarut* (celestial
   held by Brahma)   world)

Ramanuja (1050–1137), a Tamil Brahman, was a contemporary of Imam Ghazali.[12] After visiting the various Hindu centres of pilgrimage, he settled in Srirangam in the south. Initially trained in Shankara's school, Ramanuja reacted against its philosophy. Opposed to Shankara's philosophy of simple or non-qualified monism, Ramanuja propounded qualified monism, or Vishishta Advaita, according to which Brahma and Ishwara were not two but one with the name of Vishnu, the supreme, responsible for all creation and destruction. *Sat, chit* and *anand* are his attributes which can be possessed both with and without being in form. Thus, Ramanuja believed in both aspects of God, *nirguna* and *saguna*, so that He is within and beyond approach, both relational and non-relational. *Jiva* (oneself) is neither one with God nor independent, but exists as a unique reality and never losses its identity. To explain this relation Ramanuja presents the analogy of the soul and body. As the soul controls the body but is distinct from it, so Brahma controls the soul but is distinct from.

Thus, in explaining *tat tvam asi* Ramanuja takes a different position from Shankaracharya. He explains it not as oneness but as *amsa* (part) of Brahma in terms of father and son and also as soul and body. Like Ghazali, Ramanuja holds that the difference between God and man is due to man's lack of perfection. Perfection can be achieved only through effort and by the grace of God. In that position, a man can become God-like but not God as such, because some divine qualities can never be attained by man. So, in Ramanuja's philosophy, God, soul and world or universe are all distinct. *Maya* or *mithya* is nothing, and the universe is eternal, going on forever in a cyclic order. This philosophy was termed *satkhyatvad*, i.e. non-illusion but real.

Ramanuja was the first philosopher who propounded the way of Bhakti in south India as against Shankaracharya's doctrine of *jnana*, and his sect was the first of four Vaishnava sects which flourished from the eleventh to the fifteenth centuries. According to Ramanuja, Bhakti was the only way of salvation and the other two ways, *karma* and *jnana*, were just the means leading to bhakti. He gives a complete code of conduct containing sevenfold aspects to culture mind and body for spiritual perfection. Ramanuja believed not only in the Vedas and the Upanishads as scriptural authority but also in the Tamil *Prabandham* of the Alvar saints of the south.

Both Shankara and Ramanuja regarded Vishnu as the Supreme God, but on certain philosophical lines they differed sharply from each other. Shankara was the philosopher who, in spite of systematizing the philosophy of the Upanishads, tried to over-shadow the idea of God as a personal being at the cost of popularizing the concept of his Advaitvad—in which he failed because of its being beyond the common approach. On the other hand, Ramanuja opposed Shankara by claiming that his own doctrine of Visishtadvaita was the only true representation of the contents of the Upanishads. He believed, unlike Shankara, that the Supreme God is personal and that, in spite of the soul being an *amsa* or portion of God, it is never absorbed into the essence of God but retains its identity. It was perhaps due to this uniqueness of thought that Ramanuja's concept of bhakti gained much popularity.

As for Shaivism, it developed in south India from the seventh century AD onwards. During the same period it was also a dominant religion in northern and central India. Important philosophical schools, which emerged subsequently in the north, were the Trika (Kashmiri School of Saivism) founded by Vasugupta in the northwest and the Buddhistic Vajrayana and Sahajiya school in Nepal and north-east India, from which evolved the Vaishnava Sahajiya school. This was a form of non-orthodox, anti-Brahmanical Tantric Vaishnavism closely connected with the Buddhist Sahajiya school and also with the Saiva school of the Nathpanthis. Shaiva Bhakti which developed in Kashmir from the ninth to tenth centuries, exemplifies ardent Nirguni Bhakti based on inner mystical experience or *anubhava*. It is an eclectic combination of the Sankhya Yoga and the monistic Yoga. In its monistic trend Parama Shiva, both as God and Guru, occupies a central place.

A few esoteric practices (yogic or tantric) are found in ancient times in the philosophy of Sankhya and Patanjali. These were later adopted by the Siddhas and the Yogis.[13] Traditions ascribe to the existence of nine Naths and eighty-four Siddhas who are said to have emerged in early medieval times almost simultaneously as counterparts of each other. While the Siddhas represent the 'totality of a revelation', the Nath doctrine is founded on the trinity of Shiva, Matsyendranath, and Gorakhnath. Shiva is the Adi Nath or the first Lord of the Naths, Matsyendranath is the first human guru, and his first disciple is Gorakhnath, followed by Charpatnath Gihimnath and others. The nine Naths, masters of yogic powers, emerged as independent teachers. All of them were regarded as great wonder workers having attained bodily immortality and were Gods. Their followers emerged as a cult under Gorakhnath,[14] the founder of the order of Kanphata (Split-Ear) Yogis.[15]

There also appeared a number of Shaivite ascetics who haunted cemeteries, ate from skulls, and even consumed corpses at the burning ghats. Known as Aghoris or Aghora-panthis and the ascetic order of Kapalikas (wearers of skulls), they were also called yogis but are quite different from the Nathpanthi yogis.

From the twelfth century onwards the Nath Yogis began to spread throughout northern and central India but their influence is visible only in the thirteenth century. They were part Buddhist and part Shaivite, and anti-Brahmanical. They lived in forests, but wandered in towns and also established permanent monasteries called *akharas* or *maths*. The Naths initiated members of all castes, including weavers and other low artisan castes, into their non-hierarchical order. While some of the Naths indulged in homosexuality, and also in observations such as orgies, necrophiha, scatology, bestiality, etc., most of them lead ordinary lives and disseminated the spiritual tenets of their founders.

Like the Shaiva *tantras* or Agamas,[16] the yogis also established their own *bani* or sayings in the form of the *Dohakosas* of the Siddhas and the *Jogesari Bani* of the Naths.[17] A yogic *tantra* ('chain' or 'treatise') constitutes a scriptural authority in contradiction of the Vedas, which aimed at reconciling the needs of the Kaliyuga or the existing age. Though they do not formally reject the authority of the Vedas, like the Jains or the Buddhists they consider them of no relevance. These *tantras* are essentially ritual manuals of a synthetic character uniting the Vedantic and the

Buddhist metaphysical views with a particular type of yogic practice, and also incorporating popular Hindu myths, magic, and alchemy.[18] Their main aim was to teach tantric beliefs and practices to the masses.

Some of the texts of the cult, including especially the *Siddha Siddhanta Paddhati,* formed the basis of the doctrines of the puritanical Naths and offered a common ground for the exchange of ideas with Sufis such as Shaikh Hamiduddin Nagauri and Shaikh Fariduddin Ganj-i Shakar. The discussions on different spiritual issues, particularly on the nature of the ultimate reality, enhanced understanding between the Naths and the Sufis.

The *Siddha Siddhanta Paddhati* emphasized the idea of a relationship between Advaita and Dvaita by drawing the analogy of water and bubbles.[19] In Nathpanthi terminology, the absolute spirit is called shiva and his unique power is Shakti. There is no difference between the two, since Shiva is regarded as the father of the universe and Shakti as the mother. The Creation of the cosmic system is in reality a gradual revelation of Shiva's inherent Shakti.

The prefect yogi can transform his body according to his will and is, therefore, free of disease and death. The disciples of Gorakhnath and the other Siddhas are believed to have achieved the practical aspect of this philosophy and they came to be known as the *jivanmukta* (liberated while alive), which is the state of true perfection.

Similarly, the Virashaiva or Lingayat movement, founded by Basava in Karnataka in the twelfth century, is characterized by monistic trends as well as by fervent Shaiva bhakti.[20] The five Aradhyas or great teachers of the cult were Revana (Revanacharya), Marul, Ekorama, Pandit and Allama Prabhu, who lived like Muslim *pirs* and admitted disciples called Jangamas. The Virashaivas or brave followers of Shiva were revolutionary warriors.[21]

The *Vachana*, compilations in Kannada of the sayings of the Virashaiva mystics known as Saranas reflect an ardent devotion to an invisible and all-pervading God, without giving any importance to Shaivite mythology.[22] The songs of Saranas taking refuge in Shiva are good examples of Nirguna Bhakti. The goal is not only *nirvana* or salvation but also complete merging into the essence of Shiva. Idol worship, even of Shiva's emblem or *lingam*, is of no use in their system. Allama Prabhu comments on the uselessness of offerings *(prasada)* made to a stone *lingam*. All the Saranas

Introduction   21

believed in sharing divine joys and experiencing God within the self and everywhere in the universe. But Basava is as extolled Shiva incarnate and the five Aradhyas as his transcending embodiments or manifestations.

Of similar thought was a Kashmiri woman called Lalded or Lalleswari, called Lalla, who emerged as a great Shaivite-poet in the fourteenth century. She was a contemporary of Syed Ali Hamadani who migrated from Persia to Kashmir in the 1380s. Lalded, a wandering Shaiva ascetic, belonged to a low and despised caste; she was a *bhangi* or scavenger. Deemed by the Shaivites to be a devout follower of the Kashmiri school of Shaiva-yoga, Lalded was honoured there both by Hindus and Muslims.

Lalla's doctrine and phraseology resembles that of the Nathpanthi yogis and she calls her Guru 'Gurunath' without giving his exact name. Lalla considers 'Shiva, Keshav, or Jina' as equal.[23] If we leave aside the poetic accounts of the siddhas and the Nathpanthi yogis, *Lalla Vakyani* or the sayings of Lalla are the first specimen of popular mystical poetry in old Kashmiri in northern India. Her devotion seems to be a synthesis of ancient Shiva-bhakti and some concepts of Tantric Yoga, with some Sufi influence.[24] Lalla's bhakti for Shiva finds a support in the Tantric notion of the interiorized guru (as Satguru in Shiva).

Tantric knowledge and practices were not restricted to any caste or creed but open to all kinds of people, men and women, provided they were 'qualified' for such revelation and were initiated by a 'worthy' guru.

Tantric Yoga developed from the seventh century onwards as an offshoot of Mahayana Buddhism, and slowly impregnated most schools of popular devotion in northern and southern India. Tantricism is sometimes equated with Shaktism (the cult of Shakti as the female 'energy' of Shiva). This actually integrated the ancient cult of Devis or autochthonous goddesses whose cult is linked with fertility, material prosperity and with protection against the evil forces of nature, especially disease. These Devis are to be propitiated with *bali* or blood offerings, implying the ritual killing of a domestic animal, a buffalo or goat, sometimes an owl, and also often human sacrifices. Many Devis have been extremely popular, though they with their cult are (now) deemed 'impure' and have been deprecated and vehemently opposed particularly where

Buddhistic and Jaina influence prevails. Whereas the Brahmans took no notice of such blood rites, the Buddhists and Jains opposed them due to their firm belief in the principle of *ahimsa*. And this has been inherited by all Vaishnava sects.

Sometimes Devi herself, under various names such as Chandi, Durga, or Kali, is represented as the great cosmic force (divine 'Mother' ruling universe with her bloodthirsty character). But at the same time she also appears with more amiable traits, as Sarada or Sarasvati, the lotus-seated goddess holding the *vina*. She is also conceived as a consort of a major god (especially) and united with him as his own *shakti* or 'energy'. Such goddesses conceived as Shaktis play a great part in Tantric worship. In Shaivite Tantric Yoga, Shakti is worshipped as an 'active' female principle whereas the male principle is viewed as inactive. The aim of Tantric *sadhaka* is to experience the supreme bliss generated by union of male and female principles by 'realizing' this merging within himself. But as the male principle Adi Shiva or Parama Shiva is considered as totally passive, it is essentially through the cult and rites associated with the great Devi or divine Shakti that Tantric *sadhana* can be achieved. Devi-worship in general, even when not-associated with specifically tantric yoga practices, is often referred to as the Shakta type of religion (Shaktism in modern parlance) and all Devi-worshippers are often designated as 'Shaktas'.[25]

In the Nathpanthi form of Tantric Yoga, *sahaja* is identified with the all-pervading ultimate reality (not very different from the Vedantic concept of Brahma-*atma*), which in turn is equated with Parama Shiva or Sadashiva (conceived as 'Adinath') and with the perfect, interior guru or the satguru. Siddha is a 'perfect one', an Avadhuta, 'one who has shaken off (the ties of *sansara*)' and 'one who is liberated while alive'. Tantric Yoga is also commonly known as Hatha Yoga or difficult Yoga, since extremely strenuous bodily exercises and difficult postures are usually associated with it. In this system the attainment of the supreme *sahaja* state is equated with the attainment of bodily immortality. Therefore, the question of escaping death may be taken as a salient feature and the peculiar *sadhana* prescribes various physical and physiological practices to remove disease, and decay, and to defeat death. This shifting of emphasis from *moksha* or *nirvana* to a kind of 'bodily salvation' is

Introduction 23

particularly marked in the most popular forms of Hatha Yoga advocated by Sahajiya Siddhas and even more by Nathpanthis. Both the Siddhas and Naths claim that through appropriate yogic practices, the human body can be rejuvenated and can become as changeless as a mountain and as immutable as gold. It is significant that whereas other schools of thought regard the ultimate dissolution of the body or its final dissociation with the spirit as the key to *moksha*, this class of Tantrikas seek 'liberation' in a transformed or trans-materialized body which they call a 'perfect body' (*siddha-deha*).[26] Tantrics, especially Nathpanthis, strictly hold that Yama or Kala (the personification of death) has no hold over perfect yogis. It is around this quest for immortality that all Nath yoga myths and legends revolve. This belief is also exemplified by the famous story of the fall of Matsyendranath among the wicked women of Kadali and of his rescue from the clutches of Yama by his 'disciple', Gorakhnath.[27]

Liquors of immortality, magic herbs and remedies, and alchemy were important in the more popular forms of Tantric Yoga. Tantric Buddhists used in their ritual an intoxicating drink which they called *varuni*; Vajrayana Siddhas called it simply *rasa* (juice, liquor) or *sahaja-rasa*, and they too considered the intoxication it procured as a means to immortality. The fondness of vulgar *jogis* for strong drink and *bhang* (*Cannabis indica*) is well known.

The Nathpanthis themselves seem to have integrated the archaic beliefs and techniques of ancient *rasayana* school, which is Indian name for alchemy. In this school, as in Hatha Yoga, the aim is to effect the trans-materialization of vile metal into gold with the help of a substance called *rasa* or *rasayana*, a chemical element derived from mercury. It is also believed that the transmutation of the corruptible human body into an incorruptible perfect body can also be achieved by similar methods. The followers of *rasayana* school held that postmortem 'liberation' is worthless and mere speculation and that there can be no positive proof of it, whereas bodily immortality is a positive achievement. The possibility of such achievement, according to them, was established by the eighty-four Siddhas who conquered death and remain always.[28]

There also appeared three other popular Vaishnava sects, Madhva, Nimbarka, and Vallabha, which took two forms or streams,

Vaishnavite and Krishnaite. While for Ramanuja and Madhva, Brahma or the supreme god is Narayana or Vishnu, for Nimbarka and Vallabha, it is Krishna.

As far as the Madhva Sect is concerned, it flourished in the thirteenth century in the south and was the first sect based on the *Bhagvata Purana*. Its founder, Madhvacharya (1199–1278) a Kannada Brahman, was a monist in a different way. Like Ramanuja, he also differed from Shankaracharya on issues like *maya* and *mithya*. God's position was for him non-relational and beyond approach. Though God prevails everywhere, the created things have a separate identity of their own. Thus, Madhvacharya preached the doctrine of Dvaita as against that of Advaita. With this his philosophy took yet another dimension, called *Brahmavad* meant for *Brahma Mimamsa* or *Jijnasa* (*jnana*).[29]

The Nimbarka Sect was a cult of Krishna founded by Nimbarka (c. 1130–1200), a Telugu Brahman, in the second half of the twelfth century. Having faith in Dvaitadvaita (dualistic non-dualism) he propounded the philosophy of *Bhedabhed* (different, non-different). This meant that God's position is both manifesting and non-manifesting in the cosmos. Krishna, along with his consorts (especially Radha) are to be worshipped because the different consorts represent the different aspects of Krishna's life. Yet this cult emphasized not *karma* but the way of bhakti. To make it systematic, the sect introduced *Navadha Bhakti* or the nine methods of bhakti.[30]

The Vishnu Swami Sect is said to have been related to Maharashtrian Bhagavat Dharma. It developed in the north in the later fifteenth century under Vallabhacharya (1473–1531). The sect adopted the philosophy of modified monism called Suddhadvaita (pure non-dualism). It believed in Krishna as the only God with the qualities of *sat, chit* and *anand*. Being both *nirguna* (formless) and *saguna* (formful). He is within and beyond approach. The soul is believed to have emerged from the essence of God as flame from fire and will be ultimately absorbed as salvation in the same essence.[31]

The Vishnu Swami Sect along with its offshoot, the Pushti Marga (i.e. the way of divine grace) also emphasized not *karma* but bhakti. There was no place for theory of knowledge in these sects and, therefore, they had complete faith in the scriptural authority of

Introduction 25

Bhagavad Gita and *Mahabharata* without using argumentation or logical thinking.

A new dimension was added to Vaishnavite Bhakti by a contemporary of Nimbarka, the Sanskrit poet Jaidev, at the Sena court in Bengal. His masterpiece is the poetic drama, the *Gita-Govinda* based on the stories of Krishna, Radha, and the gopis.

NOTES

1. Max Müller, *Six Systems of Indian Philosophy*, London: Longmans Green and Co., 1919, pp. 35–9. The people observed different rituals and made sacrifices of animals by reciting different verses or hymns. There was a variety of content in the Vedic hymns and a lack of uniformity in the thought and practices of different sections of people.
2. Ibid., p. 40.
3. Vedanta is considered to be the glorious period of Indian religious thought. It aimed at solving the mystery of existence on the basis of two factors, the knowing agency (*ksetrajna*) and the knowable (*ksetra*). Being the science of reality it contains all sources of knowledge, viz. experience and intuition, and covers all stages and conditions of life. It is neither religion nor mysticism, nor even theology or scholasticism but contains rudiments of scientific thought and philosophical insights about the nature of the universe.
4. Mutazalism was the first rationalistic school of Islamic philosophy. Great philosophers of this school include Wasil ibn Ata (b. AD 699), Abdal Hudhail Allaf (AD 748–840) and Nazzam (d. AD 848). See D.B. Macdonald, *Development of Muslim Theology, Jurisprudence and Constitutional Theory*, Beirut: Khayats, 1965, pp. 186–90.
5. The founder of this school was Abul Hasan Ashari who was first trained in Mutazalism but later developed his own school.
6. Epistemology, which formed an essential part of Indian philosophy, was meant for a critical assessment of the elements, sources and limits of knowledge. This was because all schools of Indian thought took ignorance to be the root cause of human suffering and sought to discover the means and processes of true knowledge by which reality could be known and misery minimized. This preceded the theory of reality, because without it metaphysical discussions were of no use.

Commenting on the first *sutra* of Gautama, Vatsyayana has well expressed the views of Indian thinkers on the subject by saying that the study of the sources of knowledge (*pramana*) was necessary, because only on this basis can we know reality and guide our actions towards desirable ends and thereby avoid suffering. Epistemology is thus closely connected with

ontology or morality and both, necessary to each other for perfection, are also linked with ethics. See Haridas Bhattacharya, ed., *The Cultural Heritage of India*, vol. III, Calcutta: Institute of Culture, 1956, p. 548.
7. For details, *The Cultural Heritage of India*, vol. III, pp. 550–9.
8. For details about the life and thought of Shankaracharya, S.N. Dasgupta, *A History of Indian Philosophy*, vol. II, rpt., Delhi: Motilal Banarsidass, 1975, pp. 1–227; also Anonymous, *Three Great Acharyas (Shankara, Ramanuja and Madhava)*, 2nd edn., Madras: G.A. Natesan & Co. (n.d.), pp. 1–93.
9. S.N. Dasgupta, *A History of Indian Philosophy*, pp. 156ff.
10. In Sufism *fana* (annihilation) does not mean absorption of oneself into the essence of God, but is taken as a stage of spiritual advancement. It is explained that there are four stages of spirituality and it is in the third and fourth stages where the devotee experiences *fana*.
11. In the *Rigveda*, the term *maya* is used in the sense of magical power and the Upanishads take it for false knowledge. In general Advaita philosophy it is taken as having no real existence and *maya* misleads men to seek the transitory pleasures of the world as if they were real.
12. For details about Ramanuja, see *The Three Great Acharyas*, pp. 95–141; Yusuf Husain, *Glimpses of Medieval Indian Culture*, 2nd edn., Bombay: Asia Publishing House, 1962, pp. 9–13.
13. *Yoga* means union, i.e. joining the *atma* (soul) and *brahma* (God). It seeks to make one's consciousness and inner self so powerful that it has direct communion with God.
14. There is a great uncertainty regarding Gorakh's place and date, but most probably he emerged in the eastern side in the eleventh century. For details, see Mohan Singh, *Gorakhnath and Medieval Hindu Mysticism*, Lahore, 1937; G.S. Ghurye, *Indian Sadhus*, Bombay, 2nd edn., 1964, pp. 128ff.
15. W.G. Briggs, *Gorakhnath and the Kanpatha Yogis*, Calcutta, 1938, pp. 228ff.

At the time of initiation the ear cartilage of a novice were split, and two enormous earrings were inserted in the holes. This was considered necessary to open a mystical channel for the development of yogic powers. During the ceremony a knife was driven into the ground and vows were recited over it by the initiate. These included a vow to protect the ears, believed to contain a network of invisible *nadis* connected to the inner organs of perfection. The rites also included the symbolic slaying of the neophyte, the washing of his entrails and the hanging of his body on a tree.
16. The Saiva Agamas are generally in the form of dialogue between Siva and Parvati: Siva reveals the esoteric doctrines and practices to his consort and disciple. Hence, Siva appears to play the part of the Adi-Guru.

Introduction 27

17. These works are contained in the *Panchavani,* the literature of the Dadupanthis. For instance, see *Basta* no. 12, compiled by Swamdas, vs 1693/AD 1636, pt. II, ff 235a–270a; *Basta* 2, compiled by Narharidas, vs 1733/AD 1676, pt. III. Photocopies of both the *Bastas* brought by me from the Dadu Mahavidyalaya, Jaipur, are lodged in the Seminar Library, Department of History, AMU, Aligarh.
18. E. Conze, *Buddhism: Its Essence and Development,* Oxford, 1951, rpt. 1959, p. 184; also Ch. Vaudeville, *Kabir,* vol. I, Oxford: Clarendon Press, 1974, pp. 126–42.
19. The bubbles appearing on the surface of water eventually merge with the latter and lose their separate identity. The relation is analogous to that between water and water-bubbles. In reality 'Parama Shiva is absolutely one.' See Mohan Singh, *Gorakhnaths,* p. 69.
20. There is much obscurity regarding Basava's early career, but it is clear that he was a minister under Bijjala (1156–67), the Kalachuri king of Kalyan. There was Jain and Brahmanical influence in the court and kingdom, but Basava was a rival of both. This led to a long conflict between him and Bijjala. Tarachand, *Influence of Islam on Indian Culture,* Allahabad: Indian Press, 1963, pp. 116–29; S.C. Nandinath, *A Hand Book of Vira Saivism,* Dharwar, 1952; and H. Thipperudra Swamy, *The Vir Saiva Saints: A Study,* Mysore, 1968.
21. For details J.N. Farquhar, *An Outline of the Religions Literature of India,* rpt., Delhi: Motilal Banarsidass, 1984, pp. 259–64; Tara Chand, *Influence,* pp. 94–100.
22. Virashaivas make no mention of the visible manifestation of Shiva described in Agamic and Puranic literature. Strict Saranas are even opposed to the worship of stone *lingams,* which they call *sthala* or fixed and, therefore, exterior *lingams.*
23. See *Lalla Vakyani* or the *Wise Sayings of Lalded: A Mystic Poetess of Ancient Kashmir,* tr. G. Grierson and Barnett, London, 1920, pada 22, p. 10.
24. Some modern scholars like R.C. Temple and Mohibbul Hasan have sought to prove a wholesale Sufi impact on Lalla's sayings, but there seems to have been a direct impact from Kashmiri Shaivism. See R.C. Temple, *The Words of Lalla,* Cambridge: Cambridge University Press, 1924, pp. 1–5; M. Hasan, *Kashmir under the Sultans,* Calcutta: Iran Society, 1959, pp. 238–9.
25. For details, see Ch. Vaudeville, *Kabir,* vol. 1, pp. 124–30.
26. See S.N. Dasgupta, *History of Indian Philosophy,* pp. 218–19. In the *Hevajra-Tantra,* the Lord explains that, although everything is empty, there is a need for the physical body because the highest bliss cannot be gained without it.
27. Vaudeville, op. cit., p. 127.

28. For further details of the yogic philosophy of *Jivan-mukti,* see S.N. Dasgupta, *A History of Indian Philosophy,* vol. 1, rpt., New Delhi: Motilal Banarsidass, 1975, pp. 245–52.
29. S.N. Dasgupta, *History of Philosophy,* vol. IV, Chapter XXV.
30. Ibid., vol. III, Chapter XXI.
31. For further details of the philosophy of Vallabhacharya, ibid., vol. IV, Chapter XXXI.

CHAPTER 1

Hindus Under Muslim Rule

Although the early Muslim historians like Hasan Nizami and Fakhr-i Mudabbir often give the impression that the Turkish conquest of India was a *jihad* (religious crusade) and that the Muslim warriors were religious heroes committed to fight for faith, Muslim rule in India was not 'theocratic'. The Ghorian conquest of India was not followed by any reactionary action inspired by religious bigotry.[1] The idea of *jihad* was politically motivated, being 'an inevitable result of the emigration of races from Mongolia and Central Asia'.[2] Certainly, there are cases of temple destruction but there are also instances of the demolition of mosques by Hindu chiefs wherever Hindu kingdoms came to power. Describing Mahi Pal's sack of Lahore, Sufi hagiographies record the massacre of Muslims, the demolition of mosques, and building of Hindu temples on their sites.[3] In the fifteenth century the zamindars in Malwa and even in areas near Delhi are reported to have converted mosques into temples.[4] Rana Kumbha claims to have 'imprisoned the *yavanis* (i.e. Muslim women) and also broken a mosque'.[5] But this was not the common practice on either side, and caused by political exigencies rather than religious hatred.

The concept of *Farr-i Izadi* (divine favour) relating to kingship was so strong that Imam Ghazali had to emphasize that kings were sent by God as His 'shadow on earth'.[6] Ziauddin Barani (1285–1356) wrote two very important works, the *Tarikh-i Firoz Shahi* and the treatise, *Fatawa-i Jahandari*, both expressing almost the same political theory. In the *Tarikh-i Firoz Shahi* the political concepts are couched in dialogues of the Sultans but the *Fatawa-i Jahandari* incorporates them in stories about Persian princes. The *Tarikh-i Firoz Shahi* rationalizes both the absolutism of kings and their use of *zawabit* (state laws). According to Barani, after the period of pious caliphs, the later caliphs and the Muslim rulers found themselves in a dilemma. If they followed the traditions of the Prophet Muhammad, they were unable to govern properly; and if, otherwise, they ruled vigorously and ostentatiously like the Iranian emperors, they violated the religious law.[7] Barani has also affirmed that theories of monarchy such as 'the Sultan is God's shadow on earth', 'religion and state are twin brothers' and 'people follow the faith of their kings', were inevitable and, therefore, the *Badshah-i Islam* could not fulfil his divine mission without depriving Hindus of higher posts and forcing Brahmans into bankruptcy and social misery.[8] Thus, for Barani only the autocratic form of government could justify Islamic rule in India. Shaikh Abdul Haq Muhaddis Dehlavi, an eminent Naqshbandi of the Mughal period, also legitimized the position of the ruler in a limited framework aiming at promoting the cause of Islam. He extolled the *badshah-i dindar* (the king upholding the faith) and said the entire community should cooperate with such a ruler in the task of spreading the *din* (faith).[9]

But the Sultans of Delhi governed India on the basis of expediency and most often made compromises when it came to political and administrative matters. It was the result of this policy that, according to I.H. Qureshi, 'Muslim and Hindu traditions were unanimous in according to the Sultan great respect and prestige'.[10] Muhammad Habib says that the foundation of the Turkish state was 'nevertheless non-religious and secular', because its basis 'was not the *Shariah* of Islam but the *Zawabit* or state laws made by the king'.[11]

When Muslim political power extended to the areas of the people of other faiths, there appeared the problem of determining the position of 'non-believers' (or non-Muslims) in the Muslim political system. In an Islamic state, Muslims were required to follow the *sharia* and perform duties prescribed by the state. But no such obligations could be expected of the non-Muslims. The latter comprised three categories: (a) *ahl-i kitab* (those who possessed some revealed book), (b) *mushabah ahl-i kitab* (those who resembled the possessors of revealed books), and (c) All other *kuffar* (infidels) and *mushrikin* (believers of more than one God).

Jurists declared that non-Muslims of the first two categories were entitled to equality in status and opportunity with the Muslims provided they agreed to pay *jizyah*. With regard to the position of the people of the third category, however, there was conflict of opinion.[12] But the consensus of juristic opinion was in favour of extending the privileges of *zimmi* to non-Muslims without any distinction.[13] Once the status of *zimmi* was accorded to a non-Muslim, it became the duty of the state to protect his life, property, and religious freedom.

Jizyah is the Arabic form of the Persian word *gezit*, which means tax. This tax had been implemented long before the time of the Prophet of Islam. Nausherwan the Sassanian emperor formulated certain rules about it and realized it in lieu of military service. When the Prophet imposed this tax as *jizyah*, he followed the same tradition.[14]

The *jizyah* was levied by the Prophet on the Christians of Najran in AH 8, and the privileges of the *zimmi* were explained thus:

To (the Christians of) Najran and the neighbouring territories, the security of God and the pledge of His Prophet are extended for their lives, their religion and their property. . . . They shall continue to enjoy everything great and small heretofore; no image or Cross shall be destroyed; they shall not oppress or be oppressed.[15]

The pious caliphs, who continued the theocentric political organization of the Prophet, maintained the same spirit. In almost all the settlements made by the second caliph, Umar Farooq, the following occurs repeatedly: 'Their religion shall not be changed; nor shall any interference be made in their religious affairs.'[16]

The fourth caliph, Ali, is said to have remarked that the blood of the *zimmi* was as sacred as that of the Musalmans.[17]

When Mohammad bin Qasim occupied Sindh in the early eighth century, the problem arose as to what status should be given to the Hindus of the place. After much deliberation it was decided to place them under the category of *Mushabah ahl-i Kitab* (those who resembled the possessors of revealed books) and thus to accord them the status of *zimmi* (protected people). Thus, the *jizyah* was levied on non-Muslims for the first time in India by Mohammad bin Qasim, as a protection tax. According to the *Chachnama*, Brahmans were employed to realize *jizyah* from local Hindus and to deposit it with the government treasury. The Brahmans, who were exempted from this tax, induced the people to pay up and those who were unwilling were asked to leave the place for other dominions ruled by the Hindus.[18]

As for the attitude of the Delhi Sultans towards *jizyah*, some later historians have argued that it was intended to punish the Hindu rebels (mainly Rajputs who revolted against the state). But to say that '*jizyah* was levied in order to degrade and insult the non-Muslim population'[19] is wrong. Quoting references from Barani's *Fatawa-i Jahandari*, Mohammad Habib has concluded that it was not designed by the Delhi Sultans to humiliate Hindus.[20] K.A. Nizami argues that the *jizyah* could not be realized during the Sultanate period as there was no 'elaborate administrative machinery' for the purpose.[21] In fact, with the passage of time the religious connotation of *jizyah* changed, and it came to be known as *karaj* (land tax). It occurs frequently in texts on contemporary *fiqh* (jurisprudence).

However, the legal position of Hindus as defined during the early Sultanate period (to be regarded as *Mushabah ahl-i Kitab* and not as *mushrikin* or *kuffar*) was maintained by succeeding generations of the Muslim theologians and rulers of medieval India. Once or twice during the whole period, some religious fanatics insisted on lowering the status, but their demand was turned down by rulers. It appears from an anecdote provided by Ziauddin Barani in his *Sahifa-i Nat-i Muhammadi*[22] that one day a delegation of leading *ulama* (theologians) of the time suggested to Sultan Iltutmish (1210–36) that 'Hindus be confronted with the alternative of death or Islam'. The Sultan consulted his wazir, Nizam-ul Mulk Junaidi, in this connection. The latter rejected the idea by saying that such actions could spur the Hindus to unite and that would pose a serious threat to the government.[23] Hearing this, the delegation then asked the Sultan to manage a strong differentiation between the (ruling) Muslims and the (ruled) Hindus and to maintain discrimination in all spheres of life. But the ulama failed in that effort too. Barani then, rather ironically, remarks that 'since no action was taken against the Hindus, infidelity, polytheism and idolatry took root among the Muslims and the faithful'.[24] However, a similar idea is reflected in another conversation of Syed Nuruddin Mubarak, as mentioned by Barani himself in his *Tarikh-i-Firoz Shahi*. He asked Iltutmish that if the polytheists were so numerous that no Muslim ruler could eradicate them, at least he should bring disgrace, dishonour, and ignominy upon them.[25]

In fact, we have no source of information except Barani on the attitude of the ulama towards the Hindus. But his account is so deeply prejudiced against the Hindus that it is difficult to put our reliance on it. In order to rationalize his attitude, he selected a ruler (Sultan Mahmud of Ghazni), a saint (Syed Nuruddin Mubarak) and a theologian (Qazi Mughisuddin) to weave his religious ideas round them and used them to express his own views. It may also be taken into account that no other historian has referred to this representation of the ulama. Even those later historians who have largely copied from Barani's account have not mentioned this incident, perhaps because it did not represent the general opinion of theologians. Barani cannot be taken as representative of the thinking of the entire class of ulama, who were generally not so rigid.[26] However, Barani reports that some nobles in Balban's court urged that idolatry be wiped out and steps be taken for forcible conversion to Islam.[27] But the Sultan was wise enough not to follow such an aggressive policy.

In fact, no Sultan from the time of Qutbuddin Aibak (1206–10) paid heed to the rigid ulama in administrative matters,[28] and Alauddin Khalji was the first to declare that religion and politics should not be mixed. His political concept in this context, as described by Barani himself in his *Tarikh-i Firoz Shahi,* is clear. The Sultan declares, 'I do not know whether the order is in conformity with the *Sharia* or contrary to it. Whatever I consider to be for the good of the people and expedient, that I decree.'[29] The Sultans of Delhi, their nobles, and even the ulama did not generally try to suppress Hinduism. The common people maintained cordial relations and, therefore, the orthodox ulama were not successful in dividing society. Since the number of the Muslims in India was comparatively very small, the strict observance of Islamic laws could have created many problems, leading to a paralysis of the administrative machinery. Jalaluddin Khalji (1290–2) openly expressed his inability to take steps for religious persecutions and said he had to tolerate Hindus bathing in the Jamuna and reciting their 'mantras'.[30]

Thus, though the theologians were given complete freedom in

civil and personal affairs (marriage, inheritance, etc.), in matters relating to the administration their jurisdiction was restricted.[31] It appears from the study of the *fatawa* of medieval India that they contain matters relating only to civil and religious affairs, leaving aside the political and administrative problems. This was for the simple reason that the Muslim governments were guided not by the *sharia* but by secular rules and regulations framed by rulers in view of the exigencies of the time. The political authorities tried to bind the theologians to the state in order to win Muslim public support, but they were not allowed to determine the administrative measures or the course of political development.

Since Hindus were not to be governed by Islamic canon law, the latter was divided into two parts, *tashrii* (religious) and *ghair tashrii* (secular).[32] Muslim rulers appointed pandits in the department of justice to assist qazis in delivering judgements in disputes among Hindus.[33] According to Baillie, the religious portion of Islamic law was applicable only to Muslims. Baillie specifically says that the *zimmi* 'are not subject to the laws of Islam. Their legal relations are to be regulated according to the precepts of their own faith.'[34] 'On this principle', as remarked by Waheed Husain, 'the Hindus were allowed to be governed by their own laws and carry on their mode of worship according to their religious rites and ceremonies. The Muslim sovereigns . . . did not interfere in the religious beliefs and customs of their non-Muslim subjects.'[35] Barani remarks that the Islamic law was not strictly enforced to subjugate the Hindus.[36] Out of several Islamic laws, one was the *qanun-i urf* or customary law. It enabled converts to maintain their earlier traditions and customs though these could be contrary to the basic principle of Islam.[37] This was naturally 'to reconcile the rigidity of law with local requirements',[38] and, in consequence, it enabled Hindus and Muslims to come closer. This was also because the Muslim rulers generally exercised their authority in the urban areas and the villages were dealt with by panchayats. Contact between ruler and populace was through government officials, as patwari, amin, qanungo, and kotwal. And the latter were mostly Hindu. The law was applied to Hindus and Muslims alike in both civil and criminal cases except in matters relating to succession, marriage, *sati*, and *devadasi*.[39]

The Ghuri conquest of northern India not only substituted one political and administrative system with another, it also motivated the transformation of socio-economic and religious life of the country. Alberuni has provided a detailed description of the social conditions before the advent of the Muslims. It appears from his account that the principle of caste formed the basis of the social structure, resulting in the total annihilation of the entire sense of citizenship and of loyalty to the country.[40]

The upper class of Indian society was represented by the four varnas, Brahman, Kshatriya, Vaishya and Shudra. Though sharply divided among themselves, these classes lived together in the towns and villages. For Manu, the Brahman was the 'lord of all varnas'. His religious and spiritual supremacy was uncontested.[41] Not only this, Brahmans were also exempted from payment of all taxes. Next to the Brahman, there was the class of Kshatriya represented by the Thakurs. This warrior section was divided into three grades: *rais*, *ranas*, and *rawats*.[42]

The remaining two castes, were given a lower place. The Vaishya was assigned the duty of agriculture, cattle-breeding, and business, either for himself or for a Brahman. The Shudra was considered a 'servant of the Brahman, taking care of his affairs and serving him'.[43] Vaishyas and the Shudras were denied access to the sacred texts.[44]

Below these varnas were eight classes of outcastes called *antyaja*, following professions like that of the fuller, shoemaker, and weaver. The lowest in the hierarchy were the Hadi, Doma, Chandala and Badhatau who were assigned work like the cleaning of the village.

Brahmans and Thakurs acquired the maximum benefits of the produce and they exploited the rest, particularly workers and peasants. All efforts were made to keep them in ignorance. Moreover, the fortified cities, towns, and villages were under the strong control of the higher castes. The depressed classes were not allowed within the city walls except at fixed times when their services were required or a supply of commodities was needed.[45]

The lower castes were reduced to the position of slavery and were considered untouchable.[46] Moreover, the religious diversity was an additional factor for the division of Indian society. Division and discrimination on social and religious grounds, and economic exploitation, brought very adverse consequences for the country.

These weaknesses gave way to the emergence of different reactionary reform movements within the country, and proved to be the basic reasons of the defeat of Indian political power. In contrast there was unity among Muslims, religious as well as social. There are two fundamental principles of Islam—unity of God and unity of social order within the *millat* (community). Muslims hold that God is one, without apparent attributes, and master of the whole universe, visible or invisible. Second, Islam preaches brotherhood among Muslims, men and women.[47] True, Muslim society was divided, but only into two broad categories, freemen and slaves. Slavery was permitted as an economic necessity. The slave could be purchased or captured in war. In theory, at least, Islam does not permit any discrimination in view of family status, education, wealth, race, nationality, or colour. This is apparent from the declaration of Imam Abu Hanifa that all free Musalmans are of one *kuf* (status).[48]

The unity of god and brotherhood among mankind proved to be useful in turning Indian public opinion towards Islam, and this opened the way for the urban as well as the rural revolutions.[49] The immediate and the most significant effect of the conquest was the liquidation of the old city-planning. The 'caste-cities'of the Rajputs turned into 'cosmopolitan cities' of the Muslims. Even if we accept K.L. Srivastava's arguments (based on mythological and other ancient Indian works like the Puranas and *Manasarita-Vastushastra*) and his conclusion that 'labourers and artisans in all ages lived in the cities and towns',[50] the fact remains that city gates were more freely open under the Turks for all kinds of workers, artisans, and labourers who practically lived with the Muslims without any social barrier. The Turkish officers needed all workers to live close to them for work in their *karkhanas* (factories), offices, and homes. Mohammad Habib has rightly observed that 'all sections of the people were living within the cities without any sort of discrimination', and 'the cities, under the new regime, were developing into thriving centres of industry and commerce . . .'.[51] The *karkhanas* played an important role in ameliorating the economic conditions of the workers and craftsmen. Artisans employed in different crafts were also rewarded for excellence. Besides, favourable conditions in Delhi also encouraged artisans to develop their own crafts.[52] Thus the Hindu artisans enjoyed, for the first time, a respectable position and better economic conditions under the new government. Besides, the substitution of forced labour by free labour must have had a positive effect on a large number of Indian masses. More and more economic and professional transactions led to interaction between Hindus and Muslims on the cultural level. Consequently, Hindus adopted some Muslim customs and vice versa.

The *sharia* made no distinction between Hindu and Muslim in everyday life. Consequently, as observed by Mohammad Habib, 'there was a landslide in favour of the new faith', so much so that 'by the middle of the thirteenth century we find large numbers of Muslim workers of purely Indian origin in every city and town'.[53] Hindus were inclined towards Islam due to certain defects in their own socio-religious system. It is significant that the cases of religious conversion were mostly in groups of weavers and butchers, either out of conviction or in reaction to existing socio-economic considerations.[54]

In fact, the Muslim rulers of India, from the very beginning, did not and could not prevail as arbitrary religious kings. For the consolidation of political power tolerance was necessary. The Arabs in Sindh appointed Hindus to state service. The realization of revenues and the maintenance of accounts were mostly in their hands.[55] It is significant that Brahmans were assigned the duty to realize *jizyah* from local Hindus but were themselves were exempt from this tax.[56]

When Arab soldiers in Sindh were unable to return to their homeland, they decided to live in India and to marry Hindu women, which led to the establishment of military colonies known as *junus* (armies) and *amsar* (cities).[57] For consolidation of power, the Arabs allowed Hindus to rebuild their temples and perform their religious obligations.[58] They also encouraged Hindu musicians, masons, painters, and physicians.[59]

Even before the foundation of the Delhi sultanate, Sultan Muizuddin bin Sam maintained friendly relations with most of the *rais* and *rawats* of the Punjab. The figure of a bull was inscribed on the reverse of coins of Muizuddin, minted in Punjab. Similarly, Tarain after his victory in 1192 continued to mint coins with the figure of goddess Lakshmi.[60] The successors of Sultan Muizuddin in India continued cordial relations with Hindus. Besides, Muslim ruler seems to have made very little change in the rural areas. In an attempt to win over the local people, assignments of land were given to Hindus.[61] Fakhri-i-Mudabbir praises Sultan Qutbuddin Aibak for befriending those Hindu chiefs who agreed to submit to his authority.[62] The Turkish nobles did not hesitate to enter into alliances with the Hindu chieftains. In this context the reference of Minhaj Siraj about the rebel Malik, Qutlugh Khan, is important.[63] Afterwards, Balban, prior to his succession, was attended by a body of a thousand *paiks* (Hindu soldiers).[64] He even sought the cooperation of Danuj Rai, the ruler of Sonargaon, against Tughril.[65] Sultan Jalaluddin's reign was short, but he was so popular among the Hindus that some Hindu horsemen offered him their services in order to suppress a revolt.[66] It is significant that Hindus joined Jalaluddin Khalji against the rebels.[67] So also Alauddin enjoyed the trust and confidence of Hindus. A Hindu official named Malik Naik, who held a high military rank, proceeded against the Mongols with 30,000 horsemen.[68] When Alauddin's nephew, Akat Khan, attempted to kill him, the Sultan was saved by Naik and his *paiks*.[69] Naile was subsequently raised to the rank of malik. K.S. Lal has rightly observed that the 'vast Empire Alauddin built up could not have been sustained but by befriending not only Hindu public opinion but also many Hindu ruling chiefs'.[70]

Under Qutbuddin Mubarak Khalji (1316–20) the position of the Hindus improved mainly because he had gained the throne with the help of the palace guards. Within a short time these guards acquired such a dominant position in the government that the Sultan was helpless to control them.[71] Ultimately, Qutbuddin Mubarak was murdered by Nasiruddin Khusrau Shah, a Hindu convert, with the help of the Barwaris and other Hindu supporters from Gujarat. This Sultan appointed his Hindu supporters to key posts, so much so that it was believed that Hindu rule had been established in Delhi.[72] The Barwaris had monopolized power during the short rule of Khusrau in 1320. Ghazi Malik declared *jihad* against the Sultan in order to get the support of the Muslims, but it appears from the accounts of Isami and Amir Khusrau that Hindu soldiers fought on both sides.[73] A.M. Husain remarks that 'Khusrau Shah's army consisted of an equal number of Hindus and Muslims'.[74]

With the advent of the Tughluqs to power, the number of the Hindu officers and army generals increased. Muhammad bin

Hindus Under Muslim Rule 39

Tughluq promoted Hindus and Muslims to important positions on the basis of merit and regardless of caste or community. His successors followed him in this and the system remained unchanged to the end of the Sultanate period. Mention should be made of the Khatris of Punjab, who held important positions since the Tughluq period.[75] Likewise Khizr Khan and his successors employed Hindus and entrusted them with positions at the court. The nobility of the Lodi Sultans was also broad based, Hindu and Muslim being included along with Afghans.[76]

There is a misunderstanding regarding the economic condition of Hindus under the sultanate. To say that all the sections of Hindu society suffered a setback after the Ghuri occupation of the country, is not correct. Certainly the Rajput feudal lords who did not submit to the victor were destroyed. Yet many chiefs who acknowledged the suzerainty of the Sultan were befriended and granted complete autonomy. It appears from Barani's work, which was written during the Tughluq period, that their prosperity increased during the fourteenth century.[77]

Moreover, Indian merchants were given the freedom to trade in Ghazni even when political relations between India and Ghazni was not good.[78] According to Mohammad Habib, when Alauddin was organizing his economic reforms, he had to depend upon the Hindu nayaks for grain and the Hindu merchants of Multan for cloth [which were] the basic commodities of the market'.[79] It is significant that the Multani traders were mostly Hindu, and there were frequent dealings between them and the Muslims, including the Turkish nobles.[80] The fact that the Hindu moneylenders were in a position to advance loans to the Muslim aristocracy,[81] cannot be ignored in this context. The role played by the Hindu–Muslim trade in the formation of harmonious relationship between the two communities was so important that it was recognized by the state.[82]

As stated, the Sultans also employed Hindus in administration. They realized that the indigenous administrative systems could not be run without the cooperation of the Hindus in different departments of administration, particularly at local levels. Any attempt to replace them would have paralysed the administrative machinery and lead to chaos. They alone could help the Turkish government in the collection of revenues and could act as intermediaries between state and peasantry.[83] According to Tara Chand, 'When Qutbuddin

Aibak decided to stay in Hindustan, he had no other choice but to retain the Hindu staff which was familiar with the civil administration, for without it all government including the collection of revenue would have fallen into utter chaos.'[84] The Turks in India had to largely depend on local Hindu government officials, even when they were generally not assigned high posts in the administration. The Sultans also enlisted Hindu soldiers in the Muslim army.[85] Habibullah writes, 'On his way to Lakhnauti Balban had a *levee en masse* in Awadh and enrolled about two hundred thousand men as archers, carriers and also as horsemen and infantry. It is reasonable to assume ... that a portion ... came from the non-Muslims.'[86] The Sultans also often employed Hindu mercenaries in their wars. For instance, Razia and Altunia tried to regain Delhi with the help of the Khokhars and the Jats of Punjab.[87] Moreover, Hindu chiefs were favoured by the Muslim rulers and they became reliable allies of Muslim rulers.[88] The observation of Titus in this context is even more important: 'We not only read of Hindu troops being employed by Muslim rulers, but ... men of both religions freely began to enter each other's service.'[89]

During the period of Alauddin Khalji, Hindus were employed in the revenue and other departments of the government. It appears from an inscription of VS 1373/AD 1316 found in Ladnu (Jodhpur) that Alauddin had appointed a Hindu named Sadharna as his treasurer.[90] Such appointments continued under the Tughluqs. Ghiyasuddin Tughluq who employed Hindus in his army is said to have despatched a force comprising Hindus and Muslims to fight the Mongols.[91] He also issued orders that no *kharaj* or *charai* should be demanded from the Hindu khuts and muqaddams, as they shared a huge burden of state work.[92]

Isami says that Muhammad bin Tughluq favoured Hindus with important positions in state services.[93] He also asserts that a Hindu named Ratan was given an important assignment in Sehwan (Sindh), probably as Governor.[94] According to Firishta, Bhiran Roy, commander of the Gulbarga Fort, enjoyed the confidence of the sultan.[95] The sultan appointed a Hindu named Dharadhar as naib wazir of Deogir and the head of the *Diwan-Usloob*.[96] Samar Singh Jain, who held the post of commissioner under Mubarak Shah Khalji and was later sent to Telangana by Ghiyasuddin Tughluq, was appointed governor of Telangana by Muhammad bin Tughluq.[97]

Despite Firoz Shah's effort to streamline the state policy in the light of *sharia*, the finance and revenue departments of his government continued to be run by Hindu petty officials.[98] Firoz Shah also appointed Rajputs as his personal bodyguards. Barani says that Rai Bhiru Bhatti, a relative of Firoz's mother, was employed as the head of the bodyguards.[99]

The Turkish Sultans of Delhi gave religious freedom to the Hindus. Even in the imperial city of Delhi, Hindus bowed before their idols, blew their conches, bathed in the river Jamuna, and carried on the religious processions without hindrance.[100] Old temples like those of Mahoba and Khajuraho were kept intact and the new temples were allowed to be constructed during this period. The three Jain images discovered in Etah contain dated records of their installation in VS 1335/AD 1278.[101] Moreover, a fragment of a bilingual inscription in Persian and Sanskrit, found in the Purana Qila of Delhi, reports the endowment of 12 *bighas* of land to a temple dedicated to Sri Krishna.[102] Firoz Shah's protest that 'the idolatrous Hindu . . . had built new temples in the city and the environs',[103] is itself proof that no step was taken for destruction of places of worship during this period. Sultan Sikandar Lodi once thought of damaging a religious place of the Hindus at Kurukshetra. But his chief theologian, Mian Abdullah of Ajodhan, decreed, that it was not permissible to ruin a temple of long standing.[104]

There was not only religious tolerance but due response and recognition were also given to the Indian thought and culture. At the court of Alauddin Khalji Hindu astrologers were respected and, on the occasion of festivals, Hindus and Muslims were invited together to the palace.[105] It appears from the Jain accounts that the leader of the Digambar Sect, Puran Chandra Suri, commanded respect at Alauddin's court. Besides, the Sultan is also said to have invited Acharya Mahasen to his court and to have held a religious discourse with him.[106] Moreover, Alauddin was the first Sultan to marry a Hindu Kamla Devi, the ex-queen of Rai Karan Baghela, the ruler of Gujarat.[107]

Muhammad bin Tughluq is said to have participated in the religious festivals of the Hindus. He is the first Sultan of Delhi, about whom there is a definite contemporary evidence given by Isami for his participation at celebrations of Holi.[108] Barani says, 'By the reign of Muhammad bin Tughluq, the Hindu gentry had attained a status which excited jealousy among the Muslims',[109] so much so that Isami had to remark: 'The Sultan destroys the Muslims in his attempt to patronize the Hindus'.[110] However, Jain scholars such as Raj Shekhara, Bhim, Mantri Bhanak, Mahendra Suri, Bhallarka Sinha Kirti, Somaprabha Suri, Somatika Suri, Sena Suri and Jinprabha Suri were also patronized by the Sultan.[111] Jinprabha who used to recite Persian and Sanskrit verses in the durbar occupied a high position in the court.[112] Muhammad bin Tughluq took interest in Hindi learning. Ziauddin Nakhshabi's *Tutinama* (Account of a Parrot), a book of fifty-two short stories in Persian adopted from Sanskrit, is the most notable work of his reign. According to Firishta, the Sultan had women of many races in his harem: Arabian, Georgian, Turk, European, Chinese, Afghans, Rajputs, Bengalis, Gujratis, Telanganis and Maharashtrian, and he could talk to them in their own languages.[113]

Jain gurus continued to enjoy royal favour even under Firoz Shah, who is said to have honoured at least three eminent Jain scholars, Gunabhadra Suri, Munibhadra Suri, and Mahendra Suri, the third being a reputed astronomer and mathematician.[114] The Sultan had also keen interest in Hindu literature and Hindu philosophy. He brought Sanskrit works from the Jwalamukhi temple of Kangra and ordered translations into Persian. A book known as *Dalail-i Firuzshahi* on astronomy and astrology was translated from Sanskrit into Persian during his reign. Books on music and wrestling were rendered into Persian from Sanskrit.[115] Barani's account of Firuz's sixth regnal year shows that

The (Tughluq) Sultans confer on them responsible offices including governorship of provinces.... Thus, the Hindus enjoy all luxuries, employing Musalmans as their servants and keeping them in attendance at their houses. They also carry on an unrestrained and open propaganda of their books and disseminate their teachings, preferring Hindu philosophy to Islamic literature.[116]

However, the reign of Firoz Shah also witnessed some action against the liberal trends of thought, which was gaining ground during his time. A Hindu *daroga* (inspector) of Uch named Nawahun was killed simply because of his liberal views towards religion.[117] One Ahmad Bihari was killed due to his *Wahdat-ul Wujud* belief. If Ahmad Bihari's murder was to prevent the development of liberal ideas in Muslim circles, the killing of Nawahun was certainly a precautionary measure against the secular Bhakti thought that was gaining ground during the time of Firoz Shah.[118]

In subsequent periods the growth of liberal ideas took further steps, as is evident from the case of Lodhan (Brahman) who was killed in the time of Sikandar Lodi because he had challenged the monopoly of Islam as the only true religion by saying that 'Islam is a true (religion) and my religion is also rightful'.[119] The executions of Ahmad Bihari, Nawahun, and Lodhan were serious events in the religious history of India, but should not be taken as individual cases of religious persecution. The concepts of such people, both Hindu and Muslim, and particularly the remark of Lodhan, implied the basic idea of Sufi and Bhakti thought, i.e. the unity of religion (*Wahdat-i Adyan* or *Sarva Dharm Samabhava*), and a meeting of leading ulamas was called in the case of Lodhan to consider the problem and to take action. K.S. Lal has, however, exonerated Sikandar Lodi for this punishment, as it was the only incident of this kind that took place after 1500. He remarks, 'Even in this case Sikandar Lodi had acted judiciously, he had condemned Lodhan only after a long trial.'[120]

The religious policy of the Lodi Sultans was thus generally tolerant and liberal except the above instance under Sikandar Lodi. During his reign a treatise on medical science, the *Tibbi-i Sikandarshahi*, was prepared by physicians of India and Khurasan.[121] It is important to note that it was by his time that Hindus began to study Arabic and Persian and the Muslims became interested in the study of Sanskrit and Hindi. This would later give birth to a new language, Urdu. Consequently, the roots of empire went deeper and the seeds of Hindu–Muslim unity were to bear rich fruit during the Mughal period.

The first Mughal ruler, Babur, was also basically liberal minded. Although he declared the war against the Hindu rulers like Rana Sanga and Medini Rao of Chanderi as *jihad* and, after victory, assumed the title of Ghazi (Muslim victor), such terms were used not for religious purpose but to boost the morale of Muslim soldiers. Even Akbar used these terms when he led expeditions against Hindu rulers. That Babur was moderate in religious matters and had no prejudice against Hindus is borne out by his attitude towards the autonomous Hindu rajas. He had won over Adam Gakkar and Sangur Gakkar, who fought for him along with their troops in the battle of Khanva. On the other hand, it was the generosity of Babur that when Rani Padmavati, the widow of Rana Sanga, sought his support for her son Vikramajit who was being harassed by his brother, Babur not only received her envoy with honour, but offered her Shamsabad in place of Bayana, as was desired by the Rani herself.[122] It is said that Babur advised Humayun to continue the policy of religious tolerance.[123] During Humayun's stay in Iran, Shah Tahmasp also suggested that he 'rear the Rajputs', since 'without gaining control over the zamindars it is not possible to rule in Hind'.[124]

Humayun, in his turn, advised Akbar to be kind and considerate to the Rajputs, as loyalty was ingrained in their character.[125] It was on this commandment of his father that Akbar built a strong bridge of friendship with the Rajputs. He created a new Rajput nobility in which men like Raja Todar Mal, Raja Birbal, Bhagwandas, and Man Singh enjoyed a position no lower than that of Muslim nobles, even princes. But the attitude of the ulama in religious matters for power politics was also responsible for Akbar's liberal policies. His approach to all religions took the shape of practical liberalism when, according to Badauni, 'compulsion in religious matters was forbidden', and one was free 'to go over to any religion he pleased'.[126] Akbar identified with not one but all religions to an extent that the leaders of other communities were for long under the impression that each of them had won his faith.[127] The policy of reconciliation and adjustment with the Hindus was based on the theory that the Emperor as God's representative had to treat all his subjects without discrimination of faith and creed. Yet this dangerous concession to an alien faith was opposed by the ulama who were fighting for Islamic superiority. The idea of the religious monopoly of Islam was rejected outright by Akbar with the argument that sensible men were present in all religions and 'some true knowledge was everywhere to be found'.[128]

Akbar's liberal policy was practically unique, as it represented not only tolerance but also acceptance of the importance of socio-religious systems of India in order to accomplish a fusion of the various classes of Indian people. Akbar's policy of matrimonial

Hindus Under Muslim Rule

alliance with Rajput princesses, pursued for political motives, nevertheless had a deep psychological impact on his non-Muslim subjects. The Rajput princesses entered the royal palace, enjoyed full liberty to follow their own religious practices and celebrate their own festivals, accompanied by Akbar himself. Similarly, the banning of the practice of enslaving and converting prisoners of war in 1562,[129] the removal of pilgrimage tax in 1563, the abolition of *jizyah* in 1564,[130] and permission to non-Muslims along with the Muslims for further construction of religious places, proved to be a turning point in medieval Indian history. With these acts Akbar created an atmosphere of common citizenship, Hindus and Muslim. Thus the whole policy of Akbar gave a different complexion to his political efforts for territorial expansion, as he came to be regarded as an Indian ruler in India.

Thus on the whole Muslim rulers avoided interference in the religious practices and social affairs of Hindus. Instead they took care of the religious sentiments of Hindus and tried to win over their confidence by taking personal interest in their socio-cultural activities. Some went so far that they were identified not as foreigners but as Indians. This was necessary for the foreign Muslim rulers to run the government smoothly and successfully in India. The result was that the masses who did not stand for the cause of Indian rulers during the Turkish invasion, were attracted to the Muslims and gradually mingled with them. In fact, there was no communal tension or riot as such throughout the period of Muslim rule in India.

NOTES

1. Old Hindu towns were not destroyed but expanded with new colonies of foreign Muslim immigrants. Habibullah writes: 'Exaggerated report of destruction of temples and the establishment of the abode of God had a definite propaganda value; it facilitated recruitment in Central Asia by holding out prospects both of religious glory and of worldly riches'. A.B.M. Habibullah, *The Foundation of Muslim Rule in India,* Allahabad, 1989, p. 32; also Aziz Ahmad, 'Theocracy Versus Autocracy', *Journal of Indian History,* vol. XVIII, part III, 1939.
2. K.A. Nizami, *Some Aspects of Religion and Politics in India during the Thirteenth Century,* Delhi: Idarah-i Adabiyat-i Dehli, 1978, p. 90.

3. Aziz Ahmad, *Studies in Islamic Culture in the Indian Environment*, Delhi: Oxford University Press, 1964, p. 94.
4. Abbas Khan Sherwani, *Tarikh-i-Sher Shahi*, Eng. tr. Elliot and Dowson's *History of India*, rpt., vol. IV, Delhi: Low Price Pub., 2001, pp. 403–4.
5. R.C. Majumdar (ed.), *The Delhi Sultanate*, Bombay: Bharatiya Vidya Bhavan, 1960, p. 639.
6. For details, see A.A. Rizvi, *A History of Sufism in India*, vol. II, Delhi: Munshiram Manoharlal, 1983, pp. 353–4.
7. *Fatawa-i-Jahandari*, tr. Mohammad Habib and Mrs. Afsar Khan, *The Political Theory of the Delhi Sultanate*, Delhi: Kitab Mahal, n.d., p. 39.
8. For Barani, it was one of the primary duties of Muslim kings to redeem the inherently sinful and evil nature of kingship by rooting out paganism, polytheism, and idolatry. Since Hindus were the worst enemies of God and His Prophet, they were to be looted, enslaved, or killed, and the Brahmans (leaders and instigators of idolatry) massacred. See Ziauddin Barani, *Tarikh-i Firozshahi*, ed. Sir Syed Ahmad Khan, Calcutta: Bib. Indica, 1862, pp. 41–2, 290–1.
9. For details, see A.A. Rizvi, *Sufism*, vol. II, pp. 363–5.
10. I.H. Qureshi, *Administration of the Sultanate of Delhi*, Lahore: Ashraf, 1942, pp. 43, 47; also M. Aziz Ahmad, 'Theocracy Versus Autocracy'.
11. Mohammad Habib, *The Political Theory of the Delhi Sultanate*, Allahabad: Kitab Mahal, n.d., Introduction, p. VI. In support of his view the author quotes Barani: 'A State law (*zawabit*) in the technique of administration means a rule of action which the king has imposed as an obligatory duty upon himself for realizing the welfare of the state, and from which he absolutely never deviate', p. 64.
12. Imam Shafa'i restricted the application of the *zimmi* law to the *Ahl-i Kitab* and the Zoroastrians. Imam Abu Hanifah and Imam Ahmad bin Hanbal extended its application to all except the infidels of Arabia. For them, the sword or Islam were the options. Imam Malik and Qazi Abu Yusuf adopted the most liberal attitude and accorded the status of *zimmi* to all non-Muslims, without the distinction of Arab/non-Arab. K.A. Nizami, p. 308.
13. *Zimmi* is derived from *zimma* which means contract. After conquest a Muslim conqueror entered into a contract with the conquered, which guided his relations with him. By paying the stipulated tax non-Muslims became free subjects of a Muslim state and were treated like Muslims in all transactions of daily life. The government was responsible for their personal security and religious freedom. K.L. Srivastava, *The Position of Hindus under the Delhi Sultanate (1206-1526)*, Delhi: Munshiram Manoharlal, 1980, p. 59.
14. Such taxes were levied in many other countries with different names in the middle ages; France, Germany, and England. According to the Islamic system, by paying this tax non-Muslims were exempt from the military

service that was compulsory for the Muslims in a Muslim state. The rights of protected people in a Muslim state included the protection of life and property, religious freedom, and non-interference in personal law. Moreover, the *bait-ul mal* (treasury) had to care for those who were unable to take care of themselves. It was for these obligations that *jizyah* was demanded from non-Muslims. Persons of less than 20 and more than 50 years of age were exempt; women, the poor, the handicapped, and mendicants were also exempt. Having been exempted from military service, those who rendered this service or contributed to the welfare of the state, were also exempted from this tax. For details about the nature and imposition of *jizyah* in India during the Sultanate period, see K.A. Nizami, *Aspects of Religion, and Politics*, pp. 313–15.

15. For the full message of the Prophet and its authenticity, see Shibli Nomani, *Maqalat-i Shibli*, vol. I, Azamgarh: Dar-ul Musannafin, 1955, pp. 188–9.
16. Ibid., p. 191; also Shibli's *Al Faruq*, vol. II, Azamgarh: Dar-ul Musannafin, 1956, p. 155.
17. As cited in *Maqalat-i Shibli*, vol. I, p. 191.
18. Ali bin Hamid bin Abu Bakr, *Fathnamah-i Sindh*, commonly known as *Chachnama*, ed. N.A. Baloch, Islamabad, 1982, pp. 160–4; Eng. tr. Elliot and Dowson's *History of India*, rpt., vol. 1, Delhi: Low Price Pub., 2001, pp. 184–7, 460.
19. Srivastava, *Position of Hindus*, p. 89.
20. Mohammad Habib, *The Political Theory of the Delhi Sultanate*, p. 69.
21. K.A. Nizami, *Aspect of Religion*, p. 35. I.H. Qureshi, *Administration*, p. 119.
22. This was written in 1353–4 and is preserved in manuscript form in the Raza Library, Rampur. It deals mainly with the life of the Prophet Muhammad, but also refers to the religious, social, and political ideas of the author himself. For details see S. Nurul Hasan, *Sahifa-i Nat-i Muhammadi* of Zia-uddin Barani', *Medieval India Quarterly*, vol. 1, no. 3, 1950, pp. 100–5.
23. Nizam-ul Mulk Junaidi explained the futility of this idea by saying, '. . . at the moment India has newly been conquered and the Muslims are so few that they are like salt (in a large dish). If their advice was acted upon, the Hindus might unite and confusion could arise. Then the Muslims would not be able to suppress it. It is, however, possible when the Muslims are powerful enough, to offer the Hindus the choice of "death" or "Islam".' Ibid., p. 103.
24. For the Persian text, ibid., pp. 104–5; and Eng. tr., pp. 101–3.
25. For details of this conversation, Barani, *Tarikh-i Firozshahi*, pp. 41–2.
26. The attitude of the Muslim theologians was determined by what they found in books on *fiqh* (jurisprudence) written outside India. No Indo-Muslim scholar sought to study the relationship between Muslims and non-Muslims in India. Even the *Adab-ul Harb-wa Shujaat,* which contains

48 Bhakti Movement in Medieval India

some information about the position of the *Zimmi* in a Muslim state, makes no reference to the Hindus. Fakhr-i Mudabbir talks about Sabians, Christians, and Jews, but does not mention the vast Hindu population even though the work was compiled in India. Of the four main schools of Muslim law, the *Hanafi* was most liberal in its attitude to non-Muslims, while the *Shafa'i* represented the other extreme. Barani was probably more inclined towards *Shafa'i* thought, because it vindicated his own prejudices. The fact that of all the medieval sultans, he singled out Mahmud of Ghazni—around whom to weave his political ideology—was perhaps due to the latter's *Shafa'ite* leanings. But the majority of ulama in India were *Hanafi*, and their attitude to non-Muslims was liberal. K.A. Nizami, *Aspect of Religion*, pp. 317–18.

27. Barani, *Tarikh-i Firozshahi*, Calcutta, 1862, pp. 72, 74, 75.
28. Although there was no priestly class in Islam, some ulama regarded themselves responsible for the enforcement of the Islamic way of life and principles. K.M. Ashraf, *Life and Condition of the People of Hindustan*, Delhi: Jiwan Prakashan, 1959, pp. 67–8.
29. Barani, *Tarikh-i Firozshahi*, p. 296. For details of Alauddin's conversation with Qazi Mughisuddin, ibid., pp. 290–1.
30. For details, see Barani, pp. 70–9.
31. Reuben Levy, *The Social Structure of Islam*, 2nd edn., Cambridge: Cambridge University Press, 1957, p. 262.
32. N. Baillie, *Digest of Muhammadan Law*, London, 1875, p. 174; also Agha Mahdi Husain, *The Tughlaq Dynasty*, Calcutta: Thacker, 1963, p. 14.
33. Wahed Husain, *Administration of Justice During the Muslim Rule in India*, rept., Delhi, 1977, p. 15; Muhammad Bashir Ahmad says, 'The system of employing pandits to explain the law in civil cases among the Hindus was introduced by Sultan Iltutmish on the Abbaside model.' *The Administration of Justice in Medieval India*, Karachi, 1951, p. 127; also Ameer Ali, *A Short History of the Saracens*, Delhi: Kitab Bhawan, 1977, pp. 188, 422. The Hanafi School of Islamic jurisprudence recognizes the appointment of non-Muslim judges for the disposal of suits among the *zimmi*. The muqaddam acted as both the committing and trying magistrate. A.B.M. Habibullah, *Foundation*, p. 272.
34. Baillie, *Digest*, p. 174.
35. Wahed Husain, *Administration of Justice*, pp. 147–8.
36. Barani's observation deserves to be quoted at length: 'In the capital (Delhi) and in the cities of the Musalmans the customs of infidelity are openly practised, idols are publicly worshipped and the traditions of infidelity are adhered to with greater insistance than before. Openly and without fear, the infidels continue the teaching of the principles of their false creed; they also adorn their idols and celebrate their rejoicing during their festivals with the beat of drums and *dhols* and with singing and

dancing. By paying merely a few *tankas* as the *jizyah* they are able to continue the traditions of infidelity by giving lessons in the books of their false faith and enforcing the orders of these books. . . . The desire for overthrowing infidels and knocking down idolators does not fill the hearts of the Muslim kings. . . .' See his *Fatawa-i Jahandari*, Eng. tr. Muhammad Habib, *The Political Theory of the Delhi Sultanate*, Aligarh, 1960. Advice XI, p. 48.
37. For details, M.B. Ahmad, *Administration of Justice*, pp. 73–4.
38. Ibid., p. 74.
39. Srivastava, *Position of Hindus*, p. 78.
40. Alberuni, *Kitab-ul Hind* (Alberuni's *India*, written at the time of Sultan Mahmud), ed. E.C. Sachau, Delhi: S. Chand, 1964, vol. I, p. 101; vol. II, p. 137.
41. The *Manusmriti* was compiled in the third or the fourth century probably by not one but many authors.
42. K.A. Nizami, ed., *Politics and Society During the Early Medieval Period (Collected Works of Mohammad Habib)*, vol. I, Delhi: People's Publishing House, 1974, p. 61.
43. Alberuni, *Kitab-ul Hind*, vol. II, p. 136.
44. Alberuni says that 'every action which is the privilege of a Brahman, such as saying prayers, reciting the Vedas and offering sacrifices to fire, is forbidden to them to such an extent that if a Shudra or Vaishya is proved to have recited the Vedas, he is accused by the Brahmans before the magistrates who ordered his tongue to be cut off', vol. II, p. 125.
45. The *Manusmriti* states that '. . . at night they shall not walk about in villages and in towns. By day they may go about for the purpose of their work.' Chap. X, p. 62.
46. According to Alberuni, they were 'considered illegitimate children': vol. I, p. 101.
47. There were mainly three kinds of discriminatory exceptions in the case of women: inheritance, witness, and divorce.
48. As cited by Mohammad Habib, *Political Theory*, p. 34.
49. For details ibid., pp. 74–94.
50. Srivastava, *Position*, pp. 24–5.
51. Cf. Mohammad Habib, *Political Theory*, p. 74.
52. Barani mentions the progress of arts and crafts in Delhi and praises artisans for their skills. He claims that Delhi's artisans excelled in manufacturing weapons, garments, and rosaries. Barani, *Tarikh*, p. 365. Isami also says that Delhi's craftsmen, artists and scientists acquired fame in foreign countries. See his *Futuh-us Salatin*, ed. Usha, Madras, 1948, pp. 445–6.
53. Mohammad Habib, *Political Theory*, p. 56. He argues that 'the increase in the size of Friday mosques and idgahs during the thirteenth century

testify to a growing mass of Muslim workers', and that 'by the end of Iltutmish's reign, all Friday mosques were overcrowded and the congregations used to spread out into the adjoining open land'.
54. There is, in fact, no shred of evidence to prove any organized effort of rulers or ulama or even Sufis for conversion. Block conversions of Hindus are generally attributed to Sufis because of fabricated *Malfuz* accounts of a later period. This issue will be discussed in detail in subsequent pages.
55. *Chachnama*, pp. 160–4.
56. Elliot and Dowson's *History of India*, vol. I, pp. 469, 476–7; Muhammad bin Qasim had appointed Siskar, former minister of Raja Dahir, as his advisor. See Aziz Ahmad, *Studies in Islamic Culture in the Indian Environment*, Delhi: Oxford University Press, 1964, p. 101.
57. Elliot and Dowson's *History of India*, vol. I, p. 464.
58. Ibid., p. 469.
59. Srivastava, *Position of Hindus*, p. 12.
60. A.B.M. Habibullah, *Foundation of Muslim Rule in India*, p. 235. The practice continued and Alauddin Khalji also allowed inscriptions in Sanskrit on his coins. E. Thomas, *The Chronicles of the Pathan Kings of Delhi*, Delhi: Munshiram Manoharlal, 1967, p. 172.
61. Mahdi Husain, *Tughlaq Dynasty*, p. 11.
62. Cf. *Tarikh-i Fakhr-i Mudabbir*, ed. E. Dension Ross, London, 1927, p. 26.
63. Minhaj Siraj writes about the Malik thus: 'When he sought safety and protection in the Santur mountains, Rana Ran-pal (Ranapala), the Hindu, who held the chieftainship among the Hindus—and it was the usage among that people to protect those who sought shelter with them—assisted Malik Kutlugh Khan.' *Tabaqat-i Nasiri*, vol. II, ed. Abdul Hai Habibi, Kabul, 1343 AH, p. 306; Eng. tr. Raverty, vol. II, p. 839.
64. Barani, *Tarikh-i Firoz Shahi*, p. 55.
65. Ibid., p. 87; also K.S. Lal, *Studies in Medieval Indian History*, Delhi: Ranjit, 1966, p. 206.
66. Barani, *Tarikh*, p. 182.
67. Agha Mahdi Husain writes, 'Occasionally the Hindus formed the rank and file of a rebel prince, such was the case with Malik Chhajju. When he revolted against Jalaluddin Khalji, he recruited Hindus freely in his army. With enormous followers he marched against the Khalji ruler.' A.M. Husain, *Tughlaq Dynasty*, p. 11.
68. Mohammad Habib, *Political Theory*, p. 150, in his article in *Aligarh Magazine*, Aligarh: AMU, October–December, 1931, p. 8; tr., *Khazain-ul Futuh*, Bombay: Taraporewala, 1931, p. 26. It was due to the presence of a large number of Hindu soldiers in the imperial army that Ala-ul Mulk advised the Sultan not to move out of the capital to repel the Mongol attack which had surrounded Delhi. Barani, *Tarikh*, pp. 255–7.
69. Ibid., p. 273.
70. K.S. Lal, *Studies in Medieval Indian History*, p. 206.
71. Ibid., p. 208.

72. With reference to Maulana Ziauddin, K.S. Lal says that idol worship was begun inside the palace. The Parwaris placed idols in the mosques and insulted Muslim religious feelings. 'Nasiruddin Khusrau Shah', *Journal of Indian History*, vol. XXIII, part 3, 1944, pp. 174-5.
73. Isami asserts that there were Hindu generals like Gulchandra in the army of Ghazi Malik. *Futuh-us Salatin*, p. 378; I.H. Qureshi *Administration*, p. 145. Similarly, Amir Khusrau claims that the army of Khusrau Shah consisted of many Hindu generals, such as Ahar Deo, Amar Deo, Narsia, Parsia, Harmar Parmar, and Rai Rayan Randhol, *Tughlaqnama*, ed. Syed Hashmi Faridabadi, Aurangabad, 1938, pp. 128, 131.
74. Mahdi Husain, *Tughlaq Dynasty*, p. 421.
75. I.H. Siddiqui, *Authority and Kingship Under the Sultans of Delhi*, Delhi: Manohar, 2006, pp. 61, 62, 72-7, 98, 105, 114-15, 138-41; 'The Composition of Nobility Under the Lodi Sultans', *Medieval India: A Miscellany*, vol. IV, Aligarh: AMU, 1977, pp. 53, 64, 66.
76. Siddiqui 1977, pp. 66ff.
77. Barani, *Fatawa-i Jahandari*, Eng. tr., p. 47.
78. Nizami, *Some Aspects*, p. 319.
79. Ibid, p. xxi.
80. Barani, *Tarikh-i Firoz Shahi*, p. 120.
81. It is said that the Turko-Persian nobles even in the early Sultanate period accumulated enormous debts to Hindu bankers and that the brokers, 'Multanis' and *Sahs*, during the time of Alauddin Khalji's economic reforms, figured among the wealthiest and most important subjects. Ibid., pp. 120, 284.
82. For details, Iqtidar Husain Siddiqi, 'Social Mobility in the Delhi Sultanate', *Medieval India*, vol. I, 1992, pp. 30-3.
83. Agha Mahdi Husain says, 'The Muslim governing class consisting of the Sultan and the *Waalis* (provincial governors) had their sphere of control limited to towns, it was the Hindu chief who was the link between the provincial governor, usually a Muslim, and the Hindu peasant.' *Tughlaq Dynasty*, p. 12.
84. Tara Chand further says that since the Muslims did not bring with them 'artisans, accountants and clerks, their buildings were erected by Hindus . . . their coins were struck by Hindu goldsmiths and their accounts were kept by Hindu officers. Brahman jurists advised the king on the administration of Hindu law and Brahman astronomers helped in the performance of their general functions'. *Influence of Islam on Indian Culture*, p. 137. Agha Mahdi Husain specifically says that Hindus 'acted both as assessors and collectors of revenue and they controlled the local administration of the Muslim State in India'. *Tughlaq Dynasty*, pp. 10-11. Besides, Sultan Aibak also appointed a Rana from Banaras as Sahib-i barid (head of the intelligence service), though some were opposed to his appointment to such an important post. *Lubab-ul Albab*, ed. E.C. Browne and Mirza Muhammad Qazvini, London, 1906, pp. 113-14.

85. Srivastava, *Position of Hindus*, p. 136. Barani says Hatya Paik and Brinjtan Kotwal, Balban's nobles, were elevated to high positions and received high salaries. *Tarikh-i-Firozshahi,* pp. 210–12.
86. A.B.M. Habibullah, *Foundation of Muslim Rule*, p. 265.
87. Ibid.
88. M.T. Titus, ed., *Indian Islam*, 2nd edn., Delhi: Oriental Books, 1979, p. 152.
89. For instance, the Muslim ruler of Malwa in his attack on the Bahmani kingdom employed 12,000 Afghans and Rajputs, whereas Deo Raj, the ruler of Vijaynagara, recruited Muslims, assigned lands to their chiefs and built a mosque at his capital as a means of encouragement. Ibid., p. 152.
90. *Journal of Indian History,* vol. XV, part 2, 1936, p. 183.
91. Agha Mahdi Husain, *Tughlaq Dynasty*, p. 73.
92. Barani, *Tarikh*, pp. 429–30.
93. Isami, *Futuh-us Salatin,* ed. A.S. Usha, Madras, 1948, p. 515. The Sultan appointed a Hindu named Sri Raj as his Nazir and one Mehta as administrative officer in Karnal. Barani, *Tarikh*, p. 523; Agha Mahdi Husain, *Tughlaq Dynasty*, p. 335; A. Rashid, *Society and Culture in Medieval India (1206–1556)*, Calcutta: Firma, 1969, p. 228.
94. Agha Mahdi Husain, *Tughlaq Dynasty*, p. 224. The nature of the post was not specific, but the appointment itself was opposed by some Muslim officers who ultimately got him murdered.
95. Firishta, *Tarikh-i-Firishta,* Newal Kishore Press, 1281 AH, vol. I, p. 246.
96. Barani, *Tarikh*, p. 501.
97. Agha Mahdi Husain, *Tughlaq Dynasty*, p. 316.
98. Cf. Aziz Ahmad, *Studies in Islamic Culture in the Indian Environment,* Oxford: Clarendon Press, 1967, p. 102.
99. Barani, *Tarikh*, pp. 587, 595; Afif, *Tarikh-i-Firoz Shahi,* ed. M. Wilayat Husain, Calcutta, 1890, pp. 103-4. Firoz Shah honoured a Hindu Zamindar, Rai Ziarain, for helping him in his Bengal expedition. Afif, op. cit., p. 111.
100. Barani, *Tarikh-i Firoz Shahi,* pp. 216–17. We have already quoted from Barani the conversation of Sultan Jalaluddin Khalji with Malik Ahmad Chap regarding his helplessness concerning the heretic practices of the Hindus.
101. *Annual Report of the Archaeological Survey of India, 1922–1923.*
102. Ibid., 1909–10, p. 131.
103. *Futuhat-i Firoz Shahi,* text with Eng. tr. Shaikh Abdur Rashid, Aligarh: AMU, n.d., p. 11.
104. Abdullah, *Tarikh-i Daudi,* ed. Shaikh Abdur Rashid, Aligarh: AMU, 1954, p. 29; also Ahmad Yadgar, *Tarikh-i Shahi,* ed. Muhammad Hidayat Husain, Calcutta: Bibliotheca Indica, 1939, pp. 130–1.
105. Yahya Sirhindi, *Tarikh-i Mubarak Shahi,* ed. M. Hidayat Husain, Calcutta, 1931, p. 79.

106. Cf. K.M. Pannikar, *A Survey of Indian History,* Bombay: Asia Publishing House, 1956, p. 131.
    Jain sources appreciate Alp Khan, Alauddin's governor in Gujarat, for permitting the reconstruction of the temples destroyed during the Muslim invasions. S.C. Misra, *The Rise of Muslim Power in Gujarat,* 2nd edn., Delhi: Munshiram Manoharlal, 1982, pp. 68–9.
107. The sultan married his son Khizr Khan to Deval Rani, the daughter of Kamla Devi. Srivastava, *Position of Hindus*, p. 77 and n. 5.
108. Isami, *Futuhat-i-Firoz Shahi,* p. 515.
109. Barani, pp. 504–5; Qureshi, *Administration,* p. 195.
110. Isami, *Futuhat,* p. 44. The appointment of Hindus on important posts was also not liked by Barani, op. cit., pp. 504, 505.
111. Agha Mahdi Husain, *Tughlaq Dynasty,* p. 316.
112. Ibid., pp. 322–3. Another Hindu courtier, Raghava Chaitanya, who was proficient in 'mantras', tried to create such conditions for Jinprabha Suri to leave the court, but failed.
113. Firishta, *Tarikh,* vol. II, pp. 369–70. Firishta is not corroborated by any contemporary or near contemporary source.
114. Mahdi Husain, *Tughlaq Dynasty,* pp. 147, 323.
115. R.C. Jauhari, *Firoz Tughlaq (1351-1388),* Agra: S. Agrawala, 1968, p. 156; Aziz Ahmad, p. 219.
116. Barani, *Fatawa-i Jahandari,* p. 323.
117. Hamid bin Fazl-ullah, *Siyar-ul Arifin,* Delhi: Razi Press, AH 1311, pp. 159-60: when Syed Makhdum-i Jahanian was seriously ill, Nawahun came to see him and prayed for his long life thus:

خدای تعالیٰ حضرت مخدوم را صحت دید، ذات پاک مخدوم تم اولیاء است چنانکه محمدﷺ ختم
انبیاء بود

Syed Makhdum's younger brother, Syed Sadruddin Raju Qattal and his followers noted the words and claimed that by calling the Muhammad the last Prophet he had become a Musalman. Thus, the formal declaration of accepting Islam had been demanded from him. But when Nawahun refused to do so and fled to Delhi for refuge, Raju Qattal along with some witnesses followed him thereafter his brother's death.
    Though the other ulama, particularly Shaikh Mohammad bin Qazi Abdul Muqtadar, contended that since Nawahun had not formally accepted Islam, the law of heresy did not apply to him, Raju exercised his influence and prevailed upon the ulama for a decree of execution of Nawahun.
118. It appears from the description of *Futuhat-i Firoz Shahi,* p. 8 that the action was confined to the personality of Ahmad Bihari and his followers. That it was perhaps only a precautionary step taken by Firoz Shah against the Wahdat-ul Wujudi movement on the whole, was pointed out by Shaikh Sadruddin and his followers.
119. Firishta, *Tarikh-i,* vol. 1, p. 185; *Tarikh-i Daudi,* p. 59; Khwaja Nizam-

uddin Ahmad, *Tabaqat-i-Akbari*, vol. I, rpt., Calcutta, 1973, pp. 222–3. It appears from these sources that a Brahman named Bodhan or Lodhan was sent by Azam Humayun, the governor of Lakhnauti, to Sultan Sikandar Lodi (who was then in Sambhal) with the charge that he had declared اسلام حق است و دین من نیز درست است

Sikandar then called a meeting of the leading ulama, where it was decided that the person should be killed if he did not accept Islam.
120. K.S. Lal, *Twilight of the Delhi Sultanate*, Delhi: Asia Publishing House, 1963, p. 191.
121. Abdullah, *Tarikh-i-Daudi*, p. 40.
122. Satish Chandra, *Mughal Empire 1526-1748*, part 2 of *Medieval India*, Delhi: Har Anand, 1999, p. 45.
123. K.A. Nizami, *Akbar and Religion*, Delhi: Idarah-i Adabiyat-i Dehli, 1989, p. 13.
124. Satish Chandra, op. cit., p. 111.
125. Ibid.
126. Badauni, *Muntakhab-ut Tawarikh*, ed. Molvi Ahmad Ali, Calcutta: Bibliotheca Indica, vol. II, 1865, p. 392.
127. Akbar maintained good relations with Hindus and their holy men from the beginning. See, Shahabuddin Iraqi, 'Akbar's Relations with Non-Sufi Saints of India', in *Islamic Heritage in South Asian Subcontinent*, vol. II, ed. Nazir Ahmad and I.H. Siddiqi, Jaipur: Publication Scheme, 2000, pp. 122–36.
128. Badauni, *Tarikh*, pp. 256–8 says that Akbar was particularly influenced by the doctrine of transmigration of souls; he had approved of the saying that 'there is no religion in which the doctrine of migration has not taken firm root'. He refers to Debi and Purukhotam who instructed Akbar in Hindi. They had impressed upon his mind the importance of the theory of metempsychosis and that of the sun as a symbol of power.

It is significant that whereas Abul Fazl mentions the names of some Hindu saints and scholars under the first out of the five categories of people, Muslim religious leaders like Abdul Qadir Badauni, Shaikh Abdun Nabi, and Qazi Sadruddin are declared bigots, not 'beyond the narrow sphere of revealed testimony', and their names have occurred under the last category. See *Ain-i Akbari*, Eng. tr. Jarrett, vol. 1, book 2, p. 608.
129. Abul Fazl, *Akbarnama*, Eng. tr. H. Beveridge, vol. II, Delhi: Oriental Books, 1972, pp. 159–60.
130. It is significant that Akbar gives convincing arguments regarding these two measures. About the abolition of the pilgrimage tax he says that it would amount to non-interference and giving freedom to Hindus in religious matters; and about *jizyah* he says that since the Hindus were also serving the state by taking part in wars, there was no justification for levying this tax on them. Ibid., pp. 190, 203.

CHAPTER 2

Sufism in India

In his systematic account of Sufism in the twelfth century, Imam Ghazali (AD 1058–1111), the mystic philosopher, differentiated between the *ulama-i zahir* (externalist scholars) and *ulama-i batin* (saints or mystics), meaning that while the former proceed from knowledge to action, the latter proceed from action to knowledge.[1] Ghazali emphasized that true knowledge can be achieved only through personal experience, and that theological doctrines are proved, not by speculative methods, but by direct knowledge with which God floods the heart.[2]

In the thirteenth century there appeared three very important figures in the history of Sufism: Shaikh Shihabuddin Suhrawardi (d. AD 1234), Shaikh Muhiuddin Ibn-i Arabi (d. AD 1248), and Maulana Jalaluddin Rumi (d. AD 1273), who provided Sufism its philosophical grounding. Ibn-i Arabi propounded in his two famous works, *Futuhat-i Makkiya* and *Fusus-ul Hikam*, the philosophy of *Wahdat-ul Wajud* (the unity of existence as the manifestation of God). He was the first mystic to interpret the doctrine of *al-Wajud* (being). As for Rumi, the popularized Sufi mystic ideas in his famous *Masnavi* that remained popular in the Sufi circles of Delhi even in the fourteenth century.[3] The *Awarif-ul Ma'arif* of Shaikh Shihabuddin Suhrawardi, on the other hand, is a treatise on the moral and ethical aspects of Sufism. It has fixed the connotation of mystic terms, explained the aims and objectives of mysticism, and formulates principles for institutional organization. This treatise was, therefore, readily accepted by the mystics of all schools including the Chishti saints as the best guide.[4]

In India, Sufism was introduced and popularized by two eleventh-century Sufis, Shaikh Ali Hujwiri of Ghazna and Shaikh Safiuddin Gazruni. The former settled in Lahore where he composed his famous, *Kashaf-ul Mahjub*, the first treatise on Sufism in Persian.[5]

The latter lived in Uchh in south Punjab. His *dargah* became a place of pilgrimage, but the Gazruni *silsilah* could not gain popularity. By the twelfth century, the Sufis organized themselves into *silsilahs* (fraternities or orders), each called after a great Sufi Shaikh to whom the followers traced their spiritual descent. Two of the *silsilahs* introduced in India just after the formation of the Delhi sultanate in the beginning of the thirteenth century were the Chishti and the Suhrawardi.

The Chishtia *silsilah* was founded by Khwaja Abu Ishaq Shami (AD 940) in Chisht, a village near Herat. It was brought to India by Khwaja Muinuddin Sijzi[6] who established a Chishti mystic centre in Ajmer even before the Turkish conquest of India. Under his able successors, such as Shaikh Qutbuddin Bakhtiyar Kaki, Shaikh Fariduddin Ganj-i Shakar, and Shaikh Nizamuddin Auliya, the *silsilah* spread far and many Chishti mystic centres were established in northern India.[7] On the other hand, the Suhrawardi *silsilah* was founded by Shaikh Najibuddin Abdul Qahir Suhrawardi (d. AD 1169) in Suhraward (a town in Jibal), but was developed by his nephew, Shaikh Shihabuddin Suhrawardi (d. AD 1234). He sent many of his disciples to India but Shaikh Bahauddin Zakaria alone succeeded in establishing the order firmly in India, particularly in Multan and Sindh.[8] Later, some other important *silsilahs* like the Firdausi, the Qadiri, the Shattari, and the Naqshbandi also emerged, and in time spread to different parts of the country and built up their own centres, the *khanqahs, jama'at khanas*, and *zawiyas*.[9]

INSTITUTIONAL STRUCTURE OF SUFISM

The establishment of *khanqahs* was an integral part of the Sufi *silsilahs*. Having been effectively organized on a large scale, they became centres of mystic activity and forums for the regulation of the corporate life of the Sufis. Hence, the formation of such training centres had to be based on certain principles, even if the *khanqahs* of different orders were organized on different patterns. Shaikh Shihabuddin Suhrawardi in his *Awarif-ul Ma'arif* gives seven basic principles for *khanqah* organization.[10] The Shaikh (spiritual teacher) was the central figure and ultimate authority of the *khanqah*, responsible not only for the entire administration of the centre, but also for affiliated branches across the country. He was, therefore, highly respected, and was called with the title of *Shaikh-ul Islam* to denote his spiritual position and power.

The Shaikh was required to possess the requisite qualities and qualifications. Shaikh Nizamuddin Auliya used to tell his disciples that a Shaikh must be acquainted with Islamic sciences and a knowledge of the Quran, *hadis* (Prophetic traditions) and *fiqh* (jurisprudence) was necessary. Any instruction given by the Shaikh that was inconsistent with the Quranic injunction could be turned down by the *murid*.[11] It may be noticed that these were the qualifications to be possessed by the ulama also.

In order to maintain their spiritual identity, Shaikhs would adopt some special articles of daily use, the *khirqah* (patched frock), the *sajjadah* (prayer-carpet), the *nalain-i chubin* (wooden sandals), the *tasbih* (rosary) or the *asa* (wooden stick) as mystic insignia, and whomever was entrusted with these articles at the time of the Shaikh's demise came to be regarded as the spiritual successor. Previously, the appointment of chief successor was made from amongst senior and highly qualified disciples, but later, as pointed out by Mohammad Habib, some Shaikhs began to appoint 'their own sons as their successors, and thus mysticism ceased to be a spiritual urge and degenerated into a comfortable and recognized hereditary trade or profession, which catered to the needs of the ignorant and the credulous'.[12]

In the Suhrawardi *silsilah* the hereditary succession had become an accepted tradition. The founder of the order, Shaikh Najibuddin Abdul Qahir, had appointed his nephew, Shaikh Shihabuddin, his chief *khalifa* and *Sajjadah-nashin*. Shaikh Bahauddin Zakariya's son, Shaikh Sadruddin Arif (d. AD 1285), succeeded him as his chief successor in Multan, though his disciple, Jalaluddin Surkh Bukhari (d. AD 1291), founded a separate Suhrawardi centre at Uchch. Shaikh Sadruddin too was succeeded by his son, Shaikh Ruknuddin Abul Fath (d. AD 1335). As Shaikh Ruknuddin had no son, after his death a struggle for succession began between a grandson of the Shaikh's brother and a nephew. The problem became so serious that the matter was referred to Muhammad bin Tughluq for arbitration. Both parties went to Daulatabad to argue their claims. The Sultan decided in favour of Shaikh Hud who was sent back to Multan with state honours to take charge.[13]

There was generally no bitter struggle among the men of different orders for spiritual control of their respective areas. Whenever such a situation arose, it was resolved by mutual understanding.[14] The Chishti and the Suhrawardi saints maintained mutual respect and cordial relationships among themselves in spite of ideological and temperamental differences. For instance, once Shaikh Ruknuddin Multani was called by Sultan Mubarak Shah Khalji who was on bad terms with Shaikh Nizamuddin Auliya and wanted to turn public opinion against him by setting up a rival *khanqah* in Delhi.[15] But the situation turned out differently. Amir Khurd says that when Shaikh Nizamuddin heard about this he went out to receive Shaikh Ruknuddin near the Hauz-i Khas-i Alai, and they exchanged cordial greetings. Later, the Suhrawardi saint went to see the Sultan, who asked him, 'Whom did you meet first in the city?' The Shaikh replied, 'The best among the citizens'.[16] Thus the Sultan's intention of creating differences between the two holy men could not be fulfilled.

However, methods were prescribed for the initiation of members into the mystic circle. The disciples of a Shaikh in a *khanqah* were supposed to have complete faith in their *pir* as the spiritual authority. They were to regulate their religious and worldly lives according to his instructions. The *murids* were generally divided into two categories, *muqiman* (inmates or permanent residents) and or *musafirin* (visitors). From the latter the Shaikh did not expect anything more than honest dealings and regular performance of religious duties. From his permanent disciples, however, he demanded complete detachment from worldly ties, and a surrender of the self for the cause of the *khanqah*.[17]

Permanent members were also divided into three grades, *Ahl-i khidmat*, *Ahl-i suhbat*, and *Ahl-i khalwat*, according to their standing and the nature of the tasks assigned to them in the *khanqah*. Usually a senior disciple was given charge of general supervision of the *khanqah* administration. He assigned duties to the inmates, looked after guests, and arranged for the distribution of *futuh* (unasked for charity). A strict discipline was maintained in the *khanqah* and elaborate rules were laid down for this purpose.[18] The Shaikh often overlooked minor acts of irregularity, but in the cases of disciples of higher rank he kept a vigilant eye on every aspect of their thought and action, and action was taken against those found guilty of the slightest irregularity.[19] Khilafatnama (certificate of succession) was conferred on a dedicated *murid* trained by the Shaikh for this purpose, and only merit was taken into consideration.[20] As evidence of authority, each of the *khalifahs* (successors) was provided a written Khilafatnama signed by his Shaikh. In his *Siyar-ul Auliya* Mir Khurd provides the texts of some Khilafatnamas, which throw light on the aims and objectives of appointing *khalifahs* to various territories.[21]

The concept of *wilayat* (spiritual dominion) was so deeply rooted in the institutional structure that the heads of the *silsilahs* dispatched their *khalifahs* to the various provinces, on *wilayats*; and they, in their turn, appointed their subordinate *khalifahs* in *qasbas* and cities. Thus, a spiritual hierarchy of Sufi mystic leaders came to be established. Territorial distributions on a large scale give an idea of the exactness with which areas of spiritual supervision or control were determined.

For their maintenance a *khanqah* generally depended on a *waqf* or endowment. If a *khanqah* had no *waqf*, the Shaikh either instructed his disciples to earn their livelihood on their own or allowed them to beg or sit in the *khanqah* on *tawakkul* (trust in God). If a *khanqah* had no Shaikh and was run by an *ikhwan* (a group of men of equal spiritual status), the same three means were open to them.[22] Some Chishti *khanqahs*, that received large amounts of *futuh* provided better meals for their inmates and visitors. Consequently, the *langar* (open kitchen) became a regular feature of *khanqah* life; it distributed free food to the people. The tradition of a *langar* among the Indian Chishtis was, however, probably established by Shaikh Farid. There is no reference of any *langar* in the *khanqah* of Shaikh Muinuddin Chishti or of Shaikh Qutbuddin Bakhtiyar. Even Shaikh Farid's *langar* did not function regularly due to unavailability of the fund of *futuh*. In the beginning Shaikh Nizamuddin did not have a *langar*, but later when enormous funds were received, he established a rather good *langar*, as we shall see. There were, however, certain prescribed rules for the acceptance of *futuh*. It could not be aspired for, it could not be in the form of a guaranteed payment or immovable property, and it had to be utilized and distributed immediately after being received. Shaikh Farid is said to have been very particular in distributing all that he received as *futuh*. He used to say that his *khanqah* was not a storehouse for royal gifts. It was the practice at the *jama'at khana* of Shaikh Nizamuddin Auliya that on every Friday everything in the store was given away to the poor and the house was cleared and swept.[23] As far as the personal family life of the Chishti saints is concerned, most of them lived in poverty and did not own houses of their own.[24] This was because they considered the possession of private property an obstacle to spiritual advancement. They subsisted mostly on *futuh*. Shaikh Hamiduddin Nagauri was probably the only exception, who adopted cultivation in preference to *futuh*. On the other hand, Shaikh Farid was also the only Chishti saint who, forced by his circumstances, permitted his disciples to distribute *zanbil* (a dried and hollow gourd functioning as a bowl) and to collect food.[25] Even incurring of debts for household expenses was not allowed.[26] In fact, most of the Chishti saints were so absorbed in their mystic activities that they could not give proper care to their families and family members. Deprived of fatherly care and affection, many sons and dependants of such saints turned into worldly people. If the only son of Shaikh Qutbuddin was 'unworthy of his father', a grandson of Shaikh Farid was a drunkard and a grandson of Shaikh Najibuddin was a vagabond.[27] The way in which Shaikh Badruddin Ishaq was treated by the sons of Shaikh Farid[28] shows that they were guided by material considerations rather than moral and spiritual ideals. This was due to the indifferent family atmosphere in which they were brought up.

The Sufis and the State

According to Barani, spiritual life was to be attained through humility, poverty, and self-abasement, whereas to the king a degree of pride, arrogance, and self-glorification were necessary, implying that the co-existence of spirituality and kingship was impossible.[29] It is significant that the Sufis also generally considered that spirituality was not meant for the rulers and the ruling class; they generally maintained a distance from the court, and the rulers and nobles were not welcomed in the *khanqah*. Some Sufis like Shaikh Sharfuddin Yahya Maneri were, however, of the opinion that they could be intermediaries between the ruler and the masses.[30]

The renunciation of the world (*tark-i dunya*), the basic principle of Sufism, meant detachment not from worldly life as such but from worldly desires and materialism. It was for this reason that the Sufis led a family life and yet remained indifferent to wealth, politics, and government service. But there was difference of approach between the Chishtis and the Suhrawardis. While most of the Suhrawardi saints had no hesitation in visiting the royal courts and accepting government service, the mystics of Chishti *silsilah* generally abstained from these involvements.

The Chishtis

After the fall of the caliphs, the Muslim state, turned into a largely materialistic and exploitative enterprise negating the true spirit of Islam. Besides, there were legal objections to the service of the state which found expression in Imam Ghazali's work. According to Ghazali, 'almost the whole of the income of the Sultans is from prohibited sources . . . (even) *jizya* is realized through such cruel means that it does not continue to be permitted'.[31] Consequently, all services paid from such sources of income were deemed illegal. And then there were moral and ethical considerations. Government jobs distracted a mystic from his single-minded pursuit of God. He would also be cut-off from the masses, which was the main context of his activity. He would also cease to be independent and would be bound not to go against government policies.

Owing to these considerations, Chishti mystics severed all contact with the rulers and governments. It is said that Khwaja Muinuddin Chishti was once forced by his sons to proceed to the court and to obtain necessary documents from Sultan Iltutmish to settle a dispute over some reclaimed land in their possession. But the Khwaja did not visit the court.[32] Shaikh Qutbuddin Bakhtiyar Kaki visited the court of Iltutmish only once, and that too because of unavoidable circumstances.[33] While the Shaikh extended his moral support to the Sultan in his welfare projects, he would not associate with the administration.[34] Shaikh Fariduddin Ganj-i Shakar (1175–1265) not only maintained his distance from the court, he also wanted his disciples not to associate with kings and princes.[35] But the Shaikh is said to have had cordial relationship with Balban, who respected him a great deal. He is also reported to have written a letter of recommendation to Balban.[36] Shaikh Nizamuddin Auliya also maintained distance from the court. His clear instruction to his senior disciples was: 'You will not go to the doors of the kings and will not seek their rewards'.[37] But a new dimension of relationship began in the time of Alauddin Khalji (1296–1316). It appears from both the historical and hagiological accounts that the Sultan respected Shaikh Nizamuddin (d. 1325).[38] Though in the beginning he was suspicious of him and his popularity,[39] after having been convinced of the Shaikh's innocence, Sultan Alauddin was so impressed by him that he directed the princes like Khizr Khan, and Shadi Khan to become his disciples, and to celebrate the occasion a grand feast was arranged, with the permission of the Shaikh himself.[40] This indicates that both sultan and Shaikh gave immense importance to this unique relationship. Following this trend, however, a large number of nobles also became disciples of the Shaikh. According to the conclusion drawn by I.A. Zilli, 'the members of the royal household, the nobility and the government servants constituted roughly 20 per cent of the total recorded number of his disciples'.[41]

However, the Chishti saints were particularly against accepting *jagirs* or government service in order to remain independent. Shaikh Qutbuddin refused to accept a land grant offered to him by Iltutmish.[42] Shaikh Hamiduddin Nagauri preferred to pass his days in poverty rather than accept anything from the Sultan.[43] Shaikh Farid's reply to Ulugh Khan's offer of villages was, 'There are many who deserve it; give it to them.'[44]

Shaikh Nizamuddin Auliya also refused to accept royal grants 'If I accept this, the people would say: The Shaikh goes to the garden; he goes to enjoy the view of his land and cultivation. Are these acts proper to me?'[45]

The Shaikh's instructions to his disciples were clear: 'Do not accept any village or stipend or favour from kings and officials. It is not permitted to a dervish.'[46]

Similarly, the explicit order of the Chishti Shaikh to his followers was to stay away from state appointments. He dealt with offenders strictly, either by cancelling his Khilafatnama or by expelling him.[47] Shaikh Qutbuddin emphatically declined the post of *Shaikh-ul Islam* offered him by Sultan Iltutmish.[48] Another contemporary mystic, Shaikh Hasan, is also said to have stayed away from being appointed as qazi.[49] Shaikh Nizamuddin Auliya demanded from his senior disciples a promise to abstain from the service of kings.

Sufism in India 63

This gave such a definite shape to their character that some years after the Shaikh's demise, when Muhammad bin Tughluq desired to associate the Chishti saints with the administration, they declined the offer and this became the main reason of conflict between the two. However, the *farman* to migrate from Delhi to Daulatabad could not be disobeyed, and all the Chishtis, with the exception of Chiragh-i Delhi, went to the Deccan.[50] It was afterwards that many of the saints changed the policy and, when provincial governments were established, accepted endowments from the founders of the provincial dynasties, and jagirs became almost an integral part of many of the *khanqahs*.[51]

It may be pointed out that among the early Chishtis only the *khalifas* were required not to enter state service. Lay murids like Amir Khusrau and Hasan Sijzi were permitted to work in the government in different capacities. As regards the cases of above two personalities they enjoyed the personal affection of Shaikh Nizamuddin Auliya and were not mystics of high rank. Nor were they granted the Khilafatnama which barred a disciple from government service.[52]

For cash gifts, however, an exception was made. Earlier, the Chishti saints rarely and reluctantly accepted cash from rulers.[53] But Shaikh Nizamuddin seems to have accepted it without any hesitation. On several occasions Sultan Alauddin sent huge amounts to the Shaikh, and he readily accepted.[54] This was obviously for distribution amongst the needy. That the establishment of Shaikh Nizamuddin was wealthy or magnificent seems an exaggeration, but the maintenance of a big *khanqah* along with *langar* could not have been possible without the patronage of the ruling class. It is evident from several sources that the enormous *futuh* at the disposal of the Shaikh actually came from members of the royal household and from civic officials. Merchants from abroad also made offerings in cash.[55]

Sultan Ghyasuddin died in 1325 and was succeeded by his son, Muhammad Tughluq; Shaikh Nizamuddin too was succeeded soon after by Shaikh Nasiruddin Chiragh-i Dilli. Mystic and Sultan could not understand each other, and the result appeared in the form of mutual conflict. The Chishti *silsilah* had to suffer so much that the Shaikh laments by giving the names of a number of *langars* which had then ceased to exist.[56]

Shaikh Nasiruddin proved to be the last great Chishti saint, and after his death in 1356 the central organization of the order broke down. The institution of chief successor also ceased to exist, as the Shaikh could not appoint a successor. Provincial centres with their local and limited jurisdiction developed in different parts of the country.[57] For instance, as described by Syed Bashir Hasan, the Chishti *silsilah* was well established in Malwa.[58]

Mystic writings hardly contain precepts for the political figures of the time, perhaps because they considered them distant from spiritual circles. However, Chishti saints generally advised rulers and nobles in indirect ways, in the guise of stories, or wrapped in the traditions of the Prophet. Two statements of Chishti saints are of significance: 'Entrust the country to a God-fearing minister' and 'The Prophet says that if any old woman goes to bed hungry in any town of a kingdom, she will hold the collar of the ruler on the Day of Judgment.'[59]

Shaikh Abdul Quddus Gangohi (Chishti, Sabri), wrote letters to Sikandar Lodi, Babur, and Humayun. In a letter to Sikandar Lodi, he reminded the Sultan of his duties as a ruler. An hour spent by rulers in the pursuit of justice was more commendable than sixty hours of prayers by others, he said. He emphasized that the welfare of state depended on the Sultan, and that if a monarch neglected to protect the weak, the holy, the ulama, and the mystics, the world would become anarchic.[60] It was perhaps in this spirit that the Shaikh subsequently advised Babur to take up the revenue administration according to the practices of the first four caliphs and to reserve all high offices for Muslims. Hindus were not to be given control over the finance and revenue departments, but to be reduced to the status of a revenue and *jizyah* paying class. He suggested that Hindus should be forced to dress differently from the Muslims, and that they should be restricted to their traditional trades and professions.[61]

The Suhrawardis

Contrary to the traditions of Chishtis, the Suhrawardis mixed freely with the rulers and accumulated wealth. When their peers objected, they replied, 'Poison does not harm (him) who knows the antidote.' They argued that they thereby helped the poor to get their grievances redressed by the Sultan and brought about a change in the outlook of the Sultans themselves.[62] Inspired by the Quranic verse, 'Obey God, obey His prophet and obey those with authority amongst you', Shaikh Najibuddin Abdul Qahir, the founder of Suhrawardi order, exhorted his disciples to revere their rulers and abstain from finding fault with them. He was of the opinion that rebellion against a ruler, even if he were cruel or unjust, was not permitted.[63]

Thus, a tradition of mixing with rulers and taking part in political affairs was already in place outside India by Shaikh Najibuddin, and his disciple Shaikh Shihabuddin followed suit.[64] This tradition determined the attitude of the Indian Suhrawardi saints towards the state. The early Turkish Sultans needed the support of the religious classes in order to consolidate their political power in India. Since the Chishti saints held aloof, the Sultans turned to the Suhrawardis, who readily extended their support and accepted administrative posts. Though Shaikh Bahauddin Zakariya accepted the post of *Shaikul-ul Islam* to run a *khanqah* for the distribution of charity and provide assistance to travellers, Syed Nuruddin Mubarak Ghaznavi was appointed to this post to supervise charity in the metropolis, and he was popularly called Mir-i Dehli.[65] Similarly, Maulana Majduddin consented to perform the duties of *Sadr-i Wilayat*.[66]

Syed Nuruddin Mubarak was a frequent visitor to the court of Iltutmish. He used to deliver sermons in the royal presence.[67] At the same time he is also said to have declared that the way the rulers lived, and the etiquette observed at the court were contrary to the principles of *shariat*. He exposed the irreligious character of those practices considered 'essentials of kingship' لوازم امور بادشاهی by medieval Muslim rulers. His denunciation was, in fact, of all those principles and ideals of Persian civilization that had permeated the Muslim society and had conditioned the political ideology of the governing classes. It was not only difficult but almost impossible for Iltutmish to resolve the contradiction between Muslim political theory and practices that had appeared after the fall of the *Khilafat-i Rashida* (pious caliphate). The sultanate itself was an un-Islamic institution. Aware of this, the historian Ziauddin Barani, was constrained to declare that sovereignty was never possible without the practice of non-Islamic customs,[68] and, for the same reason, Syed Nuruddin was also prepared to accord sanction to such practices, provided the monarch tried to act on what he called the four principles for the protection of the faith (چهار عمل دین پناهی).⁶⁹

However, when Sultan Iltutmish's attempt to consolidate the empire brought him into conflict with the Turkish nobles and slave-officers, Shaikh Bahauddin Zakariya, though living in his *khanqah* at Multan under Nasiruddin Qubacha, supported the cause of Iltutmish. In concert with Sharfuddin, the qazi of Multan, the Shaikh wrote to Iltutmish probably inviting him to invade Multan.⁷⁰ But the letter was intercepted by Qubacha. The qazi, being a government servant, had to pay the usual penalty for treason, but the Shaikh escaped. The reasons were more political than spiritual. The Shaikh was so popular among the people of Multan that his execution might incite rebellion in the newly acquired territories of Sindh and might also provide a plea to Iltutmish for expediting a move into Multan for which he was already planning. Thus it was the fear of political and popular reaction that prevented Qubacha from taking action against him.

After Iltutmish's annexation of Multan, however, Shaikh Bahauddin Zakariya developed close personal contact with the Sultan and accepted the honorific title of *Shaikh-ul Islam*.⁷¹ The Shaikh also cooperated with the administration in dealing with the Mongol problem and saved the town of Multan from destruction.⁷² Besides, he was probably the richest Shaikh of the land, because enormous *futuh* flowed into his *khanqah*. He is said to have had a *khazana* containing boxes full of gold *tankas*. The local administration of Multan looked to him for help in times of hardship⁷³ and provoked robbers to kidnap his son and demand a ransom.⁷⁴ In fact, Shaikh's resources were no less than those of a medieval Iqtadar.

An account of the Suhrawardi *khanqah* at Multan will reveal its basic principles and approach to life. Contrary to the Chishti *jama'at-khana*, it was a state institution, magnificent and better organized.⁷⁵ The *khanqah* had large stocks of cereal in its granaries and its treasury was full of gold and silver coins. When contemporary mystic thought could not reconcile itself to the idea of accumulating wealth and at the same time claiming to be the spiritual head of the people, Shaikh Bahauddin Zakariya made every possible effort to convince his critics that it was not the wealth itself that mattered but its proper use for the welfare. Yet the fact is that he failed to condone this contradiction in his career and character.[76] His arguments carried little weight with the Chishti, who rejected the idea of accumulating wealth as negation of the true spirit of *tawakkul* (trust in God). Even the argument of Shaikh Ruknuddin Multani that when all sorts of people visited him he too required money apart from his learning and spiritual ability,[77] seems not to have been convincing: only a small part of *futuh* was distributed among the needy, the major part remaining in the *khazana*. It may also be borne in mind that the Suhrawardi *khanqah* was hardly open to common people or the Shaikh accessible to them. Shaikh Bahauddin was fond of good food, but did not keep an open table. Only those invited by him could eat with him.

The difference of approach between the Chishti and the Suhrawardi saints is also apparent in their approach to family life. We have seen that owing to financial constraints the Chishti saints did not pay due attention to their children, while the Suhrawardi saints, having enough wealth and resources, provided all kinds of facilities including good education to their children. It is said that when Shaikh Bahauddin Zakariya died (in AD 1267), he left millions for his sons.

It is not that all Suhrawardi saints who were fond of the good life involved in politics, or that all Chishtis were opposed to it. Men like Shaikh Sadruddin Arif, Shaikh Wajihuddin Usman Sunami, and Shaikh Salahuddin Darvesh of the Suhrawardi order developed an aversion to wealth and working for the administration. Shaikh Sadruddin, being the son and successor of Shaikh Bahauddin Zakariya, was the richest of them all, but realizing the validity of the criticism against accumulation of wealth, he distributed all the riches inherited from his father in charity.[78] Similarly, some Chishti saints took jobs with the government without hesitation. It is said, 'Almost all the descendants of Shaikh Fariduddin were enrolled in the imperial bureaucracy; the descendants of Sayed Mahmud Kirmani . . . (also) followed the same path. Of the smaller fry there was no reckoning.'[79] Besides, we have seen that enormous *futuh* sent by Alauddin Khalji was accepted by Shaikh Nizamuddin Auliya. It is significant, as observed by I.A. Zilli, that some important Suhrawardi families, who were quite flexible in this regard, were conspicuous by their absence from the government service as compared to the Chishtis who were opposed to it.[80]

However, with the advent of Shaikh Sadruddin's son and successor, Shaikh Ruknuddin Abul Fath, there was a return of the traditions of Shaikh Bahauddin Zakariya. In certain respects he even crossed the limits fixed by his grandfather. From the time of Alauddin Khalji to the days of Muhammad Tughluq, he was frequently in touch with men of the ruling class. During the critical situation created by Bahram Aiba's rebellion (1327-8), the Shaikh and his family took the side of Sultan Muhammad Tughluq against the rebels. This pro-Sultan behaviour in a time of rebellion was so apparent that the rebels were provoked to kill him.[81] Ibn Battuta says that immediately thereafter the Shaikh was granted a *jagir* of a hundred villages by the Sultan,[82] which was indeed by way of reward for the services rendered by him to the government.

But there was another aspect also of Shaikh Ruknuddin's character. After crushing Bahram Aiba's rebellion, the Sultan wanted to punish the citizens of Multan but the Shaikh pleaded for mercy so that the Sultan pardoned them.[83] Even before this, while Khwaja Karak extended his moral support by way of blessings to Alauddin Khalji in his political mission against Sultan Jalaluddin Khalji,[84] Shaikh Ruknuddin used his political influence to rescue the lives of the family members of Jalaluddin after his murder.[85]

Anyhow, Shaikh Ruknuddin's close contact with the government and his holding of a big *jagir* brought the Suhrawardi *silsilah* under the supervision and direct control of the ruler, and it became no more than a state sponsored institution. Ibn Battuta says that Shaikh Ruknuddin never allowed anyone to stay in his *khanqah* without receiving permission from the *wali* (governor) of Multan.[86] This restriction imposed by the government changed the entire character of the Suhrawardi organization in India. As for succession to the spiritual *gaddi*, this too came under state control after the death of Shaikh Ruknuddin, as we have noticed.

The favourable attitude of Muhammad Tughluq to Shaikh Hud as successor of Shaikh Ruknuddin made him lead a luxurious life for years. This was ultimately reported by Imad-ul Mulk, the governor of Multan, to the Sultan, who issued orders for the confiscation of the Shaikh's property. The governor forcibly recovered wealth from the relatives of the Shaikh and searched his house, where he found among other costly things a pair of women's shoes studded with gems. When the Sultan sought an explanation for this the Shaikh attempted to leave the country for Turkistan but was arrested en route and executed by the order of the Sultan.[87]

With the execution of Shaikh Hud, the Multan branch of the Suhrawardi order collapsed. Of course, during the reign of Sultan Firoz Shah Tughluq (1351–88), the position of the branch was revived to some extent, as Shaikh Sadruddin, another descendant of Bahauddin Zakariya, was appointed Shaikh-ul Islam and was respected by the Sultan.[88] But the fact is that it could never revive its earlier spiritual position.

As far as the Uch branch of the Suhrawardi order is concerned, it came into prominence under the leadership of Sayyed Jalaluddin Bukhari, popularly known as Makhdum-i Jahanian. He proved to be a different kind of religious leader who did not accept the title of Shaikh-ul Islam in Siwistan, offered by Muhammad Tughluq, on the pretext of proceeding on *Haj*.[89] On his return, however, he developed cordial relations with Firoz Shah, the reigning king, apparently for the purpose of helping the poor.[90] At a time when Jam Juna and Baubhina, the leaders of the Samma, created a serious problem for the kingdom on the Punjab and Gujarat borders and entered into alliance with the Mongols, Sayyed Bukhari prevailed on them to surrender and also subsequently interceded in securing a pardon for them.[91] But the Samma did not fulfil their promises of good conduct. When Firoz Shah went on his second Thatta campaign, Jam Juna and Baubhina again sought the help of Sayyed Bukhari who came from Uchch to the imperial camp at Thatta and secured the Sultan's mercy for the Samma leaders.[92]

Thus, the religious influence and prestige of Sayyed Bukhari went a long way in establishing peace in Sindh and securing the submission of the Samma leaders. Firoz Shah's favourable attitude towards the saint was not only for political considerations but also out of a spiritual conviction. The attitude of his younger brother, Sayyed Sadruddin, popularly called Raju Qattal, was, however, quite different, as we have seen discussed in the context of his prevailing upon the ulama to secure a decree of execution of a Hindu *daroga* of Uchch for challenging the monopoly of Islam. Raju Qattal's purpose was to impose Islam on an unwilling person, which reflected the moral weakness and spiritual decline of the regime and revealed a dangerously parochial and exclusive attitude towards religion. He threw away all the norms of tolerance and brotherhood of the Muslim mystics of his own order.

Thus, after Makhdum-i Jahanian Sayyed Jalaluddin Bukhari the Suhrawardi *silsilah* entirely lost its spiritual and moral force, a few decades later becoming transformed into a ruling dynasty. After the collapse of the Tughluqs the empire began to disintegrate. The Lodi Afghans established a semi-independent kingdom at Samana under the leadership of Shah Lodi, while the descendants of Timur claimed a right over certain portions of Punjab. In Multan Mughals and Afghans contended for supremacy. It was in this critical situation (particularly in Multan) that the nobles elected Shaikh Yusuf Zakariya, a descendant of Shaikh Bahauddin Zakariya, as their ruler in 1443. The transformation of a spiritual order into a ruling dynasty was indeed a unique development in Indo–Muslim history, but it was the logical culmination of the process of subordinating spirituality to politics that had started much earlier. The election of Shaikh Yusuf was due to the influence and prestige that the family of Shaikh Bahauddin Zakariya exercised over Multan and its adjoining territories. After coming to power, Shaikh Yusuf engaged in statecraft, increasing the number of retainers and enlarging his army.[93]

Already in possession of Dipalpur and Lahore, Bahlul Lodi occupied Delhi in 1451 and began to consolidate his power. So it was difficult for Shaikh Yusuf to remain independent in Multan. Rai Sahrah, a powerful chief of the Langa tribe of Baluchistan, suggested a matrimonial alliance with the Shaikh in order to strengthen his position against Bahlul Lodi, which he conceded. Later by fraudulent means Rai Sahrah imprisoned Shaikh Yusuf,[94] but somehow the Shaikh managed to escape and found shelter with Bahlul Lodi (1451–89). The Lodi Sultan received him with the courtesy which the fugitive prince of a respectable family deserved.[95]

With the escape of Shaikh Yusuf from Multan the central organization of Suhrawardi *silsilah* disintegrated. But the order subsequently developed in Delhi and Gujarat and succeeded in winning over a large number of followers, amongst the people and the rulers. It was more successful in Gujarat than in Delhi, because the new ruling dynasty needed the moral support of spiritual people to integrate the heterogeneous social elements of Gujarat into a coherent polity. The Suhrawardi saints extended their cooperation to the rulers and in return received enormous jagirs, gifts, and endowments.[96] In Delhi not only Shaikh Yusuf but many others like Shaikh Samauddin, Shaikh Ishaq, and Shaikh Abdul Wahab settled and they were patronized by the Lodi Sultans. Bahlul Lodi even entered into matrimonial relationship with the Suhrawardis by giving his daughter in marriage to Shaikh Abdullah, the son of Shaikh Yusuf.[97]

Shaikh Yusuf was still anxious to revive his political position in Multan and persuaded Sultan Bahlul to wage war against the Langas. The Sultan did so but nothing could be achieved.[98] The Langas themselves, aware of the pre-eminent position which the family of Shaikh Bahauddin Zakariya occupied in the religious life of Multan, tried to win over the favour of the *silsilah* and exploited its influence in controlling the nobles, zamindars and traders of the place. In 1523 when Babur issued an order to Mirza Husain Arghun, the governor of Thatta, to annex Multan, Mahmud Langa sent Shaikh Bahauddin Qureshi and Maulana Bahlul to dissuade the Mirza from attacking his territory. The emissaries were received with respect but their request was not conceded.[99]

Shaikh Samauddin, a *khalifa* of Shaikh Kabir, was one of the most outstanding Suhrawardi saints. Though Bahlul Lodi and his nobles often visited him, he did not accept their presents. But it was not possible for him to remain indifferent towards Sultan Bahlul who had supported the Suhrawardi order at a time when it had been uprooted from its homeland. The Shaikh advised the Sultan to follow the path of virtue and rectitude, which he conceded very humbly.[100] Sultan Sikandar Lodi also had great faith in Shaikh Samauddin. Before ascending the throne, he went to him for his blessings.[101] The Shaikh extended his moral support to the Lodis in dealing with contemptuous chiefs like Sultan Husain of Jaunpur.[102] Besides, Haji Abdul Wahhab, a descendant of Sayyed Jalaluddin Bukhari, who came to Delhi from Multan during the time of Sikandar Lodi, received a cordial reception from the Sultan and was highly respected by him.[103] Yet when differences arose the Sultan took no time to declare the saint as no more than a slave, though the Sultan also had to face the serious consequences of the curses of the saint.[104] This reflects another aspect of the relationship between the holy men and the rulers.

On the other hand, Jamali, an eminent disciple of Shaikh Samauddin, was a courtier by temperament and a poet by profession. For spiritual rather than poetic achievements, he was on good terms with Sultan Sikandar Lodi.[105] Jamali wrote an elegy on the death of his patron, Sikandar Lodi, which also contained a contemptuous reference to his successor, Ibrahim Lodi who had developed hatred and indifference towards the mystic poet. Jamali later tried repeatedly to win over the confidence of the Sultan but did not succeed. He retaliated later in a *qasida* by expressing his delight at the death of the sultan at the battlefield of Panipat. When Babur came to power, Jamali, forgetting his patron, the Afghan ruler, wrote panegyrics in Babur's praise as never before. Jamali also helped Babur in his military operations in 1527.[106]

Jamali was sent 'with royal letters of encouragement to Dudu and her son Jalal Khan' on 21 April 1529.[107] His presence in the court on the occasion of a royal feast is also recorded by Babur.[108] When Babur died (AD 1530), Jamali attached himself to Humayun and showered poetic praise on him too.[109] Jamali joined Humayun on his Gujarat campaign, and died in the camp in 1535, leaving a rich legacy for his sons.[110]

Jamali's two sons, Hayati and Gadai, were also associated with the court.[111] Gadai was so attached to Humayun that when Sher Shah ousted him from India, Gadai also left for Hejaz. But Hayati changed his loyalties with the change of dynasty and turned to the Surs and became one of the 'most trusted' attendants of Salim Shah. With the restoration of Mughal power in India, Hayati disappeared from the scene (and died in AD 1551), but Gadai came back from Hejaz and joined Bairam Khan who appointed him Sadrus Sudur in spite of the strong resentment of Abul Fazl and Badauni.[112] When Hemu was brought before Akbar, Gadai persuaded the Emperor to kill him with his own hands 'for such an act would have great reward'.[113] Gadai's position in the court was so high that when Syed Muhammad Ghaus Gwaliori visited the court at Agra, he discredited him in the eyes of Bairam Khan.[114] In the conflict between Akbar and Bairam Khan he became a close counsellor of the Khan-i Khanan.[115] After the fall of Bairam Khan, Gadai went to Jaisalmer but later returned to Delhi where he died in 1568.[116]

The Firdausis

The Firdausi *silsilah* traced its spiritual descent from Shaikh Saifuddin Bakharzi (d. 1260) of Bukhara. The order was founded in India by Khwaja Badruddin of Samarqand, who settled in Delhi and had a cordial friendship with Shaikh Nizamuddin Auliya. There appeared a number of *khalifas* in succession but the most outstanding figure of this order was Shaikh Sharafuddin Yahya Muneri (1263–1381), a disciple of Shaikh Najibuddin Firdausi. The disciples of the Shaikh established a network of small *khanqahs* from Bihar to Sunargaon and elsewhere in India.[117]

Shaikh Maneri maintained cordial relations with the rulers for the purpose of serving the poors.[118] Yet he did not hesitate to criticise them when necessary.[119] During his long life, he witnessed the rise and fall of three dynasties and about eleven Sultans of Delhi, but his relations with Muhammad bin Tughluq and Firoz Shah were particularly important.

Muhammad bin Tughluq issued a *farman* to the muqta of Bihar to construct a *khanqah* for Shaikh Sharafuddin and to assign the pargana of Rajgir for the maintenance of the *khanqah*.[120] It appears from the Shaikh's *maktubat* (collection of letters) that he maintained a correspondence with the Sultan.[121] In one of his letters, the Shaikh has indirectly warned the Sultan against the harmful effects of wealth and power and advised him not to try and follow in the footsteps of the Pharoahs.[122]

The Shaikh wrote two letters to Firoz Shah advising him to be impartial in dispensing justice.[123] But he was disappointed by the Sultan's misuse of judicial powers and to the execution of two Sufis, Shaikh Ahmad Bihari and Shaikh Izz Kakoi, for their *Wahdat-ul Wujudi* thought. The Shaikh's objection to the incident was expressed in surprise that 'the town where blood of such godly persons was shed, should continue to enjoy prosperity for long'.[124] When Firoz Shah heard the Shaikh's resentment, he consulted the ulama who advised him to summon the Shaikh from Bihar to account for his conduct. A *farman* was issued to this effect, but was cancelled due to the intervention of Makhdum-i Jahanian Sayed Jalal Bukhari.[125] It was perhaps at this juncture that the shaikh returned the *sanad* of the *jagir* to Firoz Shah.

One of several disciples of the shaikh was Shaikh Muzaffar who in 1395-6 wrote two letters to Ilyas-Shahi Sultan of Bengal named Ghiyasuddin Azam Shah (1389-1409). In one, he reminded him to be holy and pious like Firoz Shah; in the other, he advised him that high government posts should not be given to Hindus.[126]

The Qadiris

The Sufis of the Qadiri *silsilah* were late to arrive in India: they settled in Uch and Bidar in the Deccan in the fifteenth century.[127] In the Deccan, after the transfer of the capital from Gulbarga to Bidar in 1424, Mir Nurullah was given a royal welcome in the court of Sultan Ahmad. According to Firishta, the Mir was given the title *Malik-ul Mashaikh*, along with official superiority over all other Sufis of the south including the descendants of Gesu Daraz.[128] The Sultan gave his daughter in marriage to the Mir. His father, Shah Kalimullah and brothers, Shah Habibullah and Shah Muhibullah, joined him subsequently. His brothers were married to two other royal princesses. All these Sufis continued to enjoy considerable power and position under the Bahmani Sultan. However, at the end of the reign of Sultan Alauddin Humayun (1461), Shah Habibullah was executed by the Sultan because of his extending political support to his enemy, Prince Hasan Khan.[129]

Shaikh Abdul Qadir Sani (the second), the son and successor of Shaikh Muhammad al Husaini, not only resigned from government service but also returned all *farmans* of grants and stipends to the Langa ruler of Multan. He declined the Sultan's invitation to the court in order not to disturb his ascetic life.[130] The Shaikh's grandson, Shaikh Hamid (d. 1571), was showered with gifts and grants due to his great popularity in Multan, which he distributed among the people. Early in Akbar's reign Shaikh Gadai, the Sadr-us Sudur, succeeded in summoning the Shaikh to Agra and the Shaikh cursed both Shaikh Gadai and his patron Bairam Khan.[131]

Akbar used the influential Sufis of the order in his political interest. He offered them stipends and revenue free land grants. For instance, Syed Ismail Gilani, a renowned Qadiri of Punjab, was granted 1,000 *bighas* of land by Akbar at Firozpur.[132] Besides, as in the case of a dispute between the two claimants of Shaikh Ruknuddin's spiritual succession in the Suhrawardi order, which was settled by Muhammad bin Tughluq, a similar controversy between the two sons of Shaikh Hamid, Shaikh Qadir and Shaikh Musa of the Qadiriya order, was decided by Akbar, and the latter was declared as the successor. Afterwards, Shaikh Qadir passed some remarks against the Emperor, who consequently dubbed him 'ignorant' and asked him to leave the empire. At this the Shaikh resigned his *madad-i ma'ash* grant.[133]

Shaikh Musa lived permanently at Akbar's court at Fatehpur Sikri and remained a friend of Abul Fazl who wrote in detail about him after his assassination early in 1602 by the Langa rebels at Uchch, mentioning that he had achieved the rank of amir.[134] Shaikh Musa's famous disciple, Shaikh Abdul Haq Muhaddis Dehlavi (1551-1642),[135] also came in contact with Abul Fazl and Faizi' but the eclectic trend in religion that had developed at the court disgusted him and he refused to take part in the conflict between Abdun Nabi and Makhdum-ul Mulk.

After the death of Akbar, in 1619-20 Jahangir invited Shaikh Abdul Haq to pay him his respects and rewarded him with lavish gifts and honours.[136] Before his death, however, Jahangir became alienated from the Shaikh and his son, Shaikh Nurul Haq, whom he exiled to Kabul we do not know why. It seems that Shaikh Nurul Haq, qazi of Agra, was accused of friendship with the rebel Prince Khusrau. After the accession of Shahjahan to the throne not only were Shaikh Abdul Haq and his son allowed to return to Delhi, but the latter was reappointed qazi in Agra.[137] Shaikh Tajuddin Ajodhan subscribed to the view of most of Akbar's nobles that the Emperor was the 'Perfect Man', thereby becoming a target of Badauni.[138]

However, during the governorship of Ali Mardan (1651-7) when there occurred a severe famine, the starving people of Kashmir, led by Haji Bam, burnt alive the governor's Hindu *peshkar* (secretary), Shahjahan summoned the leading Kashmiri Muslims including Mir Muhammad Ali Qadiri (d.1559-60) to Delhi for an investigation of the incident. On his way to Delhi, Mir Muhammad visited Shaikh Muhammad Masum, the son of the Mujaddid, at Sirhind. Dissatisfied with the administrative measures of Shahjahan and Dara Shukoh, these men became friends, but no action was taken against any one, and the Mir returned to Srinagar with renewed prestige.[139]

In 1634, the court ulama persuaded Shahjahan to sentence Mulla Shah (d. 1661), an eminent disciple of Miyan Mir, to death for blasphemy. Dara Shukoh, who later became the Mulla's disciple, suggested the Emperor not take any action without consulting with Miyan Mir, and thus the issue subsided.[140] Afterwards, both Shahjahan and Dara Shukoh visited Mulla Shah twice at Kashmir in 1645 and in 1646. The Shaikh also visited Lahore at the Emperor's invitation.[141] Mulla Shah's association with Dara Shukoh had increased the hostility of the orthodox ulama towards Sufism, even though Mulla Shah's own importance as a Sufi remained intact.

After Dara Shukoh's defeat by Aurangzeb in 1658, the new Emperor took action against Dara's friends and associates. Mulla Shah became a target, and an order was issued to the governor of Kashmir to send him to Delhi. The Shaikh was somehow rescued from going to Delhi, but Aurangzeb continued to condemn Mulla Shah for his *Wahdat-ul Wujudi* beliefs.[142] On the other hand, Aurangzeb extended his favours to Hajji Shuhrat and assigned a village to him in Mathura.[143]

The Shattaris

The Shattari *silsilah* was founded by Shaikh Bayazid Bistami (AD 753–845) as *Tariqat-i Ishqiah* in Iran. It was introduced in India during the Lodi period by Shah Abdullah, who have it the name *Shattari*. In order to give the order a popular base the Shah made a tour of many parts of the country and finally settled at Mandu (Malwa). His successors developed the *silsilah* in different parts of northern India.[144]

In a discussion on the ten cardinal principles of the Shattari *silsilah*, Shaikh Bahauddin in his *Risala-i Shattaria* emphasizes the importance of 'resignation', 'contentment', and 'seclusion'. But these principles were hardly followed by the holy men of the order. They freely associated with the kings and the government and accepted *jagirs*. Thus there was a great contradiction between their principles and practical life, which they, like the Suhrawardis, tried to reconcile by saying that the welfare of the people obliged them to behave so.[145]

When Shah Abdullah reached Chittor in 1442–3, Sultan Mahmud Shah Khalji was besieging the fortress. The Shattari saint blessed the Khalji Sultan and remained with him till the fort was captured.

The Sultan sent him to Mandu where Abdullah developed close contact with the ruler of Malwa, Sultan Ghiyasuddin (1469–1501) and dedicated to him his famous, *Lataif-i Ghaibia*.[146] Other saints of the order followed suit. Shaikh Bahauddin left his native place for Mandu at the request of the ruler. Syed Muhammad Ghaus Gwaliori (d. 1563) felt no hesitation in mixing with the rulers and the bureaucracy. He was the first Shattari to develop contact with the Mughal emperors. When Babur's forces besieged Gwalior in 1526, the Shaikh sided with the invader and suggested a strategy to the Mughal generals to make Tatar Khan surrender.[147] Shaikh Phul, the elder brother of Syed Ghaus, was one of the closest associates of Humayun[148] who showered 'royal favours' on him. The Shaikh lived with the Emperor, joined him in his expeditions, and was ready to exercise influence in favour of the government whenever needed.[149] Jahangir speaks about these two brothers with respect and regard, though Abul Fazl has castigated them in most derogatory terms.[150]

The incidence of Shaikh Bahlul's death due to performing the duties of a plenipotentiary, increased Humayun's attachment to his brother, Shaikh Muhammad Ghaus. When Sher Shah ousted Humayun and political power passed to the Afghans, the Shaikh left Delhi for Gujarat[151] but remained loyal to Humayun. It was for this reason that Humayun did not forget the Shaikh and entered into a respectful correspondence with him; the Shaikh responded in the same manner.[152]

After Akbar's accession to the throne, Shaikh Muhammad Ghaus visited the Mughal court in 1558, where he was received with honour by Akbar.[153] But Shaikh Gadai, the Sadr-us Sudur, became jealous. Badauni remarks that this the advent of Ghaus was for Gadai 'a case of opening a shop above his own shop'.[154] Taking advantage of his influence, Shaikh Gadai discredited Shaikh Gwaliori's position in the eyes of the Regent, Bairam Khan, as we have seen. The shaikh was forced to go back to Gwalior where he had a big *jagir* yielding a huge revenue.[155] The Shaikh's son, Shaikh Budh Abdullah, joined military service. He was initially appointed a mansabdar of 1000 and was soon promoted to the rank of 3000. At one stage he played the role of ambassador to Mirza Shahrukh of Badakhshan. During the reign of Jahangir, the Shaikh retired to Gwalior, where he died in 1612.[156]

As stated, Abul Fazl speaks about Shaikh Muhammad Ghaus along with his elder brother, Shaikh Bahlul, in derogatory terms. He calls him a 'boastful simpleton',[157] and seems to be inclined to prove that Akbar had no sincere attachment to the Shaikh. The reasons for this are not known, though the Shaikh had fully identified with the Mughal elite and had served them from the very beginning. Even in his last days, at the age of eighty, the Shaikh persuaded Fattu (Fateh Khan Masnad-i Ali) to surrender Chunar Fort to the Emperor.[158]

When Shaikh Muhammad Ghaus was in Gujarat his views clashed with the orthodox opinion of the theologians. Consequently, Shaikh Ali Muttaqi issued a *fatwa* imploring Mahmud III (1537-54) of Gujarat to kill the Shaikh for violation of *Sharia*. The Sultan referred the case to Sayyed Wajihuddin Alavi for his opinion, who tore up the *fatwa* with the comment that this it did not apply to him.[159] Wajihuddin was a disciple of Shaikh Ghaus and his attachment to the Shattari *silsilah* not only silenced opponents but also enhanced the Shaikh's position in society.[160]

As a leading scholar of his time, Wajihuddin (d. 1589) was respected by the rulers of Gujarat. His greatest contribution was that he established a *madrasa* which became one of the biggest seminaries of the country. In order to maintain its independent character, he avoided seeking state assistance, though whenever offered he did not refuse it. Wajihuddin's attitude to the state formed a reconciliation between the two rival approaches of the Chishtis and the Suhrawardis or Shattaris themselves. He considered state service neither 'sinful' nor 'sacrilegious', but a 'distraction of a serious nature'.[161] His son Shaikh Abdullah, and grandson Shaikh Haider, however, accepted cash gifts and land grants.

Once Jahangir himself visited the *khanqah* of Shaikh Wajihuddin at Ahmedabad. The royal visitor threw enormous gifts and *jagirs* to Shaikh Haider and his relatives, which they accepted.[162] Later there followed daily stipends to the Shaikh.[163]

Shah Pir (1632) of Meerut, a strong supporter of Jahangir, enjoyed the faith of the Emperor. K.A. Nizami's conclusion that there is no 'reference to the Shattari saints during the reigns of Shahjahan and Aurangzeb' has been questioned by S.A.A. Rizvi, who asserts that the leading Shattaris, Shaikh Isa (d. 1621), Shaikh Burhanuddin (d. 1678), Shaikh Abdul Latif (d. 1655), and Shaikh

Muhammad Ashraf (d. 1667) continued to function during this period and some of them enjoyed royal patronage.[164]

However, the *silsilah* was not organized on a popular base. It appealed to scholars and rich men but not the masses. The *mashaikh* of the order fixed their target on palaces and mansions and identified with the state.

The Naqshbandis

The Naqshbandi *silsilah* emerged as an offshoot of the *Silsilah-i Khwajagan* organized by Khwaja Ahmad Ata Yasvi in Central Asia in the twelfth century. It was popularized by his disciple, Khwaja Bahauddin Naqshbandi (1318–89) among Turks and Mongols. His impact on the *silsilah* was so deep that it came to be called the Naqshbandi *silsilah*.[165] Babur's conquest of India opened way for the migration of many Sufis of this order from Central Asia to India. But the order was firmly organized in India by Muhammad Baqi or Baqi Billah (1564–1603).

The Naqshbandis were mystics who considered it imperative to have contact with the rulers in order to influence their thoughts and actions. Keeping in view that the policies of rulers had a deep impact on society, the Naqshbandis played an important role in shaping their religious outlook during Mughal rule. Babur's father, Umar Shaikh Mirza, was a devoted disciple of Khwaja Ubaidullah Ahrar who, according to Babur himself, accompanied his father 'step by step (so that) most of his affairs found lawful settlement'.[166] Babur was deeply attached to Khwaja Muhammad Qadi, a Khalifa of Khwaja Ahrar. After his conquest of India, Babur invited Khwaja Ahrar's descendants to a feast in Agra and gave them rich presents. He sent a copy of the *Baburnama* to Khwaja Kalan.[167] Whenever he was in trouble, he turned to this *silsilah* for solace.[168] Babur's tradition was continued by his descendants. When Khwaja Khawand Mahmud, a descendant of Khwaja Ahrar, came to India, Humayun received him with honour.[169]

In the early years of Akbar's reign many Naqshbandi saints obtained high posts in the civil and military administration. For instance, Khwaja Husamuddin was given a high position in the military and civil services. Later he married a sister of Abul Fazl. At the end of the sixteenth century he served in campaigns in the

Deccan under Abdur Rahim Khan-i Khana and held a mansab of 1000.[170] In general, they retained their loyalty to Akbar and even supported his liberal policies after 1579.[171] Before Akbar's death, Khwaja Khawand Mahmud came to Agra where he initiated a number of eminent Mughal nobles including Mirza Aziz Koka. Some of the prominent ladies of the harem such as Salima Begum and Gulrukh Begum also joined the *silsilah* as disciples.[172]

There came a new dimension in the history of the Naqshbandi *silsilah* with the arrival of Khwaja Baqi Billah (1564–1603) from Kabul in the closing years of Akbar's reign.[173] Though he established a *khanqah* in Delhi in 1599 and developed contacts with prominent nobles like Nawab Murtuza Khan and Farid Bukhari, he did not yield to their persuasion to enter government service.[174] Shaikh Abdul Haqq Muhaddis Dehlavi (1515–1642) was an eminent disciple of the Khwaja. His theory of legitimizing the position of a ruler appears to be in a limited framework aiming exclusively at promoting the cause of Islam. The Shaikh extolled the *badshah-i dindar* (the king upholding the faith) by saying that the entire community should cooperate with such a king in the task of strengthening and spreading the *din*. The ulama should help by expounding the laws of the *sharia*, the dervishes should pray, the army should fight and artisans, cultivators and merchants should actively perform their duties.[175]

With the joining of the mystic order by Shaikh Ahmad Sirhindi popularly known as Mujaddid-i-Alf Sani (1564–1624), however, political activity began in the *khanqah*.[176] As a renovator of Islam he disagreed with Akbar's religious experiments and sharply reacted to them.[177] In fact, the Shaikh's vision was confined to *shariah*. His attitude towards the liberal trends was uncompromising. It is not surprising that in a letter to Hirdaya Ram the Shaikh differed from him on the issue of identifying Ram with Rahim,[178] because he could not tolerate or compromise even with the ulama and the Sufis who deviated from the *sunnah*.[179]

The Shaikh wanted to involve the ruler and his nobles by holding the view that the *sharia* could be restored and protected by the ruler, for 'the King is to the universe what the heart is to the body', and the elite were to advise the king to follow the *sharia*.[180] He sought to meet the king and to join his courtiers in order to get the rule of *sharia* implemented. Accordingly, he wrote a number of letters to Mughal nobles like Shaikh Farid (Murtaza Khan), Khan-i-Khana, and Mirza Aziz Koka, exerting them to convince the king of his mission.[181] However, the clash with Akbar was specifically about interference in Muslim religious matters and his assuming the position of religious head. It is significant that some Hindu nobles had the same reaction.[182]

In the beginning of Jahangir's reign the Mujaddid wrote letters to the leading political figures that the accession of the new Emperor they should avail of the golden opportunity to streamline the administration in accordance with the *Sharia*.[183] He also wrote to Nawab Murtaza Khan and through him to Jahangir, welcoming his accession and expressing deep concern at what had happened during the previous regime.[184] That Jahangir had made a commitment to the Naqshbandi saints on his accession is verified only by Jesuit accounts.[185]

For about fourteen years after Jahangir's accession, the attitude of the Emperor towards Shaikh Ahmad Sirhindi is not known but, all of a sudden in 1619, Jahangir decided to put the Shaikh behind bars in Gwalior.[186] The reason why Jahangir did not take notice of Shaikh Ahmad's movement before 1619, was perhaps his growing popularity due to circulation or 'publication' of the first two volumes of his letters (in 1617 and 1619) and due to the changes brought about in court politics with the evolution of the so-called Noor Jahan Junta. The charges labelled by Jahangir himself against the Shaikh were as follows:

'At this time (May–June 1619) it was reported that an impostor, Shaikh Ahmad by name, had spread the net of fraud and deceit in Sirhind and ensnared a number of devotees of worthless appearance, and sent to every city and district as his Khalifa. . .'.[187]After being released from imprisonment, however, Shaikh Ahmad was given money and permission to stay at the court by Jahangir.[188] He had discourses with him on religious matters, as is evident in some of his letters.[189] How far Jahangir was influenced by the Shaikh's thought is not known, but he did not follow Akbar's policy of religious experiments. Opposed to Mujaddid's theory for the kings and their responsibilities, Miyan Mir considered the Emperor the 'Perfect Man', though he also urged him to be just and to safeguard the interests of his subjects and his empire.[190]

There seems to have been interaction between Khwaja Muhammad Masum, son of Shaikh Ahmad, and Aurangzeb.[191] He addressed six letters to Aurangzeb. When the prince proceeded on his Qandahar campaign (1649–52), the saint wrote him a long letter in which he emphasized the superiority of 'protecting the frontiers' to sitting in *chillah* (contemplation).[192]

Another important saint of the order, who played a role in the politics of eighteenth century, was Shah Waliullah (1703–62).[193] His political thought was based on two kinds of sources—those of orthodox Sunnis and those of leading Muslim philosophers. His own contribution was to suggest ways and means of establishing the domination of orthodox Sunnis in the government.[194] For peace and prosperity Shah Waliullah suggested certain virtues be mastered by a king who should be careful about appointing army commanders and town administrators.[195] He was deeply concerned with the decline of Mughal rule in India and, therefore, tried to awaken Ahmad Shah (1748–54) to revive Muslim power. In a letter to the Emperor and his ministers, he suggested that some traditional schemes be adopted in the administration.[196] He advised a reduction of *jagir* lands and extension of *khalsa* area, condemned the practice of farming out revenues, and suggested a reorganization of the army. He also argued for bold administrative measures to reduce corruption.

Shah Waliullah was neither a separatist nor exclusivist, but his political mission was to see the restoration of Sunni dominance over the world, starting in India.[197] His call for a return to Arabic, Arab dress, and the Arab way of life was a reaction against Irani and Hindu influence on the Mughal government. He believed that the elimination of those elements would restore Sunni dominance in every sphere of life.

SUFIS IN INDIAN SOCIETY

Sufism emerged not as a challenge to Islam, to the Quran, or to the Prophet, but simply as a movement against the formal or external attitude of the ulama. It developed certain peculiar features, through which dynamic and progressive elements entered the social structure of Islam. Muslim theologians, being unaware of the changing trends of the time, seldom tried to reconstruct their socio-religious thought accordingly—thus reducing Islam to a set of lifeless rituals and ceremonials. The Sufis stood for a direct and natural approach to religion. Thus, whereas the ulama maintained the Islamic concept of equality and brotherhood within the *umma* (community), the Sufis extended this to non-Muslims. They also tried to replace the static theology by progressive ideas in order to achieve universal character. The sharp division between the two trends of thought represented by the ulama and the *mashaikh* is evident from the discussions that took place on the issue of *sama* (audition party) at a *mahzar* (convention of the learned) in the court of Ghyasuddin Tughlaq.[198]

We have seen the distinction made by Imam Ghazali between *Ulam-i Zahir* (externalist scholars) and *Ulama-i Batin* (saints or mystics). They had different roles in society as shown by Amir Khusrau, a political and spiritual figure, in the following lines:

The righteous Ulama ... are the source of enlightenment for thousands of people and the light of the community.... The documents drafted by these scholars are issued to legalize the collections of money for the royal treasury.... As for the missionary work done by the Sufis, it has merit lasting till the day of resurrection.... Their blessing and prayer increase the power and grandeur of the Empire and also strengthen its foundations...'.[199]

Isami observed that all monarchs and their kingdoms lay under the protection of a saint; and the first step of providence, when it wished to destroy a country, was to effect the saint's presence.[200] Thus, for him the death of Nizamuddin created troubles for Delhi in the time of Muhammad bin Tughlaq,[201] and the prosperity of Daulatabad, prior to the revolt against the Sultan from 1324 onwards, was attributed to the presence of two Shaikhs, Burhanuddin and Ziauddin.[202]

For medieval chroniclers one of the most important criteria in evaluating a Sultan's reign was the treatment of the holy men of religion. Despite the faults of Alauddin Khalji, the only reason, for his continued success was, as conceived by Barani, his growing attachment to Shaikh Nizamuddin and that the Shaikh had graced his political authority.[203] The great spiritual power of a shaikh could become a threat to the authority of the sultan and was termed Sultan-ul Mashaikh or Sultan-ul Arifin (in the case of Shaikh Nizamuddin, for instance). The spiritual governance in the *khanqah* and the control of spiritual *wilayat* reflect the pattern of state administration.

The attention of Muslim mystics from the very beginning seems to have been directed to removing racial distinctions, class superiority, and religious differences. Constituting the ideological base of the Sufi attitudes to society were belief in the essential unity of all religions (*wahdat-i adyan*), so that a categorization of people into 'believers' and 'non-believers' was of no importance,[204] and the idea of universal brotherhood.

It would not be wrong to say that the wounds made by Muslim warriors in the body of Indian society was healed by the Muslim mystics. When Balban was organizing his court on the Iranian pattern, differentiating between Turks and non-Turks, Shaikh Farid opened the door of his *khanqah* to all without distinction of caste or community. *Khanqahs* thus emerged as centres of cultural synthesis, where ideas were freely exchanged.

It may also be noted that while Alberuni, an authority on comparative religion, understood the Hindu religious thought in philosophical perspective, the Sufi approach was psychological and emotional. They were concerned more with emotional integration than with ideological synthesis, and for that reason perhaps, they appeared to be more interested in Hindu religious practice than Hindu theology. The Sufis never indulged in *munazra* or theological controversy of any kind. They neither studied Hinduism as such nor gave any assessment of its credibility. As a principle of *wahdat-ul adyan*, they respected all religions and occasionally quoted a Hindu theory or a Hindu story in their conversations.

For the Sufis, India was neither *Dar-ul harb* nor *Dar-ul Islam*, but God's earth with all sorts of people. The two spheres in which their liberal ideas found the full expression were religion and language. There are instances when the Sufis showed a deep and genuine appreciation for the multi-religious and multi-lingual character of Indian society. They were fond of Hindi. They appreciated Hindu devotional songs composed by the Bhakti saints. In the case of language too, wherever the Sufis settled they adopted the local dialects to communicate with local people. Thus, they also played a vital role in the growth of Indian languages.

The Muslim mystics were practically involved in *khidmat-i khalq* (social service) which they regarded as the object of all spiritual exercise. When asked to explain the highest form of *ta'at* (religious obligation), Shaikh Muinuddin Chishti said it was 'nothing but feeding the hungry, providing clothes to the naked and helping those in distress'.[205] Elaborating the same view, Shaikh Nizamuddin Auliya is said to have stated that 'devotion to God is of two kinds: *lazmi* (obligatory) and *muta'addi* (communicable)'.[206] While the first covers personal religious activities and its benefits go to the devotee alone, the second brings comfort to others. Thus the mission of the leading Sufis was to inspire people to emancipate themselves morally. They equated the service of mankind with devotion to God. Their care for people in need increased their popularity. Their understanding of Hindus and Hinduism brought them close to many. Moreover, the Sufi faith in a pacific or non-violent approach has been the essence of Indian philosophy, apparent in the following remark of Shaikh Nizamuddin Auliya: 'If a man puts thorns (in your way) and you do the same, there will be thorns everywhere.'[207]

This principle was demonstrated by the Sufis in their own lives. They tried to impress, both by precept and example, the fact that a true mystic should strive to create affection in the hearts of the people. Shaikh Farid once told a visitor, 'Do not give me a knife, give me a needle. The knife is an instrument for cutting and the needle for sewing together.'[208] The Sufi principle of *ahimsa* was extended to animals: they disapproved of the slaughter of animals. It was due to this faith in *ahimsa* that the Shaikh turned vegetarian and he exhorted his disciples again and again to do likewise.

To come in direct contact with the common people, the Shattari saint, Shah Abdullah had adopted some unique methods. While the Sufis of other orders used to settle in one place attracting people to their *khanqahs*, Shah Abdullah travelled from place to place, beating drums, asking if there was 'anyone who wishes to be shown the way to God'.[209] Some Sufis appear to be deeply concerned with poverty, especially among cultivators. Shaikh Abdul Haqq was of the opinion that tax relief for cultivators was more praiseworthy than the same amount being dispensed in charity to *dervishes*. He reminded rulers that to them peasants were as important as an army.[210] Hazrat Bari, one of the mentors of Dara Shukoh, also urged his royal disciple to take care of the cultivators whose taxes swelled the imperial treasury.[211]

Khwaja Muinuddin Naqshbandi for his part urged that a sultan dispense equal justice to Muslims and non-Muslims.[212] Shaikh Ahmad Sirhindi confined himself to religion and the ruling class, whereas Shah Waliullah addressed all sections of Muslim society, soldiers, artisans, Sufis, ulama, and commoners (both men and women), and advised them to act strictly according to the laws of *sharia*.[213] He analysed the evils of the economic system and indicated two main reasons for chaos: the pressure of parasites on the public treasury and the burden of heavy taxation on the peasants and merchants. The Shah also suggested ways and means for social and economic reform. According to him *adl* (equality and justice) and *tawazun* (moderation) were the crucial factors to be applied in all spheres of life.[214]

Many of the Sufis of different orders adopted Indian customs and practices. The practice of bowing before the Shaikh, presenting water to visitors, circulating a *zanbil* (a hollow gourd), *mahluq kardan* (shaving the head of new entrants to the mystic discipline), holding *sama* (audition parties) and doing arduous ascetic exercises were closely similar to Buddhist and Yogic practices.[215] Shaikh Sharafuddin Maneri of the Firdausi order lived an ascetic life for several years eating green leaves and wild fruit in the Rajgir hills of Bihar.[216] The Shattari saint Syed Muhammad Ghaus, a man of ecstasy, had also undergone a rigorous spiritual discipline for twelve years on the lower slopes of the hills of Chunar.[217] Shaikh Farid Chishti and later Shaikh Abdur Rahman Qadiri practised the arduous *chilla-i makus* (the inverted *chilla*) in which the body was suspended upside down by a rope in a well for an entire night. Shaikh Rahman would dig a grave and cover his whole body with earth while totally absorbed in prayer.[218] The Qadiris practised many forms of breath control which they have attributed to Ghaus-ul Azam.[219] Shaikh Bahauddin Shattari asserted that *zikr* without breath control was ineffective and that the neophyte need not confine *zikr* to Arabic or Persian words—he may also make Hindi *zikr*. He also recommended the sitting posture of the *jogis*, and outlined several magical and mystical practices for the achievement of supernatural power.[220] Syed Muhammad Ghaus's relations with the Hindus and his knowledge of Hindu mystic thought was very deep.[221]

Thus, the mystic attitude towards the Hindus and Hinduism was based on sympathetic attitude and adjustment, because they believed that all religions were different roads leading to the same destination. The belief in *ahimsa*, vegetarian diets, and giving equal status to all increased the area of contact with Hindus. Shaikh Muinuddin took two wives, and one of them was the daughter of a Hindu raja of Ajmer.[222]

There is, of course, a lack of historical evidence on the extent of the influence of Hindu mystic ideas on Muslim mystic thought. The *Jawahir-i Khamsa* (a collection of five treatises) written by Syed Muhammad Ghaus in 1522-3, gives us only a glimpse. A comparative study of Hindu and Muslim mystic practices would clarify much. The eagerness with which Muslim mystics established close relations with Hindus and tried to understand them, opened way for the evolution of a common medium for an exchange of ideas. Since the earliest accounts of the Hindi language are found in the mystic records, the early Sufi *khanqahs* in India became the birth-place of the Urdu language. In fact, the impact of the socio-cultural revolution brought about by the Sufis was nowhere so deep than in India.

NOTES

1. Shibli Nomani, *Al-Ghazali*, Delhi: Helal Press, 1914, p. 187.
2. D.B. MacDonald's article, 'The Life of Al-Gazzali', *Journal of the American Oriental Society*, vol. XX, 1899.
3. Hamid Qalandar, *Khair-ul Majalis*, ed. K.A. Nizami, Aligarh, 1959, p. 163.
4. The impact of this work in India may be estimated from the fact that for a long time it was prescribed for higher studies in religion and mysticism. The Chishti saints might or might not have taken Shaikh Shihabuddin's life as a model, his *Awarif* was undoubtedly accepted by them as the best manual on mystic discipline. Shaikh Farid is said to have prepared a commentary on it. The *Awarif* was translated into Persian for the first time by Daud Khatib of Multan, disciple of Shaikh Burhanuddin Zakaria. Later, Izzuddin Mahmud Kashani (AD 1334) translated it under the title *Misbah ul Hidayah wa Miftah-ul Khifayah,* which was published by Newal Kishore Press, Lucknow. The manuscript is available in the Maulana Azad Library, Aligarh Muslim University, Aligarh.
5. Shaikh Ali Hujwiri, *Kashaf-ul-Mahjub,* Eng. tr. Reynold Nicolson, Delhi: Taj Company, 1982.

6. For details Khwaja Muinuddin's life and career, see K.A. Nizami, *Some Aspects of Religion and Politics in India During the Thirteenth Century*, rpt., Delhi: Idara-i Adabiyat-i Dehli, 1978, pp. 181–5.
7. Ibid., pp. 185–99.
8. Ibid., pp. 220–9.
9. Though broadly used in the sense of hospice, these terms differ in connotation. The *khanqah* built by the Suhrawardis was a spacious building which provided separate accommodation for every visitor and inmate. The *jama'at khana* of the Chishtis containing a large room where all disciples slept, prayed, and studied on the floor. The *zawiyahs* were smaller places where mystics lived and prayed, but, unlike the other two, did not aim at establishing any vital contact with the local people. In the sixteenth century another type of spiritual centre came into existence, the *mahadavi daera*. These were much smaller and their primary aim was to provide place for affiliated men for their religious meditation. But the word *khanqah* is often used to denote all centres of spiritual activity.
10. For details about the importance of the *khanqah*, see Nizami, *Some Aspects*, pp. 59–61.
11. Amir Hasan Sijzi, *Fawaid-ul Fuad*, Lucknow: Newal Kishore Press, 1312/1894, p. 147.

    Here, Mohammad Habib's observation is no less important: 'Muslim mysticism in those days was a post-graduate discipline—a discipline exclusively for the Muslims who had completed their study of the theological and other sciences.' See Mohammad Habib, *Politics and Society During the Early Medieval Period (Collected Works of M. Habib)*, ed. K.A. Nizami, vol. 1, Delhi: People's Publishing House, 1974, p. 76.
12. Ibid., p. 56.
13. Ibn Battuta says that Shaikh Hud was accompanied by Shaikh Nuruddin Shirazi as the state representative, who installed him on the *gaddi* on behalf of the Sultan. This event was conducted with great pomp and show. *The Rehla of Ibn Battuta*, tr. Mahdi Husain, rpt., Baroda: Oriental Institute, 1976, pp. 90–1.
14. For details, Nizami, *Some Aspects*, p. 177.
15. Ziauddin Barani, *Tarikh-i Firoz Shahi*, ed. Sir Syed Ahmad Khan, Calcutta: Bibliotheca Indica, 1862, p. 396.
16. Mir Khurd, *Siyar-ul-Auluja*, Delhi: Muhib Hind, 1885, p. 146.
17. It was sufficient for disciples of the second category to regularly pay out *Zakat-i shariat* (2.5 per cent of their saving), while those of the first category had to pay *Zakat-i haqiqat* (all that they possessed): *Fawaid-ul Fuad*, p. 103.

    I.H. Siddiqui, 'The Pir and Murid: A Case Study of the Sufis of Suhrawardi Silsilah in India during the Thirteenth and Fourteenth Centuries', *Hamdard Islamicus*, vol. XXI, no. 3, 1998, pp. 57–77.

Sufism in India 89

18. For details of these rules, see Nizami, *Some Aspects*, p. 61.
19. Ibid., p. 215.
20. The remark of Shaikh Farid, while appointing Shaikh Nizamuddin Auliya as his successor, is important in this context: 'Almighty God has bestowed three (qualities): knowledge, wisdom, and cosmic emotion, and he alone who possesses these three qualities is qualified to discharge the duties of the *khilafat* of saints.' See Khurd, *Siyar-ul Auliya*, p. 345.

    For the same reason, a request by Maulana Fakhruddin of Bilgram for the grant of *khilafat* was turned down by Shaikh Farid because that was 'a divine trust which cannot be assigned on account of one's desires. The qualified one receives it without asking for'. Ibid., pp. 345–6.
21. For the text of *Khilafatnamas* issued by Shaikhs Farid and Nizamuddin Auliya, see Nizami, *Some Aspects*, pp. 349–52.
22. Nizami, *Some Aspects*, p. 61.
23. Ibid., p. 245.
24. For details about the family life of the Chishti saints, see ibid., pp. 199–204.
25. Hamid Qalandar *Khair-ul Majalis* (*Malfuz* of Shaikh Nasiruddin Chiraghi Dilli), ed. K.A. Nizami, Aligarh: AMU, 1959, p. 150; Mir Khurd, *Siyar-ul Auliya*, p. 66.
26. Shaikh Farid once declared, 'The dervishes prefer dying of starvation to incurring any debt for the satisfaction of their desires. Debt and Resignation are poles apart and cannot subsist together.' Ibid.
27. *Fawaid-ul Fuwad*, pp. 61, 147–8; *Khair-ul Majalis*, p. 106.
28. *Siyar-ul Auliya*, pp. 171–2, also pp. 121–2 for the way in which the sons of Shaikh Farid quarrelled with Sayyed Muhammad Kirmani for mentioning Shaikh Nizamuddin's name in the last moments of Shaikh Farid.
29. Barani, *Fatawa-i Jahandari*, tr. M. Habib and Mrs. Afasar S. Khan, in *The Political Theory of the Delhi Sultanate*, Delhi: Kitab Mahal, n.d., p. 39.
30. See the Shaikh's letter 47, cited by A.A. Rizvi, *History of Sufism in India*, Delhi: Munshiram Manoharlal, 1978, vol. I, p. 230.
31. As cited by Nizami, *Some Aspects*, p. 240.
32. The earliest source to record this episode is the *Siyar-ul Auliya* which reports that the Khwaja twice visited Delhi to meet his disciple, Shaikh Qutbuddin Bakhtiyar Kaki. The source specifically mentions that the Khwaja dissuaded Qutbuddin from informing Sultan Iltutmish about his arrival as he did not like the crowding of people at the place of his stay. So the visit to the court by Khwaja Muinuddin seems to be just a legend of a later date.
33. Iltutmish is said to have had great respect for Qutbuddin. It is also said that on his arrival in Delhi, Iltutmish welcomed him and invited him to

stay near his palace. But the Shaikh declined and the Sultan himself used to visit him twice a week. Nizami, op. cit., pp. 188–9.
34. Many hagiographic works refer to the Shaikh's keen interest in the construction of the famous *Hauz-i Shamsi* (water reservoir). See Muhammad Qasim Firishta, *Tarikh-i Farishta*, Lucknow: Newal Kishore, AH 1281, vol. 2, pp. 381–2.
35. The Shaikh used to tell his disciples, 'If you desire to attain the position of great saints, do not pay attention to princes.' *Siyar-ul Auliya*, p. 75. When Sayyidi Maula sought Baba Farid's permission to leave Ajodhan for Delhi, he unwillingly allowed him by saying, 'But keep in mind my one advice—do not mix with kings and nobles. Take their visit to your *khanqah* as a calamity. Any *durwesh* who opens the door of association to kings and nobles is doomed.' Barani, *Tarikh-i Firoz Shahi*, p. 209.
36. Mir Khurd, *Siyar-ul Auliya*, pp. 81–2.
37. Ibid., pp. 305–6.
38. Barani, op. cit., pp. 163, 331–2, 345–6; Firishta, *Tarikh*, vol. II, p. 394.
39. For details of this suspicion, see *Siyar-ul Auliya*, pp. 143–5; Barani, *Fatawa*, p. 332.
40. For details, Barani, op. cit., p. 394; Firishta, op. cit., vol. II, pp. 394–5; *Siyar-ul Auliya*, p. 144; Shaikh Abdul Huq Muhaddis Dehlavi, *Akhbar-ul Akhyar*, Delhi: Matba-i Mohammadi, AH 1332, p. 57; also Muhammad Jamal Qiwamuddin, *Qiwam-ul Aqaid* (the earliest biography of the Shaikh compiled in Deccan in 1354), as cited by K.A. Nizami in *The Life and Times of Shaikh Nizamuddin Auliya*, Delhi, 1991, pp. 107–8.
41. I.A. Zilli, 'Early Chishtis and the State', in *Sufi Cults and the Evolution of Medieval Indian Culture*, ed. Anup Taneja, Delhi: ICHR, 2003, p. 65.
42. Nizami, *Some Aspects*, p. 244.
43. It is narrated by K.A. Nizami that being touched by the distress and poverty of Shaikh Hamiduddin, the *muqta* of Nagaur offered him a plot of land and some cash, which the Shaikh declined, saying that none of his elders had accepted a government gift. The matter was reported by the *muqta* to the Sultan, who sent 500 silver *tankahs* with a *farman* conferring a village on him. That too was not accepted. Ibid., p. 187.
44. *Fuwaid-ul Fuwad*, p. 99.
45. Ibid.
46. *Siyar-ul Auliya*, p. 295.
47. Ibid., pp. 295–6. For instance, Shaikh Nizamuddin Auliya took back the Khilafatnama from Qazi Muhiuddin Kashani, the moment he found him inclined towards government service.
48. *Siyar-ul Arifin*, as cited by Nizami, *Some Aspects*, p. 246.
49. Ibid.
50. *Khair-ul Majalis*, pp. 49–56; K.A. Nizami, ed., *Politics and Society During the Early Medieval Period*, vol. I, pp. 368–71; K.A. Nizami, *The Life and Times of Shaikh Nasiruddin Chiragh*, Delhi, 1991, pp. 66–71.

Sufism in India 91

51. K.A. Nizami, 'Attitude of Muslim Mystics Towards Society and State during the Sultanate Period', *Sanskrite*, Delhi, 1996, p. 557.
52. Once in an audition party presided over by Shaikh Nizamuddin, Amir Khusrau rose in an ecstasy of joy (which was common among the Sufis at this occasion). But the Shaikh objected to this and said, 'you are connected with the world; you are not permitted to rise up (like this)'. *Siyar-ul Auliya*, p. 506.
53. Khwaja Qutbuddin Bakhtiyar Kaki did not accept coins from Malik Ikhtiyaruddin Aibak. Similarly, Shaikh Noor Turk declined to accept a bag of gold coins sent by Razia, *Siyar-ul Auliya*, p. 59, *Fawaid-ul Fuwad*, p. 161.
54. Firishta, *Tarikh*, vol. II, p. 394; also S.A.A. Rizvi, *History of Sufism*, vol. I, p. 224.
55. A.A. Rizvi, op. cit., vol. I, p. 222.
56. *Khair-ul Majalis*, ed. K.A. Nizami, pp. 87–8, 184–5, 240.
57. Introduction to *Khair-ul Majalis*, ed. K.A. Nizami, pp. 48, 66–7; K.A. Nizami, 'Chishtiyya', *Encyclopaedia of Islam*, Leiden, 1965, vol. II, p. 51; K.A. Nizami, *Life and Times of Nasiruddin Chiragh*, p. 145; Rizvi, *History of Sufism*, vol. 1, p. 175.
58. Syed Bashir Hasan, 'A Study of the Chishti Sufis in Mughal Malwa', *U.P. Historical Review*, vols. II–III, New Series, 2007 pp. 92–9.
59. *Siyar-ul Auliya*, pp. 77 and 41.
60. See, Abdul Quddus, *Maktubat-i-Quddusia*, Delhi: Matba-i Ahmadi, 1871, p. 45.
61. Ibid., pp. 236–7; A.A. Rizvi, *History of Sufism*, vol. 1, pp. 344–6.
62. Nizami, *Some Aspects*, pp. 248–9; also his 'The Suhrawardi Silsilah and its Influence on Medieval Indian Politics', *Medieval India Quarterly*, vol. III, nos. 1–2, 1957, pp. 113–14.
63. But there was contradiction in Shaikh Najibuddin's views about the rulers. Sayyed Jalaluddin Bukhari has pointed out that in spite of his close contacts with the rulers Shaikh Najibuddin Abdul Qahir Suhrawardi had criticized their court life and the sources of their income. Nizami, *Some Aspects*, pp. 249–51.
64. Ibid., pp. 252–3.
65. Shaikh Abdul Haq Muhaddis, *Akhbar-ul Akhyar*, p. 28.
66. Ibid., p. 50. The author informs that the Maulana performed the duties of this office for two years with great ability and after that he requested the sultan to relieve him from the post.
67. Barani has provided the substance of two of Syed Nuruddin's sermons which reveal that he was bold but narrow-minded, trying to force the Sultan to institute an inquisition in India. See his *Tarikh-i Firoz Shahi*, pp. 41–4.
68. Barani, *Fatawa-i Jahandari*, p. 39.
69. Ibid., p. 41.

Expounding his 'four principles', Syed Nuruddin said that the Sultan should try to uproot the idolators and idolatry. Second, vice and immorality should be extirpated and life be made impossible for criminals and bad characters. Third, only God-fearing, pious and religious-minded men should be appointed to state offices. The study of philosophy should be proscribed. Fourth, principles of equality and justice should prevail in the empire. The *Mir-i Dehli* told Iltutmish that if a Sultan instituted these four doctrines, he would be popular among the apostles and saints even if his morals were not high; but if he failed to enforce them all of his good acts would be futile and his place could not be anywhere but hell. Barani, *Tarikh-i Firoz Shahi*, pp. 41–2. It is difficult to ascertain whether the whole of this statement was made by Sayyed Nooruddin or whether Barani was attributing his own views to the great Suhrawardi saint. The uprooting the idolators and a ban on the study of philosophy do not fit in with the teachings of the Sufi saints. Moreover, in *Fatawa-i Jahandari* Barani has himself expounded most of these principles as his own.

70. It appears from Jamali's reference to the incident that the Shaikh was definitely pro-Iltutmish and had deliberately taken such a risk. This was probably due to the Sultan's early contact with the Suhrawardi saints in Baghdad. However, for details of the incident, see Nizami, *Some Aspects*, pp. 254–5.
71. Shaikh-ul Islam was both an office and a title in the Sultanate period. For the duties of the office, see Ishtiaq Husain Qureshi, *The Administration of the Sultanate of Delhi*, 2nd edn., Lahore: S.H. Muhammad Ashraf, 1942, pp. 190–1.
72. Ibid., p. 256.
73. Once the Waali of Multan borrowed some corn from the Shaikh. When the corn was being removed from his granaries, pitchers full of silver *tankas* were found hidden there. *Fawaid-ul Fuwad*, pp. 223–4.
74. It is reported by Mir Khurd that a son of Shaikh Bahauddin was kidnapped by a robber and released for a huge ransom by Shaikh Sadruddin. *Siyar-ul Auliya*, p. 159.
75. Shaikh Bahauddin's *khanqah* in Multan covered an extensive area and was well furnished. Separate accommodation was provided to all inmates and visitors. Nizami, *Some Aspects*, p. 227.
76. Once at a *mahzar* (a regal court) convened by Iltutmish Shaikh Hamiduddin Sawali took the advantage of Shaikh Bahauddin's presence to put questions to him about the accumulation of wealth, but the shaikh could not satisfy his critic. The Suhrawardi sources state that the Shaikh, in search of a satisfactory reply, invoked the spiritual guidance of his mentor, Shaikh Shihabuddin Suhrawardi. *Siyar-ul Arifin*, as cited by Nizami, *Some Aspects*, p. 228.
77. *Akhbar-ul Akhyar*, p. 66.

78. For details about Shaikh Sadruddin's attitude to wealth and the state, see Nizami 'Suhrawardi Silsilah', pp. 125–6.
79. For details, *Siyar-ul Auliya*, pp. 205–7, 215, 226, 228, 316–17, 322, 328; K.A. Nizami, (ed.), *Politics and Society During the Early Medieval Period*, vol. 1, p. 368.
80. I.A. Zilli, op. cit., p. 82.
81. For details K.A. Nizami, 'Suhrawardi Silsilah', p. 129.
82. *The Rehla of Ibn Battuta*, Eng. tr. Mahdi Husain, p. 61. For details, A.A. Rizvi, *History of Sufism*, vol. I, p. 213.
83. Barani, *Tarikh-i Firoz Shahi*, p. 479; Isami, *Futuh-us Salatin*, ed. Usha, p. 443; Yahya Sirhindi, *Tarikh-i Mubarak Shahi*, ed. M. Hidayat Husain, Calcutta, 1931, p. 100.
84. Firishta, op. cit., vol. 1, p. 100.
    Khwaja Karak was a disciple of Shaikh Ismail Qureshi, a *khalifa* of Shaikh Bahauddin Zakariya. Barani has mentioned his name among the celebrities of the 'Alai age'. *Tarikh-i Firoz Shahi*, p. 353.
85. After the murder of Jalaluddin at Kara, his sons left for Multan and remained in the fort. Alauddin sent Ulugh Khan and Zafar Khan to Multan to capture them. Realizing the critical position, Jalaluddin's sons approached Shaikh Ruknuddin Multani for refuge. The Shaikh took them to Alauddin's commanders, who conceded shelter to the family, though later none of them were spared.
86. The *Rehla of Ibn Battuta*, Eng. tr. Mahdi Husain, p. 90.
87. Ibid., p. 145.
88. Afif, *Tarikh-i Firoz Shahi*, ed. Molvi Wilayat Husain, Calcutta, 1890, pp. 96–7.
89. Shaikh Abdul Haq Muhaddis Dehlavi, *Akhbar-ul Akhyar*, p. 142; A.A. Rizvi, *History of Sufism*, vol. 1, p. 277.
90. As a state guest he enjoyed the respect of the Sultan, and huge crowds would gather to secure his recommendations to Firoz Shah. A scribe used to record the problems of the people, which was presented to the sultan, who solved them out of respect for the saint. Afif, *Tarikh-i Firoz Shahi*, pp. 515–16.
91. Ain-ul Mulk, *Insha-i Mahru*, ed. S.A. Rashid, Lahore: Idara-i Tahqiqat-i Pakistan, 1965, letter no. 99, pp. 186–8.
92. Ibid.
93. Nizamuddin Bakhshi writes, 'As the greatness of the noble family of Shaikh Bahauddin Zakariya had made such an impression on the hearts of the residents of Multan and of the zamindars that nothing short of that could be imagined.' The people elected Shaikh Yusuf Zakariya Qureshi the ruler, and had the *khutba* read in his name at Multan and Uchch and other towns. He then began to run the administration. Khwaja Nizamuddin Ahmad, *Tabqat-i Akbari*, vol. III, ed. B. De and M. Hidayat Husain, Calcutta, 1935, pp. 522–3.

94. Ibid., pp. 523-4.
95. Ibid.
96. The beginning of Suhrawardi influence on the political life of Gujarat can be traced back to 1375, when Sayyed Sikandar, a disciple of Makhdum-i Jahanian, accompanied an expedition to conquer Mangrol. He received the grant of a village by way of reward and settled there. With the establishment of the independent sultanate of Gujarat (in 1396), the Suhrawardi influence in that region increased, because the Makhdum-i Jahanian was the patron saint of Gujarat. After his accession, Zafar Khan (later Muzaffar Shah) welcomed the Suhrawardi saints and bestowed jagirs and endowments upon them. When Ahmad (1411-42) founded Ahmedabad, Sayyed Burhanuddin Qutb-i 'Alam, a grandson of the Makhdum, was requested to settle in the new capital. The moral support which Qutb-i 'Alam gave to Ahmad Shah helped him consolidate power. The Sultan bestowed on the Shaikh a village where he finally settled and died in 1453. The descendants of the Shaikh came to be known as Sayyeds of Batwa. Later more villages were added to Batwa and the whole *jagir* was made hereditary. The house of Qutb-i 'Alam became a centre of power politics, and the saints were in a position to influence public opinion in favour of certain sultans and to discredit others. Consequently, some of the sultans of Gujarat were not on good terms with Batwa, and the *jagir* was resumed probably more than once. A *farman* issued by Sultan Mahmud III in 1548 relating to succession to the *gaddi* of Batwa throws enough light on the relationship between the Suhrawardi saints and the sultans. K.A. Nizami, 'Suharawardi Silsilah' *Medieval Indian Quarterly,* pp. 144-8.
97. See *Tabqat-i Akbari,* p. 525; *Akhbar-ul Akhyar,* p. 214.
98. *Tabqat-i Akbari,* pp. 527-30.
99. Ibid., p. 540; also Firishta, vol. II, p. 330.
100. Nizami, 'The Suhrawardi Silsilah', p. 138.
101. Abdullah, *Tarikh-i Daudi,* ed. Shaikh Abdur Rashid, Aligarh: AMU, 1954, p. 34.
102. Nizami, op. cit., p. 139.
103. *Akhbar-ul Akhyar,* pp. 215-19.
104. Ahmad Yadgar, *Tarikh-i Shahi* pp. 62-4; Abdullah, *Tarikh-i Daudi,* pp. 79-80.
105. *Tarikh-i Dandi,* p. 48.
106. Babur records 'Shaikh Jamali was sent to collect all available quiver-weavers from between the two waters (Ganges and Jumna) and from Delhi, so that with this force he might overrun and plunder the Miwat villages, leaving nothing undone which could awaken the enemy's anxiety for that side. Mulla Tark-i 'Ali, then on his way from Kabul, was ordered to join Shaikh Jamali and to neglect nothing of ruin and plunder

in Miwat; orders to the same purport were also given to Maghfur, the Diwan. . . . They raided a few villages in lonely corners and took some prisoners. . . .' See *Baburnama*, tr. Mrs. Beveridge, Delhi, 1979, vol. II, p. 551.
107. Ibid., p. 665.
108. Ibid., p. 631.
109. *Siyar-ul Arifin* cited by Nizami in 'The Suhrawardi Silsilah', p. 142.
110. Shaikh Abdul Haq, *Akhbar-ul Akhyar*, p. 228.
111. For Hayati, ibid., p. 228; Badauni, *Muntakhab-ut Tawarikh*, ed. Molvi Ahmad Ali, vol. III, p. 219; for Gadai, ibid., vol. III, pp. 76–7; Shahnawaz Khan, *Maasir-ul Umara*, vol. II, ed. Molvi Abdur Rahim, 1890, pp. 539–41.
112. Both Badauni and Abul Fazl have condemned Bairam Khan for this appointment. See Badauni, op. cit., vol. III, p. 76; Abul Fazl, *Akbarnama*, tr. H. Beveridge, vol. II, rpt., Delhi, 1993, pp. 161–2.
113. Badauni, *Muntakhab-ut Tawarikh*, tr. Lowe, p. 9.
114. Ibid., p. 28; Abul Fazl, p. 135.
115. Badauni, *Muntakhab-ut-Tawarikh*, p. 31.
116. Abul Fazl, *Akbarnama*, pp. 161–2.
117. For details of the Shaikh and the *silsilah*, Paul Jackson, *The Way of a Sufi: Shurfuddin Maneri*, Delhi, 1987; Rizvi, op. cit., vol. 1, pp. 226–40.
118. The Shaikh expressed that the Sufis should be intermediaries between the ruler and the masses. Letter 47, cited by Rizvi, vol. I, p. 230.
119. For details, see Paul Jackson, pp. 111–17.
120. Rizvi, op. cit., vol. 1, p. 230.
121. Paul Jackson, op. cit., p. 114.
122. See the Shaikh's letter, quoted in Paul Jackson, op. cit., pp. 112–14.
123. Rizvi, op. cit., vol. I, p. 231. The shaikh reminded Firoz Shah of the Prophet's injunction that an hour spent pursuing justice was superior to sixty years of worship.
124. *Manaqib-ul Asfia*, as cited by Rizvi, op. cit., vol. I, p. 131.

The *Futuhat-i Firoz Shah* of the Sultan gives a different version: that Shaikh Ahmad and his followers were atheists who misguided the people in the name of solitude and renunciation. Some people in Bihar considered Ahmad to be God. *Futuhat-i Firoz Shah*, ed. Shaikh Abdur Rashid, p. 8.
125. Ibid., p. 231.
126. S.H. Askari, 'The Correspondence of the Fourteenth Century Sufi Saints of Bihar With the Contemporary Sovereigns of Delhi and Bengal', *Journal of the Bihar Research Society*, 1956, pp. 183, 186–7.
127. For details Rizvi, *History of Sufism*, vol. II, pp. 54–130.
128. Ibid., pp. 56–7.
129. Ibid., p. 57.

130. Ibid., p. 59.
131. Ibid.
132. Ibid., p. 64.
133. For details, see Badauni, op. cit., vol. III, pp. 91–2.
134. Ibid.
135. For details about the life and works of the shaikh, see K.A. Nizami, *Hayat-i Shaikh Abdul Haq Muhaddis Dehlavi*, Delhi, 1964; Rizvi, op. cit., vol. II, pp. 82–97. In 1578 a second round of religious debate started in which Abdun Nabi and Makhdum-ul Mulk emerged as the main rivals. But the Shaikh remained neutral not only in this dispute but also to the imperial religious policies as a whole. vol. II, pp. 82–97.
136. *Tuzuk-i Jahangiri*, ed. Sir Syed Ahmad Khan, 1864, p. 283.
137. Rizvi, op. cit., vol. II, pp. 87–8.
138. Badauni, op. cit., vol. II, p. 258.
139. Rizvi, op. cit., vol. II, p. 71.
140. Ibid., p. 116.
141. For details, see ibid., pp. 122–3. In 1647–8 Jahan Ara ordered a mosque and *khanqah* to be built for Mulla Shah in Srinagar. The complex was visited by the Emperor.
142. Ibid., pp. 123–4.
143. Ibid., p. 146.
144. Details about the *silsilah* are provided in *Gulzar-i Abrar* of Muhammad Ghaus, which is one of the most important *tazkiras* of Indo–Muslim mystics containing most reliable account of the *Shattaris*. Rizvi, op. cit., vol. II, pp. 151–73; K.A. Nizami, 'The Shattari Saints and their Attitude Towards the State', *Medieval India Quarterly*, vol. 1, no. 2, 1950, pp. 56–70.
145. Nizami, 'The Shattari Saints', p. 60.
146. Rizvi, vol. II, p. 153.
147. Nizami, 'The Shattari Saints', p. 61.
148. *Tuzuk-i Jahangiri*, p. 258.
149. While Humayun was in Bengal in 1538–9, he sent the shaikh to persuade his rebel brother, Mirza Hindal to join him in the war against the Afghans. The mission was not successful and the shaikh himself was killed. *Akbarnama*, vol. II, pp. 135–6. Nizami, op. cit., p. 62.
150. *Tuzuk-i Jahangiri*, p. 258. Abul Fazl says, 'Though these two brothers were void of excellencies or learning and lived in mountain hermitages ... they put saintship to sale and acquired lands and villages by fraud'. *Akbarnama*, vol. II, p. 135.
151. Badauni gives the reason for the migration: 'As Sher Shah began to give Shaikh Muhammad trouble, he left for Gujarat', but Abul Fazl suggests that it was fear that drove the Shaikh to Gujarat. Badauni, *Muntakhab-ut Tawarikh*, vol. III, pp. 4–5; *Akbarnama*, vol. II, p. 135.

Sufism in India 97

152. Humayun wrote to the Shaikh, 'With due respect I submit that nothing happened in these unfortunate circumstances upon my heart except the fact that I was deprived of your society. . . . I sincerely and earnestly hope that God will relieve me of the present miseries and we shall meet again. . . . Messages of welfare should be regularly exchanged'. These letters were provided by Shaikh Muhammad Jalal, a disciple of Sayyed Muhammad Ghaus, to Muhammad Ghausi who has incorporated them in his *Gulzar-i Abrar*. For details Nizami, 'The Shattari Saints', pp. 63–4.
153. Abul Fazl, op. cit., vol. II, p. 135; Badauni, op. cit., vol. III, p. 8.
154. Badauni, op. cit., p. 34.
155. Ibid., p. 35.
156. His elder brother, Shaikh Zia-ullah, however, chose to live in poverty.
157. Abul Fazl, op. cit., vol. II, pp. 134–5.
158. Ibid., p. 232. Badauni (op. cit., p. 62) says that Fattu was a devoted disciple of the Shaikh.
159. For details, see Badauni, op. cit., vol. III, p. 44; *Tuzuk-i Jahangiri*, p. 211.
160. Jahangir writes, 'Sayyed Wajihuddin was a Khalifa of Shaikh Muhammad Ghaus. . . . His devotion to him is a glaring example of the spiritual greatness of the Shaikh'. *Tuzuk-i Jahangiri*, p. 211.
161. Nizami, op. cit., p. 68.
162. Jahangir gives a detailed account of his visit to the Shaikh's *khanqah*. It was the time of Shaikh Haider and the occasion of the his anniversary. He gave a huge amount to Shaikh Haider for the expenses of the festival, as also some cash and land to each of his relatives. *Tuzuk-i-Jahangiri*, p. 211.
163. *Mirat-i Ahmadi*, cited by Nizami, op. cit., p. 69.
164. Rizvi, op. cit., vol. II, pp. 169–73. Aurangzeb was deeply impressed by Shaikh Abdul Latif for his strict adherence to *sharia* and banning *sama* and music. Shaikh Muhammad Ashraf, a frequent visitor to the court, was given villages as madad-i maash by the Emperor.
165. For details about the origin and early development of the *silsilah*, see Rizvi, op. cit., vol. II, pp. 174–80; Nizami, 'Naqshbandi Influence on Mughal Rulers and Politics', *Islamic Culture,* Jubilee Number, vol. XXV/1, 1951, pp. 41–52.
166. *Baburnama*, tr. Beveridge, pp. 33–4.
167. Ibid., pp. 631, 633–53.
168. Ibid., p. 62.
169. Nizami, 'Naqshbandi Influence on Mughal Rulers and Politics', p. 44.
170. For Khwaja Husamuddin, Rizvi, op. cit., vol. II, pp. 193–5.
171. Some of the saints of this order who had migrated to India after spending a few years with Mirza Hakim (Akbar's half-brother), or those who belonged to Kabul, remained loyal to him and opposed Akbar's religious policies. See Rizvi, op. cit., vol. II, p. 181.

98   Bhakti Movement in Medieval India

172. Ibid., p. 183.
173. For details about Baqi Billah, see ibid., pp. 185–93.
174. Ibid., p. 192.
175. According to the Shaikh, the king being *khalifa* (successor) of the Prophet Muhammad should obey the laws of the *sharia* and follow the directives of the righteous ulama. He should consider the Muslim treasury as a trust fund to be drawn only for items prescribed by *sharia*. The income from mines and the discovery of hidden treasure should also be spent according to the laws of *sharia*. The shaikh concluded that a healthy state treasury depended on tranquillity and the morale of the army corresponded to a treasury administered according to the *sharia*. The above matters in detail are provided with reference to the shaikh's treatise, *Nuriya-i Sultania*, by Rizvi, op. cit., vol. II, pp. 363–5.
176. For details about the Shaikh's views ibid., pp. 196–223; Irfan Habib, 'The Political Role of Shaikh Ahmad Sirhindi and Shah Waliullah', Proceedings of Indian History Congress (23rd Session, Aligarh, 1960), part I, Calcutta, 1961, pp. 209–16.
177. For details of the Shaikh's reactions to this effect, see his *Maktubat-i Imam Rabbani Mujaddid-i Alf-i Sani* (collection of Shaikh Ahmad Sirhindi's letters in Persian), Istanbul, 1977, vol. I, letter 47, pp. 123–5.
178. Cf. *Maktubat-i-Rabbani*, vol. I, letter 167, pp. 277–8.
179. Ibid. (for instance), letters 47, 48, pp. 123–6.
180. Ibid., letter 47, pp. 123–5.
181. Ibid., letters 47, 53, 54, 195, pp. 123–5, 131–4, 311–12.
182. That the Hindu nobles disapproved of Akbar's religious experiments is apparent from the fact that only Raja Birbal became a member of the *Din-i Ilahi*. Raja Bhagwan Das and his son Man Singh refused to join it. Man Singh told Akbar, 'I am certainly a Hindu. If you order me I will become a Musalman, but I know not of the existence of any other religion than these two'. See Badauni, *Muntakhab-ut Tawarikh*, vol. II, p. 364.
183. For instance, *Maktubati Rabbani*, vol. I, letters 47, 48, 53, 54, pp. 123–5, 125–6, 131–2, 132–4.
184. Ibid., vol. I, letter 47, p. 124. In a letter to Lala Beg, who had earlier supported Salim's rebellion and was still one of his confidants, Shaikh Ahmad wrote, 'If at the very beginning of (new) regime, Muslim ways are introduced . . . well and good; if delayed, the position will become very different for the Muslims', ibid., vol. I, letter 81, pp. 180–1.
185. Father Du Jarric, S.J. Pierre says, 'Accordingly, the leading noble (i.e. Shaikh Farid who was closely associated with Shaikh Ahmad), having been sent by the others as their representative, came to Prince (Salim) and promised, in all their behalf, to place the kingdom in his hands, provided that he would swear to defend the law of Islam.' *Akbar and the*

Jesuits: An Account of the Jesuit Missions to the Court of Akbar, Eng. tr. C.H. Payne, Delhi, 1979, p. 204. This is corroborated by Ferano Guerreiro, who tells that Jahangir had 'sworn an oath to the Moors to uphold the law of Mafamede (Muhammad)', *Jahangir and the Jesuits*, C.H. Payne, p. 3.
186. It appears from the Shaikh's letter that his house, garden, library, and other belongings were also confiscated. He faced the situation with confidence. He wrote to his sons and disciples not to be demoralized by this. *Maktubat Rabbani*, vol. III, letter 2, pp. 277–8.
187. See *Tuzuk-i Jahangiri*, pp. 272–3.
188. Jahangir himself says, 'I had him released (Shaikh Ahmad Sirhindi) and gave him a dress of honour and Rs. 1,000 for his expenses and allowed him to go or stay as he chose . . . and he desired to remain at the court'. *Tuzuk-i Jahangiri*, p. 308.
189. For his meetings and discussions with Jahangir, see *Maktubat*, vol. III, letter 47, pp. 380–1.
190. Rizvi, vol. II, pp. 365–6.
191. The official history of the first ten years of Aurangzeb's reign contains two references to Muhammad Masum and his brother Muhammad Said, and both are praised as deserving to be the heirs of a mystic like Shaikh Ahmad. Muhammad Kazim, *Alamgirnama*, Calcutta: Asiatic Society of Bengal, 1868, pp. 293, 595.
192. Nizami, 'Naqshbandi Influence on Mughal Rulers', pp. 49–50.
193. K.A. Nizami, 'Shah Waliullah Dehlavi and Indian Politics in the 18th Century', *Islamic Culture*, Jubilee number, vol. XXVI, 1952, pp. 133–45; Rizvi, *History of Sufism*, vol. II, pp. 252–9; also Irfan Habib's article 'The Political Role', pp. 216–20.
194. Rizvi, op. cit., vol. II, pp. 373–4.
195. The Shah suggested that a town administration should feature five classes of officers: qazi (jurist), amir (army commander), rai (governor), amil and wakil. They all should be oppointed on the basis of qualifications and competence. See *Hujjat-i Allah al-baligha*, as cited in ibid., pp. 380–2.
196. Ibid., p. 383. For the text of the letter, see K.A. Nizami, *Shah Waliullah Dehlavi ke Siyasi Maktubat*, Delhi, 1969, pp. 41–4.
197. Rizvi, op. cit., vol. II, p. 386.
198. K.A. Nizami, *Tarikh-i-Mashaikh-i Chisht*, vol. I, Delhi: Idara-i Adabiyat-i Dehli, 1980, p. 424. The same controversy had already appeared during the time of Iltutmish. Nizami, *Some Aspects*, pp. 302–3.
Maulana Jalal Rumi (1207–73) had explained the relations between the kings and the ulama thus: 'The worst of scholars is he who visits princes, and the best of princes is he who visits scholars.' Rizvi, op. cit., vol. II, p. 356. Letters from Shaikh Sharafuddin repeatedly warned Muslims to

protect themselves from the evil influence of the worldly ulama, who thronged the courts hoping for positions in the state judiciary. Ibid, vol. 1, p. 235.
199. *Aijaz-i Khusravi*, vol. IV, Lucknow: Newal Kishore Press, 1876, pp. 121–40. Barani has also defined the role of a Sufi. With reference to Shaikh Ruknuddin Suhrawardi of Multan, he says that 'the Shaikh performed well the function of the *masaikh*. The entire population of the Indus Valley from Multan and Uchch and below became attached to his sanctified place.' *Tarikh-i Firoz Shahi*, p. 348.
200. *Futuhat-us Salatin*, pp. 455–6.
201. Ibid., pp. 456–7.
202. Ibid., pp. 458–9, 461–2. We have seen that Multan was saved from the Mongols in Qubacha's time through the intervention of Shaikh Qutbuddin Bakhtiyar Kaki.
203. Barani, *Tarikh-i Firoz Shahi*, pp. 324–5, 332.
204. Shaikh Isa (d. 1621-2), disciple and *khalifa* of Mohammad Arif Shattari, explains the matter thus: 'All gods . . . and all universalities are the theophany of His attributes, it is immaterial if the god is of stone or wood.' Also, 'In the temple they do not worship other than thou. One may prostrate either before stone, clay or wood.' For this reason the shaikh was some time called a heretic or infidel. Rizvi, op. cit., vol. II, pp. 169–70.
205. *Siyar-ul Auliya*, op. cit., p. 46.
206. *Fawaid-ul Fuwad*, op. cit., pp. 13–14; also *Siyar-ul Auliya*, p. 411.
207. *Fawaid-ul Fuwad*, op. cit., pp. 86–7.
208. Ibid., p. 226.
209. *Akhbar-ul Akhyar*, p. 176. During his visits the Shah used to put on his royal robes while the huge retinue of his disciples, who accompanied him, wore military uniform and marched with banners and drums.
210. Rizvi, op. cit., vol. II, p. 364.
211. Ibid.
212. The Khwaja has reproduced the guidelines laid down in the *Zakhirat-ul Muluk* of Sayed Ali Hamadani that the *zimmi* should be treated strictly according to the examples set by Caliph Umar. Rizvi, op. cit., vol. II, pp. 366–7.
213. Ibid., pp. 384–6.
214. Ibid.
215. *Fawaid-ul Fuwad*, pp. 137, 158–9; *Khair-ul Majalis*, pp. 65–6, 150; and *Siyar-ul Auliya*, p. 66.
216. The Shaikh prescribed for his disciples severe ascetic exercises almost similar to those of the Yogis. His many letters outlined his ideas on *tajrid* (solitude) and *tafrid* (renunciation). The first required complete severence from worldly things, while the second marked total relief from minor anxiety. Rizvi, op. cit., vol. I, pp. 229, 233.

Sufism in India 101

217. Nizami 'The Shattari Saint', p. 58.
218. For Shaikh Abdur Rahman's practices, see Rizvi, op. cit., vol. II, p. 69.
219. According to Shaikh Abdul Haqq, *mujahada* (mortification) and *riyazat* (ascetic practices) were instrumental in precipitating obedience to God and the *sharia*. He appreciated the Yogis who obtained supernatural powers by strict ascetic exercises and were able to perform miracles with divine favour (*istidraj*), ibid., vol. II, p. 136.
220. Ibid., p. 156.
221. It was shocking to Badauni that the shaikh showed great respect to Hindus. He says that the Shaikh stood up to welcome every Hindu visitor. *Muntakhab-ut Tawarikh*, vol. III, p. 5.
222. *Akhbar-ul Akhyar*, pp. 24–5.

CHAPTER 3

The Bhakti Movement and the Evolution of its Thought

Bhakti thought occupies a prominent place in the social and religious history of India. But the scarcity of the authentic source material is a great problem. Controversies abound, the data to settle them is tantalizing in its meagreness. H.H. Wilson, Monier Monier-Williams, and George Grierson tried to prove that bhakti emerged in India under Christian influence,[1] but this has been challenged. Bhandarkar traced its indigenous origins and established its antiquity with the support of epigraphical and literary evidence.[2]

The Vedas give a considerable account of the conflicting trend of worship of different nature gods, but there is no reference of bhakti as such. It is said that in Vedic times there was a person named Vasu among the people called Vrishni, who taught his followers informal worship. After his death, he himself came to be worshipped as Vasudev (about 300–400 BC). Thus there emerged a separate group of people who opened the way for the rise of Bhagvatism or the Bhagvat cult, from the second century. Later in the *Narayaniya* section of *Mahabharata*, Vasudev was identified with Vishnu, and Krishna was taken as his incarnation. In the *Bhagavad Gita*, bhakti received formal recognition within the fold of traditional Vaishnavism for the first time. Though all the Puranas reflect the existence of Saguna and Nirguna Bhakti, it was in the *Bhagavat Purana* that these are particularly emphasized. The *Bhagavat Purana* is a Vaishnava text considered the basic source of bhakti. But the loving devotion to Vasudev-Krishna has a strong content and his bhakti is described as a surging emotion which chokes speech, makes tears flow and the hair stand up with exceptional excitement. In the *Bhagavat Purana*, bhakti is not a separate spiritual discipline but mingles with *karma* and *jnana*.

The Bhakti Movement and the Evolution of its Thought 103

Bhakti is described there as a balancing force between the two in the context of salvation.[3]

Bhagvatism received an impetus during the Gupta period. All the Gupta rulers from Chandragupta II (376–414) upheld the Bhagavat cult until about AD 550. The patronage they extended to the cult contributed to its spread. The bhakti age in south India is said to have lasted from the sixth century to the end of the Vijayanagara empire. In the earlier phase a number of Bhakti saints, endowed with poetic and musical talents, wandered from place to place, singing hymns in praise of different deities, and drew their followings from among the common people.

But the emergence of a distinct bhakti cult in south India was the result of the emotional fervour of the Alvar and the Nayanar or Nayanmar saints who flourished between the seventh and the eleventh centuries.[4] It is important to note that in south India bhakti thought helped the transformation of Vedic ideology into sectarian religions of Shaivism and Vaishnavism. Though opposed to each other in approach, the Vaishnavite and Nayanmars worked hard for the development of bhakti thought in south India in their own ways. While in the earlier stages of bhakti thought Shaivism was dominant, in the later phase it was fully clothed in Vaishnavism. The trend created by the Nayanmar saints later developed into a religio-philosophical system called Shaiva Siddhanta. Similarly, various Vaishnava schools were also formed, in which bhakti was grafted on the theistic interpretations of the Vedanta.[5]

The second phase of spiritual transformation appeared in the period of the Cholas, the tenth to twelfth centuries, with Shaivism as the institutional base. This is best illustrated by the Thanjavur and Gangaikondacholapuram temples. The royal authority of the Cholas is visible in these temples, which represented Shiva bhakti centres. During this period the singing of bhakti hymns became an integral part of temple ritual. Religious rivalry between the Shaivites and the Vaishnavites and the favourable attitude of the Cholas towards Vaishnavism were to continue.

A new phase began with Ramanuja (1050–1137) who tried to bring about a reconciliation between the Vedic and Tamil traditions, between Vedanta and bhakti and between the social division based on varna and the sectarian orientation of bhakti in the south. This phase witnessed not only a new category of Shudra functionaries called *sattada mudlias* (i.e. holy men without sacred threads) but also a trend of liberalization in temple worship even in the most traditional sanctuaries like Tirupati and Kanchipuram. This comprised devotional worship of the 'twelve Alvars'.[6] Thus, the Bhakti movement spread through a nucleus of great temples starting with the Pallava period, maturing in the time of the Chola–Pandya, and achieving prominence under Vijayanagara.

The evolution and early development of bhakti thought and ideology, both Vaishnava and Shaiva, took place in south India and it was brought to northern India in the medieval period.[7] This is confirmed by the northern Vaishnava sects which proudly claim to be offshoots of south Indian bhakti. We have already seen that from the seventh to eleventh centuries, the Alvar saints provided a popular base to the Vaishnava form of bhakti in the south in an intense form. The Alvars mostly belonged to the lower strata and menial castes.[8] They did not believe in caste and were opposed to the *ashram dharma* also. The Alvar saints were mystics, and the four anthologies of their hymns in Tamil is popularly known as *Prabandham*. This is believed to be the first Bhakti text.

The early twelfth-century philosophy of Vishishta Advaitavad propounded by Ramanuja was based mainly on the *Prabandham*. Ramanuja was also influenced by another mode of devotion, the *prapatti* (or complete surrender to God) which was open for all, including the Shudras. Thus, Ramanuja included the Shudras and the low caste Alvars along with the Brahmans to be taught and trained in his Sri Sampradaya (sectarian establishment). After Ramanuja, the understanding that had been developed on the content of the Vedas *vis-à-vis* the *Prabandham* could not be maintained by his followers. Some of them started giving importance to the Vedic thought, others to the *Prabandham*.

The cult split into two schools, the Tenkalai and the Vadagali. The first, giving importance to the *Prabandham* and headed by Pillali Lokacharya, remained in the south, while the second, giving importance to the Veda and led by Vedanta Desika, settled in northern India. They came to lack a liberal attitude and thus closed the door to lower caste people. At the same time, the background for the rise of a more popular Bhakti movement was also being prepared in northern India.

We have seen that Nawahun, a Hindu *daroga* (inspector) of Uchch was killed under Firoz Shah because of his liberal views on religion. When we link this to the case of Ahmad Bihari who was killed for his *Wahdat-ul Wujudi* beliefs, it becomes clear that the murder of Nawahun was a reaction to the bhakti thought that was gaining ground in the time of Firoz Shah. In the subsequent period, the new thought took further steps, as is evident from the case of Lodhan or Jodhan (Brahman) who was killed in the realm of Sikandar Lodi because he had challenged the monopoly of Islam as the only true religion by saying that 'Islam is true (religion), but my religion is also rightful.'[9] It may be borne in mind that these cases of religious persecution were intended to check liberal trends that were developing in the society.

Liberal ideas were propagated also by a number of religious teachers and reformers of different schools of thought, Muslim and non-Muslim. The greatest contribution in this context was made by the Sufis. They not only maintained friendly relations with Hindus but also tried to learn their religious thought and practices.[10]

P.R. Chaturvedi has provided instances which show that in the non-Muslim circles too, similar views prevailed.[11] It appears from his account that during those days there were a large number of premonmadi sadhus in Bengal, extraordinary men called Bauls.[12] The Bauls were a popular group of Hindu and Muslim singers. While the Hindu Bauls were Vaishnavites, the Muslim Bauls were Sufis. Both sections were 'Men of the Hearts'. They were non-dualistic, conceiving the body as the microcosm of the universe. Hindu Bauls believed that though their first guru was Birbhadara, son of Nityananda (1473–1544), they received the Baul faith from a Muslim woman called Madhava Bibi. Besides, somewhere in the same province at about the same time there had emerged another group of 'Vaishnava–Sahajiyas' who, by explaining and elaborating the term *sahaja*, were trying to popularize it on a large scale. They preferred to achieve the state of *sahaja* (the ultimate self) not through yogic practices but by a process of the divinization of human love, as represented in Radha–Krishna union.

There then appeared in the north a group of Vaishnava bhaktas known as the '*Punch Sakha*' who, in spite of having been under the impact of Buddhism, were trying to popularize ideas against caste distinctions and ritualism. A similar trend seems to have emerged in those days within Jainism. There were two religious reformers, Launka Shah (1415) and Taran Swami (1448–1515), who, in spite of having been Svetambar and Digambar respectively, tried to spread ideas against the conservative thinking and ritualistic observances not only of Jainism but also of Hinduism and Islam.[13]

The same trend was developing during those days in Kashmir. We have already discussed the role of Lalla or Lalded. The crossbreeding of Sufi beliefs with those expressed by Lalded led to the foundation of the Rishi order of Sufis in Kashmir. Its founder, Shaikh Nooruddin, popularly known as Nand Rishi (AD 1378–1439),[14] was Lalded's spiritual successor. The Shaikh's teachings are embodied in his Kashmiri verses, some of which appear to be almost identical to those composed by Lalded. It was under Lalded's influence that the Shaikh imbibed the spirit of folk Shaivism. But in popular perception and in the *Rishi-namas* of *Charar-i Sharif*, Nand Rishi is portrayed not only as a venerated Sufi but also a champion of the lower castes.[15]

Performing some ascetic exercises, the Shaikh lived in a cave in the village of Kaimuh near Srinagar. He subsisted on wild spinach and leaves.[16] He and his disciples preferred to be called Rishis.[17] The contemplative life of the Rishis was founded on the Sufi *pas-i anfas*, similar to the *pranayama* of the yogis. They remained celibate, believing that a family life was great impediment in the pursuit of a saintly life. Later many Rishis began to live in *khanqahs*, accepting land and money from the government and from their own devotees. Nevertheless, they remained involved in social service without distinction of caste and religion. Abul Fazl and Jahangir were impressed by the Rishis and praised them for planting fruit trees for the benefit of the people.[18]

On the other hand, with the growth of imperialism the Gupta rulers identified themselves with divinity by adopting divine titles. The subjects, therefore, were expected to have devotional ties to them as their personal servants (*dasyabhava*). The transformation of spiritual bhakti to God into the material service to the king is a well-researched phenomenon of the feudal polity of early medieval India.[19]

Such an assessment of bhakti has, however, been challenged by Krishna Sharma.[20] In fact, feudal bhakti was governed by the power of the king and subordinate chiefs and lords were required to fulfil

The Bhakti Movement and the Evolution of its Thought 107

administrative obligations like military service, tribute, and their presence at court. Since loyalty was linked with political interest, it could change any time. On the other hand, no such obligations were required in the spiritual sphere (*niskama bhakti*) which was bound with the spirit of *shraddha* (or the force of inner faith) and which consequently kept all such devotees united.

BHAKTI MOVEMENT IN NORTHERN INDIA

Although the medieval monotheistic bhakti of northern India had a philosophical link with the conventional bhakti of south India, they were different not only in their socio-religious ideas but also in practical life and political approach. In spirit, the followers of different schools of northern bhakti had a unity of thought among themselves. This is evident from the *Guru Granth Sahib* of the Sikhs, *Panchavani* of the Dadupanthis and other compilations which exclude the compositions of followers of conventional bhakti thought in south India. The northern bhakti saints occupied a distinct place in medieval history, emerging as revolutionary saints and giving a new dimension to bhakti thought.

Such thought emerged as a spiritual movement some time in the early fifteenth century. It developed in two distinct schools in the north, Ram bhakti and Krishna bhakti. The first upheld austere and decorous modes of devotion, while the Krishnaites laid stress on more emotional forms, singing, dancing, and going into trance.

Ram Bhakti took two forms, *saguna* and *nirguna*. Saguna bhakti meant the devotional form of worship of God's visible or material attributes. This was a form of traditional Brahmanical worship, in which it was necessary to go to the temple, worship the image, and have faith in the material form of God. This school, being represented by the conformist saints like Tulsidas, remained committed to the scriptural authority of the Vedas and emphasized the need of a human guru as religious mediator between God and man. On the other hand, Nirguna Bhakti meant devotion to one God but without a visible object, since God has no attributes and is manifested everywhere, and is to be apprehended only by inner (mystical) experience. This school was led by radical or non-conformist men like Kabir, Nanak, and Dadu, adopted an independent *path* (way) and attempted to create a religious environment acceptable to people of different castes and communities. This school rejected the scriptural authority of the Vedas, broke with past traditions, fought against social discrimination, and strove for Hindu–Muslim reconciliation. It was inspired by both Islamic monotheism and the Vedantic monism. The cult formed a spiritual movement outside the institutional fold of all religious orders.

There is no historical founder of this unique movement, but Ramananda (1400–70) is considered to have introduced it in northern India.[21] With him there came a great social revolution. There is a great uncertainty regarding his life, work, and thought due to the lack of authentic source material. It is, however, generally believed that Ramananda was born in Prayag (Allahabad) to a Kanyakubja Brahman family around 1400. His spiritual teacher was Raghavananda, of the Shri Vaishnava Sect of Ramanuja. So, Ramananda was brought up in a traditional Vaishnava school of northern India and was the fifth spiritual successor of Ramanuja after Raghavananda. But since he could not adjust to the rigid religious practices and caste distinctions maintained there, a controversy ensued between him and his teacher. He was expelled or left of his own volition. He then founded a new cult by substituting the worship of Ram for that of Vishnu and His consort and by teaching the doctrines of Nirguna Ram Bhakti to people of all castes and communities.

A large number of works are attributed to Ramananda, such as *Shri Vaishnava Matabja Bhaskar, Shri Ramarchan Paddhiti, Anand Bhashya, Gita Bhashya, Upanishad Bhashya, Siddhanta Patal, Ram Rakshastotra, Yogchintamani, Ramardhanam, Atamabodh, Adhyatma Ramayan,* and miscellaneous Hindi hymns (*pad*).[22] But these appear to be fictious, containing fabricated accounts. They are perhaps deliberately attributed to Ramananda in order to prove him a traditional Vaishnava saint. The *Hanuman Stuti* is wrongly attributed to him, since it deals with the mythological characters of *Ramayana* including specially Hanuman.

There are only three miscellaneous hymns of Ramananda that are authentic. One of these is included in the *Guru Granth Sahib*,[23] and this along with the other two are found in the *Panchavani* literature of the Dadupanthis.[24] All three hymns were composed in the same spirit of monotheism. It is significant that there is not only

The Bhakti Movement and the Evolution of its Thought 109

a rejection of the theory of incarnation and of idol worship, but also of the Smartta system and the scriptural authority of the Vedas 'Satguru', and not the human guru, is the real guide.

Tara Chand has rightly observed that Ramananda formed a 'bridge between the Bhakti movement of the south and the north'.[25] The word 'bridge' used by him is important and implies that there were symptoms of bhakti thought in northern India even before Ramananda, which we have discussed. Cunningham is of the opinion that Ramanand emerged as a reaction against the cultural conflict between Hinduism and Islam,[26] but this lacks historical testimony. It is, of course, true that in spite of the best efforts of both communities for cultural synthesis, the religious consciousness was working in their minds. Since this attitude was deep-rooted it is possible that Ramanand's ideas of bhakti were a reaction. But, at the same time, we cannot forget that the Islamic concepts (because of the Sufi saints) had been playing a vital role in the spread of liberal ideas.

The bhakti saints were particularly inspired by the two fundamental concepts of Islam, the unity of God and the equality of human beings. It is thus more probable that Ramananda's emergence was a reaction against Hindu orthodoxy. It is significant that Cunningham contradicts himself by saying on the same page that it was due to the Islamic impact that Ramananda was able to seize the idea of man's equality before God to admit all classes of people as disciples.[27] Macauliffe clarifies the issue by saying that Ramananda was in direct contact with learned Muslims at Banaras, as a result of which he was able to depart from the rigid practices of Ramanujiya Sect.[28]

Ramananda's Ram was an absolute God without attributes. His liberal outlook and informal religious obligations prepared a sound background for Hindu–Muslim unity.

But there seems to be no reality in the popular belief that Ramananda was the guru of 'twelve disciples', Kabir, Raidas, Pipa, Dhanna, etc. In fact, none of them acknowledges him or even names him.[29] In fact, Ramananda could acquire only a limited number of followers in his life, though after him the Ramanandi Sect was founded, and it developed centres at Kashi and Ayodhya.

Anyhow, during and after the time of Ramananda there appeared a series of bhakti poets in northern and central India,[30] among whom those of Nirguna-marga were Kabir (1440–1518), Nanak (1469–1539), Dadu (1544–1603), Raidas (1399–1514?), Pipa (1408–67), Dhanna (1415–1513). Most of them came from the lower social strata and they hailed from both communities. They were generally non-sectarian individuals, neither *sannyasis* nor monks but secular householders like the Sufis. They did not follow any *parampara* as such but formed a spiritual lineage, and remained independent teachers. Philosophically these saints were close to the tradition of Vedanta monism as propounded by Shankaracharya and Ramanuja, but they were not Smartta Hindus. They had no relation with any of the four popular Vaishnava sects nor were they even systematic philosophers. They used the traditional Vaishnava names like Hari and Niranjan for God, but they did not believe in Vishnu or His incarnations. They can thus be called neither Ramaite nor Vaishnavite. Their main mission was to hit the class stratification of society and to foster Hindu–Muslim unity. Their strict monotheism, opposition to Brahmanical ritualism and idol worship brought them closer to Muslim mysticism than to traditional Vaishnavism.

Another point is that these saints had no formal education and yet their ideas took an identical course: there seems to have also been a good deal of mutual understanding among them. For the reason that these saints generally belonged to the lower strata of society from both the communities, they rejected the institutional structure and practices of all religious orders.

It is an inappropriate assumption of K.A. Nizami that the 'Bhakti movement received a setback from Akbar'.[31] It was merely the *nirguna* aspect of the movement that got a setback, and, for that too Akbar was not responsible, though the process had begun in his time. In fact, the Nirguna bhakti saints not only revolted against religious orthodoxy and formalism but also occasionally challenged the scriptural authorities of both communities. It is significant that a similar revolutionary trend against the Islamic orthodoxy and dogmatism had also begun. Hence, the need for a counter revolt against such trends was felt intensely and simultaneously by conformist Hindus and Muslims and found expression in the sixteenth century in the form of religious revivalism. This was aimed at re-establishing religious authority and its pristine purity in society. For this purpose, when in Muslim circles there emerged

The Bhakti Movement and the Evolution of its Thought 111

the Mahdavi movement under the leadership of Syed Mohammad of Jaunpur,[32] amongst Hindus, the mission was taken up by Tulsidas (1532–1623) and his disciples like Nabhadas (1573–1643).

Tulsidas was a religious philosopher who led a counter revolt against the prevalent liberal and revolutionary trend in order to revive older Vaishnava traditions and establish the authority of the scriptures. Yusuf Husain has rightly observed that Tulsidas not only 'gave literary form to the religion of Bhakti . . . (but also) raised the moral level of Hinduism'.[33] The *Bhaktmala* of Nabhadas was written (in early seventeenth century) mainly to provide a consistent history of Vaishnavism from south to north, with reference to the development of different Vaishnava cults from the twelfth to the sixteenth centuries.[34] What the author deliberately did was to include among a total of two hundred saints the names of the most liberal and revolutionary saints like Kabir, Namdev, Raidas, Pipa, and Dhanna even though they were quite opposed to Vaishnava tradition. The impact of such revivalism was so deep in the sixteenth century that suitable amendments and alterations had been made in the sayings of these saints before their incorporation in the Sikh, Dadupanthi, and other compilations, which inevitably caused serious ideological variation and inconsistency. Moreover, we should not forget that this was the time when, with the change in the trend of bhakti thought and movement, the revivalist saints of the Saguna-marga occupied a dominant position over the reformist and non-conformist saints of Nirguna-marga.

NOTES

1. H.H. Wilson, *Sketch of the Religious Sects of the Hindus*, Calcutta: Sushil Gupta, 1958, pp. 100–2; Monier Monier-Williams, 'Indian Theistic Reformers', *Journal of Asiatic Society*, 1881, p. 2; George A. Grierson, 'Bhakti-Marga', *Encyclopaedia of Religion and Ethics*, vol. II, ed. James Hastings, Edinburgh, 3rd print, 1953, pp. 548–50.
2. R.G. Bhandarkar, *Vaishnavism, Shaivism and Minor Religious Systems*, Varanasi: Indological Book House, 1965.
3. S. Radhakrishnan says that though 'the path of both the *Karma* and *Jnana* find their place in the *Bhagavata Purana*, the main stress is on Bhakti'. See his Foreword to Siddheshwar Bhattacharya's *The Philosophy of Srimadbhagavat*, Shanti Niketan: Vishwa Bharati, 1960, pp. 7–8. Tara Chand has clarified that the 'Bhagwat Purana marks the transition from the

ancient religion of *karma* (action) to the medieval religion of Bhakti'—*Influence of Islam on Indian Culture*, Allahabad: Indian Press, 1963, p. 134.
4. Susmita Pandey, *Birth of Bhakti in Indian Religions and Art*, Delhi, 1982, pp. 112-40.
5. M.S. Ahluwalia, 'Reflections on Bhakti Movement in Tamil Nadu and Punjab', *Journal of Sikh Studies*, vol. XXIX, no. 1, 2005, pp. 14-15.
6. S. Radhakrishnan, *Indian Philosophy*, Delhi, 1940, vol. II, p. 708.
7. For details of Southern Bhakti, see *Three Great Acharyas*, 2nd edn., Madras: G.A. Natesan and Company, n.d.; Tara Chand, op. cit., pp. 1-28; Yusuf Husain, *Glimpses of Medieval Indian Culture*, Bombay: Asia Publishing House, 1962, pp. 1-31.
8. The greatest among the Alvars, Namalvar (about AD 800), was himself a lowly Shudra.
9. This has been discussed in the Chapter 1.
10. See Chapter 2.
11. Parshu Ram Chaturvedi, *Uttari Bharat ki Sant Prampara*, 2nd edn., Allahabad: Bharti Bhandar, 1964, pp. 220-1.
12. The Sanskrit words *vatula* (crazy) and *vyakula* (impatient) are suggested as possible roots of the word. A Hindi variation *baur* (also meaning crazy) is suggested as a closer equivalent. All are compatible with the poetry of the Bauls and their philosophy of life. S.A.A. Rizvi, *A History of Sufism in India*, Delhi: Munshiram Manoharlal, vol. 1, 1978, p. 358; S.N. Dasgupta, *Obscure Religious Cults*, 2nd edn., Calcutta: University Press, 1962, p. 161.
13. For details of their lives and teachings, see P.R. Chaturvedi, *Uttari Bharat*, pp. 222-4. The author asserts that the radical views enunciated by Launka Shah soon acquired a definite shape and his followers flourished within a century in thirteen branches, of which at least four are still alive in one way or the other. Taran Swami on the other hand was the author of fourteen treatises, a collection of which has now been published with the title *Adhyatmvani* (spiritual voice). These treatises are mostly related to Jainism, but the central theme is to emphasize the ideas of kindness and humanity which are taken as the 'light of knowledge' and 'the real means of salvation'. His followers are still to be found in Uttar Pradesh and Rajasthan.
14. Shaikh Nooruddin, whose earlier name was Nand Sanz, was a posthumous son of Salat Sanz, a low-caste village watchman (*pasban*). After being converted to Islam, Salat came to be known as Shaikh Salaruddin. Mohammad Ishaq Khan 'The Rishi Movement as a Social Force in Medieval Kashmir', in *The Making of Indo-Persian Culture: Indian and French Studies*, ed. Muzaffar Alam, Françoise 'Nalini' Delvoye and Marc Gaborieau, Delhi: Manohar, 2000, p. 134; also Chaturvedi, op. cit., pp. 255-7.

The Bhakti Movement and the Evolution of its Thought 113

15. Chaturvedi, *Uttari Bharat*, pp. 255–7.
16. Rizvi, op. cit., vol. 1, p. 350.
17. Shaikh Zainuddin, disciple of Shaikh Nooruddin, invented a distinctive dress for rishis which consisted of woollen cloth with a black and white pattern running though it. Ibid., p. 351.
18. *Ain-i-Akbari*, tr. Jarrett, vol. II, p. 170, *Tuzuk-i-Jahangir*, ed. Sir Syed Ahmad Khan, Aligarh, 1864, p. 302.
19. R.S. Sharma, 'Problem of Transition from Ancient to Medieval in Indian History', *Indian Historical Review*, vol. 1, 1974, pp. 7–8. Sharma explains: 'The ideas and practices associated with Bhakti cult can be compared to the complete subjection of the tenants to the landlords. The tenants offered a part of their produce and rendered labour services to the lord. In return they received land and protection as a kind of favour from him. . . . The Bhakti bond was further cemented by the close tie between vassals or feudatories on the one hand and the paramount ruler, on the other.' N. Subrahmaniam also views bhakti as a feudal, contractual bondage between two unequal parties, deity and devotee, the former of providing protection in return for surrender. 'Bhaktism in Medieval Tamilnad', *Medieval Bhakti Movements in India*, ed. N.N. Bhattacharya, New Delhi, 1989, p. 180.
20. Krishna Sharma, *Bhakti and Bhakti Movement: A New Perspective*, Delhi: Munshiram Manoharlal, 1987, p. 29.
21. For some details about Ramananda's life and thought, see *Saints of Northern India* (from Ramananda to Ram Tirtha). This is one in the series on world teachers, published by G.A. Natesan & Co., Madras, n.d. The work deals with more than twelve teachers including Nanak and some of his successors.
22. Of these the first three have been published, the first two by Pandit Ram Tahaldas and the third by Raghuwardas, Ahmedabad, 1929. The Hindi hymns have also been edited and published by Kashi Nagari Pracharini Sabha, 1952.
23. Macauliffe, *The Sikh Religion*, Delhi: Low Price Pubs., 1993, vol. VI, pp. 105–6 (Rag. Basant).
24. See the *Panchavani, Basta* no. 12, compiled by Swamdas in 1636, part III, f. 281a.
25. Tara Chand, op. cit., p. 143.
26. J.D. Cunningham, *History of the Sikhs*, ed. H.C.O. Garsett, Delhi: S. Chand & Co., 1955, pp. 30–1.
27. Ibid., p. 30.
28. Macauliffe, op. cit., vol. VI, p. 102.
29. Kabir refers to Namdev along with Jaidev (author of *Gita-Govinda*) as a great saint. See *Gauri* XXXVI, *Bilaval* VII, Macauliffe, op. cit., vol. VI, pp. 158, 231. Ravidas mentions the names of Namdev, Kabir, Trilochan, Sadhna, and Sain: *Asa* V, *Maru* 1, ibid., pp. 327, 339. Dhanna says that he was inspired by Namdev, Kabir, Raidas, and Sain: *Asa* 1, ibid., p. 109.

30. At about the same time in other parts of the country too a large number other teachers and mystics emerged: Chaitanya (1486–1533) in Bengal, Narsingha Mehta (1450–80) in Gujarat, Vidyapati and Umapati (about 1450) in Bihar. They belonged to the Krishna school.
31. K.A. Nizami, *Akbar and Religion,* Delhi: Idara-i Adabiyat-i Dehli, 1989, pp. 30–1.
32. For details of the movement, see S.A.A. Rizvi, *Muslim Revivalist Movements in Northern India in the Sixteenth and Seventeenth Centuries,* Agra: University Press, 1965, pp. 68–105.

    Apart from working for general religious revivalism, the Mahdavis opposed Akbar's religious experiments and condemned the materialistic approach of the court theologians.
33. Yusuf Husain, *Glimpses of Medieval Indian Culture,* Bombay: Asia Publishing House, 1962, p. 14. For details about Tulsidas and his ideas, see C.K. Handoo, *Tulsidas: Poet, Saint and Philosopher of Sixteenth Century,* Bombay: Orient Longman, 1964, and 'Tulsidas: Poet and 'Religious Reformer', *Journal of the Royal Asiatic Society,* 1903.
34. Nabhadas, *Bhaktimala,* ed. S.R. Bhagwandas, Lucknow: Newal Kishore Press, n.d. For details about the work and the author, see P.N. Dikshit, *Nabhadas Krit Bhakt Mala: Ek Adhyayan,* Allahabad: Sahitya Bhawan, 1961, and 'Gleanings on the Bhaktmala', *Journal of the Royal Asiatic Society,* 1909, 1910.

CHAPTER 4

Historical Importance of the *Sant-sahitya* or Bhakti Literature

Bhakti literature constitutes a major part of the rich heritage of vernacular literature in medieval India.[1] Its contents are similar to that of the *malfuz* literature of the Muslim mystics.[2] The works of both traditions were written or compiled almost contemporaneously, and, apart from being valuable records of their separate organizations, both constitute valuable sources of history. Undertaken by Hindu and Muslim authors without prejudice or loyalty, the work of bhakti poets is crucial for a reconstruction of our medieval Indian history. The poetry can be used not only to fill in lacunae in the regular historical sources but also to assess and evaluate the authenticity of contemporary texts.

The *Sant-sahitya* in its various forms and dialects was written in different places covering from Bengal in the east to Kathiawar in the west, and from Kashmir in the north to Madhya Pradesh and Maharashtra in the south. There are sectarian hagiological works like the various *Bhaktmalas, Bhaktnamavalis, Parchais, Varta Sahitya* of the Pushti Marga, *Qulzum Sharif* and *Bitak Sahitya* of the Pranami Sect, and other works. There are also compilations of the sayings of saints, Sufis and yogis: the *Guru Granth Sahib* of the Sikhs, the *Panchavani* of the Dadupanthis, that of Naranjanpanthis and the *Panchayatan* of the south.

Of the above sources, the sectarian hagiographies are important. Good sources of history for socio-religious developments in medieval India, they also cover important political events such as the Turkish and the Mughal invasions, political conflicts among the petty states, and their relations with the centre. Besides, they reflect various aspects of the lives of common people and their relations with and reactions against the government and its functioning.

The *Bhaktmala* of Nabhadas (1573–1643), written in VS 1680/ AD 1623,[3] provides a history of Vaishnavism but incidentally also refers to Man Singh, who ruled from 1589 to 1618 and met Agradas (teacher of Nabhadas); Maharaja Yashwant (Jaswant) Singh Rathor (1626–78) and Jagat Singh (d. 1650).[4] The meeting between Man Singh and Agradas is mentioned in the *Bhaktmala* of Raghavadas, which also mentions another meeting, between Man Singh and Nabhadas. Raghava's *Bhaktamala* (AD 1660)[5] is based on the famous *Bhaktmala* of Nabhadas, but is an improvement on it. It narrates the development of six philosophical schools, Jogi, Sannyasi, Bodh, Jain, etc., and gives a detailed account of the four radical teachers, Dadu, Kabir, Nanak, and Jagan. Nanak and Dadu, about whom there is no reference in Nabha's *Bhaktmala,* are discussed at length. This work also provides the first complete account of the Niranjanpanth.[6] There are some smaller *Bhaktmalas* of the same kind, like that of Jagga and that of Ramdas. Similarly, there are other works of the same nature, such as the *Bhaktnamavali* of Dhrudas (d. 1643), the *Kavi Mala* compiled by Tursidas Nranjani in 1655, and the *Kalidas Harzara* compiled by Kalidas Trivedi in 1718.

On the other hand, the versified life sketches written by Anantdas around 1600, of Namdev, Trilochan, Kabir, Raidas, Pipa, and Dhanna,[7] also deal with certain events of political and socio-religious importance. For instance, in Kabir's *Parchai* there is a detailed account of his conflict with the Brahmans and Mullas of Banaras on the one hand, and with Sikandar Lodi on the other. The *Dadu Janma Lila Parichaya* (life sketch of Dadu), written by Jan Gopal between 1610 and 1620 not only provides a complete and consistent account of Dadu's life and career, but also refers to the socio conditions and some political events of Akbar's time. It also speaks of the conflict between Hindus and Muslims, on the one hand, and between the qazis and saints of Sambhar (near Amber), on the other, and a prolonged ideological conflict between Dadu and Man Singh during the closing years of the sixteenth century. It ends with a narrative of the installation of Dadu's eldest son, Gharibdas, as his spiritual successor.[8] This narrative provides a detailed account of Dadu's visit to Akbar at Fatehpur Sikri in 1584 and his meetings and discourses with Akbar, Abul Fazl, Birbal, and

Raja Bhagwat Singh (Bhagwandas). Mention is also made of Dadu's impact on Akbar by showing that his order for prohibiting the slaughter of animals was a result of that meeting.[9] Another *Parchai*, the *Malukdas ki Parchai* written by Suthradas in 1727, refers to Akbar, Jahangir, Shahjahan, and Aurangzeb, dealing with the condition of the common people.

But the literature of the Pushti Marga is even more important. The two *Vartas* of this sect are particularly significant: the *Chaurasi Vaishnavon ki Varta* and the *Do Sau Bawan Vaishnavon ki Varta*.[10] The literature mainly deals with the biographies of the saints of different sects and dialogues on socio-religious problems. But it also describes public reaction against the Turkish conquest of India on religious grounds, and describes state policies, and the socio-economic system of the time. Narrated in this literature are:

(A) Events of Political and Administrative Importance

(1) Muslim invasion of India was unexpected. It weakened the political structure of the country, causing a great loss to the life and property. It destroyed Hindu religion and propagated Islam by creating awe.
(2) With the passage of time the Muslim rulers began to live with amity and goodwill with their Hindu subjects. Many Hindus were employed by the state and some Muslim officers turned to Vaishnavism.
   (i) Naraindas was appointed Diwan, though later he was imprisoned for some reason and fined rupees five lakhs. As the fine was not paid, he was whipped 500 times a day.
   (ii) Prithvi Singh in his declining age desired to go to Braj. The matter was reported by his enemies to the emperor, who dispatched him on a campaign to Kabul.[11]
   (iii) A Pathan, governor of Braj, banned the felling of trees in the Braj forests, and people were warned that anyone violating the rule would be liable to severe punishment.
   (iv) The Pathan's son became the disciple of Gosainji and followed the practices of Vaishnavism in act and deed.
(3) The political atmosphere of the country was full of confusion and chaos. The local Rajas had no harmony among them and invaded one another's territories.

(4) Akbar came to Agra from Delhi. He directed his men to gather information about Surdas. A meeting between Akbar and Surdas took place, in which Akbar offered him a village and some cash, which the latter refused. Surdas requested the emperor not to meet him again. In the conversation references were made to Agra, Delhi, and Mathura.
(5) Akbar summoned Kumbhandas, a noted Hindi mystic poet, to appear before at court in Fatehpur Sikri in order to honour him. The poet did so but was disgusted by the experience, the details of which will be discussed later.
(6) Akbar and Birbal visited Gokul to solve religious problems there.

There are also the references to court life and the harems[12] and to officials like Pauriya, Bhitaria, and Khawas. Muslim rulers are shown to be lovers of art and literature, and the people, music, song, dance and drama. The rulers accorded honours to artists in various fields. For instance, there are references to Tansen, the great musician in the court of Akbar.

(B) Events of Socio-Religious and Economic Importance

(1) The excessive use of wealth by rulers and rich people; ordinary people earned their livelihood by agriculture or by trade and commerce; labourers were unskilled and were employed on daily wages.
(2) References to money transactions, the main trade routes and means of conveyance and transportation. References to currency: mohars, rupees, tanka, kansi, etc. The means of transport: cows, buffaloes, horses, boats (small and big) and ships.
(3) Reference to thefts and robberies as common occurrences that caused insecurity to travellers and householders. Punishment was of two kinds, penalties and corporal punishment. In corporal punishment there was whipping; death sentences were carried out by hanging or burning.
(4) Reference to Islam and Vaishnavism and various sectarian organizations like Shaiva and Shakti sects. Popularity of the Vallabhite Sect in other countries—Madhodas went to Kabul for this purpose. It also appears that temples and residences of

Vaishnava saints had become the main centres for sectarian publicity, which attracted the masses and so affected society as a whole.

(5) References to different communities, the Kannaujiya, Bhatt, Sachaura, Pandey, etc. The caste system is condemned in order to make common cause with the lower classes.

(6) People are shown following their hereditary customs and ceremonials. Faith in superhuman characters and in *sati* were dominant. There were joint families; child marriage was frequent but widows were not permitted to remarry; dowry giving is gleaned from the conversation of Damodardas Sammalhor and from the character of Chaturbhujdas. There is also the reference of Dhareja to keeping a woman without marriage.

(7) There are a number of references about the things of household use—ornaments and utensils like chains of pearls, finger rings, foot rings of gold; various garments; *malmal* (silk) of Bengal and *zari* cloth. Various kinds of food preparations like *bal bhog, raj bhog* (even *juthan*) and the pots including *jhari, kasendi, banta, tishti,* and *tabkari* have also been described in detail.

Another work of this nature is *Bhao Sindhu ki Varta* of Gokul, which refers to the Raja of Krishnagarh (Rup Singh) helping Shahjahan in war.[13] There are many more *vartas* of this kind, such as the *Nija Varta*, the *Gharu Varta*, the *Baithak Charitra*, the *Shrinath ki Varta*, and the *Ashta Sakhan ki Varta*.

Similarly, the literature of the Parnami Sect[14] also constitutes an important source on medieval Indian history. It is valuable not only for the history of the seventeenth century and the thought of the sect itself, but also for the political and socio-religious developments of the time.

The first and most important work of this sect is the *Qulzum Sharif* of Prannath (1618–94),[15] compiled just after his death in 1694 by one of his disciples, Keshavadas. This is a voluminous source comprising fourteen treatises, all of which were composed in verse and in different dialects.[16]

The following is the list of the treatises in the order as they appear:

Name of the Treatise	Chaupais in Volume	Language	Year of Compilation
Ras Granth	1,010	Gujarati	1655–74
(a) Prakash	1,176	Gujarati	–
(b) Prakash	1,176	Hindi	–
Khat Ritu	230	Gujarati	1665
(a) Kalash	768	Gujarati	–
(b) Kalash	768	Hindi	1672
Sanangh	1,691	Hindi	1678–9
Kirantan	2,103	Hindi	–
Khulasa	1,019	Hindi	1683–94
Khilwat	1,094	Hindi	1683–94
Parkarna	2,484	Hindi	1683–94
Sagar	1,128	Hindi	1683–94
Singar	2,209	Hindi	1683–94
Sindhi Bhasha ki Chaupai	559	Sindhi	1683–94
Karfat	1,034	Hindi	1683–94
Qayamat Nama	667	Hindi	1687

The above treatises were written in Devanagari script, but the themes and vocabulary have been mainly drawn from Persian and Arabic sources. For instance, in *Qayamat Nama* the author quotes *Siparas* (sections) from the Quran and refers to different points contained therein. It begins with the warning of *qiyamat* (the Doomsday) to the *Mu'mins* (Muslims), when the door of repentance will be closed, and goes on to describe the history of the last eleven centuries: how Jesus Christ came first and then Muhammad, and after him the Imams. The work continues to narrate the story of Adam's fall along with a reference to 'Azazil's (the devil's) determination to destroy the human race. It then refers to the prophesies of the different religions, Islam, Christianity, and Hinduism, and an attempt is made to prove that the last prophet of the world will appear in Hinduism in the form of 'Budh Kalanki' and then the people of all religions will have a common faith.

With the titles of the first three treatises the names of the religious scriptures like *Injil*, *Zabur* and *Taurat* are also added perhaps for the reason that the religious ideas of these scriptures are specially worked out in them. The *Sanangh* has been claimed to be a new interpretation of the Quran on the basis of *Srimad Bhagvat*.

Historical Importance of the Sant-sahitya 121

Prannath also gives in his works a considerable account of the political developments of his time. In the *Kirantan* treatise, a separate account of the political career of Maharaja Chhatrasal Bundela has been provided, in which his policy of 'nationalism'and 'militarism'against the Mughals is appreciated.

Besides, there was also the tradition in the Pranami Sect of writing *Bitaks*[17] comprising the biographies of saints of the sect, including especially Prannath and his teacher, Deochand. Of seventeen such *Bitaks,* the most important are the *Bitak* written by Swami Laldas in 1694,[18] and the *Bitak* (also called *Vritanta Muktawali*) written by Braj Bhushan in 1698.[19] Other *Bitaks* were produced by Mukund Swami, Hansraj Swami, Lallu Maharaj, Jai Ramdas, Bahurang Swami, and others.

Bitaks occupy a prominent place in Hindi biography as particularly complete and authentic.[20] They represent the first interprovincial form of *Khariboli* in seventeenth-century northern India. All the *Bitaks* contain similar accounts, with some variation of language and content. These are voluminous works and the important ones are generally divided into 71 chapters of more than four thousand *chaupais* (four line compositions).

The importance of this literature lies in its dealing with the life sketches of the saints of the cult. The efforts of Prannath to infuse the spirit of cordiality and humility among the people of different religions and his ideological conflict with Aurangzeb in 1678–9 have been narrated in these sources.[21] There is also a detailed account of esoteric practices as were maintained in the cult. Incidentally, this source also refers to certain political figures and political events of the time: Qutbuddin Khan's attack on Jamnagar, and Aurangzeb's attack on Udaipur.

It is significant that whereas in our established historical accounts there is a reference to only one attack having been made by Qutbuddin Khan on Jamnagar in December 1662, the *Bitak* of Laldas specifically refers to two attacks.[22] The reference to Aurangzeb's attack on Udaipur, and its date (1679–80), are correct.[23] Besides, the well-known fact of Jaswant Singh being with Aurangzeb during his march to the North-West Frontier in 1674 for the suppression of Afghan rebels, is also provided in the account.[24]

Similarly, in the context of describing the ideological conflict between Prannath and Aurangzeb, the *Bitak* refers to certain nobles of Aurangzeb's court, Shaikh [al-] Islam, Rajvi [Rizvi] Khan, Akal Khan, Sidi Polad [Siddi Faulad], Shaikh Nizam, and many more personalities about whom we know nothing.[25] These references, therefore, require verification and testimony from other reliable sources. Similarly, Jadunath Sarkar's account of Chhatrasal Bundela[26] may also be compared with the account provided in the *Kirantan* section of the *Qulzum* and that of the *Bitaks* for a better understanding of Chhatrasal's political career.

In the same way there are a number of other works of different sects, which also provide accounts of historical importance. For instance, the literature of the Nimbarka Sect[27] speaks of Muslim rulers as materialistic and using esoteric powers (*tantrik bala*) to create awe among the Hindus, though later they started to mingle with them and showed respect to their religious systems. Prices of daily commodities were not high but labourers faced hardships as daily wages comprised just 4 or 5 paisas. Among customs and ceremonials the most important was the *Kankan Bandhan* (tying string on the wrists of groom and bride on their marriage). Besides, the literature also reflects the general interest of people in education, architecture, and music.

Similarly, the literature of the Chaitanya Sect refers to the Muslim invasion and its consequences on Indian politics and society. Muslim rulers, previously hostile to the Hindu people, later tried to socialize with them.[28] There is a specific reference to Husain Shah of Ghaur who planned an attack on Orissa and requested Sanatan Pada (a follower of Chaitanya) to accompany him, but the latter refused, saying that it would lead to temple destruction. He was imprisoned.[29]

For general administration and economic system there are references to customs houses, chaukis, the permit system, the realization of revenue, the construction of houses on contract basis. There are also references to caste, to the various customs and ceremonies, and to household affairs. The garments of mendicants were deer skins, woollen blankets, and garlands, etc. The utensils were earth bowls and *surahi*, *dima*, and *ghara*.

On the other hand, since the leaders of the Radhavallabha Sect were associated with the Mughal government,[30] their literature furnishes valuable information about political and socio-cultural life of the time.[31]

Events of Political Importance

(1) After Sher Shah, Hemu became the ruler but Humayun took over by killing him.
(2) Hasan Beg was appointed governor of Mathura by Akbar.
(3) Muslim rulers adopted the policy of tolerance towards their non-Muslim subjects. For instance, Akbar allowed Hindu rajas to construct temples anywhere they wanted and consequently a number of temples were constructed everywhere.[32]
(4) Reference is made to a certain Narwahan who had become strong enough to refuse paying the state dues and drove away the amil of the place.

There are references to *mansab, jagir, patta,* etc., to coins, and to the means of transport. Muslim and Hindu rulers are described as patrons of art and literature. Similarly, references to theft and robbery and the punishments are also found. The literature also deals with caste, the social position of women, faith in evil spirits, and household ornaments, garments, and utensils.

On the other hand, the literature of the revivalist movement, particularly that of Tulsidas, is also important. Tulsidas wrote the *Ramcharitmanas* (1576), *Vinaya Patrika* (1582), *Kalidharmadharm Nirupan* (about 1600) and *Sahitya Lahri*. They provide insights into the existing political trends and the religious life of the common people.[33]

Another very important work is the *Pothi Gyan Bani* of the Satnami Sect of Narnaul, which exists in the form of a unique manuscript copy in the Royal Asiatic Society Library, London (Hindi 1).[34] The text is in both Nagari and Persian scripts. In the latter an introductory portion in verses (running up to f. 34b) is added. The colophon at the end of the work is written in Persian, which is followed by a glossary of mystic terms. The text is written in prose and poetry. The versified portion deals with spiritual beliefs and the prose gives a code of conduct for the followers.

The Persian chronicles represent the Satnamis as a rebellious force who suddenly broke out in 1672 against the Mughals. But it appears that they had already been organized as a sect under the leadership of Gharibdas in 1657, fifteen years before their famous rebellion. There are other references to the nature and habits of the Satnamis, indicating their social position and political careers.

A number of compilations were produced during this time at the various sectarian centres, which incorporate the sayings of a number of teachers, Sufis, and Yogis. These compilations were made in different parts of the country: especially in Maharashtra, Chhattisgarh, Rajasthan, Punjab and eastern Uttar Pradesh. Of this literature, the *Guru Granth Sahib* collection of the western corpus, and the Dadupanthi and the Niranjanpanthi literature representing the central or Rajasthani tradition, form the most important part. There is a large body of Kabirpanthi sources denoting the tradition of Chhattisgarh and eastern UP. Maharashtra too had its compilation, the *Panchayatan*, which includes the sayings of Gyandev, Namdev, Eknath, Tukaram, and Ramdas.

Of the various sectarian compilations, however, the *Guru Granth Sahib*, also known as *Adi Granth*, is important. Initially compiled in Gurmukhi script by Guru Angad in 1534, and containing the sayings of Nanak and Angad, it was later enlarged, in Devnagari, by Guru Arjan (1604). Arjandev at first collected the sayings of five Sikh gurus including his own, and then invited the followers of other sects to suggest verses of their respective teachers for inclusion in the holy *Granth*. The object was to put into effect practical liberalism. But, of course, only those saints and their verses were incorporated which were not opposed to Sikh teachings. For instance, even the personal requests of Kahna, Chajju, Shah Husain, and Pilo were turned down by the guru on the ground that their views were inconsistent with those of Sikhism.[35]

Final shape was given to the *Guru Granth Sahib* by the tenth guru, Gobind Singh, in 1705. He added the sayings of his father, Tegh Bahadur, and his own. He declared at Nanded in 1708 that the *Granth* was the ultimate religious authority for all the time. It was henceforth regarded as the eleventh incarnated guru, a living testament to the *bani* or sayings of all the Sikh gurus, as well as the *bhaktas* of different schools of thought.

The original collection of the *Guru Granth Sahib* with the sayings of five Sikh and sixteen non-Sikh teachers, compiled by Guru Arjan in 1604, is preserved in Kartarpur. The main editions are:

Historical Importance of the Sant-sahitya 125

1. (a) *Adi Guru Granth Sahibji*, Gurmukhi script, ed. Bhai Mohan Singh, Amritsar.[36]
   (b) Ibid., Nagari Script, ed. Bhai Mohan Singh, Tarn Taran, Amritsar, 1927.
2. *Shri Guru Granth Sahib*, in both Gurmukhi and Nagari scripts, Shiromani Gurdwara Prabandhak Committee, Amritsar, 1952.
3. *Shri Guru Granth Sahib*, Sarva Hind Sikh Mission, Amritsar, 1937.

The content covers the religious thought of the saints of northern India from twelfth to the seventeenth centuries and comprises:

1. Sayings of the first five Sikh gurus and the ninth one; Nanak (1469-1539), Angad (1504-52), Amardas (1479-1574), Ramdas (1534-81), Arjan Dev (1563-1606) and Tegh Bahadur (1621-75).
2. Sayings of sixteen early Bhagats or saints of different schools of thought, viz., Jaidev (1119-70), Namdev (1269-1344), Trilochan (1267-1355), Parmanand (fifteenth century), Sadhna (fourteenth century), Beni (fourteenth century), Ramananda (1400-70), Dhanna (1415-1513), Pipa (1408-67), Sain (1390-1440), Kabir (1440-1518), Raidas (d. 1514) Mira Bai (1498-1546), Shaikh Farid (1173-1265) Bhikhan (1480-1573) and Surdas (1483-1563).
3. The poems of Bhattas like Mathra, Jalap, Nal, Kirat, Das, Gayand, Sadrang, and Bhikha.
4. *Ram Kali Sadd* of Sundar, hymns of Mardana and a long poem, war of Satta and Balwanda.

There are 3,384 hymns, of which 974 were composed by the first guru, 62 by the second, 907 by the third, 679 by the fourth, 2,218 by the fifth, and 115 by the ninth guru. Of the remainder the highest number of hymns is in the name of Kabir.

The hymns of the *Granth* are grouped in the following ten heads: *Japuji* (a philosophical poem of deep meditation), musical hymns, *Slok Sahaskriti, Gatha, Funhe, Chaubole, Sloks* of Kabir and Shaikh Farid, *Sawayyas* of the gurus and *bhagats*, *sloks* of the gurus, and the *Ragmala* of Guru Arjan.[37] They are arranged according to the various *ghars* or *ragas* and in according to *chaupada* (composition of four verses each) *Ashtapad* (composition of four verses each), special long poems, *vars* and *sawayyas* (both consisting of two or more *sloks* with a concluding stanza).[38]

The collection and compilation of the *Granth* is not according to subject matter and period, but according to *raga*. From this point of view, it is the only work which has a foundation on music, having musical and emotional appeal. The *Granth* contains sayings of saints of both communities from different parts of northern India: Jaidev of Bengal; Surdas of Oudh; Nandev, Trilochan, and Parmanand of Maharashtra; Beni, Ramanand, Pipa, Sain, Kabir, Ravidas, and Bhikan of Uttar Pradesh; Dhanna of Rajasthan; and Shaikh Farid of Ajodhan (now Pakpatan). Apart from being diverse in their regions, they also represent a diversity of class, caste, and occupation. Kabir was a weaver; Sadhna, a butcher, Namdev a calico printer; Dhanna a peasant; Pipa a prince, Sain a barber, Ravidas, a cobbler; Shaikh Farid a mystic, and Bikhan a Muslim scholar.

Another important text of the Sikhs is *Shri Dasam Guru Granth Sahebji* written by Guru Gobind Singh (1675–1708). It comprises 1,427 pages. Its content may be divided into twelve parts, *Jap* (in praise of God), *Akal Ustat* (in praise of the immortal), *Bachitra Natak* (wonderful drama), *War Sri Bhagauti Ji Ki* (a war poem), *Gyan Prabodh* (giver of knowledge), *Avatar* or the incarnation of God (comprising a critical account of Hindu religion and mythology), hymns in Rag Ramkali, hymns in *Sawayyas*, hymns about the Sikhs, *Shastra Nammala* (in praise of weapons), *Pakhian Charitra* (a long episode dealing with the wiles of women), and *Zafar Nama* (a letter of victory in Persian addressed to Aurangzeb).[39] In the letter the guru clarifies the Sikh religious position, saying that Hindu Rajas worshipped idols but he, the guru, was an idol breaker.[40]

The *Panchvani* of the Dadupanthis[41] is also an important source, with the largest manuscript collections. These manuscripts, compiled over time and at various centres of the Dadupanth, are available not only in Rajasthan but also in many other places.

The Dadu Mahavidyalaya at Jaipur has a large number of manuscripts which it preserves in the form of *bastas* and *gutkas*.[42] Most of this collection cannot be dated earlier than the eighteenth century, but a few manuscripts also belong to the early seventeenth century. The following list, in chronological order, gives some

Historical Importance of the Sant-sahitya 127

details of a few select manuscripts available at the institution in Jaipur:

Basta No. 12, compiled by Swamdas (Pipa-Bansi),[43] AD 1636. It appears from the contents that it originally had 425 folios, of which about 100 are in a very bad state of preservation.[44] This is a very valuable collection. It contains not only the account of the five saints traditionally recognized, but also the sayings of about eighty other saints of different schools, particularly of Gorakhnath, Surdas, and Nanak. The last three receive so much attention that they acquire parity with the prominent five. The sayings of Pipa have also been fully represented, perhaps because the compiler originally belonged to the Pipa Sect.

Basta No. 2, compiled by Narharidas, AD 1676,[45] contains a total of 568 folios, and is in a fully preserved condition. It includes the sayings of about eighty saints besides those of the traditional five saints. In addition to *sakhis* (couplets) and *sabads* (short-poems), this *basta* also includes a few rare manuscripts such as Kabir's *Bavani, Sakal Gahgari,* Goraknath's *Pran Sankali, Atma Bodh, Kafir Bodh,* Khemdas's *Sukha Samvad, Laghutnama, Chintavani,* Bajid's *Sukhnamau, Gunnam-Mala*; Narayandas's *Naomala*; Ghamandidas's *Naon Mahatma Grantha*; Chaturbhuj's *Vaisnava Mahima;* Prithinath's *Sadh Parcha Jog Granth*; Shankaracharya's *Barahma Gyan*; Jangopal's *Dhruvacharitra, Bharta Charitra*; and the famous *Gunganjanamah* of Jagannathdas. In addition there are *parchais* or life-sketches written by Anantdas and the saints covered include Trilochan, Namdev, Kabir, Raidas, Angad, and Pipa.

Basta No. 43, compiled by Jagannathdas (disciple of Laxmidas) at Didwana (Jodhpur), in 1711 has about 1,000 folios. Surprisingly, this manuscript does not maintain the panchavani order. It begins with the *sawaiyyas* of Sundardas, followed by the *sakhis* and *sabads* of Dadu, Kabir and Pragdas. Then come the *Ramaini* and *Chandaini* of Kabir, and the two *Parchais* written by Anantdas on Namdev and Trilochan. It also has Sukdev's *Lilagranth,* and Sundardas's *Vivekchintavani.*

There are many more *bastas* in the Dadu Mahavidyalaya, No. 4 compiled by Ram Dayal (of the order of Banwaridas) (1745); No. 18, compiled by Ganga Ram at Ranila (Hissar) in 1748; No. 15, compiled by Ramdas (of the order of Banwaridas), in 1755; No. 3, compiled by Charandas (disciple of Premdas), in 1762; No. 19, compiled by Mauji Ram (a Niranjanpanthi) at Sambhar (Ajmer), in 1776; No. 8 compiled by Ramghandas at Nagaur, AD 1784; and Nos. 11, 13, 14 and 34, which also belong to the eighteenth century, and are particularly important. One contains 146 *sakhis* of Qadi Kapan. The works of a seventeenth-century poet of Jaunpur, Banarsidas Jain, the *Samai-Sar, Banarsi Kavitta* and *Iman Battisi* are found in Basta Nos.13/310, 14/342 and 34/594, respectively, along with accounts of other saints. Among the *gutkas,* at least three deserve mention: No. 33 compiled by Haridas seems most important. The present copy of the manuscript is of AD 1666 and contains the works of Laldas, Bhikhan, Bajid, and Jangopal, all of the Dadupanth. No. 75/383 includes Ahmad's *Barahmasa* and 69/365 has verses of Shaikh Farid and his contemporaries. Similar *gutkas* are also found in the Kabir Mandir at Jaipur.

The Dadu Mahavidyalaya at Jaipur is not the only centre of its kind. There are several other centres particularly those at Naraina (Jaipur), Ranila (Hissar), and Narnaul (Patiala), which possess a number of Panchavani manuscripts.

Apart from the centres mentioned above, the Hindi Sahitya Sammelan at Prayag preserves similar manuscripts. An important manuscript known as the *Anbhai Sargarh* is preserved in the Panjab University Library (No.1960). Besides, the Nagari Pracharini Sabha at Varanasi also possesses several such manuscripts. One of these, No.108, dated 1504, has already been utilized by Shyam Sundardas for his *Kabir-Granthawali*.[46] Surprisingly, this manuscript of 72 folios contains the verses of only Kabir, which closely resemble Kabir's verses in one of the collections at Jaipur compiled in 1809. The latter too has only Kabir verses. But the date ascribed to the Varanasi manuscript, AD 1504, is very early, and the date given in the colophon appears written in a different hand. However, it is a very important manuscript which, along with the Jaipur collection, presents a fair recension of the Dadupanthi tradition of Kabir's verses.

With the Sabha at Varanasi there is a manuscript, No. 1406, which contains 383 folios, and is evidently a Dadupanthi work. It appears from the colophon that it was compiled by Sadhu Mansa Ram (disciple of Gopaldas) at Udaipur in AD 1740. Besides the *Panchavani*, it also includes the sayings of Gharibdas (son of Dadu), Sadhudas, Bakhna, Jangopal, Sundardas, Khemdas, and

Historical Importance of the Sant-sahitya

many other Dadupanthis. Yet another manuscript, No. 1409, contains 791 folios and was compiled by Ramdas in 1714. In addition to the *Panchavani*, the manuscript incorporates the work of Gharibdas and miscellaneous verses of fifty-six saints of different schools, as well as the *Jogesari Bani* of the Nathpanthi Yogis, the works of the Dadupanthi saints like Jangopal, Dujandas, Jagjivandas, Jaimal, Mohandas, and the famous *Sarbangi* of Rajabdas.

Moreover, there are some very important and early manuscripts in the personal collections of scholars like Purohit Hari Narayan Sharma (*Tahvildaron ka Rasta*, Jaipur) and Agarchand Nahta of Bikaner.

There are other important works which, though part of the same *Panchavani* manuscripts, are on a different pattern altogether. The most important among them is the *Sarbangi Chintamani*[47] compiled by Gopaldas (disciple of Santdas) at Sambhar in AD 1627. A copy of the manuscript containing about 365 folios is included in Basta No. 3 of the Dadu Mahavidyalaya, which is itself a copy of the original compilation made by Charan Rain (of the order of Mohan Baba Kisandas) at Hansar in AD 1724.[48]

The *Sarbangi* or *Sarvanga-yoga* of Rajabdas (1567–1689)[49] is of a similar nature. Unfortunately, the original manuscript, which is usually assigned to a late seventeenth-century date, is not available. However, a number of copies do exist in many Panchavani manuscripts both at Jaipur and at Varanasi. For instance, the Dadu Mahavidyalaya contains the work in Basta No. 3, compiled by Charandas, 1762 (ff. 322–500); Basta No. 36, compiled in 1768 (ff. 9–261); Basta No. 19, compiled by Mauji Ram, 1776 (ff. 256–488); and Basta No. 8, compiled by Ramghandas at Nagaur, 1784 (ff. 253–500).[50] Likewise, the Nagari Pracharini Sabha at Varanasi also preserves the text of the *Sarbangi* in several manuscripts, such as No. 1409, compiled by Ramdas (1714), ff. 611–790; No. 1708, compiled by Khusyaldas, 1779 (ff. 229–427); and No. 1407, compiled by Gyandas, in 1815. Among all these, the Basta No. 3 of the Jaipur collection[51] and No. 1409 of the Banaras collection are the earliest to comprise the *Sarbangi* of Rajabdas along with the *Panchavani* and the sayings of many more saints. However, the various copies of the *Sarbangi* available in these collections have very little textual variation.

Both *Sarbangis* are very compact and comprehensive compilations. They incorporate the sayings of saints, sufis, yogis and siddhas (a total of sixty-six in Rajab's *Sarbangi*). It may be noted that these mystic poets feature also in many of the complete Panchavani collections. The *Sarbangis* have also maintained the traditional Panchavani system of giving the maximum representation to the sayings of Dadu, Kabir, Namdev, Raidas, and Hardas. This shows that these works followed the traditional Dadupanthi system. Yet the *Sarbangi* appears compiled on a pattern different from the Panchavani. The first *Sarbangi*, the *Sarbangi Chintamani*, is divided according to subject into 135 *angas*, and the second into 142 or 145 *angas*. Each *anga* has also *sabads* or *padas* (short poems) in different ragas. Otherwise, the method of selection, incorporation, and arrangement remains the same as in the *Panchavani* collections.

A similar collection, the *Gunganja-namah*, was compiled by Jagannathdas[52] some time in the late seventeenth century. Like the *Sarbangi*, copies of *Gunganja-namah*, in manuscript, also form part of several Dadupanthi collections, in several bastas in Jaipur and in Banaras (compiled by Daya Ram Dadupanthi in 1790 at Naraina).

It is significant that, though the *Gunganja-namah* fundamentally bears the *Sarbangi* pattern, its compilation has distinct features. It is a collection of *sakhis* and other short verses, and the text is not divided into *ragas* but has only 179 *angas*. For the same reason, despite its 5,586 *sakhis* and other verses, it remains a smaller compilation compared to the *Sarbangi*. But, just like the *Sarbangi*, the *Gunganja-namah* also includes the verses of a number of Sufis and Siddhas (65 in all), though surprisingly not of Hardas, the famous Panchavani saint. However, it gives the foremost place to Kabir and about 400 of his *sakhis* are included, of which 86 are not found anywhere else, as against the limited six in the *Sarbangi*. These differences in compilation apart, the above works, along with all the *Panchavani* manuscripts, follow the basic pattern applied in the *Angabandhu* collection compiled by Rajabas as early as 1595. The difference between the two is that while the latter only contains the sayings of Dadu, the former incorporates accounts of a large number of other personages.

Now, like the verses of Dadu in the *Angabandhu*, the sayings in all the Dadupanthi sources, including the *Sarbangi* and the

Gunganja-namah, fall into two broad categories. There are *sakhis* on independent verses or couplets (*dohas*), and *sabads* or lyrical hymns, or short poems.

However, some other poetic forms, such as the *ramaini* (a four-line composition generally followed by a couplet), *bauni, chautisi, kavitt, aril* and the Persian *bayt* are also occasional occurrences.

The *sakhis* in these collections are expository and didactic in character and are generally divided into thirty-seven chapters, each with a sacred characteristic or spiritual connotation.[53] There are many subdivisions in each *anga*, serially arranged in these collections so as to give to the whole text a definite direction. Other compilations, like the *Sarbangi* and the *Gunganja-namah*, follow the same pattern, though the *angas* in them are differently classified. Generally the *sakhis* in all the collections are numbered throughout. They are also totalled at the end of each section to ensure that no mistake has occurred in transcribing them.

The *sabads* or *padas* are classified according to the *ragas* in which they are sung and, therefore, categorized under these *ragas*. These are: Gauri, Mali, Kalyan, Kannar, Kedaro, Maru, Ramkali, Asawari, Deogandhari, Parjiya, Sarang, Todi, Nat Narayan, Sorath, Gund, Bilaval, Suhi, Basant, Bhairu, Lalit, Jaitsari and Dhanasari.

Like the *sakhis*, the *sabas* are also numbered in each section. The musical groups under which they have been arranged are not numbered but generally follow in an order. These short poems are primarily devotional in nature and each of them is complete in itself. These two factors help the *sabads* appeal directly to readers.

The whole system indicates a degree of compactness, cohesion, and uniformity in all the Dadupanthi sources. All this makes their perusal easy. The system was not invented by the Dadupanthis, since earlier examples exist in Indian literature.[54] What the Dadupanthis really contributed was a broader application of the method in a considerably modified form. A similar classification of *sabads* into different *ragas* may also be noticed in the *Guru Granth* collection, though the *dohas* do not occur in any apparent order.

A *Panchavani* collection can broadly be divided into the following parts:

1. the traditional *Panchavani* or sayings of the five saints,
2. sayings of numerous saints of different schools of thought,

3. the *Jogesari Bani* of the yogis and the *Doha Kosas* of the siddhas, and
4. the verses of saints of the Dadupanth.

The verses of Dadu, Kabir, Namdev, Raidas, and Haridas, in that order, form a major part of the *Panchavani* collection. For other saints, generally no such order is maintained. However, they too may be tentatively divided into three groups in the following order on the basis of the volume of verses incorporated in them:

1. Gorakhnath, Surdas, and Nanak
2. Mapaji, Prithinath, Khemdas, Anantdas, Pipa, Bajid (a Muslim Pathan),[55] Bakhna (*a Muslim Mirathi*), Bharthari, Gharibdas (son of Dadu), Kamal (son of Kabir), Shaikh Farid, Qadi Kapan, Qadi Mahmud, Rajabdas (excluding his *Sarbangi*), Sojha, Madhodas, Jangopal, and Harvant.
3. Shaikh Bahauddin, Parmananda, Paras, Bihebal, Tursidas (Niranjini), Jaimal, Ramanand, Trilochan, Rangi, Angad, Vyas, Beni, Dhanna, Sadhna, Sukhanand, Narsi Mehta, Mati Sundar, Jagannathdas (excluding his *Gunganja-namah*), Som Bisa, Chhitam, Shaikh Saraf, Machhindarnath, Charpatnath, Chunkarnath, Hali Pao, Jaidev, Naraindas, Sanwaliya, Ajaipal, Bal Gunain, etc.

Other works of the same nature were compiled by the members of the Niranjani Sect at about the same time, preserved in various centres. Three manuscripts of this kind are found in the Dadu Mahavidyalaya at Jaipur, largely identical. One, compiled by Mohandas Niranjani at Sambhar (Ajmer) in 1769,[56] contains a total of 536 folios and includes sayings of Haridas, Sewadas, Tulsidas, Kabir, Ramanand, etc. The other manuscript, compiled by Mauji Ram at Sambhar in 1776, is preserved there in Basta No. 19. The third one was compiled by Hari Ramdas (grand disciple of Amardas Niranjani) in 1804 at Tehri (Didwana).[57] This is a comparatively large compilation, covering 669 folios. Apart from the sayings of almost the same Niranjani and non-Niranjani saints as are found in the above two manuscripts, it also includes the *Satik Padas* of Kabir, Namdev, and Gorakhnath. Besides, some other works of Kabir, like the *Grantha Battisi, Ram Mantra, Prachaya Chintamani,* and *Janma Bodh Patrika ki Ramaini* are also included in the manuscript.

Historical Importance of the Sant-sahitya 133

A similar manuscript is preserved in the Nagari Pracharini Sabha Library at Banaras, No. 873, which consists of 717 folios. This is also a large compilation of the sayings of Haridas, Sewadas, Kabir, Namdav, Raidas, Pipa, Jagjivan, Gorakhnath, etc. In addition the work incorporates some Parchais of Haridas, Sewadas, and Pipa. Another manuscript collection of the same kind is found in the India Office Library, London (Hindi-a-II), which consists of 571 folios.

In the Niranjanpanthi compilations there is very little textual variation. There is also much similarity in the contents of the Niranjanpanthi and Dadupanthi compilations, and the mystic poets of different orders incorporated in the two recensions are also almost the same. The only difference is that the former sources are comparatively large and many of the *padas*, *sakhis* and *remains* of the Niranjanpanthi sources are not found in the Dadupanthi collections. Even then at least half the texts of the Niranjanpanthi compilations tally throughout with those of the Dadupanth. Besides, there also appears a great similarity of pattern and method of compilation in the two recensions. The names of the *angas* and the ragas, and the arrangement are the same. Moreover, the effect of languages like Persian, Rajasthani and Panjabi on these two recensions is almost the same, and are the linguistic errors and repetitions.

Under these circumstances the Niranjanpanthi literature appears to be a part of the Dadupanthi tradition. This was perhaps for the reason that Haridas (d. 1613), the founder of the sect, lived till his death in Didwana (Jodhpur), the place of Prayagdas Dadupanthi (d. 1631), and is said to have been initiated by him into the Dadupanth before founding his own panth. Besides, the compilation of Hari Ramdas Niranjani was prepared in Didwana where some important Dadupanthi works had been compiled by the disciples of Prayagdas.

In view of the content, however, a Niranjanpanthi compilation may be divided into three parts: Works and verses of the Niranjanpanthi saints; sayings of the saints of other schools of thought and the *Jogesari Bani* of the Yogis and the *Doha Kosas* of the Siddhas.

A similar compilation was produced in Muslim mystic circles, i.e. the *Rushd Nama* of Abdul Quddus Gangohi (1456–1537), which contains, beside Persian verses, several Hindi verses.[58]

The system of incorporating the sayings of such a large number of spiritual teachers of different schools of thought in the Sikh, the Dadupanthi and other similar compilations indicates that there was a basic unity and uniformity in these collections, and these have succeeded in creating an atmosphere of practical liberalism and secularism. This was not incidental but a deliberate attempt under a determined policy, so that the spiritual lineage of different traditions as well as the ideas of different regions and periods could be fully represented. They also reveal the presence of a number of religious figures about whom nothing would otherwise have been known to us.

It may be pointed out here that while the *Guru Granth Sahib* includes the sayings of sixteen non-Sikh teachers (Jaidev, Namdev, Trilochan, Permanand, Sadhna, Beni, Ramanand, Dhanna, Pipa, Sain, Kabir, Raidas, Mira Bai, Shaikh Farid, Shaikh Bikhan, and Surdas) the Dadupanthi sources incorporate those of about a hundred non-Dadupanthi saints, including the above sixteen and the two early Sikh gurus, Nanak and Angad. A comparative and concordant study of the verses found in both sources may yield interesting and significant results. It is surprising that sources of the radical bhakti thought classified as Nirguna Rama cult, also include the sayings of Surdas (1483–1563) and Mira Bai (1498–1546), who belonged to the Saguna Krishnaites while the verses of some other important contemporary saints of the same views and of the same period, like Chaitanya (1484–1527) and Tulsidas (1532–1623), were not included. This is perhaps for the reason that they had led their own organized movements. But it is not understandable why Dadu (1544–1603) and Haridas (1512–95), the two great saints of the radical school, are not incorporated in the *Guru Granth* collection, whereas at least two early saints of Sikhism, Guru Nanak (1469–1539) and Guru Angad (1504–52) are duly represented in the Dadupanthi compilations. (Kabir, Namdev, and Raidas are the three leading figures whose sayings have been copiously included in both the sources.)

We have already mentioned that the sayings of Shaikh Farid are found in both the *Guru Granth* and the *Panchavani* compilations.[59] But there is a controversy regarding authorship. To Macauliffe, it was Shaikh Braham [?Ibrahim] who composed the *sloks* and hymns of the *Guru Granth* that bear the name of Farid.[60] K.A. Nizami too

Historical Importance of the Sant-sahitya

doubts that such a large number of verses were actually composed by Baba Farid himself, and if so, this would have been referred to by his successor, Shaikh Nizamuddin.[61]

It is true that Guru Nanak would not have met Shaikh Farid (d. 1265), but his successor, Shaikh Ibrahim. Macauliffe's contention that the author of the verses was not Shaikh Farid but Shaikh Ibrahim [known as Farid Sani (the Second)] is not convincing. K.A. Nizami's contention is also based on a wrong assumption. The verses contained in the *Guru Granth* fall between the thirteenth and the sixteenth centuries. So, it seems rather more appropriate that Baba Farid himself was the author of the verses. Besides, when the veses contained in *Saba Sanahil* (1561) are taken as the Shaikh's compositions, there remains no reason to doubt about his verses in the *Guru Granth*, compiled in 1604 by Guru Arjan. Moreover, one of the *Panchavani* compilations clearly mentions a collection of Shaikh Farid's verses being written by 'Shaikh Farid Ganj-i Shakar'.[62]

It may be pointed out that many of the Dadupanthi sources are now found only in copies and unless the original manuscripts are found it will be difficult to ascertain when the texts were finally fixed in that tradition. That Dadu (1544–1603) himself would have put anything in writing is doubtful. However, it is almost certain that attempts were made by some of his early disciples, particularly by Mohanji 'Daftari' (the scribe), to have an up to date record of their master's preaching perhaps from 1575 onwards.[63] The first collection of Dadu's verses, *Harde-Bani*, was prepared on the basis of these records by his two disciples, Santdas and Jagannathdas. But as the verses were not properly arranged a revised text, *Anga-bandhu*, was prepared by Rajabdas in 1595 (about a decade earlier than the compilation of *Guru Granth*) in which the whole was re-arranged in thirty-seven *angas*. After Dadu's death, however, a series of such compilations were made in which not only the sayings of Dadu and his followers were included, but also those of many other teachers of different schools of thought. Since there appears no major textual variation between the earliest available manuscripts and the later copies, it may be inferred that the texts were standardized just after Dadu's death in the early seventeenth century.

Most of these sources were compiled in places on the main trade routes of the period. The leading teachers of bhakti thought are reputed to have been much travelled people, and are supposed to have often followed these routes.[64] It is to be assumed, therefore, that they came into contact with one another's literary heritage. This is evident from the fact that their sayings find mutual representation in Sikh, Dadupanthi and other similar collections. In addition the praise that these saints have for each other suggests a good rapport. The tours made by the saints brought them in close contact with different sorts of people and they observed the conditions in which people lived in villages. They expressed their views in satire against all sorts of evils.

From the linguistic point of view there is a kind of uniformity in this literature written in different local dialects. The regional languages, Gujarati, Marathi, and Rajasthani, adopted the Devanagari script which was generally used to write Hindawi and its offshoots, Purbi Hindi and Awadhi. The Punjabi dialect, Gurmukhi, also appears to have adopted a modified version of the Devanagari.

In spite of all the care and precaution taken by compilers and copyists, interpolations and alterations have casually crept into the text.[65] This happened not only in the Dadupanthi compilations but also to the *Guru Granth* and other sources. These modifications were perhaps inevitable in the wake of the great Vaisnava revivalist movement led by Tulsidas and other conservative, in the course of the sixteenth century. Hence it is likely that the alteration and modification in the sayings may have occurred under the Vaisnavaite influence and not when they came to be recorded.

These sources unfold a panorama of spiritual traditions and depict continuity as well as variety coming down from their prototype of yore. The religious beliefs and ideas of the common people as well as the impact of the expositions of the leaders of various movements and sects on the social pattern is gleaned from these sources. These compilations serve as an important source material for significant social-economic data. They reveal political developments and social customs. It also appears that there were several elements of continuity and change in society which have a great relevance to our present-day life.

Of special interest to a study of religion and society is the fact that this material can be used to prepare standard texts of the verses and sayings of various saints. It could also be utilized to explore ideas hitherto unknown which still lie untapped. They help us analyse the complex socio–religious phenomena caused by the interaction between the Sufi tradition and the representatives of Bhakti. An in-depth study of the rise of syncretic trends in medieval India is possible on the basis of this literature. The material gives a message of universality and peaceful co-existence for all kinds of people.

However, it is very unfortunate that the larger part of the vernacular literature is lying unpublished, unclassified, and uncared for in various libraries and private collections.[66] For this very reason no extensive use has been made so far by modern historians. The search for and publication of all such source materials would be very helpful not only for preparing a consistent history of socio–religious developments and cultural life of medieval India, but also to lend a new dimension to our understanding of the political, economic, and administrative systems of the time. Not only this, these sources, particularly the different compilations and other sectarian works, are also helpful for a study of the evolution of a common culture in the medieval period in general and particularly after the establishment of Mughal rule.

So, for preservation and better utilization of this vast source material in reconstructing our medieval Indian history, there needs to be a thorough search. The important sources, particularly the direct historical accounts, may be edited and published, and of the remaining ones a descriptive and classified catalogue may be prepared. There can also be prepared extracts from important Bhakti sources bearing on social and cultural life of medieval India. Similarly, Hindi texts and verses, and Persian couplets can be edited and presented to the world of scholarship.

NOTES

1. There are different kinds of vernacular sources, in four broad categories: regional works of political, administrative and socio-economic importance; *Premakhayan* literature consisting of the various love-stories; the *Sant Sahitya* in different forms; and individual Hindi works of Saints and Sufis. For details of these sources and their historical importance, see *The Sarbangi of Rajabdas,* ed. Shahabuddin Iraqi, Aligarh: Granthayan, 1985, pp. 17–99.

2. For details of *malfuz* literature, see Mohammad Habib, 'Chishti Mystic Records of the Sultanate Period', *Medieval India Quarterly*, vol. I, no. 2, October 1950, K.A. Nizami, *Khairul Majalis*, Aligarh, 1959.
3. Nabha's *Bhaktmala*, ed. S.R. Bhagwand Prasad, Lucknow: Newal Kishore Press, 1913; P.N. Dikshit, *Nabhadas Krit Bhaktmala: Ek Adhyayan*, Allahabad: Sahitya Bhawan, 1961; and 'Gleanings on the *Bhaktmal*' *Journal of the Royal Asiatic Society*, 1909, 1910.
4. Nabha's *Bhaktmala, Chhappaya* 155.
5. Manuscript copies are found in some of the *Panchavani* collections. It has been published, but details are not known.
6. The author's collection of *Sawaiyyas* forms another account providing valuable informations regading the members of Dadu's family at Naraina.
7. For the text of these *Parchais*, see The *Panchavans* of the Dadupanthis, Basta No. 2, compiled by Narharidas in 1676 part III, ff. 369a–392b. On the literature, Tirloki Narayan Dikshit, *Parchai Sahitya*, Lucknow, 1957.
8. Jangopal, *Dadu Janma Lila Parichaya*, Jaipur: Mangal Press, 1949.
9. For details, ibid., *vishrams* 4–11.
10. The authors and the dates of these *vartas* are not definitely known. It is said that the first was written by Hari Rai Pramit and the second by Bitthalnath some time in the sixteenth century. Some scholars speak of the second *varta* having been written by Gokulnath, but this is rejected by Dhirendra Verma particularly for the reason that there are certain references of Aurangzeb's time. 'Kya Do Sau Bawan Vaishnavon Ki Varta Gokulnath Krit Hai', *Hindustani*, vol. 2, part 2, 1932. It is also possible that such references were later added to the original text. Hence, it seems more appropriate that the *vartas* were perhaps written not by one but by many persons at different times. Both were edited by Dwarkadas Parikh, though the first was published by the Agrawal Press, Mathura, 3rd edn., 1960 and the second by the Sudhadvait Academy, Kankraul, in 3 parts, 1951–3.
11. See the *Do Sau Bawan Vaishnavon ki Varta*, ed. Dwarkadas Parikh, Kankraul: Sudhadvait Academy, 1953, p. 342.
12. It appears from the *Do Sau Bawan Vaishnavon ki Varta* that Rani Rup Manjari was another Hindu wife of Akbar, and a follower of Shri Gosain Ji.
13. See the *Bhao Sindhu Ki Varta* of Gokul, ed. Dwarkadas, Saurashtra: Sri Raj Singh Star Printing Press, vs 1965/AD 1908, p. 307.
14. For details of this literature, See F.S. Growse, *Mathura: A District Memoir*, Delhi, 1979, pp. 30–40; and S. Iraqi, 'Historical Importance of the Literature of Pranami Sect', *Islamic Culture*, Hyderabad, vol. LXXV, no. 4, October 2001, pp. 97–104.
15. Prannath's *Qulzum Sharif* is also known as *Qulzum Swaroop* or *Tartamya Sagar*. The original manuscript is preserved in the Dhami Mandir at Panna in Bundelkhand and a number of copies are found at different

Historical Importance of the Sant-sahitya 139

centres of the Pranami Sect. It was edited by Matabadal Jaiswal and published by Balam Ji from Bankura, 1965.

16. Pramanath's other works, as attributed by the *Khoj Report of Kashi Nagari Pracharini Sabha* (Varanasi, 1924–6 and 1936), are *Pragat Bani, Brahma Bani, Bis Girhon ki Haqiqat, Raj Vinod,* and *Virat Charitamrit.*
17. *Bitak* means history, which in method of writing is similar to the *malfuz* literature of the Muslim mystics. *The Sarbangi of Rajabdas,* ed. S. Iraqi, Aligarh: Granthayan, 1985, pp. 29–30, 92–3.
18. *The Bitak of Swami Laldas,* ed. Matabal Jaiswal, Bankura, 1966.
19. *The Bitak of Braj Bhushan,* ed. K.D. Sharma, Jamnagar: Pranami Dharm Sabha, 1931.
20. We have discussed above the other hagiographies in Hindi like the two *vartas* of the Pushti Marga.
21. Laldas, op. cit., pp. 5, 10, 38.
22. Ibid., pp. 42, 65. According to Jadunath Sarkar, an army was dispatched by Aurangzeb in December 1662 under Qutbuddin Khan Khweshgi, the faujdar of Junagarh, against Rai Singh who had disposed for himself Raja Chhatrasal, Jam of Nawanagar, and had expelled the Mughal officers posted there to collect the tribute and administer the port. *History of Aurangzeb,* vol. III, Calcutta: MC Sarkar & Sons, 1912, p. 26.
23. Laldas, op. cit., Chapter 49, p. 1; and J.N. Sarkar, op. cit., vol. III, pp. 225–6.
24. Sarkar, op. cit., vol. III, pp. 157–8; Laldas, op. cit., Chapter 50, p. 31.
25. Ibid. An account of these nobles is provided by J.N. Sarkar, op. cit., vol. iii, which is based on Persian chronicles. Besides, the *Bitak* also refers to several other personalities in the same context like Bakhtawar, Shaikh Khidr, Ghulam Muhammad, Jahan Muhammad, Pathan Fath Muhammad, about whom there is no reference in regular historical works.
26. Sarkar, op. cit., vol. V, Calcutta, 1924, pp. 390–9.
27. For details about the sect and its literature, see R.G. Bhandarkar, *Vaishnavism, Saivism and other Minor Religious Systems,* Delhi: Skylark, 1965, pp. 62–6; Din Dayal Gupta, *Ashtachhap aur Vallabha Sampadaya, Sammelan,* Prayag, 1, pp. 42–9; and Vijendra Snatak, 'Nimbarka Sampradaya', *Hindi Sahitya ka Vrihat Itihas,* pt. 5, ed. Diwendranath Sharma, Varanasi: Nagari Pracharini Sabha, 1974, pp. 113–38.
28. Some important sources on this sect are *Bhakti Rasamrta Sindhu* and *Ujjavala Nilmani* by Rupa; *Gopal Champu* and *Sata-Sandarbha* by Jiva; *Shri Govinda Lilamrta* and *Shri Chaitanya Charitamrta* by Krishnadas Kaviraj, and *Shri Haribhakti Vilas* by Gopal Bhatta.

    M.T. Kennedy, *The Chaitanya Movement,* London: Oxford University Press, 1925, pp. 123–47; D.C. Sen, *Bengali Language and Literature,* rpt., Delhi, 1986, pp. 444–565; and *Chaitanya Charitamrita* (Bengali Biography of Chaitanya), tr. Jadunath Sarkar as *Chaitanya's Life and Teachings,* Calcutta: M.C. Sarkar & Sons, 1932.

29. *Shri Chaitanya Charitamrita*, p. 236.
30. The Radhavallabha sect was founded by Hita Harivansh (1502–52) some time in the first half of the sixteenth century. Many of the saints of this sect had attained position and power in the Mughal government. For instance. Paramanand held a *jagir* and a mansab of 500 sawar under Humayun:
    शाह हुमायूँ के हैं चाकर ।। खिजमत पाई रिझाये नासरः ।
    मंसब दियों कियों बहुप्यार ।। पंज सदी के हते असवार ।।
    Later he was made the Raja of Thatta and given a mansab of 3000. Sundardas, a Kayastha by caste, was a Diwan under Abdur Rahim Khan-i Khana and was respected by Akbar also.
    खानखाना के हते दिवान । अकबर शाह करै सम्मान ।।
    Shri Rasik Ananyamal of Bhagwat Mudit, ed. Lalita Prasad Purohit, Vrindaban: Venu Prakashan, 1960, p. 22. The author of this work held the post of Diwan under Shujaul Mulk Subedar of Agra.
31. For details about the sect and its literature, see Lalita Charan Goswami, *Shri Hita Harivansh Goswami: Sampradaya Aur Sahitya,* Vrindaban: Venu Prakashan, 1957; and Vijendra Snatak, 'Radhavallabha Sampradaya', in *Hindi Sahitya Ka Vrihat Itihas*, pt. 5, ed. Divendranath Sharma, Kashi: Nagari Pracharini Sabha, 1974, pp. 161–99.
32. The reign of Akbar is praised in the following lines of *Shri Rasik Ananyamal*, p. 44:
    तिनके राज सबै सुख पावै ।। आप आपन धर्मन सब ध्यावैं ।।
    सब राजन को आज्ञा दीनी । देवस्थल की रचना कीनी ।।
33. *Ramcharitmanas*, tr. (of Abstracts) C.K. Handu, *Tulsidas: Poet, Saint and Philospher of Sixteenth Century*, Bombay: Orient Longman, 1964, pp. 120–40; Savitri Chandra, 'Tulsidas's concept, of Rulership', *Medieval India and Hindi Bhakti Poetry: A Socio-Cultural Study*, Delhi: Har Anand, 1996, pp. 116–28.
34. The first folio of the manuscript mentions the title, *Pothi Gyan Bani*, but on the last page it is *Bhen Gyan Bani*. At the end of the text the name of Bhawanidas Satnami is given as the copyist, but no mention is made of either the original compiler or the date of compilation. Some abstracts from the manuscript were provided to me earlier by Irfan Habib, on which was based my 'The Satnami Sect of Narnaul', *U.P. Historical Review*, vol. 1, no. 1, 1982, pp. 23–30.
35. For details, see Sher Singh, *Philosophy of Sikhism,* 2nd edn., Jullundur: Sterling Publishers, 1944, pp. 63–4.
36. This was the early edition used by E. Trumpp in his English translation, *The Adi Granth,* London, 1877. Macauliffe in his *Sikh Religion* (pp. vii and xiii) has criticised Trumpp by quoting a letter from Bhai Hazara Singh, according to which his translation was 'not only generally incorrect but also injurious to our religion'. In the same letter, Macauliffe's work is appreciated for the care taken to keep 'the rendering in accordance with

Historical Importance of the Sant-sahitya 141

the Sampradai arths (i.e. traditional interpretations of the Sikh Gyanis)', which shows that his translation of the *Guru Granth,* which was prepared with the help of the Sikh Gyanis, was to make it acceptable to the Sikh Sabha. Macauliffe's *The Sikh Religion* is in six vols., Delhi: Low Price Pubs., 1993, vols. 1 to 5 cover the life and sayings of the Gurus and the sixth deals with sixteen non-Sikh teachers such as Kabir and Raidas.

37. The *Ragamala* is an index of the *ragas* and *raginis* which is different from the generally accepted Hindu classification of *ragas.* According to this index, there are six main *ragas* which have thirty *raginis* (wives), and the sons of these are 18, 10, and 20, so that the total comes to 84.
38. For further details, Sher Shah, op. cit, pp. 67–8.
39. *Sri Dasam Granth Sahibji,* compiled by Bhai Mani in 1716, first approved edition, Amritsar: Sikh Singh Sabha, 1925.
40. The abstract of some of these treatises are provided by Macauliffe, *The Sikh Religion,* vol. V, pp. 260–332. On p. 205 the text of the *Zafar Nama* is provided. This is substantiated by the *Dabistan-i-Mazahib* (p. 246) which, in the days of the sixth Guru, states 'Sikhs have neither idols nor temples for idol'.
41. *Panchavani* is a term the Dadupanthis use to denote a compilation containing the *bani* (sayings) of the 'five saints', Dadu, Kabir, Namdev, Raidas and Haridas. It also incorporates the sayings of a large number of other religious figures. For details of this literature, see Shahabuddin Iraqi, 'Historical and Religious Dimensions of Dadupanthi Sources', *Islamic Culture,* vol. LXX, no. 3, 1997, pp. 37–66.
42. I am indebted to Swami Luxmandasji, *mantri* of the Sanchalan Samiti of Dadu Mahavidyalaya, for informing me that these manuscripts were brought from time to time from different places by several Dadupanthi saints. A list, with details about each, has been prepared by the *mantri,* which he shows to all who wish to see the manuscripts. But the details about the manuscripts given in the list do not seem to be very accurate and a close verification is imperative.
43. Swamdas originally belonged to the Pipa Sect, but in the manuscript he is a disciple of Chainji, and it seems that he later became a follower of the Dadupanth.
44. The details about the work are found in the colophon at the end of the manuscript, mostly illegible.
45. The title mentioned in the secretary's register is *Prakirna Rachna* (a large compilation). It also appears from the register that the manuscript was found by pujari Gopaldas. Some other details about the process of compilation occur in the work at two places, at the end of Dadu's sayings, and at the end of Gharibdas's sayings.
46. This was published by the Nagari Pracharini Sabha in 1928. It is based on the above manuscript but is also supported by another manuscript of the same nature, dated 1824. The latter is also preserved in the same

collection, No. 109. It may be noted that although the two manuscripts are 320 years apart, these are only minor textual variations in them.
47. Like *Panchavani, Sarbangi* is also a term which means a compilation containing all the *angas* or parts prescribed for the expression of mystic ideas.
48. These and other details are given at the end of the present copy of the manuscript.
49. Rajabdas (Rajab Ali Khan), a prominent mystic poet of Rajasthan, belonged to a Pathan family of Sanganer (near Amber, Jaipur). This ardent disciple and companion of Dadu Dayal was a junior officer in the army of Bhagwandas and Man Singh. He collected the sayings of his teacher and also wrote a number of his own works. For details of his life and works, see the introduction to the *Sarbangi of Rajabdas,* ed. S. Iraqi, Aligarh: Granthayan, 1985, pp. 55–60.
50. There are many more Bastas in the same collection comprising the complete or incomplete *Sarbangi,* such as Basta No. 23 compiled by Brahmadas, 1789 (ff. 128–355); Basta No. 10, compiled by Banidas, 1790 (ff. 227–442); Basta No. 4 (ff. 381–402), and so on.
51. This Basta contains about 145 *angas*, a total of 2,791 *sakhis*, 890 *sabads* or *padas,* 173 *slokas* and 73 *bayts.* In addition some *kavitts* and *arils* are also occasionally found.
52. Jagannathdas was a great scholar and philosopher. He was previously a Kabirpanthi and lived in Varanasi. Subsequently, he migrated to Amber (near Jaipur) where he became a disciple of Dadu. He was the author of many works which are found in several *Panchavani* manuscripts. S. Iraqi, 'Historical and Religious Dimensions of Dadupanthi Sources', p. 61.
53. For details of these *angas* see ibid., pp. 45–6.
54. In the *Dhammapada* of the Buddhists, the *gathas* are classified in *vaggos* (Skt. *varga*) according to subject. A similar classification occurs in the Tamil *Tirukkural* of Tiruvalluvar, which is made of three distinct parts, following the ancient *trivarga* or the three aims of human life, *kama, artha* and *dharma.*
55. Bajid is famous for his *arils* and a collection of his 135 *arils* has been published in the *Panchavani* collection, ed. Swami Mangaldas, Jaipur: Dadu Mahavidyalaya, 1948, pp. 66–99.
56. This is evident from the colophon given after the sayings of Haridas. See f. 152 of the manuscript (in the Dadu Mahavidyalaya, Jaipur).
57. These details are found in the colophon of the manuscript (in the Dadu Mahavidyalaya, Jaipur).
58. A detailed study occurs in the introduction to the Hindi translation entitled *Alakh Bani,* by A.A. Rizvi, Aligarh: Bharat Prakashan Mandir, 1971. For a critical study of the source, Simon Digby, 'Abd Al-Quddus Gangohi (1456–1537 A.D.): The Personality and Attitude of a Medieval Indian Sufi', *Medieval India: A Miscellany,* vol. 3, 1975, pp. 38–66.

Historical Importance of the Sant-sahitya   143

59. For the sayings of Shaikh Farid in the *Guru Granth*, see Macauliffe, op. cit., vol. VI, pp. 391–414 (with four *pads* in *Raga Asa* and *Raga Suhi* and 130 *sloks* bearing the name of Farid) and in the *Panchavani*, Basta No. 12, compiled by Swamdas, AD 1636, part III, ff. 315b–316b.
60. Macauliffe, op. cit, vol. VI, pp. 356–7.
61. K.A. Nizami, *The Life and Times of Shaikh Farid-uddin Ganj Shakar*, Aligarh, 1955, pp. 121–2; also Rizvi, op. cit., vol. 1, pp. 328–9.
62. Basta No. 12, f. 315.
63. See *Dadu Sampradaya ka Samkshipt Parichaya*, ed. Swami Mangaldas, Jaipur: Rajata Jayanti Samiti, 1952, p. 9.
64. Ramdev, the Marathi poet of the fourteenth century, is said to have travelled from the south to the Punjab, where he lived and taught for some time. Some of the temples dedicated to him are found in Delhi and its surroundings. Likewise, Kabir is reported to have gone up to Maharashtra. Dadu Dayal, who lived in Rajasthan (mainly in Amber), perhaps originally belonged to Ahmedabad and travelled widely in the north. As the Sikh tradition records, Nanak made extensive tours and had met some important religious figures of his time. The tradition of travelling extensively was also maintained by later leaders as part of their religious obligations.
65. For example, in the case of Kabir, where *padas* which recall his miraculous escape from the attempts on his life, or those describing the legend of the Vaishnava saint and 'martyr' *prahlad*, are obviously hagiographic and their authenticity is doubtful. Similarly, the verses that allude to the mythical *bhaktas* of Hari–Vishnu, such as Sukhdeva and Hanuman, cannot be taken into consideration, as we know that Kabir gave no importance to the Brahmanical scriptures and Hindu gods.
66. Many of the manuscripts, particularly the older ones, are deteriorating. They are not in a condition to be moved to a new location. However, I ventured to study them and have managed to make copies of some of the earliest available manuscripts from the Dadu Mahavidyalaya at Jaipur, particularly Bastas 2, and 12, and a portion of 3 containing the *Sarbangi* of Rajabdas, for research at the Department of History, AMU, Aligarh.

CHAPTER 5

Kabir and His Followers

The pre-eminent mystic of medieval India, Kabir (1440–1518) gave a new impetus to the Bhakti movement in northern India. But as is well known, Kabir's life history is shrouded in mystery. The scarcity of authentic source material is the main cause of this. Abul Fazl's *Ain-i-Akbari* (1598) is the first historical record that refers to Kabir, in the context of his two different tombs, one at Puri in Orissa and the other in Oudh. In both references Kabir is a *muwahid* (or monotheist).[1] It is significant that the Muslim chronicler was cautious about Kabir's faith. He declares him a *muwahid*, not a Muslim. This shows that there was confusion about Kabir in Muslim circles in the sixteenth century, and he was not clearly acceptable as a Muslim.

Similar testimony comes from Abdul Haq Muhaddis Dehlavi's *Akhbar-ul-Akhyar* (compiled in the last phase of the sixteenth century) which refers to Kabir as neither Muslim nor *Kafir*, but a *muwahid*.[2] However, Kabir's verses were already read or quoted in sufi circles in Delhi and Agra in the beginning of the sixteenth century.[3] It is interesting that though the author of the *Datbistan-i-Mazahib* (c. 1662) also declares Kabir as a monotheist and Julaha *Nizad* (born in a Muslim weaver's family); he places him in the general Vaishnava tradition by calling him a Vaishnavite saint and a *bairagi* (or Hindu ascetic).[4] Another late Persian work, the *Khazinat-ul Asfiah* of Ghulam Sarwar, refers to Kabir as 'Shaikh Kabir Julaha' and a disciple of Shaikh Taqi (himself a Julaha from Manikpur, d. 1574).[5]

Whereas in Persian sources Kabir's position is confused, early Hindi sources call him clearly a Julaha (Muslim weaver). Contemporary figures such as Raidas, Pipa, and Dhanna also refer to Kabir as Julaha.[6] Rajabdas in his *Sarbangi* (around 1673) writes:

जुलाहा ग्रभे उत्पन्यो साध कबीर महामुनि[7]

However, in later Hindi literature Kabir's position also became confused, but in a different way and for a different motive. Nabhadas in his *Bhaktmala* (*c*. 1623) devotes a full stanza to Kabir.[8] Nothing apparently is spoken of his life but only of his boldness of character and impartial views. The author asserts that Kabir rejected the whole Brahmanical tradition, including the division of society into castes and that he judged both religions, Hinduism and Islam, with impartiality. Later Priyadas, commenting on Nabha's *Bhaktmala* in 1712, narrates a long story about how a *turk* managed to become the disciple of Ramananda. This happened in the wake of the Vaishnava revivalist movement from the last phase of the sixteenth century onwards and Nabhadas had deliberately included in his *Bhaktmala* the names of the most liberal and revolutionary thinkers such as Namdev, Kabir, and Raidas in order to include them in the Vaishnava tradition. The whole legend from Kabir's miraculous birth to his becoming the disciple of Ramananda is woven to Hinduize him and to show he was not born *a mleccha* but a brahman. Kabir himself had not wanted to be identified as either Hindu or Muslim: he referred to himself in his verses as *Kori* and *julaha* (a Hindu as well as a Muslim weaver). He calls God Ram and Rahim.[9] He associated himself with a movement that conformed neither to Hinduism nor Islam, but to a universal religion.

However, Kabir was neither a *sannyasi* nor a monk. He was a *grihastha* (householder) like the Sufis. He was aware of his family responsibilities and maintained his family profession of weaving, though much of his time seems to have been spent in the company of the *sadhus*. Influenced by the Sufi concept of *tark* (renunciation), Kabir believed in detachment, not from worldly life as such, but from worldly desires and materialism. It was for this reason that he led a family life but adopted an attitude of indifference to worldly pursuits.[10] He asserts that pride should also be abandoned in this condition: 'Kabir, what availeth it to abandon worldly love, if pride be not also abandoned....'[11]

Such liberal views were a challenge to conservative people, and therefore, severe steps were taken against him. Kabir had to face prolonged conflict and petty persecutions from the leaders of both communities.[12] It is said that after they failed, they even sought the support of the state by complaining to Sikandar Lodi. It is significant that this complaint said, 'those who paid heed to what

Kabir said remained neither Hindu nor Muslim'.[13] Kabir was thus accused of causing trouble.[14] His migration from Banaras to Maghar is said to have taken place due to a decree issued by the Sultan in 1518, but there is no historical evidence to prove it. It is believed that it was to challenge the famous superstition that to die in Kashi would merit entry to heaven, and to die in Maghar would lead to rebirth as an ass. So he left Banaras for Maghar, saying, 'What (difference is there between) Banaras and the barren Maghar, if God be in the heart.'[15]

Kabir was not satisfied with the traditional system of religious knowledge which, to him, led to controversies. He says, 'I am not skilled in book knowledge, nor do I understand controversy.'[16]

It was perhaps in this spirit that Kabir thought it better not to touch pen or paper.[17] But it is more probable that he was not in a position to take up his academic career in a systematic manner. However, he asserts the personal experiences above all by sayings:

मैं कहता हूं आखिन देखी, तू कहता कागज की लेखी।[18]

And yet Kabir was familiar with the basic concepts of both the religions, because he spent most of his time in religious activities, receiving and serving *sadhus* and mendicants, as is evident from the complaints made by his mother and wife.[19] On this basis, however, Kabir was able to have a good knowledge and understanding about Indian religions.[20] He freely uses the technical terms of both Muslim ideology and Hindu Philosophy.[21]

As compared to other bhakti poets, much has been written on Kabir by scholars of different schools and they all have different opinions about him. One school makes him a great mystic, another speaks of him a *darshanik* (philosopher). There are other scholars who see him as a socio-religious reformer, but others are of the opinion that Kabir's mission was only to preach.[22] Some other scholars have tried to prove him a yogi. There is even a controversy among them as to which sort of yogi Kabir was.[23] The author of *Dabistan-i Mazahib* speaks of him a *bairagi* or wandering ascetic.[24] There are, however, many references in Kabir's own accounts, which indicate that he was against the yogis and their practices as a whole.[25]

The period when Kabir emerged is noted for what is called the schism of the soul and schism of the body politic, and the response of the reformers was positive. So, Kabir was the product of both the destructive and constructive elements of his age, a great revolutionary and an uncompromising saint. The complexity of ideas that crept into his mind did not leave him at ease to be a systematic thinker. Thus, Kabir's aim or mission should not be taken static but rather varied and dynamic. He was deeply concerned with the socio–religious issues of the time.

Kabir addressed the people of all castes and communities. He tried to establish a strict monotheism and monism: God is one, without attribute, found everywhere. 'There is no God but Him, the One creation', he said. Also, 'Kabir is a child of Ram and Allah'. Or, 'Kabir loudly proclaims, there is the same God for the Hindu as for the Muhammadan.'[26]

Kabir also believed in a God without attributes: 'This world is defiled with impurity; pure is God alone who has neither form nor limits.'[27] Like the Sufis, he says, 'Kabir, were I to make the seven oceans my ink, the trees of the forest my pens, and the earth my paper, I should not succeed in writing God's praises.'[28]

In describing the qualities of God as saviour, merciful, bountiful, happy, and perfect. Kabir comes very close to the God's names as contained in the Quran. His monistic ideas, besides, were based on the Vedantic concept of *tat tvam asi* (thou art that), his mode of expression seems to be very close to that of the Sufi *Wahdat-ul Wujud*. Kabir says, 'God Himself is the fire, himself the wind. . . .'[29] Kabir most often says the nature and essence of God is 'Light': 'Every heart is gladdened by God's light. . . .'[30] This is resounds with the Sufi concept of God as *Nur-i-Qahir,* whose essential nature consists in 'perpetual illumination'.

This concept of God led Kabir to believe in God as transcendent and beyond approach. But he also presents Him as one with whom personal interaction can be developed 'Enjoy yourself in intercourse with the Lord.'[31] In fact, wherever Kabir has described God as being close to the heart of the devotee, he appears to be, in spirit, under the Sufi impact. Two of his hymns are important in this context: 'Kabir having searched and searched himself, hath found God within him' and 'Hari dwelleth in the South, Allah hath His place in the West. Search in your heart, search in your heart of hearts; there is His place and abode.'[32]

It was due to this concept of God in Kabir's mind that he discarded idol worship and its associated rituals[33] but also the incarnation theory which was its basis. He declared that the incarnations of God did not concern him, because his 'Master is such a Lord as hath neither father nor mother'.[34] That Kabir's Ram was not that born in Dasrath's family but was universal, is explicitly expressed: 'Kabir, call Him Ram, who is omnipresent; We must discriminate in mentioning the two Rams; The one Ram (God) is contained in all things; the other (i.e. Ramchandra son of Dasrath) is contained only in himself.'[35]

Thus, though Kabir has used popular Vaishnava names such as Ram and Hari for God, he did not believe in Vishnu or his incarnations as such and, therefore, he cannot be called a Vaishnavite. 'The Jogis cry out "Gorakh, Gorakh"; the Hindus repeat "Ram, Ram" and the Musalmans have Khuda. But Kabir's God is all-pervading.'[36]

Kabir's concept of *maya* was based on that of Shankaracharya. But, while Shankara believed in *maya* as neither real nor unreal, Kabir admitted its existence by saying: 'Worldly life is like a dream, but believing the world to be real, I attach not myself to it...'.[37] It is specifically expressed by him that soul and God are separated by *maya* and when it is thrown away they are reunited. Kabir attaches no importance either to *avagaman* (transmigration of the soul) or heaven, but to absorption into the essence of God: 'The soul is not born, though men think it is; It is free from birth and death. When the idea of birth and death depart from man's mind, he shall for ever be absorbed in God.'[38] This covers the famous Sufi concept of *fana-fit-tawhid*, annihilation into the essence of God.

Like other radical figures, Kabir also rejects the scriptural authorities of both the communities. He took the scriptures to be biased and leading to conflict among different religionists. 'The *Smriti* is the daughter of the Vedas; she has brought a chain and a rope for men, and has of herself imprisoned them in her capital....'. He also said, '... they are good riders who keep themselves aloof from the Vedas and the books of the Musalmans'. Then again, 'The Musalmans accept the *Tariqat*; the Hindus, the Vedas and Puranas; but for me the books of both the religions are useless.'[39]

This was because Kabir believed in *anubhava jnana*, or direct knowledge from personal experience. He emphasized:

पोथी पढ़ि पढ़ि जग मुआ पंडित भया न कोय।
एकै आखर पीव का पढ़ै सु पंडित होय।।

(People were dead by studying books, but no body could become the learned. Those who understood the meaning of one word of God, became the learned.)[40]

Kabir also discarded Sanskrit, the language of the Vedas and Upanishads, and the language of the brahmans. As an alternative medium of expansion, he emphasized the importance of *bhasha*, the language of the masses.

संसकीरित है कूप जल, भासा बहता नीर

(Sanskrit is like the water of a well, whereas *bhasa* is flowing water.)[41]

Note that Kabir uses the term Sanskirit.

Kabir rejected the Brahman and Mulla as professional mediators between God and man. He has substituted the human guru with Satguru, God himself. In fact, his position is clear regarding the complete identification of spiritual teacher with divinity. He says:

गुर गोबिंद तो एक है, दूजा सब आकार।[42]

Kabir categorically condemns the Brahmans of Banaras. 'They carry rosaries on their necks and glittering brass utensils in their hands; They should not be called saints of God, but the cheats of Banaras.'[43] Again, 'You wear *tilaks* on your foreheads, carry rosaries in your hands, and put on sectarian dress. People think that God is (simply) a toy.'[44]

Kabir also ridicules the qazi thus: 'O Qazi, nothing is done by mere talk; it is not by fasting and repeating prayers and the creed that one goes to heaven.'

'O Qazi, your one God is in you, but you behold Him not by thought and reflection. Mad on religion, you do not heed why your life is of no account.'[45]

To the Jogis, he says: 'Jogis kill themselves wearing matted hair; but they know nothing of God.' 'You depend on a club, earrings, and patched coat;

In error you wander in Jogi garb. Put away devotional attitudes and you're your suspension of breath.'

'Make silence your earnings, mercy your wallet, and meditation your cup; take your body as patched coat; make the Name (of God) your support. O Jogi, practice such Jog.'[46]

Kabir is particularly against all kinds of customs and ceremonies. Says Kabir, why perform so many ceremonies? Forsaking all other essences hold the great essence of God's name.[47] He is against Muslim ceremonies and the Haj.[48] He also denounces the custom of veiling: 'Stay, stay, my daughter-in-law, veil not your face! She who preceded you used to veil her face; follow not in her footsteps.'[49] For animal slaughter he remarks: 'When God produces His record, what shall be the fate of him who violently kills animals and calls it lawful?'[50]

Kabir seems to have been also concerned with the environment and, therefore, he forbids cutting of leaves and trees: 'You cut leaves, O flower girl; in every leaf there is life. . . . Brahma is in the leaves, Vishnu in the branches, and Shiva in the flowers. You destroy three Gods in our presence; whom do you worship. . . .'[51]

Kabir thus denounced the whole system and all norms of institutionalized form of religion. He laid strict conditions by saying that only those could go with him who had burnt their own religious house and cultural identity:

जो घर फूके आपना, चले हमारे संग ।[52]

The Nirguna Bhakti meant for devotion to one God without any visible object with the spirit to apprehend Him by the inner (mystical) experiences. Kabir's bhakti was ideal in this respect, for which he wanted to dedicate the whole of his life.[53]

Kabir was so steadfast in his devotion that he believed that true devotion would itself illumine the devotee's heart with all sorts of knowledge and good actions. There should be no consideration of reward and punishment in spiritual observances or in having faith in heaven or hell. In fact, as union with God was the main object, Kabir did not lay any importance on heaven or hell. 'What is hell and what heaven, the wretched places.' As long as man desires to go to heaven, so long shall he delay dwelling at the feet of the Lord.'[54]

That the true bhakti cannot be achieved by formalities is described in many of his verses. In the process of spiritual perfection in Sufism, the role of a Shaikh was always important.

Kabir went further, considering the position of the guru no less than that of Govinda (God). This was because he considered God the Satguru, as we have seen. Besides, there are several verses in Kabir's account in which he, like the Sufis, has expressed a deep consciousness of sin within the heart and a profound sense of his unworthiness before God. A sense of self-consciousness or self-respect is also expressed in many of his verses. Some of his verses also reflect the Sufi concept of *tawakkul* (trust in God).[55]

Kabir was a practical man believing in action rather than theory. He adopted a strict approach to those who preached without practising. कथनी कथी तो क्या भया, जौ करनी न ठहराइ (What is the use of that speech which does not correspond to action).[56] The unity of preaching and action represents a great moral force for uniting human beings.

Kabir has set ideal examples of ethical and moral values by saying:

जहं दया तहं धरम है, जहं लोभ तहं पाप।
जहं करोध तहं काल है, जहं खिमां तहं आप।।

(No religious faith is fit without mercy, selfishness carries only sin; revenge leads to destruction and forgiveness to God.)

सांच बराबर तप नहीं, झूट बराबर पाप।
जाकै हिरदै सांच है, ताकै हिरदै आप।।

(No worship is better than honesty, and no sin is equal to telling a lie; God is only with those who are honest.)

ऐसी बानी बोलिए, मन का आपा खोइ।
अपना तन सीतल करै, औरों की सुख होइ।।

(Speak in a soft language that appeals to others and satisfies yourself.)[57]

This is the reason why Kabir was held in high esteem by Hindus and Muslims alike, and was followed by figures from Dadu to the satnamis.

Selfless devotion and freedom from worldly attachment were considered by sufis to be the most important preliminary steps to be taken to prepare the self for spiritual advancement. The same spirit seems to be running in the thought of Kabir, when he speaks thus:

Lay hold on your sword, and join in the fight,
Fight, o my brother, as long as life lasts ...
In the field of this body a great war is going on
against passion, anger, pride and greed.
It is in the kingdom of truth, contentment and purity
that this battle is raging, and the sword that rings forth
most forcefully is the sword of God's name.[58]

The most important factor of spiritual life is emotion and the literature of Sufism is full of such references. As the Sufis considered it religious faith (*aqeeda*) and practice (*amal*), Kabir took it as *sadhan* (means) and *sadhya* (object). Tara Chand has rightly observed that like the Sufis, Kabir too invites his fellow travellers to inebriate themselves with the wine of love and throw worldly discretion to the winds.'[59] He considered love superior to religious knowledge.[60]

For the Sufis love is like wine which should necessarily be utilized for spiritual perfection. They also believed that intoxication or a trance caused by love is necessary for a mystic to be absorbed in the deepest meditation to God. A similar symbolic expression of love may be noticed in other phrases. 'My mind is intoxicated with God's elixir'; or 'Drink God's elixir, O Kabir' and 'Turning from the way of the world I have obtained this wine, a cup of which causes divine intoxication.'[61]

There are many verses, in which Kabir describes how one goes out of one's senses and what sort of things can be experienced during spiritual intoxication.[62] Besides, the Sufis usually believed that it is with the help of love that the soul realizes its unity with the Ultimate Reality and finds his individuality merged in it. Amir Khusrau's famous verse bearing this idea is:

من تو شدم تو من شدی، من تن شدم تو جاں شدی
تا کس نگوید بعد ازیں من دیگرم تو دیگری

The same idea has been well depicted in the following verse of Kabir:

... (as) God and Kabir have become one,
No one can distinguish between them.[63]

The idea is clarified in the following verse:

Kabir and His Followers

जब मैं था तब हरि नहीं, अब हरि है मैं नाहि।
सब अंधियारा मिटि गया, जब दीपक देखा माहि।।

(There remained no more the consciousness of myself, when God was realized within self; The whole darkness ended, when the heart was enlightened by the grace of God.)[64]

At a stage in the process of spiritual perfection the devotee feels that when his soul is absorbed in the essence of God, the destiny of both also became identical. Kabir has expressed this stage very well in the following verse:

हरि मरि हैं तो. हमहूं मरि हैं। हरि न मरैं, हम काहे को मरि हैं।।[65]

With regard to other matters too, Kabir seems to have been inspired by Sufi concepts. In fact, the motivation of all of his spiritual and social views was conditioned by the two fundamental concepts of Islam and Sufism, 'unity of God', and 'unity of human being'. The liberal ideas of the Sufis suited Kabir. Westcott says that 'his condemnation of pride and commendation of humility are much more in accordance with the teachings of Sufi saints than with the practice of the Hindu *pandits*'.[66] Tara Chand also says that the 'expression of Kabir's teachings was shaped by that of Sufi saints and poets'.[67]

Kabir has emphatically argued that the superiority of a man is determined not by birth but by action.[68] The concept of *Insan-i Kamil* (perfect man) as defined in Sufism seems to have been also well reflected in many of his verses. He lays even more strict conditions for a devotee to become perfect: 'Every servant of God ought to be perfect like God Himself.'

As a result, he says, 'it so happened to me that God did what was pleasing to my mind'. Not only this, at this stage God is bent upon fulfilling his wishes: 'Kabir, once whose mind is pure as Ganga water, God follows him, saying, "Kabir! Kabir"!'[69] Such ideas remind us of Iqbal's concept of *Khudi* and his verse:

خودی کو کر بلند اتنا کہ ہر تدبیر سے پہلے
خدا بندے سے خود پوچھے بتا تیری رضا کیا ہے

In spite of the fact that Kabir derived much from Sufi traditions, he could not follow them all. The Muslim mystic systems were too varied and well planned to be imitated fully by a person like Kabir who was neither willing nor in a position to do so. Hence, there seems to be little weight in the assessment of Tara Chand that Kabir had experienced all the conditions which the Muslim mystics describe.[70] In spite of the fact that Kabir's love was deep, he could not follow all aspects of Sufism. It appears from a passage of *Khazinat-ul Asfia* of Ghulam Sarwar that though Kabir taught the Sufi doctrine of *wisal* or union (with God), he was silent about its counterpart, *firaq* or separation.[71]

There is no doubt that Kabir contributed much to the development of Sufi traditions in India.[72] It was by his time that the condemnation of polytheism, idol worship and caste distinction became frequent and emphatic. But an even more important aspect of his contribution is an adequate and simple fusion of Indian Vedanta and Muslim Tasawwuf which he brought together successfully. Kabir's emergence marks a new era in the history of Indian thought. Though the Bhakti movement was already popular in northern India under Ramananda and others, Kabir gave a new impetus and orientation by introducing to it some vital elements of Sufism such as communal harmony and universal brotherhood.

Kabir refused to recognize the superiority of brahmans and rejected the notion that birth in a superior caste was due to good actions in previous life. He advocated full equality between brahmans and Shudras and became a champion of the downtrodden. He tried to awaken the people about the duplicity and hypocrisy of the priests exploiting people's religious sentiments to serve their own ends. This crippled human dignity and had caused a spiritual degeneration. His attitude to caste discrimination may be judged as a vehement denunciation of the system.

Kabir was a contemporary of the three Lodi Sultans (1451–1526). He criticised the Muslim state and its officials. He gives his political philosophy in a very abstract form by saying, 'There is no king equal to God; . . . they make false display.' Also, 'To use force is tyranny though you call it lawful.'[73]

Kabir contemptuously refers to the Sultans who maintained great splendour in their courts, and their nobles, and to Hindu chiefs paying homage to them.[74] Corruption and turbulence in administration, specially in the revenue department, are reflected in his poems.

Kabir refers to revenue officials such as the shiqdar, munsif, karkun and patwari,[75] and their misdeeds. About the shiqdar, he says,

एकु कोट पंच *सिकदारा*, पंचे मागहि हाला ।[76]

Regarding the munsif, Kabir says he was dishonest in meting out justice to the people, and there was a system of imposed *bishtala* (forced labour) on the peasants:

नव डांडी दस मुंसफ घावहि, *रहयति* बसन न देही ।
डोरी पूरी, बहु बिटाला लेही[77]

Kabir noted with distress how people were exploited by the government machinery. He saw the reasons for the misery of the cultivators:[78]

गांई (गांव) कु ठाकुर खेत कु नेपै, *काइथ* खरच न पारै ।
जारि *जेवरो* खेति पसारै, सब मिलि मोकौं मारै हो राम ।।
खोटी *महतो* बिकट बलाही, सिर कसदम का पारै ।
बुरो *दिवान* दादि नहि लागै, इक बाधै इक मारै हो राम ।।
धरम राइ जब लेखा मांग्या, बाकी निकसी भारी
पंच किसाना भजि गये हैं, जीव धर बांध्यों पारी हो राम ।।

In the above lines, Kabir refers to the high-handedness of the village zamindar (Thakur) and the patwari, muqaddam, and diwan. He says that the Thakur (village headman) measured the fields with the old method of *jevaro* (i.e. Jarib) and the kayath (Kayasth) drew the balance all the time.[79] When the affected cultivators objected, the mahattras and the diwan had them bound and beaten. Kabir also says that the poor had no access to the higher authorities for making their complaints.

Kabir's reaction against the corrupt and oppressive role of the local authorities and the revenue officials were based on personal experience. He voiced the sufferings of all. For this reason perhaps, Sikandar Lodi tried to check abuses and ordered the land to be properly measured and the rent be fixed accordingly. He introduced a land survey with a uniform land measure, the *Sikandari gaz*. Besides, he summoned the muqaddams and the patwaris of the villages of certain parganas to explain the actual position of their villages. The Sultan also ordered that none should press the peasants for forced labour.[80] Another important outcome was the great concern of Sher Shah over the tyranny of village revenue officials.[81]

A spirit of anxiety and hostility is evident in Kabir's words against the political authorities who were exploiting the common people and the peasants. His targets, apart from the priestly class, were rich merchants, and feudal lords both Hindu and Muslim. He named the Bohras and the Banias as exploiting moneylenders, and among the Muslims he included both the Turkish immigrants who looked down on Indians, and the converted upper-class Muslims.[82] Kabir says that by oppression and discrimination these elements had made the country a living hell.

Kabir was against the accumulation of wealth. 'Curse on this body, curse on this wealth, curse on these worldly things', and 'With all your earnings, ready money, and buried treasures, you will take nothing with you.'[83] He tells moneylenders who keep a careful record of his account that they forget the account they must render to God.[84]

'Your sins will increase by a quarter day by day, just like the interest of a Bohra. That sharp Bohra will (thus) make you liable to pay amounts you will never be able to repay.'[85]

This reminds us of the existing system of usurious loans and the compound rates of interest leading to the heavy indebtedness of the needy. Similarly, Kabir has also repeatedly reacted against the business dealings of Banias.[86]

Kabir criticises those who are proud of their wealth, power and family status.

कबीर गरव न कीजिए, ऊंचा देखि अवास।
ऊंचे कुल क्या जनमिया, जो करनी ऊंचि न होइ।[87]

The word *kul* implied a family that was financially sound, of high status. The people of such families were generally associated with *samants* (Hindu landlords) and *amirs* (Muslim royal officials) and enjoyed power in the autocratic political system. In Kabir's opinion, 'men (who) wear gaudy robes and chew betel leaves and betel nuts without (reciting) the name of one God, will certainly go to hell'.[88] He says it is futile 'to be proud of lofty houses, or of high bred horses, or of a *chhatra* (royal umbrella) over one's head'.[89]

Kabir and His Followers

Kabir rejects the notion that the elite had the right to rule.[90] He warns 'those people at whose doors *naubat* is played ten times a day, at whose gates proud elephants stand, and before whom drums and other instruments are played when they move out: their pride is of no use, as death is the ultimate reality.'[91]

Kabir marked the disparity between the rich and the poor.

If a poor man goes to a rich man,
The latter, though opposite him, will turn his back.
If a rich man goes to a poor man,
The latter respects, even invites him (warmly)[92]

Kabir has emphasized the value of satisfaction and contentment with what one has got. Similarly, he also asserted the need in maintaining one's dignity, and asked the poor to maintain their self-respect by working. He says, 'poverty could be made bearable by self-labour and by chanting the name of Hari'.[93] He criticizes the *sadhus* of the *Kali* age, who haunt the doors of royalty like hungry cows in a green field:

राजदवारै यौं फिरै, ज्यौं हरहाइ गाइ।[94]

Kabir disliked all governments, but his influence, observes Tara Chand, 'continued to spread under the Mughal rule'. Akbar 'attempted to make it (Kabir's ideology) a religion approved by the state'.[95] Akbar's *Tauhid-i Ilahi* seems to have been an echo of Kabir's philosophy.

Kabir was popular during his lifetime and afterwards both among the Hindus and the Muslims. His verses were quoted at meetings in Sufi centres in Delhi and Agra from the beginning of the sixteenth century. It is because of this popularity that his sayings have been incorporated in large measure in various compilations like the *Guru Granth*, the *Panchavani* and that of the Niranjanpanthis.

It is true that the ideas of Kabir attracted a large number of followers. Kabir himself says that he made many disciples and followers, though all of them failed to perform the true devotion.[96] But he was not responsible for the foundation of the Kabirpanth. He was in fact against any institutionalized form of religion. 'A true saint', he said, 'need not go on pilgrimage and should not be called *mahant*. He should be busy in imparting the seeds of religion to his disciples.'[97]

Thus, the formation of Kabirpanth is a later development. Despite the fact that there is no certainty with regard to the origin and development of the panth, most of its branches ascribe their origins to one or other of the disciples of Kabir. It may, however, be assumed that the panth was founded some time in the seventeenth century, and developed thereafter into various branches.

There are two main divisions of the Kabirpanth, the Chhattisgarh and the Kabir Chaura (in Kashi). There are many sub-divisions of both of them, which flourished subsequently in many parts of the country. The branches attached to the Kabir Chaura section include the Lahar Tara (Shivapur), Maghar (Gorakhpur), and Kabir Bagh (Prayag, Allahabad). The branches related to the Chhattisgarh section are the Damakhera, Mandala, Kawardha, Kudarmal, and Bamini. The branches which have now detached their relations from the aforesaid section are said to be the Hatkesar, Kabir Niranaya Mandir (Burhanpur), Kabir Chaura (Jagdishpuri), and Kabir Math (Luxmipur Baghicha, Rusra, district Darbhanga). Besides, there are other branches which are said to have originally developed as independent ones, just like the Kabir Chaura or the Chhattisgarh. These are the (1) Bhaktahi at Dhanauti (district Saran), (2) Fatuha (district Patna), (3) Bidupur (district Muzaffarpur), (4) Vachan Vansh (Rusra), and (5) Acharya Gaddi (Barayya, district Jaunpur).[98]

The development of the panth was not confined to the above branches, but a large number of *maths*, were attached to established centres and also developed in many other parts of the country. The *maths* related to the Kabir Chaura are said to have spread in the urban centres of UP such as Saharanpur, Hardwar, Kanpur, Jhansi, Bulandshahr, Ghazipur and Gorakhpur. Similarly, the *maths* of the Chhattisgarh division spread almost everywhere in central India: Kudarmal, Ratanpur, Hatkesar, Mandala Vamni, Dhamdha, Kharasia, Kawardha Sagar, Parkota, Khaupa, Hardi, Nagpur, Jubbalpore, Bharatpur, Gwalior, etc. Besides, many *maths* related to the centres at Dhanauti and Bidupur are found in the province of Bihar. There are also other *maths* attached to Fatuha and Gaya.

Maths related to the centres in Saurastra and Gujarat were located in Ahmedabad, Khambat, Nadiyad, Baroda, Bharauch, Surat, Jamnagar, Rajkot, Junagarh, Bhavnagar, etc. This was under the impact of the Chhattisgarh section, because they consider Kabir no less than Ram or Krishn. Other *maths* of the panth were founded in Bombay, Poona, Hyderabad, Multan, Lahore, Karachi, Bangalore, and Gauhati.

The popularity of the panth seems to have confined to UP, Bihar, central India and to some extent to Gujarat. The reason why it did not get the same popularity elsewhere was largely due to the setback inflicted by the powerful local religious systems. In Bengal and Orissa, the Dharam sect and Vaishnava Sahajiya were popular. In Punjab, Sikhism and in the south Virashaiva and Vaishnava Dharma were powerful. So the setback to the panth in these places was but natural. But still there are some Kabirpanthi *maths* in Siyalkot and Gurdaspur.[99]

With the establishment of such a large number of Kabirpanthi centres and *maths* in many parts of the country, the followers of the sect increased and numbers rose to the hundreds of thousands. According to the Census of 1891, the total number of the Kabirpanthis in UP was 955[?].[100] The table of the census report tells us not only about their number but also about the places of their activities during those days.

A study of the table shows that the number of Kabirpanthis in Bulandshahr, Ghazipur, and Aligarh was higher than elsewhere. But Kashi, Gorakhpur, etc., with the main branches of the panth, have been left out altogether. It appears from the census report of 1901, however, that the total number of them throughout the country was 850,000 of whom 500,000 were living in the Central Provinces.[101] Moreover, it is reported by Brigs that there were no less than 600,000 Kabirpanthis in the Central Provinces alone in 1911.[102] As the conversion of the people to the sect continued, ever increasingly their number now seems to be no less than a million.

Among the persons belonging to the panth, there are Brahmans who hold important positions in various centres of the cult. But the majority are from the lower castes. As Kabir belonged to a weaver's family, most of the Kabirpanthis have hailed from the weaving castes, and it is often called as the 'weaver's religion'. There are also Telis (oilmen), Dhobis (washermen), and Chamars (cobblers) and members of other castes as well, such as Ahirs, Kurmis, Lodhis and Kachhis, who are farmers and cultivators.[103]

Not only were the religious ideas expressed by Kabir given a different shape his followers certain rules and regulations were formulated, which clearly stood against his own fundamentals. This was largely because local traditions were working simultaneously with Kabir's varied and extensive influences, which helped paint his picture in a particular colour.

The Kabirpanthis tried to give a formal shape to the sect with the creation of an institutional structure. They adopted certain rituals and dogmatic practices. Thus a movement that had begun with liberalism was absorbed in ritualism. Contrary to Kabir's condemnation of fasting, the Kabirpanthis began to observe the *Poornima Varat*, taking it as the true means of salvation. A small book, *Poornima Varat*, was published by the Chhattisgarh section, and it is recited like the *Anant Varat* of the Vedic religion. Similarly, they perform the *arti* twice a day in almost the same manner as in Vaishnava temples. Some *strotas* are prescribed to be read out on the occasion of this service.[104]

Besides, while Kabir was entirely against the system of reciting *mantras*, in the Panth a sort of network of these *mantras* is spread in the performing of daily physical needs.[105] The spiritual life of the twice-born castes is recognized and they are subjected to the rules of caste from the time when they receive the *mantra* and sacred thread (*janeo*) from their guru. Only those who have received the initiatory *mantra* and a *kanthi* (rosary of beads of *tulsi* wood) are admitted as the members of the cult. The Brahmanical *mantra* invested to a new Brahman candidate may not be communicated to those who are not Brahmans, and so is the case with other Kabirpanthis. Like any Hindu caste, the initiatory *mantra* whispered into the ear of a new entrant serves as a bond with other members and also suggests a privileged position. Beside these, some *Gayatris*, such as *Adi Gayatri, Prabhat Gayatri, Madhyana Gayatri*, and *Sandhya Gayatri Mantra* have also been composed[106] for use in the *maths* many times a day. It is surprising that most of these *sumirans*, in form identical with Vedic hymns but different in content, are attributed to Kabir himself.

Moreover, just as the Brahmans wear upon their forehead the sign of the God whom they worship, the Kabirpanthis wear the *dwadash tilak* (which differs from place to place). There are many other formal observances such as *tika arpan, chauka* service, *panparwana, jot-prashad*, etc., to which many traditional explanations (mostly miraculous) are attached.

Kabir is himself worshipped by the Kabirpanthis. His picture and *charan padooka* (wooden sandals) are worshipped twice a day in many centres of the panth. Besides, in the Kabir Chaura of Jagdishpuri there is a temple in which are placed the idols of Ram, Lakshman, and Sita and they are regularly worshipped by the *sadhus* of the sect. These practices are performed differently by various branches. The two main sections of the panth have always tried to maintain their individuality, so much so that even in Rajputana, where both exist side by side, the former is known as *mul* (original) and the latter *bachan bansh* (*stem* of the world). Although the mul section draws more disciples from the upper castes, and the bachan bansh from the lower, the followers of the latter are rather contemptuous of the former, saying that they have not followed Kabir. Similarly, the former does not recognize the gurus of the latter and neither do its followers visit the centres of the latter. It is significant that a sort of difference is also maintained in the pattern of their names—the word used after the names of the followers of the Kabir Chaura is 'das', while those of Chhattisgarh apply 'nam'. The *dwadash tilak* also differs and a sort of differentiation is also maintained in dress.

In the Kabir Chaura section, when new interants are admitted they are provided with *kanthi* and *tilak*, and some *mantras* are whispered in their ears. There also takes place the *puja* and a brief *arti* service. More or less the same practices are observed in the Chhattisgarhi branches, though in a more elaborate and complicated form. But among the Fatuha, Dhanauti, Burhanpur, and other branches, there is no system like this except that the *mahant* at the time of admission whispers some *mantras* in the ears of newcomers and then the *prashad* is distributed. With regard to the *chauka* service, both the sections of the panth accept its spiritual importance and celebrate it on occasions of both happiness and sorrow. But the Fatuha, Dhanauti, Burhanpur, and Jaunpur branches do not have much faith in it. Even where the service is observed, there seems to be a lot of difference from the arrangement of articles down to preparations and the performance.

There are also differences among various centres in the importance given to the gurus. Both the divisions worship Kabir's picture, his *charan padookas* (a pair of wooden sandals) and *samadhi*. But in the other branches, only the *arti* is given to live gurus. There is again a difference between these branches and the two main divisions with regard to the modes of giving *samadhi* to the gurus. But there is a sort of unity in giving *samadhi* to the *mahants*, and the dead bodies of ordinary members are thrown into water; no Kabirpanthi is cremated after death.

Kabir's social ideas provided a sort of banner under which all classes of people could move together. This ideal needed further extension, but was narrowed down by his followers. Theoretically, in the Panth there is no consideration of caste or creed, but this does not happen. Members of the lowest castes, such as the Mehtars, Doms and Dhobis, are not permitted to wear the *kanthi* of the panth. Besides, it is said that previously all the members of the sect ate together at the conclusion of a *chauka* service, but now, in some centres, different *chaukas* are arranged for different castes[107] even when a man embracing the order is required to leave his previous caste and its observances altogether.[108] In the Kabir Chaura, however, it is said that at the *chauka* service all members do eat together, but still, the Muslims have to arrange their meals separately. The same system seems to be maintained in the Fatuha *math*, where the Muslims are taught freely but live and eat separately.

NOTES

1. *Ain-i-Akbari,* tr. H.S. Jarrett, 2nd edn., vol. II, Calcutta, 1949, pp. 141, 182. On p. 141 Abul Fazl states that because of catholicity of doctrine and his charisma Kabir was a friend to both Hindus and Muslims. At another place the chronicler writes that Kabir, the *muwahid,* lived in the reign of Sikandar Lodi.
2. Once Shaikh Rizqullah Mashtaqi (1491–1581) asked his father, Shaikh Sadullah a contemporary of Kabir, whether he was a Muslim or Kafir. The reply was that he was a *muwahid.* See Abdul Haq Mohaddis Dehlavi's *Akhbar-ul Akhyar* (a collection of short biographies of certain Sufis, compiled written in 1590–1), ed. Muhammad Abdul Ahad, Delhi: Mutabai Press, 1914, p. 300, Urdu tr. Subhan Mahmood, Delhi, 1990, p. 591.
3. Ch. Vaudeville, *Kabir,* vol. I, Delhi: Oxford University Press, 1974, p. 34.
4. See Mobad, *Dabistan-i-Mazahib,* Kanpur: Munshi Newal Kishore, 1904, p. 200 where Kabir, called a *bairagi,* is mentioned as:

کبیر جولاہہ نژاد کہ از موحدان مشہور ہند است، بیراگی بودہ

5. See Ghulam Sarwar, *Khazinat-ul-Asfiah* cited by G.H. Westcott, *Kabir and the Kabirpanth*, Calcutta: Susil Gupta, 1953, pp. 15–16.
6. For references by Raidas, Pipa, and Dhanna to Kabir, see Macauliffe, *The Sikh Religion*, vol. VI, rpt., Delhi: Low Price Pubs., 1993, pp. 109, 119, 342.
7. *The Sarbangi of Rajabdas*, ed. S. Iraqi, Aligarh: Granthayan, 1985, *slok* 13, p. 610.
8. For the whole text on Kabir, see *Nabha's Bhaktamala*, ed. S.R. Bhagwan Prasad, Lucknow: Newal Kishore Press, 1913, *Chappay* 60, p. 479; also *Chappay* 36, p. 282, where Kabir's name occurs in the enumeration of the disciples traditionally attributed to Ramananda.
9. The matter has been discussed in Chapter 4.
10. See *Sri Raj, Gauri* VI, Macauliffe, vol. VI, pp. 142, 145.
11. Ibid., p. 302.
12. F.E. Keay, *Kabir and His Followers*, rpt., Delhi: Mittal Publication, 1995, pp. 40–1; also Westcott, *Kabir and the Kabirpanth*, p. 20.
13. Macauliffe, *The Sikh Religion*, vol. VI, p. 132.
14. Ibid., p. 133; Keay, op. cit., p. 43.
15. *Dhanasari* 3, Macauliffe, vol. VI, p. 224.
16. See Kabir's hymn, Bilawal II, Macauliffe, vol. VI, p. 229.
17. मसि कागज छूयो नहीं, कलम गह्यो नहीं हाथा, A *Kabir Bijak*, ed. Sukdev Singh, Allahabad: Nilam Prakashan, 1972, *sakhi* 171, p. 163.
18. As cited by Hazari Prasad Dwivedi, *Kabir*, 2nd edn., Bombay: Hindi Granth Ratnakar, 1947, p. 175.
19. According to the Sika tradition quoted by Macauliffe (pp. 127–8) both of them were full of anxiety, because of Kabir's indifference to his profession. They forced him to give up at least his extra religious activities. *Gauri* II, *Gaund* VI, ibid., pp. 216, 235.
20. R.K. Verma, *Kabir ka Rahasyavad*, 9th edn., Allahabad: Sahitya Bhawan, 1961, p. 20.
21. According to Tara Chand, 'Kabir used both Sanskrit and Persian terms' and 'employed both forms of *bhasha*, i.e. Sanskritized Hindi and Persianized Urdu'. Tara Chand, *Influence of Islam on Indian Culture*, Allahabad, 1963, p. 159. Keay has estimated that more than 200 words of Persian, Arabic, and Turkish origin current in those days are used in Kabir's *Bijak* only. Keay, op. cit., p. 51. Holding the same view, Tara Chand concludes that 'an analysis of these words shows how deeply his mind was imbued with Sufi doctrines'. Tara Chand, p. 153.
22. Verma, op. cit., p. 35; Shyam Sundardas, *Hindi Sahitya*, Prayag: Indian Press, 1956, p. 87; Govind Trigurayat, *Kabir ki Vichardhara*, Kanpur: Sahitya Niketan, 1952, p. 131. The author holds that revolution was part of Kabir's life.
23. Verma, op. cit., pp. 68–91 tries to prove Kabir a hathayogi, while others

speak of him a rajayogi. There are still others particularly among the Kabirpanthis, who say he observed Shabd Surati Yog.
24. *Dabistan-i-Mazahit*, p. 200.
25. For instance, *Sarath*, I, Bilawal VIII and *Ramkali*, VII, Macauliffe, vol. VI, pp. 217, 231, 243.
26. For these references, Kabir's *slok* CXXXIII, *Prabhati* II, and *Asa* XXIX in ibid., pp. 299, 277, and 212 respectively.
27. Kabir's *Bhairo*, 3, Macauliffe, vol. VI, p. 258.
28. Kabir's *slok* LXXXI, also *Ashtapadi*, 11, in ibid., pp. 268-9, 290.
29. *Gauri*, XXXIII, ibid., p. 157; also *Gauri* XL, ibid., p. 160. Kabir says, 'on my tongue dwells God, in my eyes dwells God, and in my heart dwells God'. For this and other such references Macauliffe, op. cit., pp. 160, 248, 276.
30. *Basant* 1, ibid., p. 269.
31. It appears from a hymn of Kabir, *Gauri* IX, that though God is without attributes, one may have interaction with Him. Macauliffe, p. 147.
32. See *Bhairo* VII, *Brabhati* 11, ibid., pp. 260, 276.
33. 'Says Kabir, why perform so many ceremonies.... You wear *tilak* on your forehead, rosaries in your hands, and (put on) sectarian dress. People think that God is simply a toy.' *Bhairo*, VI, Macauliffe, op. cit., p. 259.
34. *Gauri*, LXX, Macauliffe, op. cit., vol. VI, p. 179.
35. Kabir *slok* no. CXC-1, Macauliffe, op. cit., vol. VI, p. 308.
36. *Bhairo* XI, ibid., p. 263.
37. *Asa* XXVII, ibid., p. 210. For the influence of *maya* as elaborated by Kabir, *Bhairo*, XIII, ibid., p. 263.
38. See *Asa* I, ibid., p. 196; also *Gauri* IX, ibid., p. 147.
39. For all the three references, see Kabir's hymns, *Gauri* XXX and XXXI, and Acrostic no. 5 in ibid., pp. 156, 182.
40. *Kabir Granthawali*, ed. P.N. Tiwari, Prayag: Hindi Parishad, 1961, *sakhi* 33-3, p. 241; also *Kabir Granthawali*, ed. Shyam Sundardas, Varanasi: Nagari Pracharini Sabha, 1975, *sakhi* 19-4, p. 30, This idea of Kabir reminds us of the Sufi approach to God:

در کنز و هدایه نتوان دید خدارا. آئنهٔ دل بین که کتابی به از این نیست

(You cannot see God in *Kanz* or *Hidayah*. Look into the mirror of the heart, for there is no book better than that.)
41. We have mentioned that the line is popular and often quoted, but it is not found in any of the authentic sources on Kabir
42. *Kabir Granthawali*, ed. P.N. Tiwari, *sakhi* 1-28, p. 139.
43. *Asa* II, Macauliffe, op. cit., vol. VI, p. 196.
44. *Bhairo* VI, in ibid., p. 259.
45. For these two references, see *Asa* XVII and XXIX, ibid., pp. 205, 211.
46. For these references, see *Sorath* 1, *Bilawal* VIII and *Ramkali* VII, ibid., pp. 217, 231 and 243.
47. *Gauri*, V and IV, ibid., p. 145.

48. Kabir *sloks* CXCVII and CXCVIII, ibid., p. 309.
49. *Asa* XXXIV, ibid., pp. 213–14.
50. Kabir *slok* CXCIX, ibid., p. 309.
51. Kabir, *Asa* XIV, ibid., pp. 202–3.
52. Kabir *slok* LXXXIII, Macauliffe, op. cit., vol. VI, p. 291; also *Kabir Granthawali*, ed. P.N. Tiwari, *sakhi* 5-13, p. 160.
53. For instance, see *Gauri*, VI, VII and VIII, in ibid., pp. 145–7.
54. See Gauri X, Macauliffe, op. cit., vol. VI, p. 148;
    The following description of heaven in Kabir's account through use of negatives shows that he had no faith in it: 'Everybody says he is going to heaven; I know not where heaven is. . . . I know not where heaven's gate is, nor its moat, nor its plastered fortress.' *Bhairo* XVI, Macauliffe, op. cit., vol. VI, pp. 265–6.
55. For instance, *Asa* XVI, *Kedara* VI, ibid., pp. 204, 257.
56. *Kabir Granthawali*, ed. P.N. Tiwari, op. cit., *sakhi* 33–4, p. 241; also *Kabir Granthawali*, ed. Shyam Sundardas, op. cit., *sakhi* 18–1, p. 29.
57. For these references, *Kabir Granthawali*, ed. P.N. Tiwari, *sakhis* 15–33, p. 190, 15–16, p. 187, and 15–75, p. 195.
58. Quoted by Tara Chand, op. cit., p. 160.
59. Ibid., p. 161.
60. 'My Guru has taught me the subject of love, now there is nothing to be read out'. Verma, op. cit., p. 35.
61. *Sri Rag* II, *Gauri* VIII and Kedara III, Macauliffe, op. cit., vol. VI, pp. 143, 147, 256, respectively.
62. For instance, हरि रस पीया जानिए, उतर नाहि जाय खुमार। मै मंता घूमत फिरौ, नाहि तन की सार।। *Kabir Granthawali*, ed. P.N. Tiwari, *sakhi* 12–15, p. 178.
63. Macauliffe, op. cit., vol. VI, p. 139.
64. *Kabir Granthawali*, *sakhi*, 9, p. 166.
65. Verma, op. cit., p. 27.
66. G.H. Westcott, *Kabir and the Kabirpanth*, p. 29, fn. 3.
67. Tara Chand, p. 151.
68. *Gauri* VII, Macauliffe, op. cit., p. 146.
69. Kabir *sloks* CXLIX, LXXI, and LV. Macauliffe, op. cit., vol. VI, pp. 301, 289, 286.
70. Tara Chand, op. cit., p. 161,
71. Passage cited by Westcott, op. cit., pp. 15–16.
72. J.N. Farquhar considers Kabir as one of the most popular Indian propagandists of Sufism in India. *An Outline of the Religious Literature of India*, rpt., Delhi: Motilal Banarsidass, 1984, p. 284.
73. *Bilawal* V, *Asa* XVII, and *slok* CLXXXVII. Macauliffe, op. cit., vol. VI, pp. 230, 204 and 307, respectively.
74. *Kabir Granthawali*, ed. Shyam Sundardas *pads* 122, 299 and 330, pp. 97, 142 and 150 respectively.
75. A shiqdar was the head of a pargana. Sultan Bahlol Lodi appointed

shiqdars in the conquered parganas of Kampil, Patiali, Shamshabad, Saket, Jalesar and Kol. Sikandar Lodi appointed Mian Zaitum (an Afghan) in AD 1489 as shiqdar of the newly-founded capital of Agra. I.H. Siddiqui, *Some Aspects of Afghan Despotism in India,* Aligarh: Three Men Pubs., 1969, p. 141. A munsif was the head of pargana Civil Court and heard appeals in civil and revenue matters. The karkuns were clerks who maintained revenue records such as the area under cultivation. The patwaris kept records of the cultivators and their arable lands. Abdul Halim, *History of the Lodi Sultans of Delhi and Agra,* Delhi: Idara-i Adabiyat-i Dehli, 1974, pp. 248–9.

76. Ram Kumar Verma, *Sant Kabir,* Nagari Pracharini Sabha, 1902, p. 151.
77. Ibid.
78. Macauliffe, op. cit., vol. VI, pp. 251, 253; *Kabir Granthawali,* ed. S.S. Das, *pada* 222, pp. 121–2.
79. For instance, see the following verse:

काइथ कागद काढ़िया, लेखा बार न परि।
जब लग सांस सरीर में, तब लग नांव संभारि।।

Kabir Granthawali, ed. P.N. Tiwari, op. cit., *sakhi* 21-3, p. 213.
80. For these references, see Abdul Halim, op. cit., p. 249.
81. For details, Abbas Khan Sarwani, *Tarikh-i-Sher Shah,* tr. B.P. Ambashthya, Patna: Patna Research Institute, 1974 pp. 16–25.
82. Savitri Chandra Shobha, ed., *Medieval India and Hindi Bhakti Poetry: A Socio-Cultural Study,* Delhi: Har-Anand, 1996, pp. 24–6.
83. See *Bilawal* IX, *Kedara,* VI, Macauliffe, op. cit., vol. VI, pp. 231, 257. Also *Asa* XVI, ibid., p. 204, *slok* CXLIV, p. 300; also *Kabir Granthawali,* ed. P.N. Tiwari, p. 144.
84. *Kabir Granthawali, sakhi* 17-7, p. 28.
85. *Kabir Granthawali,* ed. S.S. Das, *pada* 108, p. 94.
86. H.P. Dwivedi, *Sant Kabir,* Bombay: Hindi Granth Ratnakar 1960, p. 159.
87. Ibid., *sakhi,* 12/10, p. 46; *Kabir Granthawali,* ed. P.N. Tiwari, *sakhis* 15–23, p. 188 and *sakhis* 33-7, p. 242.
88. Kabir *slok* XXXIV, Macauliffe, op. cit., vol. VI, p. 283.
89. For this and other such references, Kabir, *Bhairo* II, and *sloks* XXXVII, XXXVIII, and CXII, ibid., pp. 258, 283-4, 295.
90. Dwivedi, op. cit., *sakhi* 24-20, p. 21.
91. Ibid., 12-2, p. 31.
92. Kabir, *Bhairo* VIII, Macauliffe, op. cit., vol. VI, p. 260.
93. Dwivedi, op. cit., *sakhi* 12-47, p. 52.
94. *Kabir Granthawali,* ed. P.N. tiwari, *sakhi* 21-18, p. 213.
95. Tara Chand, op. cit., p. 165.
96. Kabir *slok* XCVI, Macauliffe, op. cit., vol. VI, p. 293.
97. As cited by Kedarnath Dube, *Kabir aur Kabirpanth,* Prayag: Hindi Sahitya Sammelan, 1965, p. 161.

Once Kabir condemns those gurus who make disciples by taking *Gurudakshina*. He points out that religious leaders have become very rich and lavish, which has no value in true religion. *Hindi Sahitya ka Vrihat Itihas*, vol. IV, ed. Divendranath Sharma, Kashi: Nagari Pracharini Sabha, 1974, p. 133.

98. Kedarnath, p. 209.
99. H.A. Rose, *A Glossary of the Tribes and Castes of the Punjab and North West Frontier Province,* Delhi: Lal Publishers, 1985, vol. II, p. 19.
100. The table of the report is reproduced by Kedarnath, op. cit., pp. 208–9.
101. R.V. Russell, *Tribes and Castes of the Central Provinces of India*, vol. I, Delhi, 1975, p. 237.

   It is stressed by Westcott that the actual number would have been even more than what is contained in the census report of 1911.

102. W. Brigs, *The Chamars*, cited by Westcott, op. cit., p. 2.
103. Ibid.
104. These *strotas* are cited by Makanji Kuber, *Kabiropasana Padditi*, Bombay: Venkateshwar Press, 1948, pp. 265–7.
105. All such *mantras* feature in ibid., pp. 163–5, 166.
106. For the contents of these *Gayatris*, ibid., pp. 158–61.
107. Keay, op. cit., p. 109.
108. For this reason perhaps in some places the Kabirpanthis of a particular caste formed a separate group within the sect, and the members of lower castes like the Mahars and Pankas are accustomed to eating and marrying among themselves.

CHAPTER 6

Nanak and His Followers

Guru Nanak (1469–1539) was non-conformist with a vision. Unlike other religious leaders with radical views, he preached a missionary religion and gave an organized fight to traditional Hinduism. His philosophy of life was based on his own personal experiences. Like Kabir, Nanak rejected asceticism. 'They who eat the fruit of their labour and share it with others, Nanak, recognize the right way.'[1]

Nanak presents his thoughts with remarkable consistency. Whereas the other radical thinkers only criticised the existing systems without suggesting alternatives, Nanak's approach was positive and practical, with a definite aim and socio-religious programme in mind. He founded a new religion that helped unite the robust peasantry of Panjab. He regulated the community life of his followers who were required strictly to worship together in congregation and to dine together.

Nanak's political views were broad-based and were well-founded on a drive for spiritual regeneration towards a new life of grace (*nadar*). Nevertheless, he drew a large number of religious metaphors from political life. To Nanak, the true king (*padshah*) was God, in whose presence sultans, khans and other officers became dust. God Himself elevated some people to rule and chose others to become wandering beggars. Kingship in Nanak's view was thus not evil, but, like some Sufis, he reminded rulers to be just and not be concerned with the acquisition and display of power alone. The following references from Nanak's account may be cited in this context: 'Kings under the influence of pride make many expeditions.' 'One may be styled a lord, an emperor, or a king . . . all this would be false display.' Also, 'Excellent horses, elephants, lances, musical instruments, armies, macebearers, and attendants are worthless and vain shows. . .'.[2]

Nanak had worked as a Modi (in charge of the state granary)

under Daulat Khan Lodi, a noble of Sultan Ibrahim Lodi, and he blamed the Sultan for not protecting his subjects in the battle with Babur. Nanak refers to Babur's invasion on India as a shocking incident: 'Babur ruled over Khurasan and terrified Hindustan. The creator takes no blame to Himself; it was death disguised as a Mughal who made war on us.'[3] 'Bringing a bridal procession of sin, Babar hastened from Kabul and demanded (by force) the wealth (of India) as his bride. . . . They (the people) sing the paeans of murder and smear themselves with the saffron of blood.'[4] Referring to the consequences of Babur's invasion, Nanak says, 'If a tyrant slay a tyrant, there is no grievance; but if a ferocious lion falls upon a herd (of cattle), the master of the herd is accountable.'[5] This is evidently in the context of Ibrahim Lodi's defeat at the battle of Panipat in 1526, for Nanak the latter is 'master of the herd' who did not protect his subjects. 'The dogs of (Ibrahim) Lodi have spoiled the priceless inheritance; when they are dead, no one will remember them.'[6]

Nanak's eye-witness account in the *Guru Granth* of the battle between the Afghans and the Mughals constitutes a contemporary source of information demonstrating Indian reaction to Babur's victory. The destruction of life and property was painful for Nanak. He laments, 'Where are those sports, those stables and those horses? Where are those bugles and clarions? Where are those who buckled on their swords and were mighty in battle? Where are those scarlet uniforms?'[7]

Nanak gives a graphic description of the sufferings of the people and the atrocities committed by the invaders. Being himself in Syedpur (Aminabad) during the third invasion of Babur in 1521, he reacted as an eye-witness to the plunder of the place. He reports that the invading armies killed several men and women and massacred innocent Indians like animals.[8] It appears that the war was not confined to the battlefield but extended to common places and that the women were targets of attack. Nanak laments that Hindustan was like a diamond destroyed by Pathans and Mughal invaders. He ponders why, when people were crying in pain and suffering, God was not concerned, and in anguish asks God why did He not save Hindustan from Babur's attack as He had saved Khurasan.[9] Obviously, there was an awareness of political events and developments abroad, and also a sense of regional identity. The accounts of *Babur-vani* in the *Guru Granth* fills in the lacunae of the existing political history, which gives military details along with the sufferings of the people.[10] Besides, there are interesting references to priests praying for divine intervention but the Mughals were victorious.[11]

Like Kabir, Nanak condemned the oppression of Muslim rulers and their officials, calling them butchers. He once said, 'the modern age was a knife and the kings butchers. The sense of justice had taken wings'. 'The *rajas* prey upon the *rayat* like lions and their *muqadams* act like dogs. Royal agents inflict wounds with claws of power and the dogs lick the blood and relish the liver.'[12]

Nanak says the Muslim rulers were tyrannical,[13] the people were afraid of the hakims, and the diwans had the controlling power. The *Guru Granth* highlights that these officials were cruel, greedy, and proud of their wealth and power.[14] There was no interaction as such between ruler and ruled, except for collection and payment of taxes. The full payment of land revenue was compulsory for the cultivators and, if they expressed their inability to pay, they had to suffer arbitrary punishment at the hands of the officials concerned.

Let it be clarified here that Nanak was not against the structure of political power but only against the actions of some of the holders of power. In the villages, apart from the big landlords and cultivators, there were also landless labourers who had to move on after their work was finished and had no rights, because, Guru Arjan remarked, 'the field belongs to its owner, and the watchman leaves when his work is done. Even though the watchman strive vigorously, he shall not become owner of the field.'[15] The labourers earned in kind, and their daily wage, as mentioned by the guru, was 3 seers each.[16] The practice of crop sharing was also prevalent during those days.[17]

After the crop was ready, a mark (*thappa*) was put on the field before the crops were cut so that the partners in land would get their due share. To quote, 'from the name of one God the nine treasures are produced, and man obtains the marks of His favour'.[18]

It is significant that like Kabir and Nanak, Surdas, who was a conformist of Krishnaite school, also reacted against the corrupt dealings of Mughal officials with the peasants. His criticism was more categorical:

Nanak and His Followers 171

अहंकारी पटवारी कपटी, झूठी लिखत *बही* ।

The arrogant and mischievous patwari writes a false *bahi* (account book).

Surdas says, 'the Amin (land assessor) is dishonest, the Mustaufi (accountant) is high handed, the Kotwal is deceitful, and plunders everything.' The revenue collectors and even the wazir (noble) had become part of corruption, *papi*. Surdas declares that all of them conspire against the peasants, and send the ahadi (messenger) who is like an agent of Yamaraj (the god of death) to collect arears from them. If they do not pay, a military contingent is dispatched, which surrounds the village and arrests the peasants. Surdas mentions in detail how the various account books—the *awaraja*, the *minzalik*, *syaha*, and *mujmil* are manipulated to show a balance in favour of the state. He also refers to the Thakur who plunders the peasant like others, and imprisons even respectable men like the Mahtos in the village.[19]

Another important conformist of the Ramaite *saguna* school was Tulsidas, who later in his *Kavitavali* denounced the raja as *bhumichor*, i.e. land-grabber. He says that the people were harassed by tax collectors who acted like human devils:

बलि मिस देखे देवता, कर मिस मानव देव ।[20]

However, it appears from the references to officials in the *Guru Granth* that there was wide circulation of money, and coins were used to purchase goods from shops. Owing to poverty, people depended on moneylenders, and so were exploited by the *Shah*. (बंधन शाह सनची धनुजै) When in need people took loans but were mostly not in a position to repay the money. This is almost in the same spirit as described by Kabir.

However, references in the *Guru Granth* show that the local shopkeepers also acted as moneylenders. The importance of moneylenders in the market shows that indebtedness was a serious social problem. There are also the references to Banjaras in the *Guru Granth*, indicating that trade and commerce were not confined to the local markets in the rural areas but was extended to wider trade networks in urban areas.

After Nanak and Angad, however, there were three Sikh gurus

contemporary to Akbar—Amardas (1552–74), Ramdas (1574-81), and Arjan (1581–1606). All of them maintained cordial relations with Akbar who was impressed by their teachings and by the spirit of reform and social service through the *guru ka langar* (community kitchen) which he had seen at Govindwal.

Akbar granted land in Amritsar to the Sikhs for their religious organization. He also assigned the revenues of several villages to the daughter of Guru Amardas as a marriage gift, and sought his blessings for the Chittor campaign in 1567.[21] Akbar visited Govindwal[22] twice to meet Sikh gurus: once he met Amardas, with whom he dined and from whom he accepted a robe of honour; and the second time he met Guru Arjan.

It is interesting to note that just as a complaint about Kabir was made to Sikandar Lodi by the religious leaders of both communities, so too a complaint was made to Akbar by some qazis and pandits against Guru Arjan.[23] But the liberal minded Akbar found no fault with the guru and his religious activities. Instead he appreciated his spiritual and social work and, during his second visit to Govindwal in 1598, favourably considered his suggestion for a reduction in the land tax of the parganas of Punjab.[24]

After Akbar's death, however, the cordial relationship between the Sikh gurus and the Mughal rulers came to an end. In fact, hostility rose with the beginning of Jahangir's reign, led to the interference of both sides in the affairs of each other. This was the time when Guru Arjan thought of expanding and re-organizing Sikhism by introducing certain changes. He transformed the customary offerings of the followers into a systematic tax or tribute and started a systematic network for converting the people into the cult. The author of *Dabistan-i Mazahib* records that before the time of Guru Arjan, 'no *bhet* (in the form of tax) was accepted from the Sikhs, but only offerings were given by them according to their own discretion (to their gurus). Arjanmal in his time appointed a person to the Sikhs of each town in order to collect a tribute from them', which was personally delivered by them to the guru at an annual function. The author writes that the people, 'through the mediation of that *masand*, accepted to become the Sikh disciples of the guru, and the great *masands*, through whose mediation a large number of people became Sikhs of the guru, appointed their own deputies, so that in every place and locality through the mediation of the *masands'* appointed deputies, made the people Sikhs of the gurus (who would be) *meli* of that *masand*.'[25]

In view of these developments, Jahangir's impression of Guru Arjan, as recorded in his memoirs, becomes significant.[26] The account suggests that a kind of negative impression against the guru was already in the mind of Jahangir, and when he showed favour to Prince Khusrau during the course of his rebellion,[27] he was punished by Imperial order.

However, as far as the execution of Guru Arjan is concerned, there is no reference in the Sikh tradition to Jahangir being responsible for it. Bhai Gurdas admires Guru Arjan for his patience in bearing the torture but says nothing about his execution. In the *Bachittar Natak*, an autobiography of Guru Gobind Singh, composed in the last decade of the seventeenth century, there is a reference to the execution of Guru Tegh Bahadur but this text too is silent about that of Guru Arjan.[28] The *Dabistan* in 1640s states that Jahangir had imposed a heavy fine on Guru Arjan which he could not pay and consequently, 'he was tied up and kept in the desert of Lahore (until) he died due to the heat of the sun and summer and the torture of the local officials' in 1606.[29]

Keeping in view the references found in the Sikh tradition, the *Dabistan's* account and Jahangir's later generosity to Hargobind (releasing him from imprisonment)[30] appear to indicate that Arjan's capital punishment was later commuted to a heavy fine and that it was the governor and his subordinates who were responsible for torturing the guru.

The son and successor of Guru Arjan, Guru Hargobind (1606–44), set a trend of militancy and organized an army of his own at Ramdaspur (now Amritsar) for armed resistance. According to the *Dabistan-i Mazahib*, 'the Guru had seven hundred horses in his state; and three hundred horsemen and sixty musketeers always remained in his service (for security)'.[31] He also 'collected arms, equipment and horses, [and] trained his people in the technique of fighting by organizing regular training exercises'.[32] Thus, Hargobind transformed the Sikh cult into a Sikh corps in which adherents were to act as 'saint soldiers' or 'soldier saints'. Sikhs believed that the guru's followers would attain heaven, and the guru himself declared, 'On the Day of Judgement my disciples will not be asked about their deeds'.[33] For an identity of his own, the guru girded two swords as symbols of spiritual as well as temporal authority, *piri* and *miri*, representing a combination of bhakti and *shakti*.[34]

Thus, the impulse that Hargobind gave to the Sikhs separated them entirely from the Hindu fold and linked them with the politics of militancy. The guru added two new features to Ramdaspur. Opposite the Harmandir, he constructed a high platform which came to be known as *Akal Takht* (the immortal throne). On this throne the guru held court to conduct the temporal business. The other feature was the construction of a fort called Lohgarh for defence.

All such works of Guru Hargobind collectively represent a departure from the functioning of his predecessors, which made him conspicuous in the eyes of Jahangir and his officials. According to the *Dabistan-i Mazahib*, Hargobind 'became involved in many activities, 'one of them was that he adopted the style of soldiers and, contrary to his father, girded the sword, employed servants and took to hunting'. Consequently, Jahangir 'sent Hargobind to [the fort of] Gwalior, [also] on account of the demand for the balance of the fine he had imposed on Arjanmal. He remained there for twelve years'. Also 'during this period the *masands* and the Sikhs went [to Gwalior] and bowed before the wall of the fort. At last Jahangir, out of benevolence, released the Guru'.[35]

After Jahangir's death (in 1627), Hargobind's relations with Shahjahan were cordial, but soon afterwards he became involved in an armed conflict with the Mughal administrators of Lahore province on the issue of the seizure of some horses belonging to his disciples.[36] Under imperial orders, a Mughal commandant attacked the guru at Ramdaspur, which was not successful. Even then the guru thought it better to leave for Kartarpur. There too he was attacked by the Mughal forces. Although the two Mughal commandants were killed in the battle and the guru was victorious, he realized that the Mughal authorities would not leave him at ease. He decided to leave Lahore and to go to Kiratpur in the small principality of Hindus (Nalagarh), where he lived for eight or nine years and died in March 1644.

The fiscal policy of Guru Arjan and the army organization of Guru Hargobind certainly made a great impact on the political development of India, in a way leading to the formation of a kind of separate Sikh state within the Mughal empire.

The conflict between the Mughal government and the Sikh organization continued during the time of Hargobind's successors. In 1658–9, Har Rai (1644–61) is believed to have supported Dara Shukoh during his flight to Panjab. Aurangzeb called him to the court, but he sent his elder son, Ram Rai, who was detained as a hostage in Delhi. Har Rai appointed his younger son, Har Kishan (1661–4), as his successor, and he too was summoned by Aurangzeb to Delhi. Aurangzeb had decided to patronize Ram Rai and granted him revenue free land in present-day Dehra Dun.[37] On Har Kishan's death, Ram Rai disputed with Tegh Bahadur for succession, but the latter succeeded in becoming the ninth Guru in 1664.

Guru Tegh Bahadur (1664–75) maintained the political and militant character of Sikhism even more strongly. His reverence for his father's sword and his repeated injunction that his followers should obey the bearer of his arrows reflect this. The aspiration to sovereignty is more clearly evident from the application to his name of the title of *Sachha Padshah* (true king). Not only this, the guru also issued certain *hukmnamas* to the *masands* of the Sikh *sangats*. There are twenty-two such orders of Tegh Bahadur.[38] In most of the cases these constitute directives for the supply of materials required for holding religious meetings. Some also furnish valuable information about the duties and functions of the *masands* who acted as intermediaries between the Sikhs and the guru.

In his efforts to consolidate Sikhism, Tegh Bahadur had turned first to the Khatris settled in cities outside Panjab and then to the Jats of Delhi. The Guru having interacted with a Muslim saint named Adam Hafiz, gave protection to fugitives, and they interfered in the affairs of the empire.[39] Thus, imperial troops marched against them and they were defeated and imprisoned. The Muslim saint was banished and the Sikh Guru was put to death as a rebel in November 1675 in Delhi.[40]

The tenth and the last guru was Gobind Singh (1675–1708). The tragic end of his father made a deep impact on his mind, but he remained in peace for about a decade. He then decided to make a thorough structural change in the body of Sikhism. Gobind Singh evolved a theory of struggle for the purpose of providing his followers a moral justification for the use of force against enemies. The theory was elaborated by incorporating into it certain elements like the concept of God as the mightiest warrior and the investiture of weapons with divinity. God was the wearer of all weapons and His might was represented as unmatched by anyone else.

The Guru declared that the purpose of his life was to work towards *dharma*, to raise the virtuous, and to uproot the wicked.[41] For the cause of his *dharmayudh* or religious crusade, he had invited Rajput chiefs of the Shivalik hills to join hands with him. For the fear of royal wrath and because of a bias against the increasing power and influence of the guru, however, they organized themselves against the Sikhs and often sought royal support to suppress them. It is said that the guru had to fight fourteen battles against the hill chiefs and Mughal forces.

Like his father, Gobind Singh also issued *hukamnamas* to the Sikh *sangats*. The *sangats* of Chittagong, Sondeep, and Sylhet were asked to send offerings collected on various accounts, including fine quality cloth, swords, and matchlocks, a war elephant, and gold and cash. All the *masands* were bound to visit the guru personally at the festival of Baisakhi and Diwali, and some of them were required to bring with them batches of foot soldiers and horsemen.[42] Bhai Nandlal, who spent several years in the guru's camp, depicts him as both saint and a king (*badshah darvesh*).[43]

Guru Gobind Singh gathered round him the best literary talents of his time to translate into Panjabi heroic ballads from the ancient epics and Puranas in order to inspire his followers with the martial spirit and enthusiasm for the *dharmayudh*. But such religious war was not communal at all. It was purely political and directed against the Mughals or the hill chiefs, in defence. In his letter to Aurangzeb Gobind Singh clearly says, 'Helplessly, as a last resort, I came forward and took to arms. When all the means have failed, it is lawful to take the sword in hand.' He also added, 'spill not the blood of anyone ruthlessly, lest your own blood be spilt with the sword'.[44] In the same manner, the imprisonment or execution of some of the Sikh gurus by the Mughals also should be taken not as religious persecution but as political reaction.

However, Guru Gobind's declaration at the end of his translation of the *Krishnavtar* (1688) is important: 'I have translated into the vernacular the Dasam Skandh (tenth part) of the *Bhagvata* with no other intention except that of *dharmayudh*.'[45] Once more he declares in the same spirit: 'I am the son of a brave man, not of Brahman; I (wish) that when the end of my life comes, I die fighting in a mighty battle.'[46]

These compositions were not confined to writing but were also sung in daily congregations of the Sikhs at Anandpur by some *dhadis* (balladists), who with their warlike actions excited the emotions of the fellow Sikhs. In such a dramatic atmosphere Gobind Singh, in a morning congregation of the Baisakhi festival of 1699, called upon the then present Sikhs with a naked sword in hand to offer their heads for sacrifice. Though this was sudden and unexpected, five men surrendered to this call. Then the guru brought them out of the gathering, dressed them like warriors with swords hanging by their sides (one to each of them) and baptized them. The baptized Sikhs were called 'Singh' (the lion), and their new organization was declared the Khalsa.[47] The guru himself received baptism from the hands of the first five, known as *panj piyare*, and thus became one of the Singhs. The system that any five Singhs could initiate others proved to be very effective, and within a short period thousands of Sikhs entered the order which formed the nucleus of a new community, the Khalsa.

While adopting military measures Gobind Singh increasingly depended on the Jats, which was apparent from his efforts to place them on a par with Khatris and with Brahman Sikhs. The preponderance of Jats in the Khalsa was ensured by his confrontation with the Rajput chiefs of the hills and the faujdars of Aurangzeb.

However, by adopting, as a uniform external appearance, all the five symbols beginning with the letter 'k' (*kesh, kangha, kara, kirpan* and *kachchha*) and taking the surname 'Singh' and a new salutation, the guru's followers were not only bound together more closely in a community with a separate identity, but also stood with a common spiritual father and mother in Guru Gobind Singh and his wife. The guru declared the Khalsa to be the heir of everything he possessed, because he himself owed everything to them. The point to be kept in mind is that the term Khalsa was used for the Sikhs initiated by the guru himself and not by the *masands*. So, a direct link with the guru was necessary. The Khalsa were instructed not to have any connection with the *masands* and their followers (*masandis*). This code of conduct not only removed the system of mediation, but also separated the Khalsa *sangats* from other Sikh *sangats*. Of course, the new organization strengthened the unity and integrity among the guru's followers, but it also led to an internal tussle between those who accepted the new order and those who remained outside.

The developments at Anandpur had already become so conspicuous that by the end of 1693 the news-writer of Sirhind was asked to report about the activities of the gathering crowds of that place. Aurangzeb, then in the Deccan, also ordered the faujdars to ensure that no crowds gathered at Anandpur.[48] Besides, a Mughal force was sent to Anandpur, but the young commander of the force was disheartened by Gobind Singh's unexpected preparation for battle and left the place without a fight. Another expedition was sent, but that too failed, because by that time some hill chiefs themselves had revolted against the Mughals. The Mughal commander, Husain Khan, was defeated and killed by the rebel chiefs who were supported by a small contingent sent by the guru.[49]

On the other hand, the increasing number of armed Singhs at Anandpur, particularly at Diwali and Baisakhi, posed a threat to the hill chiefs themselves. Since they found it difficult to fight on their own they approached the Mughal faujdars. But, all such efforts proved to be of no effect. The number of Singhs further increased, so much so that it created a problem of shortage of daily commodities and, therefore, they had to raid the neighbouring villages for food and forage.[50] The hill chiefs felt restless but were helpless. Ultimately, they decided to approach Aurangzeb for protection. Thus, the imperial and the vassal forces combined to attack Anandpur. A long blockade and assurance of good conduct induced the guru and his followers to leave the place by the end of 1704. While crossing the flooded stream near Ropar, the guru was attacked by some Mughal troops. His wife and mother, and his two younger sons were separated from him, and he reached a village called Chamkaur. The guru was again pursued and attacked, and all his followers and his two elder sons fell fighting at Chamkaur. The two missing younger sons are said to have fallen into the hands of Wazir Khan, the Mughal faujdar of Sirhind, who put them to death.

When Gobind Singh clarified his position by writing a letter, the

Nanak and His Followers 179

Zafarnama mentioned above, to Aurangzeb and the emperor himself came to know of the mishap with the guru, he thought of appeasing Gobind Singh. He sent special messengers with orders for Munim Khan, Governor of Lahore, to persuade the guru to meet him in the Deccan. But on his way to the Deccan, in Rajasthan, the guru heard of the emperor's death which occurred in February 1707.

Gobind Singh met Aurangzeb's son, Bahadur Shah, in Agra and helped him in the battle of Jajau (in Agra). Since he was assured by the new Emperor that he would get Anandpur back, he accompanied him on his Rajputana campaign in November 1707. The Guru remained close to the imperial camp for about a year, but Bahadur Shah was yet not in a position to do anything for him, and avoided him under one pretext or the other.[51] The guru stayed behind the imperial camp near Nander on the banks of Godavari, where he was assassinated by a Pathan on 7 October 1708. On this occasion, all the Sikhs and the Khalsa gathered and, thus, the differences between the two came to an end. The guruship, was thereafter vested in the Khalsa and the *Guru Granth*.

The activities of Guru Gobind Singh during the last two years of his life appear to have been inconsistent with his previous career and character. Events like the journey to the south to meet Aurangzeb, his support for Bahadur Shah in the battle of Jajau, and his being with him on the Rajputana campaign and from there to the south, require justification.

The reason for the guru's *Zafarnama* to Aurangzeb is clear. He wanted to apprise the Emperor of the misfortune faced by him in Punjab due to the frequent wars. He briefs the emperor as to how he was attacked jointly by the hill chiefs and the imperial officials. The guru's complaint was mainly against the imperial officials who, having forgotten the promises made at the time of their attack on Anandpur, were actively helping the hill chiefs against him. He held the Emperor responsible and accountable (to God) for the acts of his own officials. The guru challenged the Emperor's sense of justice and religiosity and, side by side, 'wanted to see the Emperor personally, with the retinue of one thousand horsemen'. He requested the Emperor to issue orders so that no obstacle might occur in his way.[52] Though there was no verbal or written reply, it seems that some sort of understanding occurred between the two, because soon afterwards the guru set out for the south.

The letter reveals that the united front made by the hill chiefs and the government officials against him, and the disastrous consequences faced by him were sufficient ground for a diplomatic move for peace. The death of Aurangzeb was a check on this move for a while, but for the same purpose the guru joined Bahadur Shah and helped him in the battle of Jajau and remained with him to the end of his life, though he could not achieve what he had desired.

There were two factors that gave a setback to the Sikh movement, one being internal conflict for the spiritual succession, and the other state interference in its affairs. Conflicting claims for succession had started with the demise of Guru Arjan. His elder brother, Prithi Chand claimed to be his successor and thus became a rival of Hargobind. Dhir Mal, a grandson of Hargobind, preferred to remain in the good books of the Mughal court and made a separate centre of his own in Lahore, as against Tegh Bahadur who took over Hargobind's office at Kiratpur.[53] For his pro-government stance Dhir Mal was assigned (in the early 1640s) some revenue-free land at Kartarpur by Shahjahan.[54] Besides, Ram Rai, the elder son of Har Rai, also thought it better to be pro-establishment and he too was granted revenue-free land in Dehra Dun. Apart from the rival claimants (called the *minas*) from the Sodhi family of Ramadas, there were the *udasis* (ascetics) who traced their origin to Guru Nanak through his son Sri Chand. Then there were the followers of Hindal, who did not show reverence even to Guru Nanak and tried to sidetrack the Sikh movement. One thing that was common to all dissidents was that all of them adopted a pro-government policy.

It was under these circumstances that the successors of Guru Arjan shifted the centre, of their activities to the east of the river Sutlej, providing new lands to the Sikh movement. Moreover, places like Patna, Anandpur, and Muktsar, and Nanded were associated with the last guru. Thus the transformation of Sikhism that began with Guru Hargobind due to external interference and internal disunity reached its climax under Guru Gobind Singh.

Politics and militancy continued even after Gobind Singh. During the time of Banda Singh, in the Sirhind Sarkar, 'countless people like ants and locusts gathered round him (who) were ready to fight and to be killed for his sake'.[55] But the Mughal government was too strong for the rising power of the Sikhs. Banda Singh could not resist for long the armies of Bahadur Shah and Farrukh Siyar. He was defeated, captured, and put to death in Delhi in 1716. Then the Sikhs were generally depressed, but the struggle continued until the cult established itself as a ruling power in 1764. It evolved its own political system, which may be termed a theocratic confederate feudalism.

Like Kabir, Nanak was a monotheist and monist, believing in that God is one, without attributes and everywhere manifest. 'There is but one God whose name is true, the Creator . . . immortal, unborn, self-existent.'[56] He also said, 'Millions of men give millions upon millions of descriptions of Him, but they fail to describe Him.'[57]

Nanak did not believe in the *avatar* theory and he rejected the idol worship which was the outcome of the concept of God taking physical form: 'My brethren, you worship goddesses and gods; what can you ask them? and what can they give you? Even if a stone be washed with water, it will again sink in it.'[58]

Nanak had no faith in Heaven or Hell as reward or punishment after death but he believed in attaining salvation within one's lifetime (*jiwan mukti*). The condition laid down by Nanak for a man to reach such a state of mind is strict, and the devotee who qualifies becomes a 'perfect man' close to divinity. 'Joy and sorrow are the same to him. He is ever in bliss and never in woe. . . . Honour and dishonour affect him not. A King and a beggar are alike to him. Whatever is the will of God is the best to him. Such a man, says Nanak, may be said to have attained salvation.'[59]

Nanak enjoins upon his followers to live as ideal men, not as ascetics but as householders depending on their own labour. While narrating the ten stages of human life, he says that 'in the seventh he collects things for a house to live in'. 'He alone, O Nanak, knows the (right) way, who eats the fruit of his earnings and shares it with others.'[60]

Within the cult, was required hard work and honest dealings in the professions which included not only trade but also agriculture. But at the same, Nanak was also against the accumulation of wealth 'Nanak says, man must depart; why amass property and wealth?'[61] Every Sikh was expected to voluntarily contribute to the common fund at the disposal of the guru or the local *sangats*. This contribution was made by rich and poor at the rate of one-tenth of their income, though an individual might willingly contribute more.

The institutions of *sangat* and *pangat* (i.e. mixed congregations and inter-dinning) started by Nanak and continued by his successors not only had a wholesome effect on the lives of the Sikhs but also presented a new social structure based on liberal and secular values. The system was a direct incentive to the promotion of social solidarity.[62] Besides, it was Nanak's clear directive to adopt social service for all without discrimination. The *Guru Granth* suggests three *marga* (ways) of pious life—remembering *Name* (God), *kirtan*, and social service, of which the last was the most important. The spirit behind it was not less than what was maintained by the Muslim mystics.

Nanak refused to recognize any restriction based on birth. He asserts that every man, irrespective of his position in the caste hierarchy, was eligible for salvation. Those who took shelter in God were equals: 'Perceive (in all men) the light (of God). Do not ask (a man's) caste for, in the hereafter, there is no caste; caste and status are futile, for the one (God) watches over all.' And also 'we having taken shelter in God are neither high, low, nor in between. We all are God's servants.'[63]

Nanak rejected outright the very idea of impurity attached to any human being and refused to admit anyone being untouchable: 'Nanak is with those who are low-born among the lowly; Nay, who are lowest of the low; how can he rival the great.'[64]

Defining the conduct of Brahmans and Kshatriyas, Nanak says that while the brahman is one who knows the transcendent lord, performs deeds of devotion, penance, self-restraint and humility, the quality of a Kshatriya is to have bravery and charity. Here Nanak redefines varnas as something related not to birth but to worth. He says, 'As a man soweth so shall he reap; as he earneth so shall he eat. . . . Men are judged according to their acts.'[65]

Nanak and other Sikh gurus did not accept the scriptural authority of the Vedas and the Puranas. The *Guru Granth* alone has been regarded and maintained as religious scripture in the Sikh cult.[66] However, Nanak's own opinion about the authority of early scriptures is indicated in the following declaration: 'Some read the Vedas, some the Puranas . . . (but) I know not and never know anything than thy name (O, God).'[67]

According to the *Janam Sakhis* or 'life stores' of Guru Nanak,

Nanak constantly referred to the writings of Kabir.[68] But the *Janam Sakhis* contain much legend and there is no evidence to believe that Nanak ever met Kabir. A mention of Kabir is found in the writings of the third guru, Amardas who says: 'Nama, a calico-printer, and Kabir, a weaver, obtained salvation from the Perfect Guru (God). Knowing God they embraced His word, and lost their consciousness of caste.'[69]

Nanak castigates professional brahmans as greedy and selfish. He says that their greed was never satisfied. The innocent and ignorant were forced to satisfy their demands. Most Brahmans were neither learned nor sincere to their religion, and religious ceremonies performed by them just a commercial service. Like the brahmans, the qazis were condemned by Nanak[70] for their fraudulent life and love of wealth. Mention is made of their being extortionist and tyrannical and practising falsehood.

Nanak noticed a unique tendency of the mind of religious authorities of both communities: as agents of God, they were proud of their religions garb, considering themselves a means of providing the favour of God and a place in paradise to their followers.[71]

It was for this reason that Nanak, like other radicals repeatedly speaks of himself having inspiration directly from God who alone was his Master.[72] 'God Himself is the Guru and He Himself is the disciple (Sikh)'.[73]

It was perhaps due to this reason that after Nanak's demise, the subsequent Sikh teachers as guru became one with Nanak in spirit by leaving their own identity. Nanak was regarded to have absorbed in Guru Angad who after his death entered into Guru Amardas, Amardas to Guru Ramdas and Ramdas to Guru Arjan, by giving them the name of Mahal, the first Mahal being Nanak. The concept of guruship, was institutionalized after Nanak in Sikhism and played a definite role in transforming a spiritual movement into a political and even militant movement.

Another important issue taken up by the Sikh gurus was the matter of conversion. Poor Hindus had converted to Islam either to get relief from the payment of *jizyah* or to escape punishment. Some changed their faith in order to retain their jobs. To please Muslim rulers, they had begun to wear blue cloth. They could thus live a double life. Nanak says: 'You wear a *dhoti* and a frontal mark, and carry a rosary, yet you eat the bread of mlechhas. You perform the Hindu ceremony at home, read the Quran in public, and associate with Muhammadans.'[74]

Such Hindus lived with the Muslims, ate meat and recited the Muhammadan prayers, but at home they still practised the caste rules and did not allow anyone to enter their kitchens.[75] Thus, while in public the converts acted as Muslims, in private life they continued Hindu religious customs and practices. So in most of the cases they were neither fully Hindu nor completely Muslim. The Guru advised people not to live like this. 'Lay aside hypocrisy, repeat God's name, and you shall be saved.'[76]

It is significant that though the Sikhism was distinct from traditional Hinduism, its followers hailed from all the four varnas of Hindu social order and were bound together by a common allegiance to the new faith. But this was the theoretical position, and in spite of common worship and dining in the Sikh *sangats*, their social relations in practical life was hardly better than what was maintained in the traditional social order. The pattern of matrimonial relations also remained the same.

That during those days women were not accorded much respect is reflected in the discourse between Guru Amardas and Bibi Bhani.[77] Young girls were forced to become Ramadasis or Devadasis to serve God. They were made to dance in temples and were exploited by the custodians of the temples. It was due to this reason that in Nanak's writings women have received a respectable place. Pointing out their degraded position which had weakened the family life and, consequently, the social life as a whole, Nanak offered them respect as mothers and dignity as partners of life. 'It is by woman that we are conceived and born . . . , it is she who keeps the race going on . . . why call her low from whom are born kings and great men?'[78] Guru Amardas opposed the veiling of women and led a campaign against *sati*. The same view was later also expressed by Guru Arjan and Guru Govind Singh.[79]

In 1699 Gobind Singh enforced the idea of equality by instituting the Khalsa as an order consisting of all his followers. According to this system, all of them belonged to a new caste community which was not to be identified with any of the four varnas. The Khalsa followers were not only equal among themselves but were also collectively as important as the guru himself. Thus, the ideal of equality was established by Gobind Singh. But the Sikh social reform movement started by Nanak was a long way from establishment of complete equality.

NOTES

1. *Sri Rag.* Macauliffe, *The Sikh Religion,* Delhi: Low Price Pubs., 1993 (rpt.), vol. 1, p. 72.
2. Ibid., pp. 297, 299.
3. *Rag Asa,* ibid., p. 119.
4. *Tilang,* ibid., p. 109.
5. *Rag* Asa, ibid., p. 119.
6. *Rag Asa,* ibid., p. 119.
7. *Rag Asa,* ibid., p. 115.
8. Ibid., p. 109 (Tilanq). Nanak specifically says that women who used to adorn their hair with vermilion and roam about in palanquins had to have their heads shorn and their wails rent the air.
9. Macauliffe, op. cit., vol. 1, p. 119.
10. *Baburvani* refers to the four hymns of Nanaks describing Babur's invasion of India. Three of these are found in *Asadi War,* pp. 360 and 417–18, and the fourth is in *Tilang,* pp. 722-3 of the standard text of *Sri Guru Granth Sahib;* also Macauliffee, op. cit., vol. 1, pp. 15–19, 109.
11. *Rag Asa,* Macauliffe, op. cit., vol. 1, p. 115.
12. *Majh ki War,* Ibid., p. 170.
13. Ibid., where Nanak refers to the Muslim rulers as cruel as butchers in their treatment.
14. Macauliffe, op. cit., vol. III, p. 403.
15. Ibid., p. 135.
16. Ibid.
17. Guru Arjan refers to 'gathering of the crop, whether it be green, half ripe or fully ripe and fit to be cut'. Ibid., p. 103.
18. Ibid., vol. 1, p. 263.
19. For details of this approach of Surdas, Savitri Chandra, 'Social Life as Reflected in the Works of Surdas', *Medieval India and Hindi Bhakti Poetry: A Socio-Cultural Study,* Delhi: Har-Anand, 1996, pp. 82–98.
20. Savitri Chandra, 'Tulsidas's Concept of Rulership', ibid., pp. 116–28.
21. Khushwant Singh, *A History of the Sikhs,* vol. 1, London: Princeton University Press, 1963. K.A. Nizami, *Akbar and Religion,* Delhi: Idara-i Adabiyat-i Dehli, 1989, p. 31.
22. The Govindval Nagar was established in 1552 by Amardas on the bank of river Beas.

23. Macauliffe, op. cit., vol. III, pp. 81-4.
24. According to Sujan Rai Bhandari, 'orders were issued to the Finance Minister that a reduction of twelve to ten be made in the *jama* and the revenue collectors be instructed to give remissions to the peasants accordingly'. *Khulasat-ut Tawarikh* (compiled in 1696), ed. M. Zafar Hasan, Delhi: G. & Sons, 1918, p. 425. Abul Fazl too refers to Akbar's meeting with Arjan but does not mention any suggestion from him about the reduction of land tax. He, however, refers to the reduction of the *jama* made after Akbar's visit. The previous increase of the tax was cancelled. *Akbarnama*, ed. Molvi Abdur Rahim, Calcutta: Asiatic Society, 1877, vol. III, part II, pp. 746-7.
25. Mobad, *Dabistan-i Mazahib* (MS), Lucknow: Newal Kishore Press, 1877, p. 233. This text asserts that as 'other means of acquiring wealth and influence, Arjanmal dispatched his followers to foreign countries to be keenly engaged in trade'. It says his transactions as a merchant were extensive, though confined to the purchase of horses in Turkistan. Mobad's account of Sikhs is mainly based on information collected in 1643-4, when he met Hargobind at Kartarpur. He claims to have been closely acquainted with the seventh Mahal (Guru), Har Rai (1644-61), pp. 237-8.
26. *Tuzuk-i Jahangiri*, ed. Sir Syed Ahmad, Aligarh, 1864, p. 34.
27. According to the Sikh tradition, Prince Khusrau was nominated Akbar's successor; he was then on his way to Kabul; he asked Guru Arjan for financial support to meet his travelling expenses. With some reluctance the guru provided him Rs. 5,000. Macauliffe, op. cit., vol. III, pp. 84-5.
28. Macauliffe, op. cit., vol. V, pp. 286-306; Indu Bhushan Banerjee, *Evolution of the Khalsa*, Calcutta: A Mukherjee, 1947, vol. II, pp. 177-88.
29. Mobad, op. cit., p. 234.
30. Ibid., p. 234. Apart from the reference to 'heavy fine on Arjanmal', Mobad once again, while giving the reason of the imprisonment of his son, Hargobind, says that it was on account of the 'demand for the balance of the fine he [Jahangir] had imposed on Arjanmal'. The word 'balance' is noticeable.
31. Ibid., p. 235.
32. Fauja Singh, 'Foundation of the *Khalsa* Commonwealth, Ideological Aspects', *The Punjab Past and Present,* vol. V, part 1, 1971, p. 201.
33. Mobad, op. cit., p. 239; J.D. Cunningham, *A History of the Sikhs* (ed. Garett), Delhi: S. Chand, 1955, pp. 50-1.
34. With reference to the *Punjab Sikhian*, no. 39, it is generally said that when Ramdas, on his north Indian tour, met Hargobind in Srinagar, Garhwal, in about 1634 and asked him the reason of this change, he replied, 'Internally a hermit and externally a Prince. Arms mean protection to the weak and

destruction to the tyrant.' Hearing this Ramdas said, 'This appeals to my mind'. Ganda Singh, 'Development of Sikh Thought', *Punjab Past and Present,* vol. II, part 1, 1968, pp. 17–18.
35. Mobad, op. cit., p. 234.
36. Ibid., p. 234. J.D. Cunningham, *A History of the Sikhs*, pp. 51–2.
37. J.S. Grewal, *The Sikhs of the Punjab*, Cambridge: Cambridge University Press, 1994, p. 69.
38. The photocopies of all these orders have been published with English translation by Ganda Singh: *Hukmname*, Patiala: Punjabi University, 1967, pp. 76–91. All are undated and the places from where they were issued are not mentioned.
  In one of the orders the word, 'Khalsa' has been used for the people who held the Guru's teachings as 'true' or 'pure'. This contradicts the general belief that the term *'khalsa'* in Sikhism was invented by the tenth guru, Gobind Singh. He used the term in a different connotation, as we shall see subsequently.
39. J.D. Cunningham, op. cit., p. 58.
40. J.S. Grewal, op. cit., pp. 72–3.
41. *The Bachittar Natak,* Macauliffe, op. cit., vol. V, p. 305.
42. For details Ganda Singh, op. cit., nos. 33–65.
43. For details, *Kulliyat,* ed. Ganda Singh, as cited by Fauja Singh, op. cit., pp. 207–8.
44. The *Zafarnama* or the letter of (moral) victory, composed in Persian verses, is contained in the *Dasam Granth*, a compilation of the Guru's writings. The English translation is given by Macauliffe, op. cit., vol. V, pp. 201–6; for critical evaluation, J.S. Grewal, *From Guru Nanak to Maharaja Ranjit Singh,* Amritsar, 1972, pp. 62–6.
45. Cited by Ganda Singh, op. cit., p. 19.
46. Macauliffe, op. cit., vol. V, p. 312.
47. *'Khalsa'* is an official term (of Arabic derivation, meaning 'pure') used by Muslim rulers to specify territories under direct imperial control (as against those assigned to nobles and chiefs). But here the term bears an entirely different connotation, 'a militant Sikh theocracy'. For details Indubhushan Banerjee, *Evolution of the Khalsa*, Calcutta: A. Mukherjee, 1947.
48. J.S. Grewal, *The Sikhs of the Punjab*, p. 74.
49. *The Bachitra Natak,* Indubhushan, op. cit., vol. II, pp. 183–6.
50. J.S. Grewal, op. cit., p. 78.
51. Macauliffe, op. cit., vol. V, pp. 234, 235.
52. Indubhushan Banerjee, op. cit., vol. II, pp. 142–3.
53. Tegh Bahadur soon left Kiratpur in 1664 and settled in Bakala, a village in the Bari Doab. But due to opposition from his two nephews, Dhir Mal and Harji, he had to leave Bakala and go back to Kiratpur. There too, he

was disliked by his brother, Suraj Mal. So, during the first year of his Guruship, Tegh Bahadur had to make a new centre in Makhowal in the territory of the chief of Kahlur (Bilaspur). Grewal, op. cit., pp. 69–70.
54. Grewal (op. cit., p. 66) refers to the text of Shahjahan's order issued in 1643 and contained in *Makhaz-i Tawarikh-i Sikhan.*
55. Khafi Khan, *Muntakhab-ul Lubab,* vol. II, eds. Kabiruddin Ahmad and Ghulam Qadir, Calcutta: Bib. Ind., 1874, p. 672.
56. *The Japji,* Macauliffe, op. cit., vol. 1, p. 195.
57. *Japji,* III, ibid., p. 197.
58. *Sorath Ashtapadi,* ibid., p. 336.
59. *Gauri, Sukhmani,* V, IX-7, as cited by Ganda Singh, op.cit., p. 8; *Gauri Ashtapadi,* Macauliffe, op.cit., vol. 1, p. 301.
60. *Majh ki War* and *Sri Rag,* Macauliffe, op. cit., vol. 1, pp. 279, 72.
61. *Sri Rag,* Macauliffe, op. cit., vol. 1, p. 22, also pp. 275, 277, 300.
62. Guru Angad paid special attention to these institutions, and Amardas made it mandation for all visitors to participate in the *langar* even before meeting the guru. Ganda Singh, op. cit., p. 14.
63. Hew McLeod, *Guru Nanak and the Sikh Religion,* Oxford: Oxford University Press, 1968, p. 209.
64. *Sri Rag,* Macauliffe, op. cit., vol. 1, p. 186.
65. *Suhi,* Macauliffe, op. cit., vol. 1, p. 11.
66. The point has already been discussed in detail in Chapter 5.
67. *Rag Ramkali,* Macauliffe, op. cit., vol. 1, p. 348, also *Gauri Ashtapadi* and *Sorath Ashtapadi,* ibid., pp. 296, 335.
68. A hymn cited by Macauliffe (op. cit., vol. 1, p. 114), shows Nanak mentioning the name of Kabir along with Jaidev, Namdev, Trilochan, Raidas, and Sain. But the hymn does not figure in the *Guru Granth.*
69. *Sri Rag, Ashtapadi,* Macauliffe, op. cit., vol. II, p. 160.
70. For reference to the qazis, *Majh ki War,* Macauliffe, op. cit., vol. I, pp. 38-40.
71. *Gauri Ashtapadi,* ibid., pp. 299, 300.
72. *Rag Sorath,* Macauliffe, op. cit., vol. I, p. 332.
73. Grewal, op. cit., p. 51.
74. *Slok* XVI, Macauliffe, op. cit., vol. 1, pp. 239–40.
75. Ibid., p. 240.
76. Ibid.
77. Macauliffe, op. cit., vol. 11, p. 146.
78. Ganda Singh, op. cit., pp. 14–15.
79. Ibid., p. 15.

CHAPTER 7

Dadu and His Followers

Dadu (AD 1544–1603), a close contemporary of Emperor Akbar, was another great non-conformist man of the Bhakti movement.[1] Dadu is a Turkish word, which means brother or servant. According to traditions he was an adopted son of Lodi Brahman of Ahmedabad. The author of *Dabistan-i-Mazahib* calls him a *naddaf* or Muslim cotton carder, and provides a very brief but significant account of him, which reads thus:

> Dadu was by birth a *naddaf* and lived at Naraina (a town in Marwar). He adopted the ascetic life in the time of the Emperor Akbar and made many disciples. He forbade the practice of idolatry among his followers. He also prohibited the eating of flesh and sought to avoid causing pain to any living creature. He did not require the abandonment of secular pursuits, nor forbid marriage. People were free to remain celibate or to marry, to withdraw from the world's business or engage in it as they saw fit and his disciples embraced both classes.[2]

Like Kabir, Dadu too was a householder with family responsibilities. He is said to have been the disciple of Buddhan or Viridhanand, but in the opening lines of his *Bani* (sayings) he declares himself a disciple of Satguru (God): 'Worship be paid to Niranjan, homage to the Divine Guru. . . .' He also declared, 'Miraculously the Divine Guru met with me: I received the token of His favour.'[3]

We have seen that Kabir and Nanak discarded and denounced the false roles played by certain gurus in religious matters; they declared God to be the guru, by using the term Satguru for the divine teacher. Dadu, too condemned human gurus, saying 'the disciple is the cow, the Guru is the milkman', and that 'the Guru draws the milk and drinks, the disciple is the goat or cow'.[4] He clarifies his position: 'Allah, Ram . . . the same is my Guru', and that 'the one Allah (to be taken as) Master and Teacher'.[5] Thus,

'Dadu's teacher is Ram, Govind, Allah: the Divine Teacher of Namdev, Kabir, and all other saints.'[6]

Kabir's ideas appear to have had great impact on Dadu and his followers. In the *Panchvani* compilations of the Dadupanthis, Kabir's sayings have been given the largest representation after Dadu's account, and his name also occurs next to Dadu in the preferential order of the Panchvani saints (i.e. Dadu, Kabir, Namdev, Raidas, and Haridas). Besides, Dadu himself has shown much indebtedness to Kabir by referring to him frequently in his sayings. For instance, 'Very dear to me is the true word of Kabir. To hear it is pure bliss: greatly do I delight in it. To Him who was Lord of Kabir is my soul wedded. In thought, word and deed, I acknowledge no other.'[7] He stated, 'who vanquishes the hostile army of the passions, such was Kabir in this age of darkness.' He also stated, 'Poor Kabir spoke his message and passed on, having given much wise counsels.'[8]

Moreover, there is much similarity in the content: many of Dadu's verses appear to be simply variants of the popular sayings of Kabir. The strict monotheistic concept that God is one and there is no difference between 'Ram and Allah', is well reflected in the verses of Dadu. 'To whom shall we compare Ram? There is no second.'[9] And also, 'Call Him Allah, call Him Ram. Leave the branches and grasp the root. Take the name of Allah Ram, and consume your deeds.'[10]

Like Kabir's remark about two Rams, 'one manifested everywhere and the other (the son of Dashrath) contained in himself', is this from Dadu: 'Everyone takes the name of Ram, but there is great difference in the use of it; One returns to earth in various rebirths; the other is united to the One.'[11]

On Kabir's pattern that 'his Master has neither father nor mother', Dadu discards the concept of physical form of God in the following manner: 'That which is born and dies is the body: it is not the indwelling Ram. He who is immune from birth or death, the same is my Master. . . . The world-Guru neither dies nor comes to life: in Him all things are created and destroyed. . . .'[12]

Dadu also believed that God had countless names, and each, when used with understanding, has something to teach us. 'The

Creator has many and diverse names. Choose the names that comes to mind; thus do the saints practise remembrance.'[13]

Most often Dadu speaks in the same spirit as that of Kabir, in terms of clarity and conviction being based on solid arguments. In his famous concept of *nipakh* (i.e. non-attachment to any religious order) too, Dadu appears to be much indebted to Kabir:

दादू ना हम हिंदु होहिंगें । न हम मूसलमान ।।
षट दरसन में हम नाहिं । हम राते रहमान ।।

(No Hindu am I, nor yet a Musalman. I follow none of the six systems (of Hindu philosophy): I am a devotee of the Merciful.[14])

This verse of Dadu brings to mind the satirical arguments of Kabir: 'The tiger, the lion, the jackal and all the rest; how many are these the Musalmans?'[15]

Like other non-conformists, Dadu was also concerned with the religious differences between Hindus and Muslims and wanted to bring the people out of the narrow limitations of religious belief and practice. According to Dadu himself, 'fierce and terrible have the people become, when they saw I was of neither faction'.[16] The same problem was also faced by Kabir on this issue, as we have seen.

Like Kabir, Dadu challenged the infallibility of the religious scriptures of both the communities, almost in the same spirit. Dadu says, 'I have diligently searched the Vedas and Koran, but the dwelling-place of Niranjan is not here but far off. . . . How many have wasted a lifetime blacking paper, producing Vedas and Puranas.'[17] Repeating the same he concludes, 'But what profits it, without love, to have read the Vedas and Puranas and other scriptures?'[18]

Thus, like other radical teachers, Dadu considered the early scriptures as biased sources that led to conflict. For the same reason, Dadu and his followers developed, on the pattern of the *Guru Granth* of the Sikhs, their own sectarian compilation known as the *Panchavani*, now regarded as their scripture and recited in the cult.[19]

The social hierarchy maintained by the caste system was a serious problem for all the bhakti teachers. Dadu also denounced the system and tried to assert the equality of all human beings in society. But he also seems to have stood for the formation of a separate class or community of like-minded teachers. By placing Namdev, Kabir, and Raidas in one category, he says, 'Those who have attained (salvation) have left the message . . . that all of them are of one faith, all are of one caste.'[20] He includes himself in that category, saying that 'the Lord of Kabir is *my soul wedded*'.[21] It is significant that not only Dadu but also other Bhakti teachers have laid much emphasis on the fellowship of their peers. Dadu says: 'Through fellowship with Hari you meet saints; through fellowship with the saints thou meet Hari.'[22] This kind of group consciousness was perhaps necessary for radical teachers to give an organized fight to the existing socio-religious systems.

Like Kabir, Dadu was not systematically educated and, therefore, was not aware of philosophical subtleties, but he dealt with the practical problems of life and spirituality. He conformed neither to Hindusism nor to Islam but emphasized the Universal religion. Dadu's concept was that the solution of all problems of human beings was determined by *karma*, the only force to check the transmigration of soul. He believed that the Lord of the Universe is also the Lord of *karma*: 'Deeds *(karma)* control the soul: the Doer controls the deeds; None is there, says Dadu, who controls the Doer'.[23] As for the position of the soul in relation to karma, 'The soul is in bondage: when set free it is even as Brahma. . . . The soul is in the power of *karma*; freed from *karma* it is Brahma. . . .'[24]

Like other radical saints, however, Dadu also refrained from the realization of 'salvation' freedom from the transmigration of the soul). His target was a perpetual vision of God and absorption into the essence of God: 'Grant me, O grant me the vision of Thyself, I desire not salvation.'[25]

Steadfast in his bhakti, which claims complete surrender to the will of God, Dadu said, 'Bhakti offered to the Lord fills the whole body. He whose very blood becomes water for the Lord's sake, whose very bones are dried up, the same shall find Him.'[26]

Thus, Dadu emphasized that true bhakti was not possible without losing one's personal identity in God. To attain such a state, the life of a devotee should be completely regulated and self-disciplined. 'This much do of thyself. Bring body and mind into a state of calm; Restrain the senses, and cultivate a simple mode of living.'[27]

Dadu has also described the gradual process of spiritual advancement in the following verse:

Day by day be intoxicated with Ram, day by day let your love increase; Day by day drink the essence of Ram, day by day behold the mirror within the body; Day by day forget the limitations of the body, day by day let the senses be repressed; Day by day let the devices of the mind perish, day by day will the glory be revealed. When the soul leaves the company of the body and takes its seat in the regions of Hari, Then is it devoid of fear: no limitation can possess it.[28]

In such devotion there is no place for reward or punishment by way of heaven or hell. Dadu says, 'Be not over eager for heaven, nor afraid of hell.'[29] This was perhaps because only the union with God and nothing else was the aim. 'If one serves Ram, he becomes Ram.'[30]

In some of his verses the identity of human soul with God has been expressed: 'I and my worshipper are not two; We are wholly one.' 'The soul and the Beloved are not separate: they dwell together.'[31]

Dadu's spiritual concepts and terminology seem to have been drawn from both Hindu and Muslim sources. In his section on spiritual knowledge, the four states of spiritual advancement of the soul in apprehension of God are walking, dreaming, dreamless sleep, and absorption into the essence of God.[32] These correspond with the four stages of the Vedanta as well as those of the Sufis: *Shariah*, *Tariqat* (the way), *Marifat* (Gnosis), and *Haqiqat* (the Truth). Dadu declared, 'The Guru has made clear to the disciple the meaning of the four states.'[33]

The importance of living and doing good deeds has been emphasized by almost all the bhakti saints. Dadu speaks of it even more forcefully in the following verses: 'You will not have this body again and again, O foolish one. Why do you squander it idly?'[34] and 'How priceless is this life. . . . O Man, such a life will not come again, why then cast away this precious jewel?'[35]

There are frequent references in Dadu's account emphasizing the ethical and moral values needed to be a teacher. His ideal is not withdrawal from the world but to live in harmony. Dadu defines a perfect saint is one who need not assume the outward garb of professional priests: 'All else is vain; not by the garments he wears will he find Him.' The saint must be pure, because without brightness a mirror cannot reflect. He should be selfless, thinking not of himself, but of others: as sun and moon, fire, air and water, night and day, food and shelter, all minister to the need of others, so the true saint should do. Like his Master, he should be patient and forgiving, watching not men's faults but bearing with their shortcomings. He should look upon all men as equal. 'I regard not Hindu and Turk as two'.

'When one has lost what was one's own and abandoned all pride of birth, when vainglory has dropped away, then is one face to face with the Creator.'

In short, Dadu wanted that Godly character should be reflected in all aspects of a saint's life in such a way that there should remain no difference between the two. 'The image of the Master is in all His servants; the saint, His servant, is not other than Himself.'[36]

Like the theoretical norms, the practical social aspects of Dadu's teaching and its bearing on a man's dealing with his fellowmen is also very significant: 'There is no reproach in following an occupation, if one knows how to do it right, there is joy in work.'[37] 'Render good deeds and service of others to Him to whom they are due',[38] Dadu advises. 'The wise man first thinks, then acts: the fool acts first, then thinks. He who acts without thinking is put to shame; he who thinks and then acts is honoured.'[39] It is in Dadu's concept of sin, as revealed in the section of his *Bani* entitled *Supplication,* that moral values are specifically outlined. Sin is not only weakness, folly, or ignorance but a force. It is the root cause of *ahamkara* (the ego). 'With what face shall the soul present itself before you against whom it has offended?... Nothing have I done for that end for which you created the world.'[40]

Dadu emphasizes self-control, and good conduct is due to all creatures. In the section of his *Bani*, entitled *Goodwill*, he says, 'To abandon selfhood, to give up worldly desires in body and mind, To cherish goodwill towards all creatures: this, says Dadu, is the sum of religion. He who bears no enmity to any creature is the true saint. There is but one spirit: There is no enemy.'[41]

As reported by Mobad, there was a unique practice among the followers of Dadu. 'When a member of the sect dies, their custom is to place him on a bed and carry him out to the jungle. They say,

Dadu and His Followers

it is good that the wild animals should feed upon him and satisfy their hunger.'[42] This is verified by the following verse of Dadu:

दादू मरणा तहां भला । जहां पसु पंखी खाइ ।[43]

Dadu was a Nirguna Bhakt, but his political thinking was not that of Kabir or Nanak. He did not hesitate to associate with the elite. Though Dadu was associated with Sambhar for a long time from 1568 to 1579, he left the place for Amber (capital of Jaipur), where he received a warm welcome on the shores of the Maota lake from the ruler, Raja Bhagwandas, then a commander in Emperor Akbar's army.[44] This was also the time when Dadu attracted the attention of Akbar, who in conversation with Bhagwandas expressed his desire to see and talk to him. Jan Gopal of the Dadupanth gives a detailed account of Dadu's visit on an invitation from Akbar and the subsequent series of his meetings and discourses with Akbar at Fatehpur Sikri in 1584. Abul Fazl, Birbal, and Raja Bhagwat Singh (? Bhagwandas) also participated in these discussions on social and spiritual matters.[45]

It is true that there is no reference to this meeting in any of the Persian chronicles, but the same has happened with many other such cases of discourses with Akbar, like Swami Bithalnath (1515–85), Swami Haridas, and Kumbhandas (d. 1583),[46] obviously because they did not belong to the elite of the time. But Jan Gopal's *Dadu Parichaya* explicitly narrates in its eight chapters the whole process of how the meeting was arranged at the instance of Raja Birbal and by the efforts of Raja Bhagwandas and one of his faithful retainers named Suja Kinchi, giving the year of the meeting as VS 1642/AD 1584.[47] Moreover, the meeting is also mentioned by Dadu himself in one of his verses:

अकबर साह बुलाईया । गुर दादू को आप ।।
सांच झूठ ब्यौरो हुवै । तब रह्यो नांव प्रताप ।।

(The Emperor Akbar himself invited Guru Dadu. Discussions took place on reality and falsehood, then the superiority of (God's) name was established.[48])

Contemporary historical accounts record the presence of Akbar and his nobles at Fatehpur Sikri from February 1584 to August

1585 when Prince Salim was married to Man Bai, daughter of Bhagwandas, who played a vital role in the meeting between Akbar and Dadu. Besides, the preliminary interview with Abul Fazl and Birbal gives a practical and realistic touch to the meeting. In the case of a distinguished Jain scholar named Hiravijay, who visited Akbar's court in 1582, Abul Fazl had played the same role: the scholar was 'made over to his care until the sovereign found leisure to converse with him'.[49]

This meeting fits in with the development of Akbar's religious policy at that time, when the *Ibadat Khana* had started and *Tauhid-i Ilahi* was taking shape. Cow slaughter was prohibited, and abstinence from eating meat was enjoined on certain days. Under these circumstances, Jan Gopal's claim that the Emperor's order prohibiting animal slaughter was issued under the influence of Dadu seems to be justified.

On the basis of the traditional biographies Narayandas presents Dadu in frequent contact with the royal figures of the time,[50] which reflects his association with the court. Even before meeting Akbar, Dadu had impressed Raja Bhagwandas of Amber, and later made some local Rajput rulers his disciples (Sundardas the elder, Hapaji, etc.). Thus, while within Rajasthan Dadu enjoyed the patronage of local rulers and nobles, he was extended respect outside, particularly at the Mughal court.

There are shreds of evidence in Dadu's own account, that reflect his political ideology. For instance, just like the unity of God at spiritual level, Dadu has also emphasized the need of a single political authority at the worldly level:

There would be peace only if there is unity of political authority; if there is duality (or double authority), no one can remain happy due to the ensuing conflicts. With one political authority there is tranquility in the city (state); the king and the subjects are happy and there is light everywhere.[51]

Secondly, while Dadu feels pride in being a subject of Raja Ram, he advises him self-restraint in order to govern the state effectively: 'Dadu, Rawat (*rayat*) of Raja Ram, never forsakes (his) name; take care of your soul and you can control the village (state) very well.'[52] Obviously, Dadu accepted at the social level the ideals and the institutions of government.

On the other hand, it appears from Jan Gopal's account that Dadu had to face opposition from Hindu and Muslim leaders, on the one hand, and Raja Man Singh's dislike for him, on the other. On the death of Bhagwandas, his successor Man Singh came to Amber. The whole populace arrived to meet him but not Dadu, which was taken as discourtesy. There were other complaints also against Dadu. 'He disregards caste rules, and makes no difference between the Hindus and the Muslims.'[53] This complaint is very similar to that made against Kabir to Sikandar Lodi by religious leaders. Thus, there appeared a prolonged conflict between Dadu and his opponents. This forced him to leave Amber and wander from place to place for about ten years.

Dadu first went to Marwar, where he made some new disciples among whom there were two Rathor noblemen, Rao Man Singh, and Kishan Singh of Merta. From Marwar, he went to Bikaner, where the Rao of Bhuratiya met him and proposed he settle permanently in his village, but Dadu declined. During this visit an important incident took place: Sundardas the Elder became his disciple. Sundardas's life is not given in Jan Gopal's account but Raghava's *Bhaktamala* narrates a story according to which he was a Rajput prince from Bikaner and had served in the imperial military force at Kabul.[54] Having lost his throne in a battle, Sundardas along with his family priest, Prahladdas, renounced the world, and both came to Dadu. Sundardas became Dadu's disciple and Prahladdas, the disciple of Sundardas.[55]

Both Sundardas and Prahladdas are said to have been associated with the Thambha of Ghatra (now in Alwar), to which the Dadupanthi Nagas trace their origin. Another Rajput disciple of Dadu was Prince Hapaji, the youngest son of Bhagwandas of Amber, who also renounced the world after meeting him. Narayandas tells of him having left as a prince a spiritual lineage recognized at the court.

However, Dadu's conflict with Man Singh had such an adverse effect on his mind that he refrained from any contact with the ruling family of Amber. During his journey, when Dadu passed on from Sambhar, though he accepted the invitation of Rathorani, Queen of Amber, to meet her, he left the place soon afterwards without even informing her.[56] Dadu finally settled at Naraina in 1602, where he died next year in 1603.

It remains to be clarified that there also was a dispute between the Rajput and non-Rajput followers of Dadu on the issue of following Rajput traditions. Since Dadu was clean-shaven wearing mendicant's dress, it was suggested at one of the annual Dadupanthi festivals at Naraina that all celibate members of the order should shave off their mustaches and wear the ascetic garb in order to follow the guru's example. This was also to maintain an outward uniformity. But the idea was opposed by Kevaldas and Hirdaya Ram, the two Naga leaders in the spiritual lineage of Dadu's Rajput disciple, Sundardas the elder who had maintained his moustaches throughout. Since most of the saints in their branch of the order belonged to the Rajput clan, they also maintained mustaches as a sign of the clan's valour. Hence, the dispute between the two sides was not resolved, and Kevaldas led his men away to hold a separate festival in another place. After five years, however, Jait Sahib was able to bring them back into the fold by compromising on Rajput traditions. Thus, while many of the fighting saints of India often posed a fierce visage with little or no clothes and unkept hair and beard, in the Dadupanth Kevaldas's men were allowed to be militant ascetics as well as fully clothed and mustachioed Rajputs.

Another Rajput prince, Hapaji also renounced the world after meeting with Dadu. But after twelve years when he returned to visit his native place and camped with his followers outside the city, his ruler brother invited Hapaji to the court where he so impressed the members of the thirteen noble houses of Amber that they declared him the founder. Though requested by all to stay, the saint left Amber leaving behind a few disciples to carry on the above 'noble house'.[57]

Thus, whereas individual Rajputs were allowed to maintain important aspects of their social identity, Hapaji and his followers ensured that the Dadupanthi spiritual authority was to be treated no less than the temporal authority in the local court.

Dadu was greater than the cult bearing his name. When asked by Gharibdas and others at the time of his death how the system was to be sustained while there were followers of both communities, Dadu replied, 'Retain this form of mine which you behold.'[58] But after his death, there appeared internal conflict and a struggle for power among his family members and followers at the Khalsa

Dadu Dwar at Naraina. Both Jan Gopal and Rajabdas speak of Gharibdas (d. 1636), Dadu's eldest son, being appointed by general consent as spiritual head of this centre.[59] But he soon resigned and nominated Kewal Ram, one of Dadu's followers, his own successor. This was challenged by Miskindas the second son and successor of Dadu. Being thus removed from the office, Kewal Ram founded a separate seat of his own, which was called *Gharibdasot*, while the original seat under Miskindas came to be known as *Miskindasot*. It was in fact a common practice throughout in the case of disputed succession that the rival candidate set up a separate *gaddi* (seat) of his own. However, when Miskindas was deposed, he favoured not his own son, Faqirdas, but one of his followers, Chaitandas. But Dhani Bai, the wife of Miskin and mother of Faqirdas, stood for family rights and succeeded, after Miskin's death, in having Chaitandas removed from office and Faqirdas appointed as the successor. On Faqir's death, Dhani Bai herself took possession of the *gaddi*, though she was soon removed from the office and Jait Ram, popularly known as Jait Sahib, was appointed as *mahant* by a general election in 1693.

It is clear that for about ninety years from 1603 to 1693, Naraina Dadu Dwara remained with the Dadu lineage. But during the whole period, there was much confusion and instability due to a lack of proper leadership. Neither Gharibdas nor his successors were capable of managing the affairs of the sect. There was no regular system of election, and no unity. The role played by Miskindas and his wife Dhani Bai in the sect appeared as a great embarrassment to the sincere and loyal followers of the sect. It was in these circumstances that in 1693 the control of the Naraina Dadu Dwara passed absolutely from Dadu's descendants to one of his followers, Jait Ram or Jait Sahib, who was unanimously elected as *mahant* of Naraina.

On the other hand, like other saints and their cults mentioned earlier, Dadu and the Dadupanth had also to face the process of Hinduization. His Muslim origin was gradually blurred and, at the same time, his Brahman birth was emphasized. For this the place of Dadu's childhood and youth was transferred from Rajasthan to Gujarat and his personal life was shrouded in myth. There also appeared the trend of gradual elimination of Islamic elements from the Dadu tradition. The Hindu element was so emphasized that the contribution of Islamic thought to the enrichment of Dadu's sayings was either ignored altogether or confused. Thus, the sect turned in the direction of Hindu orthodoxy and formalism. The result was that, while the number of Dadu's Muslim followers was considerably larger, their enrolment ceased with his death, and within a century, particularly after the death of Faqirdas who served as the last link with the Muslims, their names almost disappeared at least from the Khalsa branch at Naraina. With the emergence of Jait Sahib in 1693, the Dadupanth turned to be an exclusively Hindu cult.

The growing requirement of celibacy as a norm of the sect gave an impetous to the process of Hinduization. Dadu imposed no rule of celibacy on his followers. Mobad explicitly states that he 'neither enjoyed nor for bade marriage'. But the ascetic ideal was enforced by the personal example of Gharibdas as well as that of 'Aunt Hawwa', the 'two sisters', and Rama Bai. There was only the exception of Faqirdas at Naraina, who advocated the ideal of marriage.[60] Thus, even during the time of Dadu's family celibacy was dominant. The accession of Jait Sahib the first of an unbroken succession of celibate *mahants* outside Dadu's family, marked the final victory of the Hindu ascetic ideal.

Another aspect was the growing sectarian consciousness of the cult. This is evident from all Dadupanthi works, including specially the Raghava's *Bhaktamala* in which a delibderate effort has been made to compare the Dadupanth with the four popular Vaishnava sects mentioned earlier.

However, Jait Sahib (1693–1732) was a powerful leader with political skills, and he was able to bring many groups of Dadu's followers together. He remained in authority for about forty years and organized the cult. He established it as a distinct institution by framing regulations. Under Jait Sahib, apart from spiritual men there emerged a group of armed ascetics known as Dadupanthi Nagas who formed a separate organization within the cult. On annual festivals of the order at Naraina, these Nagas were given specific instructions by the *mahant* about the deployment of troops for different political and administrative purposes. They were organized basically to protect the interest of the sect.[61]

Dadu and His Followers 201

Jait Sahib was succeeded by Kishan Dev (1732–53) during the time of Sawai Jai Singh, the ruler of Amber. It was due to a royal decree regarding the compulsory marriage of the heads of religious orders that Kishan Dev had to leave Naraina for the neighbouring kingdom of Marwar (Jodhpur) where he founded a new Thamba near Merta and remained there till his death in 1753.[62] When dissensions arose after the death of Sawai Madho Singh in 1767, Chain Sahib, a disciple of Kishan Dev, returned to Naraina and took over the charge of the *gaddi* from the officiating *mahant*. Chain Sahib died in 1780 and meanwhile, the members of the Dadupanth, who had spread not only throughout Jaipur and Marwar but also to the north, were gradually being involved in more serious struggles for their existence.

Dadu is said to have left after him 152 disciples, of whom 52 founded different settlements known as Thambhas. There are only four recognized Dadu Dwaras (centres), those at Naraina, Amber, Sambhar, and Bairana (Bachhum), whose special status is due to a historical association with Dadu. The *akharas* or monastic retreat (literary court, arena) were established from the time of military organization of the sect. Other centres are known by such general names as *sthan* (place) or *math* (monastery). There appeared four main divisions or settlements of the sect—Khalsa, Virakt, Uttarardha and Nagas. There were also a large number of casual or lay members of the sect.

Apart from the Nagas, who formed a separate system within the sect, the Panth mainly consists of Khalsa and Uttarardha. The term Khalsa, denoting the original sectarian establishment at Naraina, seems to have come into use at a time when the rapid growth of the order in the north, followed by the rise of Nagas as militant force, was felt to be a menace to the purity of the original tradition.

The Khalsas do not generally engage in commerce, but have agricultural and landed interests. Involved in various forms of business, they travel much from place to place. Some of them are directly engaged in the service of Dadu Dwara at Naraina, which possesses many villages deriving large revenues.

The Uttarardha (northern), founded by Banwaridas in Ratiya (Hissar), is a wealthy and enterprising section, engaged in agriculture, medicine, teaching, banking, and commerce. Thus, most of the centres are economically self-supporting.

THE NAGAS AS MILITANT FORCE IN THE DADUPANTH

The Dadupanth produced both scholars and soldier-saints, and both of them enjoyed special favour from the ruling class of Jaipur. But they differed from each other in approach. The scholars served the princes only as Ayurvedic physicians, while the soldier-saints or 'Naga' warriors maintained loyalty to their sovereigns and remained associated with the Jaipur state as soldiers and tax collectors.[63]

This was not an innovation in the Dadupanth. Armed ascetics known as 'Naga' have been found in many religious orders from the sixteenth century onwards, and they played vital roles in political wars. The Dadupanthis were, however, the last to become armed ascetics. Once they entered this profession, they occupied a prominent place and were not easily disbanded. It was due to their activities that there appeared a rapid growth not only in number of Dadupanthis but also in material prosperity, which naturally marked a spiritual decline.

However, as we have seen, the Dadupanthi Nagas had already been formally organized under Jait Sahib. It was during his tenure that a number of Vaishnava *bairagis*, had formed a powerful confederacy at a place of pilgrimage situated about halfway between Amber and Jaipur. It is quite possible that the Dadupanthis would have come in contact with and influenced by such *bairagis*, as many of them later joined the organization. Anyhow, a fighting force of the order was formally recognized and an attempt was made to expand it by way of further recruitment.

The Dadupanthi Nagas were so powerful that when there was any disorder a contingent was sent from Naraina. This is evident from the document about a piece of land being gifted by Raja Sawai Jai Singh as a religious endowment to the Dadupanthis in 1718 at Chimanpura (district Chatsu). In another document of 1733 found in the same district, mention is made of the farming of taxes by the Dadupanthi Nagas.[64]

With the death of Jait Sahib in 1732 and the incompetence of his successors, the authority of the guru at Naraina over the Nagas waned, and power began to be exercised instead by individual Nagas under whose guidance not only training of the members in the art of warfare started but also a vigorous process of recruitment of potential candidates as warriors. Children were trained in the use

Dadu and His Followers 203

of arms on a large scale.[65] Some of these military commanders were actually the founders of different clans into which the Naga fighters were divided, such as Kevaldas of Udehi and his disciple Hirdaya Ram, who started the militant movement from Ghatra.

As mentioned above, a powerful body of armed *bairagis* was already established in Jaipur under Raja Sawai Jai Singh. The Dadupanthis are said to have joined them and to have shared with them and quarrelled over the spoils of war. Later they became strong enough to maintain a military establishment of their own. According to the oral tradition, there was a terrible massacre of the Dadupanthis during the time of Raja Isri (? Ishwari) Singh (1743–50) at Fateh Tiba, just beside Jaipur, on the occasion of a religious festival. This happened during one of the attacks made by Madho Singh of Mewar (Udaipur) on Jaipur against his half-brother Ishwari Singh, before his final victory of the place in 1750. Apart from this unconfirmed story, there is sufficient historical background to believe that there must have been at that time a strong body of armed Dadupanthis. The victims are not stated to have been professional warriors, but in that case there would have been hardly the need to massacre of harmless saints.

From 1776 the Nagas under Ram Krishandas acted as tax-farmers in the pargana of Bhawani Shankarpura (close to the scene of the Fateh Tiba disaster) for cash advances to the state.[66] In 1779, the Dadupanthi Nagas were more systematically organized under the leadership of Santokhdas, who remained a *mahant* of all the Nagas in all the later wars till 1818.

In the same year, the Jaipur state had to face a fierce attack from the Mughal force under the command of Murtaza Ali Khan, sent by Mirza Najaf Khan, naib wazir at Delhi, in order to establish the Mughal authority over there. This was the time when the state was already under the pressure of several problems like the encounters with the Jats and the Marathas and the constant demands for arrears of tribute from the imperial exchequer. The battle was fought at the place of Khatu, in which the Dadupanthis were also engaged as first regular engagement and they showed great valour. Many of them, along with their leader Mangaldas, were killed,[67] though the battle was won and Murtaza Ali fled.

In the years that followed Jaipur and surrounding states remained engaged in constant battle. This proved to be a good opportunity for the Nagas to engage in active warfare. Their recruitment continued with fresh levies, which enhanced their fighting strength. Thus, about fifteen years after their first appearance in the battle at Khatu, the Nagas were retained on the basis of land and cash grants, for their military service as well as for tax-farming to the state. Most often they provided considerable loans to the state treasury, which was repaid most often in the form of writs for the appropriation of revenue from certain villages or districts.[68] The professional character and career of the Dadupanthi Nagas is also evident in the foundation of a large *akhara* by Santokhdas at Naraina in 1787–8, which was no less than a military barracks to be used for the accommodation of the fighting Nagas.

The Dadupanthi Nagas were also engaged in the battle of Tonga (Lalsot) in 1787, in which Count de Boigne, a commander of Mahadji Sindhia, was defeated. It is said that they also formed part of the allied armies at Patan in 1790. In fact, these Nagas had practically become a necessity of the state which called on them repeatedly. They were also used to maintain law and order at the places of disturbance.

In 1797 a large force of the Dadupanthi Nagas under Santokhdas enrolled in the service of Jaipur state. Then, they were officially required to maintain a contingent of 5,000 Naga warriors or even more up to 7,000 or 10,000 assembled troops.[69] Colonel Tod speaks of 7,000 Dadupanthis holding the fort of Khandala (Shaikhawati) for Raja Pratap Singh. They were paid at the rate of half an *anna* a day, later one *anna*. The money was not paid individually to the Nagas, but the total sum was given to the guru, to be distributed to the local treasurers of the respective *beras* (camps). However, the state grant was regarded merely as supplementary source of income, since many of the Nagas were earning money from agriculture, moneylending, and other occupations.

At the time Nagas were also engaged for collecting revenues for the state. They were posted at various important places, including areas of disturbance and turbulence, in order to maintain law and order. Not only this, they were in a way a standing force, ready to fight at any time for the state. Two thousand Nagas accompanied Raja Jagat in his expedition to Marwar, and earned distinction by their victorious assault on Jodhpur. The Nagas also shared in the defence of Jaipur when it was attacked by Amir Khan.[70]

The Nagas were present when a fort at Khiror was attacked and conquered by the Jaipur force; they suffered a loss of 270 killed and 44 wounded. The high proportion of deaths in this battle reminds us of the Naga ideal of the decisive attack, whatever the consequences, which they displayed in almost all wars.

Unlike the Sikh soldiers of the Khalsa, the Dadupanthi Nagas found their temporal authority not at the sectarian centre but at the court of a ruler, though employed or engaged with the consent of the guru. It was Rajput rulers and nobles who commanded Naga soldiers on the battlefield, though sometimes gurus accompanied them to boost their morale. For them it did not matter who was in power: but was sufficient to extend loyalty to the state authority, as directed by the guru. Moreover, they did not change masters as did the Gosains and Bairagis. True, self-interest was a motivating factor, but they displayed a very great sense of loyalty to the Jaipur Raj.

The reasons for this mutual dependence are understandable. Apart from historical and regional causes idealizing the royal authority, the Dadupanthis developed as a vital military force during the period when the Nagas from many other traditions had already set the trend to serve rulers in large numbers. The collapse of the Mughal rule in the eighteenth century not only made the ascetic leaders rise to prominence, it enabled the armed ascetics to make demands on the populace. Eventually, groups of militant *sadhus* became part of the princely states. But when external wars ceased as a result of the Treaty of 1818 with the East India Company, the number of Nagas in the service of Jaipur was reduced, and those who remained reverted to their traditional occupation as collectors of revenue. Through the political disturbances at the death of Jagat Singh, and in the early part of the reign of Maharaja Ram Singh (1832–79), however, their services as fighters were still in demand. From 1823 their headquarters were at Ramgarh (Danta). In 1838 an attempt to reduce their numbers further led to a revolt, suppressed by a force sent from the British cantonment at Nasirabad.[71]

The Nagas played a vital role in the revolt of 1857, They fought for the British company at Jaipur. As the state mercenary troops readied for revolt, the Nagas saved the situation on their own. They also, on their own initiative, made a surprise attack on the Nawab of Narnaul (Patiala state), who was hostile to the British. They sacked the town to make profit for themselves, but this was taken as loyalty to the British officials. It appears from letter written by Colonel William Eden, then Political Agent at Jaipur and acting Agent to the Governor-General, that a body of 500 Nagas under the leadership of Chimandas accompanied him on his march to Mathura and Gurgaon, and helped restore peace.[72] Consequently, at a Darbar in Agra, a medal and *sanad* (certificate), with a gift of Rs. 500, were awarded to Chimandas.

After the death of Santokhdas in 1825, he was succeeded by his disciple Amolakdas. A dispute and dissent under him led to separatist tendencies, giving way to the appearance of four clans, each with own chief. The first was the Lalsot clan, formed in 1844, followed by Udaipur in 1848, and then by Chandsen. The original body came to be known as Nawai clan. The places from which these clans take their names are all of strategic importance, at which a large number of Nagas had been encamped for a long time.[73] Each of the four *jamaats* was required to supply a fixed quota of men to each *tahsil* to assist in the collection of taxes.[74] These four *jamaats* later became seven, with eleven *akharas*, each presided over by a local *mahant*. Lalsot had three *akharas*, Udaipur, five; Chandsen, two; and Nawai, one. But being officially connected with the Jaipur state, these divisions became formalized, each demanding its share of state grant. Thus, in spite of their internal divisions, all the Dadupanthi Nagas remained loyal to the Jaipur court.

In the days of wars, many of the Uttarardhas or northerners flocked to Rajasthan either to share with the militant prospects of the Nagas or to serve the interests of the sect in other ways. Some of them obtained *jagirs* and became landed proprietors. From the beginning of nineteenth century a prosperous group of Uttarardhas who claimed to be the descendants of Aduji of Siwan, a disciple of Banwaridas, had been permanently established in Jaipur and at Rajgarh (now in Alwar state). Others are found in many parts of Shaikhawati. The control of the panth, which seemed to have largely passed into the hands of the militant ascetics, now began to come back to the original Dadu Dwara at Naraina. Since the Nagas were fully transformed into a corps of professional soldiers with political motivations, it was necessary for those Uttarardhas and others who

Dadu and His Followers

still believed in their spiritual traditions to do something in order to strengthen and consolidate the position of the head office of the sect at Naraina.

In 1820, two years after the conclusion of the treaty which brought Jaipur under British protection, Mahant Dalai Ram was elected to ascend the *gaddi* under whom the Naraina Dadu Dwara claimed its old dignity and authority. With the disruptive influences that began to appear among the Nagas after the death of Santokhdas in 1825, there was need of a central authority. Naraina was already a place of pilgrimage for Dadu's followers from all over northern India, as was evident from annual festivals which gave unity and coherence to the different branches of the order. But the simple pillared courtyard had to be thoroughly renovated. It was due to the efforts of Thandhi Ram, a successful physician of Patiala, that a beautiful temple of white marble was constructed in 1827 at Naraina. The marble was gifted by Maharaja Man Singh, then ruler of Marwar (Jodhpur), in recognition of the medical services of Thandhi Ram to the royal household.

It may be concluded that Dadu did not believe in the human guru, though his followers after the formation of the Dadupanth held him in the concept of divine sovereignty which led to guru bhakti. Some subsequent gurus were feudal lords who were military men. The guru as military chief was regarded as a powerful authority, initiating young men into the order and training them in military practice. The trend of devoted service to a spiritual master thus became transmuted into that of dedicated military service to a warrior chief by his followers.

As objects of veneration, however, the Naga chiefs of Dadupanth differed from those of the Shaiva and Vaishnava traditions, the latter being ideally considered incarnations of Shiva or Vishnu. Since the Dadupanthi Nagas rejected this myth they had to seek another source of symbolic power. For this reason perhaps they ultimately turned to the political and militant authority of Jaipur. Taken into the Jaipur administration with state grants and as recognized divisions of its military force, the Dadupanthi Nagas had enough material incentive for loyalty to the state. The authority they derived from the Jaipur court made them less flexible in their political allegiance to the state than the Shaiva and Vaishnava Nagas who moved from one state to the other for short-term profit.

Moreover, since the gurus of the Dadupanthi Nagas had established their position and prestige in the Jaipur court, their followers had to learn to fight and to serve the state as military men.

While many Dadupanthi Nagas served the Jaipur rulers as tax collectors, its scholars enjoyed royal patronage and were exempt from the payment of taxes as mendicants. The position of scholars and soldiers of the sect in the Jaipur state structure is well depicted by the story of Mani Ramji (disciple of the great scholar, Nischaldas) narrated by Narayandas. As a physician, Mani Ramji earned enough wealth which he expended on a number of his dependants. When the state's tax officer came to make an assessment, he saw him feeding a long line of beggars. The officer asked him, 'If you give everything away to the poor, you will have nothing left for yourself.' The reply of the saint was, 'If it turns out like that, then I will join the line of beggars myself.'[75]

As religious sect, the Dadupanth had a firm institutional base within the political structure of Rajasthan. Since it drew support no less from the ruling class than from a popular following, it suffered the transitory nature of any religious order that depends on state authority.

NOTES

1. For details of Dadu's life and teachings, see W.G. Orr, *A Sixteenth Century Indian Mystic: Dadu and His Followers,* London: Latterworth Press, 1947 Jan Gopal, *Dadu Janma Lila Parichaya,* Jaipur: Mangal Press, 1949; and P.R. Chaturvedi, *Uttari Bharat ki Sant Parampara,* 2nd edn., Allahabad: Bharti Bhandar, 1964, pp. 488–501.
2. Mobad, *Dabistan-i Mazahib* (Persian MS), Kanpur: Munshi Newal Kishore, 1904, Chapter XII, p. 47.
3. *Gurudev Sakhis* 1 and 3; Orr, *A Sixteenth Century Indian Mystic,* p. 84.
4. *Gurudev, Sakhis* 123, 124, ibid., p. 63.
5. Ibid., p. 62.
6. Ibid., p. 74.
7. *Sabad* 34, *Piw Pichhan* 11, *Madhi* 17 and *Suratan,* 53, respectively, Orr, op. cit., pp. 72, 73, 74.
8. *Sach* 185, ibid., p. 74.
9. As cited by Orr, op. cit., p. 131.
10. *Pad* 395, ibid., p. 73.
11. Ibid., p. 141.

Dadu and His Followers 209

12. Ibid., p. 134.
13. Ibid., p. 140.
14. *The Sarbangi of Rajabdas*, ed. S. Iraqi, Aligarh: Granthayan, 1985, *Nipakh Madhi*, *Sakhi* 4, p. 415; Orr, op. cit., p. 62.
15. Ibid., p. 63.
16. Ibid.
17. *Sach, Sakhis* 98, 100, ibid., p. 62.
18. *Sach, Sakhis* 102–4, ibid., p. 166.
19. For details about the position and significance of these and other such compilations in different sectarian centres see Chapter 4.
20. *Pad* 296: 3 and *Sach Sakhi* 189, Orr, op. cit., pp. 74–5.
21. *Piw Pichhan* II, ibid., p. 74.
22. Ibid., p. 179.
23. Ibid., p. 138. According to Hindu philosophy, the caste into which a man is born is determined by the deeds done by him in previous life. Since Dadu rejected the caste system, his ideal of *karma* meant of the present life.
24. Ibid., p. 156.
25. Ibid., p. 157.
26. Ibid., pp. 167, 168.
27. Ibid., p. 169.
28. Ibid., p. 171.
29. Ibid., p. 177.
30. Ibid., p. 173.
31. Hymns 174, 206, ibid., p. 157.
32. Verses 152–9, Orr, op. cit., pp. 98–9.
33. Ibid., p. 173.
34. Hymn 338, ibid., p. 165.
35. Hymn 3, ibid., p. 166.
36. For these and other such references, ibid., pp. 182–3.
37. Ibid., p. 181.
38. Ibid., p. 178.
39. Ibid., p. 173.
40. Ibid., p. 184.
41. Ibid., p. 163.
42. Mobad, op. cit., p. 47.
43. *The Sarbangi of Rajjabdas*, ed. S. Iraqi, op. cit., *Sakhi* 13, p. 415.
44. Orr, op. cit., p. 30, Chapter 3.
    Of the gifts presented to Dadu, he kept nothing for himself. He asked for himself only simple food and shelter.
45. Jan Gopal, *Dadu Janma Lila Parichaya*, *Vishrams* 4–11.
46. For details about Akbar's meetings with these saints, S. Iraqi, 'Akbar's Relations with Non-Sufi Saints of India', *Islamic Heritage in South Asian Subcontinent*, vol. II, ed. Nazir Ahmad and I.H. Siddiqui, Jaipur: Publication Scheme, 2000, pp. 124, 125, 128–9.

47. According to Jan Gopal's account, Dadu and some of his disciples including Jan Goptal set out for Fatehpur Sikri in 1584 under the escort of Suja Kinchi. The company was received near the city by Raja Bhagwandas and taken to the Raja's house. Then the Emperor was informed, and by his orders Dadu was brought to the palace where Abul Fazl and Birbal conducted a preliminary interview. Impressed by Dadu's spiritual thought, both men reported to the Emperor and Dadu was then called into the royal presence, accompanied by Abul Fazl, Birbal, and Bhagwandas. After an exchange of greetings a long discussion took place on spiritual matters. The Emperor was impressed and wanted him to stay on and hold a further conversation with him. Abul Fazl suggested that Dadu be his guest; the same proposal was also extended by Raja Birbal, and finally it was agreed that Dadu should stay for a few days at the latter's house. Meanwhile, at the Raja's request, Dadu visited the *zanana* and the ladies of the house were delighted to meet him. Another meeting was arranged between Dadu and Akbar, in the presence of many other courtiers. Next morning Dadu was brought to the house of Raja Bhagwandas, where he was persuaded to stay for one more day. Next day, Dadu and his company of disciples set out for Amber, and Bhagwandas accompanied him to the outskirts of the city.
48. Quoted from *The Sarbangi of Rajjabdas*, ed. S. Iraqi, *anga* 40, hymn 6, p. 247.
49. V.A. Smith, *Akbar the Great Mughal (1542-1605)*, Delhi: S. Chand, 1958 (rpt. 1966), p. 119.
50. Narayandas, *Shri Dadupanth Parichaya*, Jaipur: Dadu Mahasabha, 1978-9, vol. 11, pp. 98-104.
51. Dadu Granthawali (based on a MS dated VS 1710/AD 1653), ed. P.R. Chaturvedi, Varanasi: Nagari Pracharini Sabha, 1966, pp. 130-1.
52. Ibid., p. 19.
53. Orr, op. cit., p. 37.
54. Narayandas, *Dadu*, vol.1, pp. 378-86.
55. Ibid., p. 396.

Another story is that Sundardas was on duty with the imperial forces at Kabul when a false rumour of his death reached his home. His wife, as a widow, committed herself to the flames. Recovering from his wounds and knowing this tragedy, the Rajput prince resolved not to return to Bikaner but to renounce the world by adopting the life of an ascetic. Laying his weapons at Dadu's feet, he became his disciple, though Dadu asked him to retain his arms and still remain his disciple. See, Orr, op. cit., Chapter IX, p. 189.

But the story, similar to that of Rajjabdas, is of a comparatively late origin. There is no reference to it in Jan Gopal's *Dadu Janma Lila Parichaya*. The story first appears in Raghava's *Bhaktamala*, which was written about half a century later. It seems to have been designed to

Dadu and His Followers 211

explain the later development of a branch of the Dadupanth into a body of armed ascetics. The Rajput warrior retaining his arms on his guru's instructions formed a link with the fighting Nagas who flourished under him and became prominent during Raghava's time.

However, Sundardas the younger (1596–1689) was another saint who returned from Kashi to Fatehpur in 1625. His father, Parmanand was a Khandelwal Mahajan of the Busar clan. The then Nawab of Fatehpur, descendant of Qayam Khan (a Chauhan Rajput converted to Islam some time in the fourteenth century) became a close friend of the saint. The local Mahajans built a house for his use with an underground *gufa* or cave. See *Sundar Granthawali*, ed. Purohit Hari Narayan, Calcutta: Rajasthan Research Society, 1939, vol. I, p. 65.

56. Orr, op. cit., p. 41.
57. For details about Hapaji, see Purohit Hari Narayan, op. cit., vol. 1, pp. 416–23.
58. Orr, op. cit., pp. 42–3.
59. The *Bhaktamala* of Ragho (Raghava) Das, written in 1713, records a visit paid to Gharibdas by Jahangir soon after his accession, in the course of a journey to Ajmer. If true, what transpired between the two is not known, but a *barahdari* (pillared courtyard) built on Jahangir's orders, and bearing on one of its walls a (now undecipherable) Persian inscription, is still visible at the Dwara. See Orr, op. cit., p. 185.
60. Among certain sections of Dadupanthis, there has been a continuous tradition of marriage from the very beginning, though these have never regarded themselves as *das* or *sevak*, but *sadhu*.
61. Orr, op. cit., p. 200.
62. Ibid., p. 193.
63. 'Naga' (Sanskrit, *nagna*, naked) was the generic name for all classes of armed ascetics (to be distinguished from the Naga tribe of Assam). The Naga never wore the sadhu's robe. He was recognized by his beard, his white shirt and *dhoti* with a leather belt around his waist, and by the sword or gun he usually carried. Displays of sword-fights remained for a long time a prominent feature of state entertainment in Jaipur. For an account of the Nagas, see Orr, op. cit., pp. 199–208.
64. Ibid., p. 200.
65. In adoption, it was necessary for the boy to be legally made over to the Panth, so that he might not be later claimed by his relatives. One of the essential features of the initiatory rite was the cutting of the *chutiya* (tuft of hair on the crown of the head) so as not to be identified either as Hindu or as Muslim. The practice generally was to adopt boys from 'clean' humble castes, from whose hands water may be drunk: Jat (cultivator), Gujar (cattle raiser), Mali (gardener) and the agricultural section of the Kumhar (potter) caste. Orr, op. cit., pp. 221–2.
66. Ibid., p. 202.

67. Ibid., p. 202. The details about Mangaldas are not known. He is said to have been associated with Sundardasa's Thamba of Ghatra, and was an influential member. Memorial stones erected in the memory of Mangaldas and others are still found on the place of encounter.
68. Ibid., p. 203.
69. Vasudev Sharma reproduces some written orders from the Jaipur rulers authorizing the specific support of the troops. See his *Sant Kavi Dadu aur Unka Panth*, Delhi, 1969, p. 235.
70. Orr, op. cit., p. 203.
71. Ibid., p. 204.
72. The letter, dated 'Camp, Jaipur, 3 August 1858', is in the possession of the Udaipur clan of Jaipur Nagas. It reads thus: 'I desire to record my testimony to the excellent and praiseworthy conduct of Chiman Dass and the *bhundarees* or heads of the Oodeypore clan of Nagas, as well indeed as of the whole body of them during the past convulsion. They formed a part of the field force sent with me towards Delhi in 1857 and behaved right well. The Nagas, indeed, together with the Rajput horse, were those on whom I could alone most perfectly rely when the Artillery men and Infantry began to leave me and desert at Pulwul. Chimandas and his fellow-leaders are well-behaved men and well-disposed to our foot, while they display a laudable allegiance to their chief and master. I take this opportunity to record my sense of their good and faithful conduct, and my personal satisfaction with their service, as well as with the *jamaut* or clan generally, and trust the Maharaja and durbar authorities will promote their interest as occasion may offer'. Orr, op. cit., pp. 205–6.
73. Ibid., p. 206.
74. There is no positive evidence, but the general practice seems to have been for a household of five to supply one member for duty at the *tahsil* and to keep a second in reserve to replace him whenever needed.
75. Narayandas, op. cit., vol. II, pp. 856–7.

CHAPTER 8

Maharashtra Dharma

The Maharashtra Dharma was a part of Bhakti movement. It emerged as a reform movement from the fold of Hinduism, for socio-religious readjustment in order to achieve a better social position for the lower class of people. It was the cult of Vitthal or Vithoba which evolved at Pandharpur in late thirteenth century and subsequently became popular in all of Maharashtra, Andhra Pradesh, and Tamil Nadu. The cult was greatly under the influence of the Nathpanthis, since the founder, Gyandev or Gyaneshwar, who was originally a Shaiva, claimed to be the spiritual descendant of Gorakhnath.[1] But this seems to be simply a spiritual tribute, since all the 'nine Naths' including Gorakhnath remained throughout in northern India, and lived in times much before Gyandev. Their influence reached western India by the end of the thirteenth century through Gorakh's later disciples and influenced Gyandev and his followers.

Gyandev seems to have become a devotee of Krishna of the *Bhagavad Gita*, on which he composed his famous versified commentary, the *Gyaneshwari*, in Marathi some time between 1290 and 1298.[2] But the conception of *premabhakti* outlined in the *Gyaneshwari* is very far from the concept that appears in the *Bhagavata Purana* with the realization of the erotic relationship between Krishna and the gopis of Braj, or between the divine pair, Radha–Krishna. This erotic perception was, in fact, unknown to the Maharashtrian tradition.

The cult was led by Sant poets who generally belonged to the lower strata of society, such as Kunbis, tailors, carpenters, potters, gardeners, barbers and even the outcaste Mahars. They challenged the religious monopoly of the Brahmans and took over the spiritual leadership. This inevitably caused a conflict with the upper classes.

The cult was initially spiritual and liberal. Namdev (1269–1344),

Eknath (1537-98), and Tukaram (1609-50) stood for simple and high-quality worship based on love and devotion. This made it a mass movement. The supreme efficacy of devotional love (*bhava bhakti*) over all other methods of nearness to God became the creed. The best sacrifice was to surrender to the will of God and claim nothing as one's own. The best mortification is that which makes the spirit humble. Neither knowledge nor yogic power, health nor wealth, nor heaven nor even *mukti* (salvation), is desirable in itself. What is desirable is to be always full of love for God and His works, including all creation, men and animals. The movement stressed moral values and considered both ignorance and having much knowledge as misleading. Eknath declared that 'knowledge without love is of no use', and Tukaram asserted that 'God is more with those who are simple and faithful than learned'.[3]

Namdev or Nama was a calico-printer at Pandharpur. He is mentioned by Kabir together with Jaydev as a great saint.[4] His sayings are contained in the *Guru Granth* and the *Panchavani*. Namdev's hymns in Marathi and Hindi are marked by deep Bhakti and contain elements which provided a base for the Nirguna Bhakti movement in northern India. His devotion centres on the name of Ram. The saint extolled the greatness of Satguru without naming any human guru. Eknath was a Brahman but was regarded as an ideal saint being called as *mahatma* or great soul. Tukaram was an agriculturist Kumbi by caste and a grocer by profession. It is said that he returned a present consisting of gold, silver, and jewels sent by Shivaji, with the remark that gold and dust were of the same value for a real saint.

At the same time, however, there emerged another important holy person named Guru Ramdas (b. 1608), whose attitude was quite different towards regional powers and the cult during the time of Tukaram and Ramdas divided into two schools, the Varkari and the Dharkari.

Apart from the four varnas, society in western India included several jatis the Kunbis, Mahars, Malis, Sonars, Lohars, Bhils, Kolis, Gujarati and Marwari Baniyas. There were also Muslims. Besides this, an effective socio-economic structure prevailed in Maharashtra, known as the *watandar* system which provided the base for the Maratha feudal order. The *watan* in Maharashtra was

Maharashtra Dharma 215

a state grant given to a person who held a certain office or rendered a service to the state.[5]

The equivalent of *watandar* was *desaka*. The Turko–Afghan conquerors of the Deccan recognized the importance of the desakas and retained the system by calling them *watandars*. The big *watandars* of Maharashtra hailed mainly from the brahmans and high caste Marathas. But there was a network of *watandars* ranging from the Chhatrapati, Peshwa, Sardar, Saranjandar and Mokasadar to Deshmukh, Patil, Deshpande and Kulkarni, which constituted a hierarchy of oppressive and exploiting elements in the Maratha feudal structure.[6]

It is, of course, true that there were political and administrative factors that helped the rise of Maratha power. The Mughal conquest of Ahmadnagar, Bijapur, and Golkunda demolished the triple wall system that had insulated the Marathas. This naturally tilted the political balance in the Deccan in favour of the Marathas.[7] Moreover, the jagirdari crisis faced by the Mughals proved helpful to the Marathas in their opposition to Mughals.[8] This crisis coincided with the disintegration of the Mughal empire and the rise of Maratha political power.

Besides, peasant discontent against the oppressive Mughal taxation supported the Maratha upheaval. With reference to Bhimsen's memoirs, Irfan Habib explained the connection between the rise of Maratha power and the rebellious attitude of the oppressed peasantry in the imperial territories. The Mughal court was often shocked to see Maratha peasants joining the *watandars* with arms and horses.[9] That the Maratha uprising had a mass base was conceded by Aurangzeb: he decried the Deccan peasantry for backing the 'robbers' and plunderers (the Marathas).[10] At the same time, the religious sentiments of Maratha peasantry were also provoked by the battle cry, 'Har Har Mahadev'.

Thus, religion with other factors played a role in the rise of Maratha political power. M.G. Ranade, G.S. Sardesai, P.V. Ranade, and Satish Chandra have discussed the Maharashtra Dharma as a contributory factor in the rise of Maratha power.[11] But the conclusions drawn by them either that the Maratha political revolution was caused by a religious movement[12] or that it 'provided only a favourable backdrop (of social unity) for the emergence of the Maratha power',[13] do not fully justify the case. V.K. Rajwade has also expressed similar opinion by saying that the ideas of Maharashtra Dharma stirred the Marathas to political independence, though he defines the *dharma* as *jaishnu* or aggressive Hinduism as against the rest of the Hindus whom he calls *sahishnu* or tolerant Hinduism.[14] This indicates that Maratha society was divided and that political issues had the support of not the whole but only a part of it. The mentioned above scholars have ignored the basic fact that the Maharashtra Dharma was then divided into two and that it was only the Varkari section that served the political cause of the Maratha *watandars*. The Varkaris sought to retain much of the old Bhagavata spirit and remained Vaishnava monotheists. They did not function as a sect but as a fraternity of pious lay people.

While the first section under Tukaram maintained passive devotion, the second led by Ramdas took an active aggressive form. Thus, when Tukaram was preaching the gospel of love, peace, and devotion his contemporary Ramdas taught the Marathas the formal worship of Rama, Hanuman, and Bhawani, and urged them to drive the foreign Muslim rulers out of the country. He aimed to liberate the Hindus from bondage and to save Hinduism, citing examples of the battle between Ram and Ravan as a *Dharamyuddh*.[15] This led the Marathas to make politics and even warfare a part of religious obligation.

Ramdas was a practical, straightforward and outspoken religio-political leader. It is said that he had toured widely. As we have seen, he met Hargobind Singh in Srinagar in Garhwal in about 1634 and was very much convinced with his idea of taking up arms. Ramdas finally settled at Chafal in the district of Satara, where he built a temple and founded a separate creed. He was the founder of the cult, involved in politics and not only spiritual teacher but also the political advisor of Shivaji. He led a movement for religious regeneration and systematically organized his order by establishing *maths* throughout Maharashtra. He called for *jaishnu* (aggressive) Hinduism as against *sahishnu* Hinduism in order to build up a political class of his followers and provide communal strength to the political leaders.

The *Dasbodh* (Awareness of Slavery) is the main work of Ramdas. It is divided into twenty chapters, each being sub-divided into ten sections.[16] The work contains a vast knowledge of sciences and arts. It also constitutes a code of conduct for his followers to be maintained both in private and public life. The *Dasbodh* is considered as one of the four Marathi Vedas, the others being Gyandev's *Gyaneshwari*, Eknath's *Bhagwat* and Tukaram's *Gatha*, though the spirit and the contents of the first are quite different. It is also regarded as a gospel of *karmayoga* (exercise of duty) and its author as a *Karmayogi*.

However, Ramdas is more famous for his poetic work. His *Ramayana* is full of vigour and rhetoric. Its *Yuddh Kanda* is specially important for its passionate appeal and for the glorification of the war waged by Ram against Ravan for a just cause.[17] Besides, a number of miscellaneous *abhangas* are also attributed to Ramdas. His hymns in praise of Bhawani and Maruti are extremely passionate and could awaken and activate the Maratha people in the struggle for the freedom. It is significant that his miscellaneous writings also constitute enough source material for analysing and re-writing the contemporary history of Maharashtra.[18]

Ramdas left his native Godavari region, for the land further south, on the banks of the Krishna. It is also possible that he was invited there by Shahaji Raje. The temple at Chafal was constructed in 1648, and it became the central place of the Ramdasi cult.[19] Masur in the vicinity of Chafal was a Bhosla fief. Ramnavami day was for the first time celebrated in Masur in 1645, and from 1648 onwards it was regularly celebrated in Chafal.

Ramdas was personally keen to establish *maths* in order to increase the strength for the struggle for an independent Maratha Raj. He is said to have established, according to one version, 800 and, according to another, 1,100 monasteries throughout the country,[20] of which 72 were important. Each had a temple of Ram and Hanuman with an attached *akhara*. Ramdas urged that such institutions, small or big, should be established everywhere.

The first eleven monasteries along with temples were constructed at Chafal, Shinganwadi, Majgaon, Umbaraj, Masur, Shahapur, Bahegaon, Shirale, Pargaon, Manpadale, and Bhorgaon, all situated on the road from Wai to Panhala. Besides, he deputed disciples and had followers in Karnataka, Konkan, Gujarat, Nagpur, Gomantaka, Tilangana, Malyal, Odya, Gokarna, Rameshvar, Somnath, Dwarka, Puri, Ujjain, Ayodhya, Kashi, Mathura and Badrikedar.[21]

People assembled in large number every evening at every *math* where the sermons propounded by Ramdas in his *Dasbodh* were delivered by the deputed monk. Besides, in the *akhara* attached to the temple, the youths of surrounding areas were taught the arts of warfare. They were engaged to develop their muscles and learn the use of the stick, spear, and sword.[22] The main mission of these *maths* was to build physical and moral strength and to inspire people to cooperate with Shivaji in his war. However, it was not the Maharashtra Dharma as a whole, as stated by V.K. Rajwade, but only the section under Ramdas that included four obligatory elements, *Deva-Shastrachara* (using of weapons like God), (2) *Deshachara* (local practices), (3) *Kulachara* (family affairs) and (4) *Jatyachara* (caste practices). The followers were required to follow all these practices.[23]

Ramdas had a large number of followers. Men associated with Shivaji had become members of the Ramdasi Sect. With this large following Ramdas was capable of turning public opinion in shaping the political future of Maharashtra.

It is significant that Ramdas admitted disciples mainly from the upper classes, because he wished to have an intelligent group of followers who could devote themselves to his cause with full commitment and could willingly sacrifice their lives as and when needed.[24] They had to take an oath of a life-long celibacy and like him sever all connection with their family. Ramdas was a religious leader who believed not in destiny but in direct action. He has emphasized the importance of effort thus:

यत्न तो देव जाणावा। अंतरी धरितां बरें।

(Effort should be regarded as God, and held within the heart.[25])

Ramdas repeatedly expressed the conviction that destiny is determined by action. If someone worked hard in the right direction, he would become immortal, a self-made God, since he is already an image of God. The divine qualities exist in every man in a dormant condition; realizing this, he should awaken such divinity in himself for the welfare of the country and the people. धर्मो धारयते प्रजा.[26] Thus, the concept of domination of action over destiny not only provided a practical base to the cult of Ramdas but also inspired his

Maharashtra Dharma 219

followers to be actively involved in his mission of religio-political activities.

The Varkaris were devotees of Vithoba whom they regarded as an incarnation of Buddha, a symbol of peace and love. Since these qualities were passive virtues, Ramdas considered them inconsistent with the prevalent situation. Such thoughts could not activate people to take up arms or fight for their rights. For that, faith in *Bhagwat-dharma* and worship of Vitthal was needed, to unite the Hindus of different castes in Maharashtra and create a bond of fellowship among them.[27]

Ramdas often compares Aurangzeb with Ravan and gives the call, 'Let the Hindus awaken and worship Ram, instead of Vithoba', who had killed Ravan and conquered Lanka with the help of Hanuman.[28] He urged his followers to worship Ram and Hanuman. Following their glorious examples, the people should regenerate Hinduism and cultivate the strength to liberate Maharashtra from foreign rule. Ramdas emphasized the need to worship goddess Kalika Bhawani, symbol of power and strength, who had killed seven demons.

Ramdas emphasized the idea that the Marathas should not resort to the Rajput way of burning their women folk after defeat. They should neither be afraid of a defeat nor be ashamed of it, because that would provide a chance for another effort to uproot the Mohammedan power.[29] This practical approach seems to have led the Marathas to adopt guerilla warfare against the Mughal forces. The Marathas were simple, with limited resources and desires. They had nothing to lose and everything to gain by war. This practical aspect of life gave them courage.

Ramdas spoke of politics in terms of religion. Shivaji raised the status of Marathi as a court language in place of Persian. His character and career can be judged by the fact that, like Ramdas, he too was a believer of goddess Bhawani. He had direct inspiration from Her, and in all hardships of his life he was guided by what this inspiration suggested to him.

As his chief advisor, Ramdas suggested that Shivaji should not confine his political ideology within Maharashtra but extend it over the country as *Hindu Rashtra.* He is also reported to have 'exhorted Shivaji's son, Sambhaji, to follow the footsteps of his father', and the advice that he gave him on this occasion has been summed up in two sentences: 'Unite all who are Maratha together' and 'Propagate the Dharma of Maharashtra.'[30] It is significant that this 'dharma' was not Vedic or the Puranic or even the traditional Maharashtra Dharma, but a quite different order, one that Ramdas often called Bhagvat Dharma or religion of action.

The first phase underlines the need of a powerful leadership to organize the political movement, and the second one highlights the political significance of the spread of the religious movement to cover the whole country. The question arises as to what the motive of Ramdas was in recommending the second feature of Shivaji's policy, and exhorting Sambhaji to propagate the *dharma* of Maharashtra. The idea was, in fact, deemed by the saint a remedy for problems that had arisen under the grave misgovernance of Sambhaji during the closing years of the seventeenth century. That, there was thus a close connection between religious and political upheaval in Maharashtra on the one hand and that there was a double character to the movement, on the others is important.

Ramdas was politically motivated to unite the Marathas on religious grounds. In the same process, the theory of 'Aurangzeb's religious persecution' was also made the talk of the town. It was a part of a larger movement of social and literary revival that was carried on very effectively by Ramdas and his followers.

A sense of cultural unity and identity had developed among the Marathas even before Shivaji. The use of Marathi as a single common language created an atmosphere for the development of a common regional consciousness. Besides, hostility at least among a section of the Marathas towards the Mughal ruling class was also working in Maharashtra which was surrounded by Muslim states from both sides. Shivaji was shrewd enough to exploit the situation. That he appealed to the religious sentiments and pride of the Marathas is evident from a number of contemporary documents.[31] Bhusan's laudatory verses equate Shivaji with Indian epic heroes and credit him with having saved Hinduism from extinction.[32] Not only Shivaji but also all other *watandars* up to Baji Rao II made the fullest use of religion and exploited the people by provoking their religious sentiments. The call of 'Maratha *rajya*' often made by Maratha statesmen was followed by the call of *Hindavi Swaraj*. This was practically motivated to provide a favourable background for the emergence of Maratha political power by infusing a strong current of militant Hindu revivalism in the minds of Maratha people. The *dharma* of Ramdas was truly militant. Ramdas defines it as a political rival to Turko–Afghan Mughal rule. In a violent outburst, he calls upon the Marathas:

मुलुख बुडवावा की बडवावा। धर्म स्थापनेसाठी।।
मरितां मरितां मरावें। तेणें गतीस पावावें।।
फिरोनि येतां मोगावें। महद भाग्य।।
मराठा तितुका मेलवावा। आपुला महाराष्ट्र धर्म बाढवावा।।

The land should either be drowned or trodden upon for the establishment of dharma. One should die while killing (enemies) and attain salvation, and enjoy great glory on rebirth. All Marathas should be united under one command with a mission to spread Maharashtra Dharma.[33]

In his *Anandavana Bhuvana*, a compilation of his verses, Ramdas declared the vision of a strong independent Hindustan being realized in his lifetime: 'A great evil has fallen upon the *Mlecchas* (Muslims). God has become the partisan of the virtuous in the *Anandavana Bhuvana* (region of bliss). Hindustan has waxed strong.'[34]

Such words were directed not against the Muslim community as such but the Mughal government under Aurangzeb. So Ramdas cannot be called communal. Shivaji's confrontation with the Mughals was not based on religious matters but for political considerations. The social relations between Hindu and Muslim in Maharashtra remained cordial, and the communal hatred was nonexistent in his time.[35]

Political considerations forced the Maratha leaders to maintain the traditions of religious tolerance and accommodation. There is sufficient evidence that Shivaji welcomed Muslims in his state. The court proceedings of 1567 lists the names of Muslim qazis who received regular salaries. Shivaji recruited many of the Muslims in his army. The first unit was a group of 700 Pathans who had left Bijapur after the treaty with the Mughals. Sidi Ibrahim was a trusted commander in Shivaji's army. Similarly, Noor Khan Beg was one of his closest confidants.[36]

The Maratha *watandars* exploited popular Hindu feelings with the use of *dharma*. They also exploited the sentiments of the peasants in order to gain active support against the Mughals, who were committing various kinds of oppression. This in fact was an argument in favour of the Marathas' own exactions, which constituted a kind legalized plunder. The Maratha sardars crossed the boundaries of their homeland to collect *chauth* and *sardeshmukhi* with the Mughal imperial seal.

The relationship between Shivaji and Ramdas was political, and they had become necessary for each other. In his political mission Ramdas provided not only moral support and a philosophical base but also physical strength. His preaching effected the unification of Maratha power, which had scattered in small units. Political advantage of this situation was taken by Shivaji who ultimately succeeded in establishing an independent power. He declared himself as a Hindu ruler in 1674 and died in the same capacity in 1680. It was under the influence of Guru Ramdas that Shivaji had to say that this was 'not his kingdom but it belonged to Hinduism' and that 'it was a *Hindawi Swaraj* and the king was merely the protector of Hinduism'.[37]

NOTES

1. M.G. Ranade, *The Rise of the Maratha Power*, Bombay: Bombay University, 1961, pp. 81–5.
2. *Gyaneshwari*, ed. V.K. Rajvade, Bombay, 1990. Some *abhangas* (lyrical hymns) and the *Amritanubhav* are also attributed to Gyandev.
3. Ranade, op. cit., pp. 87–92.
4. Cf. *Pads* 48.1, 198.4, *Kabir Granthawali*, ed. P.N. Tiwari, Prayag: Hindi Parishad, 1961, pp. 28, 115. For a life sketch of Namdev and his sayings, M.A. Macauliffe, *The Sikh Religion*, rpt., Delhi: Low Price Pubs., 1993, vol. VI, pp. 17–76 and pp. 69–70. Namdev's song speaks of an idol broken by the Turks, which seems to have been in the context of Alauddin Khalji's attack on Deogir. Namdev, though often taken as Gyandev's contemporary, belonged to the fourteenth century. He is said to have travelled in northern India, specially in Panjab.
5. See A.R. Kulkarni, *Maharashtra in the Age of Shivaji*, Poona: Deshmukh Prakashan, 1969, pp. 28–31.
6. Feudalism has been well defined by S. Nurul Hasan, *Thoughts on Agrarian Relations in Mughal India*, rpt., Delhi: People's Publishing House, 1990, pp. 1–8.

   Agriculture being the major source of production all the social classes

related to the Maratha agrarian system, *mirasdars, uparis, balutedars* and *inamdars*, were also theoretically known as *watandars*. But the *watandars* as a whole represented a feudal class which lived on the appropriation of the rural surplus. Among them were intermediaries between the peasants and the higher *watandars*. P.V. Ranade, 'Feudal Content of Maharashtra Dharma', *The Indian Historical Review*, vol. 1, no. 1, 1974, pp. 45–6.
7. Ibid., p. 47.
8. The *jagirdari* crisis was caused by the failure of the Mughal state to maintain a balance between income and expenditure. The available surplus realized by the state was insufficient to meet the costs of administration. See Satish Chandra, *Parties and Poitics at the Mughal Court (1707-1740)*, 4th edn., Delhi: People's Publishing House, 2002, pp. XII–XVII.
9. Irfan Habib, *The Agrarian System of Mughal India, 1556-1707*, Bombay: Asia Publishing House, 1963, pp. 347–9.
10. Ibid., p. 350.
11. Ranade, *Rise of the Maratha Power*, pp. 78-92; . G.S. Sardesai, *The Main Currents of Maratha History*, rev. edn., Bombay: Phoenix Publications, 1949; pp. 14–18. P.V. Ranade, 'Feudal Content of Maharashtra Dharma', op. cit., no. 1, pp. 44–50; and Satish Chandra, op. cit., p. 29.
12. M.G. Ranade, op. cit., p. 92; Satish Chandra, op. cit., p. 29.
13. P.V. Ranade 'Feudal Content', p. 44.
14. Ibid., p. 48.
15. N.K. Behere, *The Background of Maratha Renaissance in the 17th Century*, Bangalore, 1946, p. 166.
16. It seems that the *Dasbodh* originally contained only seven chapters which were later revised and enlarged into twenty chapters by the author. This impression comes from the words, शब्दाची आला ग्रंथाचा रोवट, which occur at the end of the seventeenth chapter, ibid., Behere, pp. 167–8.
17. Ibid., p. 168.
18. Ibid., p. 168
19. Ibid., p. 160.
20. Sardesai, op. cit., p. 61; Behere, op. cit., p. 160.
21. Ibid., p. 161.
22. Ibid., p. 62; Behere, op. cit., p. 160.
23. As cited by G.S. Sardesai, op. cit., p. 18.
24. Behere, op. cit., p. 160.
25. Ibid., p. 161.
26. Ibid., pp. 161–2.
27. Ibid., p. 163.
28. Ibid., p. 164.
29. Ibid., p. 167.
30. M.G. Ranade, op. cit., p. 78.
31. P.V. Ranade, op. cit., p. 49.

The passion for 'Hindavi Swaraj' forced Shivaji to admire Akbar for his tolerance and broad mindedness. This is evident from his letter to Aurangzeb protesting against his reimposition of *jijya* in 1679.
32. Ibid., p. 49.
33. As cited Behere, *The Background,* p. 165.
34. As cited by P.V. Ranade, op. cit., p. 49.
35. N.K. Behere, op. cit., p. 165.
36. For more details G.S. Sardesai, op. cit., p. 69.
37. P.V. Ranade op. cit., p. 169.

CHAPTER 9

The Pranami Sect

The Pranami or Prannathi Sect was founded by Prannath (1618–94), a kshatriya by caste, at Panna in Bundelkhand.[1] He was a reformer and a champion of Hindu–Muslim unity. At the same time he was also a political figure. In 1653–5 he was the Diwan of Dholpur state. At one stage there occurred an ideological conflict between Prannath and Aurangzeb, and he was inclined to send a letter to the emperor to clarify his position, but that did not materialize.[2]

Prannath was also a scholar. He was not only well acquainted with the Vedas and the Upanishads but also had a good knowledge of the Quran and the Bible. His most important work is *Kulzum Swaroop* or *Sharif*, compiled just after his death in 1694 by one of his disciples named Keshavadas. This is a voluminous work comprising fourteen treatises, all of which are composed in verse and in different dialects of Hindi, Gujarati, and Sindhi. The treatises are written in Devanagari script, but the themes and the vocabulary are mainly drawn from Persian and Arabic sources.[3]

The *Kulzum Sharif* is a valuable source for the seventeenth century. It forms a current of medieval Bhakti literature that reflects the basic unity among different religions like Islam, Christianity, Judaism, and Hinduism. The unity of thought in ideological matters as contained in different religious scriptures is successfully drawn by Prannath with references from the Quran and the Vedas frequently quoted together.

While emphasizing the unity of religions (*Wahdat-i Adyan* or *Sarva Dharm Sambhava*), Prannath defines a Satguru as one who holds together all religions.[4] In the *Khulasa* treatise of the *Kulzum*, he goes to the extent of declaring:

जे कुछ कहया कतेब, सोई कहया बेद ।

(Whatever is said by the Quran, is said by the Vedas)

There is 'only a difference of name and ritual; Khuda and Brahma are the same'.[5]

It was due to this liberal and egalitarian outlook that Prannath was held in high esteem by Hindus and Muslims alike. A Muslim historian, Mohammad Murtaza Husain calls him a Muslim saint in the garb of the Hindus.[6] درویشی از مسلمانان در لباس هنود

At death he was buried, not cremated. His followers are Hindus and Muslims who keep away from social and religious distinctions by believing that the God of all religions is one and the same. They live and eat together and remain critical of idol worship, caste distinctions and the supremacy of the Brahmans. Like the Sikhs, the Kabirpanthis and the Dadupanthis, the followers of the Pranami Sect have no idol in their centres, only a copy of the founder's work (*Kulzum Sharif*) which they use to recite daily.

Prannath was not only a spiritual leader but also a political figure with a vision for Bundelkhand. He is also said to have maintained correspondence with Raja Jaswant Singh and Rana Raj Singh in 1674 asking their support for his *Dharmayuddh* against the Mughals. Having failed in all such efforts, he left Delhi for Bundelkhand in 1675 and made friends with Chhatrasal Bundela, Raja of Panna, who had since 1671 been a rebel against Mughal rule. The meeting between the two is said to have held in 1683 at Mau, near Chhatarpur in Madhya Pradesh.

In his work Prannath gives a considerable account of the political developments of his time. In the *Kirantan* treatise of his *Kulzum*, a separate account of the political career of Maharaja Chhatrasal Bundela has been provided, in which his policy of 'nationalism' and 'militarism' against Mughal rule is appreciated and encouraged. The enthusiasm with which Prannath condemned Aurangzeb as anti-Hindu, outlining the need to counter his actions, appears to be directed to divert the public opinion in favour of Chhatrasal and to inspire the people to cooperate with him in his crusade against the Mughals. Besides, as we have seen earlier, the biographical literature in the form of different *Bitaks* also provides a detailed account of career of Prannath and Chhatrasal and refers to political events of the time.[7]

Prannath inspired and even provoked the Hindus against Aurangzeb, referring to his religious persecution. He called upon Hindu kings and chiefs to unite and organize on religious grounds under Chhatrasal. 'O Rajas, Ranas and Raots, the religion is in danger. Run to its rescue.' He said, 'The swords of the Kshatriyas seem to have been broken. . . . The Turks are gaining the upper hand.' Further, 'In the three *Lokas* (worlds) the land of *Bharata* is *uttam* and in that the Hindu religion is supermost. (But) the crowned heads of the land are lowered in shame.'

'The Bundela Chhatrasal has heard the appeal. He has come forward sword in hand and has taken this task upon his head. God has marked him to be the general and the leader.'[8] This was a clear departure in spirit from his earlier stand on the unity of religions and was politically motivated. Prannath was obviously not against Muslims but against the Mughal ruling class. As a result, he created a strong public opinion in favour of Chhatrasal. A large number of people of the region, including his own followers, joined the army of Chhatrasal. Prannath himself remained associated with the army in order to boost the morale of his soldiers. In fact, Prannath and Chhatrasal were the product of similar circumstances, and struggled for the same cause, political independence for Bundelkhand. Having met, they proved to be helpful to, even inevitable for, each other. After the meeting there came a definite turn in the policy of Chhatrasal against the Mughals.[9]

Prannath was not only the source of inspiration and strength for Chhatrasal but also his philosopher and guide.[10] It was he who suggested Chhatrasal make Panna his capital, and by conferring the title of Maharaja on Chhatrasal, he crowned him. Prannath is said to have removed Chhatrasal's financial problems by informing him of the diamond mines near Panna.

Thus Prannath played almost the same role for Chhatrasal in Bundelkhand as was played by Ramdas for Shivaji in Maharashtra. Hostility towards Mughal rule was already working in the minds of both the saints, and Shivaji, and Chhatrasal made the fullest use of this situation and exploited these leaders and their followers. Consequently, while in their spiritual capacity they took up the cause of communal harmony, in political matters they adopted a different attitude and exploited the religious prejudice against the Mughals if not the Muslim community as such.

This dual stand explains how the peace-loving holy men and their spiritual movements can become political and even militant. The theory of the comparative universality of Hinduism with other religions like Islam and Christianity, as expressed in Prannath's *Kayamat Nama* and Ramdas's *Anandvanabhuvana*, was, in its practical form, a political instrument. It changed the nature and scope of their movements from reformist to revivalist. The infusion of a strong militant Hindu revivalism was also deliberately made to provide a favourable background for getting regional political independence for themselves and their political heads. However, the effort to divide the society of Bundelkhand along communal lines for political reasons failed, and even the followers of Prannath, who hailed from both the communities, remained intact in the sect. They still live and eat together without religious distinction.

NOTES

1. For details about Prannath's life and work, *The Bitak of Laldas*, ed. Matabadal Jaiswal, Bankura, 1966; *The Bitak of Braj Bhushan*, ed. K.D. Sharma, Jamnagar: Pranami Dharm Sabha, 1931; Bhagwandas Gupta, *Maharaja Chatrasal Bundela*, Agra, 1958, pp. 104–13; and Shahabuddin Iraqi, 'Historical Importance of the Literature of Prannami Sect', *Islamic Culture*, Hyderabad, vol. LXXV, no. 4, 2001, pp. 97–104.
2. *The Bitak of Laldas*, op. cit., Chapter 32, pp. 5, 10, 38.
3. The original manuscript of *Kulzum Sharif* is preserved at the Dhami Mandir in Bundelkhand and a number of copies are found at different centres of the Pranami Sect. It was edited by Matabadal Jaiswal and published by Balamiji in Bankura, 1965.
4. Prannath, *Kulzum, Kirantan*, v. 4.
5. Ibid., *Khulasa,* Canto 12, v. 38.

 Prannath says that Hindus and Muslims are devotees of the same God. He condemns the false ego of the people of both communities: 'The Brahmans say that they are superior and Muslims hold themselves pious. But they are no better than a handful of dust *rakh* or *khaq*', ibid., *Sanandh,* Canto 40, v. 42.

6. Mohammad Murtaza Husain, *Hadiqat-ul Akalim,* Lucknow: Matba-i Nami, 1879, p. 669.
7. For details of the Bitak literature, Chapter 4 above.
8. Prannath, *Kulzum, Kirantan,* Canto 58, vv. 1, 2, 4, 16, 20.
9. Prannath, op. cit., *Kirantan,* Section 57; *The Bitak of Braj Bhushan*, op. cit., pp. 445–6; Gupta, op. cit., pp. 106–7.
10. Gupta, op. cit., p. 107.

CHAPTER 10

The Satnami Sect of Narnaul

The Satnami Sect of Narnaul occupies a prominent place in the religious and political history of India during the seventeenth century. It was in 1672 that the Satnamis revolted against Aurangzeb, and to date now all our assessment of them has been based on the Persian historians, like Ishwardas Nagar, Saqi Mustaid Khan, Khafi Khan, and Sadiq Khan, all hostile critics of the movement. Therefore, as in the case of many other sects of the time, there is much obscurity with regard to the origin and development of the Satnami Sect. The Persian authors present the Satnamis as rebels who suddenly broke out in 1672 against Aurangzeb.[1] On the other hand, the modern historians of Mughal economic history such as Irfan Habib have tried to characterize the Satnami uprising as a peasant revolt.[2]

It appears from a Satnami text entitled *Pothi Gyan Bani*[3] that it as neither a sudden outbreak in 1672 nor a peasant uprising as such, but a well planned sectarian revolt, as the Satnamis had already been organized as a sect in 1657 (or about fifteen years before their famous rebellion).

Before proceeding to deal with the ideas of the Satnami Sect, it is important to discuss the date of its origin.[4] The date assigned to the founding of the sect by modern scholars is 1543. This is based on an erroneous identification of the Narnaul Satnamis with the Sadh Sect founded by Bir Bhan.[5] That the Sadh and the Satnami are one and the same, however, is not plausible, since by nature and ideas both stand distinct from each other. The date clearly stated in the Satnami manuscript itself for the foundation of the sect is Baisakh, Samvat 1714, corresponding to AD 1657.[6] There is sufficient reason to accept this date, as the statement of the contemporary historians that the number of Satnamis at the time of rebellion was about 'five thousand' suggests that some time had passed since the foundation of the sect.

With regard to the founder of the sect, the *Pothi Gyan Vani* describes the arrival of the Satguru 'from Poorakh (i.e. God)' in the 'country of Narnaul'.[7] It speaks of his appearance as an 'attack' on the seditious Hindus and Turks (Mughals) alike in order to establish the Satnami Panth.[8] No further details are provided in the work either on the founder of the sect or on its initial development. The Persian chronicles, of course, have much to say, but their accounts of the Satnamis are confined to the time when they took to rebellion. At that time, there are said to have been 'some four or five thousand (Satnami) householders in the pargana of Narnaul and Mewat', who were organized under the spiritual leadership of Gharibdas.[9]

The Satnamis are also often referred to by the Persian authors as 'Mundiyas'[10] who 'dress like mendicants, yet their livelihood and profession is mostly agriculture and trade in the manner of tradesmen with small capital'.[11] Regarding the composition of the sect, Mustaid Khan declares that this was a 'destitute rebellious gang of goldsmiths, carpenters, sweepers, tanners, and other mean and ignoble men of artisan castes'.[12] Khafi Khan states that 'living according to the ways of their own community [they] aspire to reach the status of a good name (*nek-nam*), which is the meaning of the word Satnam'. At the same time, he alleges that they were armed and 'did not tolerate any oppression upon them as a display of courage or authority'.[13] On the other hand, raising objections on certain so-called practices of the Satnamis, Ishwardas Nagar, a non-Muslim historian, condemns even their idea of Hindu–Muslim unity.[14]

The Satnami literature disapproves of communal differences and caste distinctions within the sect. A code of conduct with certain rules and regulations is laid down in the text. The provision of punishment indicates that these rules must have been strictly followed within the sect. The commandments declared to compel adherence to the sect and its beliefs and to make followers conform with the rules of Panth,[15] suggest that the sect inculcated a great sense of community interest and group consciousness. In order to boost the morale and courage of the members, the following commandments were declared: 'Never tell a lie', 'nor give damnatory evidence'; 'have no dread of necromancy, neither have recourse to it'; 'neither spread your hand nor bow your head before anyone for any purpose'; 'nor (even) accept charity or gifts from kings and others'; 'do not join the service of those who force you to do what they want'; 'let the tongue be employed in God's praise and not others'.[16] The faithful were also asked, to be 'content with what they possess by having self control', and were prohibited from 'the habit of seizing the wealth or property of others either by force or by cheating or theft'.[17]

Similarly, there is compassion for the poor. 'Neither inflict any harm on the poor, nor do anything which is harmful to others'; 'do not kill any innocent for wealth, nor commit any violence on your part, nor even think in these terms'.[18] But a curious distinction between the conduct expected within the community and outside is shown by the commandment that one may 'create whatever disturbance (*udam*) one liked but not where one lived'.[19]

For social distinction and in order to retain the identity of the sect, certain very strict rules were laid down. Members were instructed, never to eat or drink intoxicating substances. Opium, tobacco, and meat were prohibited. Restrictions were also imposed on chewing *pan* and on perfumes. Besides, the members were instructed not to themselves dance or to go to watch a performance. Also, 'do not indulge in singing or *tamashas* or any such thing, whether the occasion is of happiness or sorrow'. They were told. Thus it was also prohibited 'to play any kind of musical instrument, drum, pipe, flute, or even to clap'. Even fire-works were restricted at the occasion of marriage. Moreover, it was also declared that no mourning was to be done on the occasion of sorrow', 'nor were any ancestral ceremonies to be performed'.[20]

Women were permitted keep their hair but men were not allowed the beard. Young people were forbidden from 'tying or dressing their hair or wearing bangles or any kind of ornament'. They were also required 'not to use *kajal* (kohl) or *surma* in the eyes except as medicine, nor *henna* or any pigments' or any kind. Besides, the followers of the sect were also forbidden from bearing any distinctive mark on the forehead. For marriage it was declared, 'Let a woman marry once only and let a man have only one wife'.[21]

Given such a code of conduct, it is strange that Ishwardas Nagar condemns the sect for its 'extreme dirtiness, rendered foul, filthy and impure'. He states that 'in sin and immorality they see nothing wrong', and that 'they eat pig's flesh and other disgusting things (without hesitation)', so much so that even 'if a dog is served up before them, they do not show any disgust'.[22] It is, however, significant that all the rules were formulated for both men and women alike and for all occasions, birth, marriage, and death. Rules for women indicate that they were full members of the sect. However, it was finally declared that those not abiding strictly by the rules were to be debarred from the panth for life and their company to be avoided by members of the sect.[23] Even 'if a person beats the other, the latter should not retaliate. . . . If both have indulged in violence of this kind, both should be expelled (from the sect).' Later their cases were to be put before the members or *sadhs,* who would decide the matter. It was also declared that 'such offenders, whether one or two, are to be denied their property rights for twelve years'.[24]

Most of these regulations are very similar to those of the Kabirpanthis. The similarity lies not only in the ideas of self-respect and simple living but also to a large extent in the system of punishment and in the admission of women into the order. But, while among the Kabirpanthis some prefer a celibate ascetic life and others are accustomed to marry, the Satnamis as a whole are in favour of marriage and household life. The speciality of the Satnami character and career lies in the declaration not to accept charity or even a gift from anyone, and in the extreme avoidance of any display of opulence. These and other such rules give an impression that there was a specific character and a definite social position of the Satnami sect.

In spiritual matters, however, the relationship between the Satnamis and Kabir is striking. The Satnami text refers proudly to Kabir as 'watching over all devotees of God'.[25] Kabir pleaded a very monotheistic concept, which was as such followed in the Satnami scripture. It states again and again that there is only one deity to whom none is superior, and to whom alone worship is due.[26] Besides, in the spiritual tradition of the early *Sant-Sahitya* (literature of the bhakti saints), bhakti is stressed by the Satnami scripture as the most important factor in spiritual life. It defines a true devotee as 'he who remembers that *Sat* is the (real) *Banda*'.[27] The text further declares that 'life is given (to us) to hold the spiritual faith (strictly) and to remember God (always)'.[28] As to

The Satnami Sect of Narnaul 233

how much the Satnamis were steadfast in selfless devotion is apparent from the following lines: 'Listen only to what is in praise of Lord. . . . Let the tongue be employed in His praise and not others'; 'do not praise anybody in that manner which is (reserved) for the Creator'; 'seek only the will of God'.[29] This spirit of devotion must have been inherited by the Satnamis from Kabir and other early teachers of the *Nirguna Marga*. It is significant that like Kabir and other radicals the Satnamis too use the term 'Satguru' for spiritual teacher, but their declaration that Satguru was an incarnation of God, or that he appeared in the world to subdue seditious Hindus and Turks in order to establish the 'Satnami Panth',[30] does not fit in Kabir's concept of holding God himself as guru. It is, however, very close to the later beliefs of the Kabirpanthis who took Kabir not only as a teacher sent by God to save the world from all kinds of troubles but also as an incarnation or a portion of *Sat Purush* (i.e. God).[31] The natural result of this theory appeared in the shape of Kabir himself being considered by his followers the real means of salvation and, thus, the only authority to be worshipped. This idea seems to be close to the declaration made by the Satnamis that Satguru is the only God to be worshipped and remembered and even that 'no God is equal to Satguru'.[32]

However, criticism of the pandit and qazi alike for false practices, and intolerance towards the dogmatic and ritualistic observances of both religions, is also apparent in the Satnami manuscript, almost in the same spirit as is found in the literature of Kabir. Once both pandit and qazi are criticised for 'not knowing the reality of religion'. They are identified as *Zahir Bhagat* (apparent devotees), and are condemned several times for wrongly accumulating wealth and for other 'seditious activities'.[33] As for ritual, the work declares that God is the name of that who cannot be achieved through fast or pilgrimage', or with the use of the rosary.[34] The spirit with which such Satnami ideas have taken shape seems to have been directly derived from Kabir.

Similarly, to have sympathetic attitude towards all men without religious distinctions was also an important factor that figures both in Kabir's account and the account of the Satnamis. It is well known that the Kabirpanthis practically applied the idea in a way that in many of their sectarian centres, people of both communities still live together with equal rights in all matters. Whether the Satnamis also actually admitted Muslims in their circle is not known, but their writings speak clearly of 'making no differentiation between Hindu and Muslim', which is confirmed, though contemptuously, by the account of Ishwardas Nagar, as we have seen.

It is significant that the Satnamis were maintaining Hindu–Muslim unity in spite of the fact that they were fighting the Mughals. The war was purely political. That the revolt was of sectarian nature and the social base of the Satnamis was wider than the peasantry is also evident from the actual incident that provoked the revolt. It is said that in 1672, one of the Satnamis was 'working in his fields when he exchanged hot words with a *piyada* (foot soldier), who was guarding the cornheap. The *piyada* broke the Satnami's head with a blow of his stick. Then a crowd of that sect mobbed that *piyada* and beat him so much to reduce him almost to a corpse'.[35] The shiqdar then sent a contingent of troops, and thus the war started. Mustaid Khan says that though the Satnamis received great success initially, they were finally crushed by a large army. It is an exaggeration that they fought so bravely that despite the lack of all materials of war, they repeated the scenes of the Mahabharata.[36]

NOTES

1. Ishwardas Nagar, *Futuhat-i Alamgiri*, Rotograph, Aligarh: AMU, pp. 115-17; Mustaid Khan, *Ma'asir-i Alamgiri*, Karachi: Nafees Academy, 1962, pp. 114-16; Khafi Khan, *Muntakhab-ul Lubab*, vol. II, ed. Kabiruddin Ahamad & Ghulam Qadir, Calcutta: Urdu Guide Press, 1874, pp. 252-4; and Sadiq Khan, *Tawarikh-i Shahjahani*, vol. II, copy, no. 9, Aligarh: AMU, pp. 438-41.
2. Irfan Habib, *The Agrarian System of Mughal India*, Delhi: Asia Publishing House, 1963, pp. 395-7.
3. The *Pothi Gyan Bani* is preserved as manuscript in the Royal Asiatic Society Library, London (Hindi-1). For details Chapter 4, Sec. f. 51(b).
4. It may be borne in mind that there are two more sects bearing the same name: one was founded in Kotwa (Oudh) in 1775, and the other in Chhattisgarh some time between 1820 and 1830. See P.R. Chaturvedi, *Uttari Bharat ki Sant Parampara*, 2nd edn., Allahabad: Bharti Bhandar, 1964, pp. 610-22.

The Satnami Sect of Narnaul 235

5. J.N. Sarkar, *History of Aurangzeb,* Calcutta: MC Sarkar & Sons, 1912, vol. 3, p. 297; Tara Chand, *Influence of Islam on Indian Culture,* Allahabad: Indian Press, 1963, p. 192. These scholars have declared the Satnami Sect 'an offshoot' of the well-known Raidasi Sect. But the fact is that no mention of the name of Raidas is made in the Satnami work even though it specifically refers to Kabir as the 'sheltering authority of all devotees'. See Satnami manuscript, f. 49(b).
6. The date of foundation, Samvat 1714, the twelfth day of *Dwadashi Baisakh* (i.e. in the *Shukla Paksha*) is given in the colophon, in Persian, at the end of the manuscript in Arabic character. Ibid., f. 51(b).
7. Ibid., f. 1(a). Narnaul is situated in present-day Mahendragarh district in Haryana state.
8. Ibid., ff. 1(a), 25(b).
9. Ishwardas Nagar, *Futuhat,* p. 115.
10. Khafi Khan, *Muntakhab,* p. 252; Mustaid Khan, *Ma'asir,* p. 114; Sadiq Khan, *Tawarikh,* p. 438; and Ishwardas Nagar, op. cit., p. 115. The Satnami Mundiyas are apparently different from that specific sect of Mundiyas which is described by Mobad, *Dabistan-i Mazahib* (Persian MS), Kanpur: Munshi Newal Kishore, 1904, p. 251. Neither is it appropriate to call them Bairagis (wandering ascetic), because they were householders.
11. Mustaid Khan, pp. 114–15; also Sadiq Khan, *Tawarikh,* p. 439.
12. Mustaid Khan, op. cit., pp. 114–15.
13. Khafi Khan, *Muntakhab,* p. 252; also Sadiq Khan, op. cit., p. 438.
14. Ishwardas Nagar, *Futuhat,* p. 115.
15. Satnami manuscript, ff. 1(a), 44(a).
16. Ibid., ff. 9(a), 12(a), 36(a), 38(a), 39(a), 40(b) and 44(b).
17. Ibid., ff. 11(a), 26(a), 4(a), and 39(a).
18. Ibid., ff. 39(b), 44(b).
19. Ibid., ff. 44(a & b).
20. Ibid., ff. 31(b), 39(b) and 44(a).
21. Ibid., f. 37(b).
22. Ishwardas Nagar, *Futuhat,* p. 115.
23. Satnami manuscript f. 39(b).
24. Ibid., f. 40(a). The word for this punishment is *be pauti.*
25. Ibid., f. 49(b).
26. Ibid., ff. 9(a), 25(b), 26(a), etc.

It is significant that many of the names used by the Satnamis for God, including *Satnam* and *Poorakh* are similar to the Kabirpanthis' usage (*Satyanam, Satpurush, Parakh*, etc.). A similarity between these two currents of thought is also apparent from the usage of other mystical terms, like *chela, banda* (devotee); *panthpad* (the spiritual way); *sumiran* and *dhyan* (meditation and remembrance of God's name); *sareer, badan, tan, pind* (all used to indicate body), etc.

27. Ibid., f. 4(a).
28. Ibid., f. 9(a).
29. Ibid., ff. 40(a), 44(a & b).
30. Ibid., ff. 1(a) & 25(b).
31. Since the Kabirpanthis have been maintaining a spiritual lineage, not only the ultimate guru, Kabir, but even the subsequent gurus of the sect, such as Dharamdas, Surat Gopal, etc., have been placed almost on the same position. Many of the *bhajans* of the Kabirpanthis are addressed to Kabir as well as to subsequent gurus, and marked reverence is paid to the existing guru or *Gaddi Nashin* as the living representative of Kabir on earth.
32. Satnami text, f. 25(b).
33. Ibid., ff. 1(a), 4(a), 11(a).
34. Ibid., ff. 25(b), 26(a).
35. Khafi Khan, *Muntakhab*, vol. II, p. 253.
36. Cf. Mustaid Khan, *Ma'asir-i Alamgiri*, pp. 115–16.

CHAPTER 11

The Response and Reactions of Some Other Cults

The sectarian literature of the Pushti Marga[1] and the Radha-Vallabha Sect,[2] produced during the sixteenth century, admires the Mughal rulers and nobles. Both the *Vartas* of the Pushti Marga, the *Chaurasi Vaishnavon ki Varta* of Hari Rai Pramit and the *Do Sau Bawan Vaishnavon ki Varta* of Bitthalnath[3] appreciate Muslim rulers in general and the Mughals in particular for maintaining cordial relations with their Hindu subjects and employing many of them in royal services. In fact, the *sants* of both sects were associated with the Mughal government from the time of Akbar and they enjoyed royal favour. It is significant that Akbar's famous and powerful nobles, Birbal, Todar Mal, Bahari Mal, and Bhagwandas, were connected with Pushti Marga. Besides, Bhagwat Mudit of the Radha-Vallabha Sect, the author of the famous *Rasik Ananyamal*, reports that Sundardas was employed by Abdur Rahim Khan-i-Khanan as his Diwan and was respected by Akbar:

खानखाना के हते दिवान। अकबर शाह करै सम्मान[4]

The nobles of the Mughal court who were associated with the Pushti Marga tried to promote the cause of the sect. For instance, Birbal introduced Vitthaldas (also called Vitthalrai or Bitthalnath, 1515–85) to Akbar who visited the latter at Mathura, granting him the title of Goswami and assigning him the town of Gokul. A *farman* was issued in 1577 to protect the Goswami. In 1580–1 they participated in the discussions of the *Ibadat Khana*. Since he had a large herd of cows, permission was granted by Akbar for grazing his cows in both the *khalsa* and *jagir* lands. Moreover, Akbar granted the village of Jaitpura to Swami Bitthalnath in 1583.[5]

The great revivalist Tulsidas (1532–1623) of the *Saguna Marga* flourished under the patronage of Raja Man Singh and Abdur Rahim Khan-i-Khana.[6] He advocated close coordination between *sants* and the state. For him the just ruler and the true *sant* were virtually partners in a common enterprise, and the common qualities were *niti* (principle) and *vivek* (consciousness).[7]

There were other holy men whom Akbar respected, visited, or invited to the court for spiritual discussion. Some avoided the corridors of power, but there were many who did not hesitate to go to the court. In early 1552, as mentioned by Abul Fazl, Akbar met at Ghazni 'a *sant* (named) Baba Bilas who congratulated him on his external and internal kingship'.[8] Akbar is also said to have met Swami Haridas of the Sakhi Sampradaya along with Tansen, a disciple of the Swami; the meeting had taken place at Nidhivan in Vrindaban.[9] Ganga Rishi, a renowned sage whom the people of Kashmir held in high estimation, was invited to the Mughal court in 1597.[10]

There were men of other cults who expressed their disgust and anxiety when persuaded to visit the royal court. Kumbhandas (1468–1583) is said to have been one such charismatic figure called to meet the Emperor.[11] A disciple of Vallabhacharya, he belonged to the Pushti Marga, of which many of the followers were associated with the Mughal government. Inspired by his literary and devotional achievements, Akbar called him to his court to honour him. Kumbhandas appeared before the court at Fatehpur Sikri in 1581. The Emperor offered him a bag of 100 gold coins and a portion of land as an allowance for his family. But Kumbhandas refused the offer and later expressed his disgust.

भक्तनि कौ कहां सीकरी सौ काम।
आवत जात पन्हैया टूटी बिसर गयो हरि नाम।।
जाकौ मुख देखत दुख उपजै तांकौ करनी परी प्रनाम।
कुंभनदास लाल गिरिधर बिनु यह सब झूठै धाम।।

(What the devotees have to do with (Fatehpur) Sikri. By visiting the place (my) foot-wear was damaged (and) I forgot (the remembrance of) God's name. (I) had to make slatute to those whom I would even dislike to see. Kumbhandas (says that) no place has importance except the place where Girdhar (Krishna) is beholden.[12])

Akbar met Surdas (1483–1563) at Braj or Vrindaban against the

The Response and Reactions of Some Other Cults 239

latter's wishes. Though this meeting is not mentioned in the contemporary Persian sources, the author of *Chaurasi Vaishnavon ki Varta* gives a detailed account.[13] It narrates that, being influenced by a *pada* (hymn) of Surdas, recited by Tansen at Agra, Akbar directed his men to gather information about Surdas. Thereafter the meeting took place in Mathura. On Akbar's request, Surdas recited a *pada* in *Raga Bilawal* describing the transient nature of worldly affairs and the reality of the happiness that lies in devotion and surrender to God. Akbar then wanted him to recite something in his own praise. Surdas recited a *pada* of four verses but in praise of Krishna, showing his unawareness of anything else. The Emperor offered the *sant* a village and some cash, which the latter refused; he requested the Emperor not to meet him again.[14] This is testimony to the absence of restrictions at that time on the freedom of thought and expression, even under such a powerful king like Akbar.

NOTES

1. The Pushti Marga (way of divine grace) emerged as an offshoot of the Vishnu Swami Samparadaya which was propounded by Vallabhacharya (1473–1531).
2. The Radha-Vallabha Sect was founded by Hita Harivansh (1502–52) in the first half of the sixteenth century. See Chapter 4.
3. It is said that both the *Vartas* were written in the second half of the sixteenth century. These deal with the biographies of the *sants* of different sects and their conversations but they also reflect the public reaction, state politics, and the general functioning of the government of the time. Both *Vartas* were edited by Dwarkadas Parikh; the first was published by the Agrawal Press, Mathura, 3rd edn., vs 2017, AD 1960; and the second by the Sudhadvait Academy, Kankraul, 3 parts, vs 2008–10/AD 1951-3.
4. Bhagwat Mudit, *Sri Rasik Ananyamal,* ed. Lalita Prasad, Vrindaban: Venu Prakashan, 1960, p. 22.
5. For details, Shahabuddin Iraqi, 'Akbar's Relations with Non-Sufi Saints of India', *Islamic Heritage in South Asian Subcontinent,* vol. II, ed. Nazir Ahmad and I.H. Siddiqui, Jaipur: Publication Scheme, 2000, pp. 122, 124.
6. Yusuf Husain, *Glimpses of Medieval Indian Culture,* Bombay: Asia Publishing House, 1962, p. 111.
7. Savitri Chandra, 'Tulsidas's Concept of Rulership', *Medieval India and Hindi Bhakti Poetry: A Socio-cultural Study,* Delhi: Har-Anand, 1996, pp. 16–28.
8. Abul Fazl, *Akbarnama,* op. cit., vol. I, Chapter LIV, p. 597.

9. S. Iraqi, op. cit., p. 125.
10. Abul Fazl, *Akbarnama*, vol. III, p. 1092.
11. For details about the saint, see the introduction by Kantha Mani Shastri to *Kumbhandas*, ed. Braj Bhushan Sharma et al., Kankroli: Vidya Vibhag, 1954.
12. *Kumbhandas*, op. cit., p. 459; also *Kumbhandas ki Varta*, Kankroli: Vidya Vibhag, n.d., letter 233, p. 96.
13. S. Iraqi 'Akbar's Relations', p. 127.
14. Ibid., pp. 127–8.

CHAPTER 12

Interaction between *Sant* and Sufi

Before the rise of Islam in Arabia, Arabs were trading with India. As Muslims they settled along the Malabar Coast, bringing Islam to India. The conquest of Sind and Multan in the beginning of the eighth century paved the way for cultural exchange. The interaction between the two religious traditions led to cultural integration. Tara Chand rightly observes Hindus offered sweets at Muslim shrines, consulted the Quran as an oracle, kept its copies to ward off the evil influence, and celebrated Muslim feasts. Musalmans responded likewise.[1]

In fact, the early exposition of spiritual thought found in the Upanishads formed an ideological bridge between Vaishnavism and Sufism. The Sufis of several orders were so impressed by Indian thought and practices that some adopted these ideas, as we shall see. Similarly, some Kayasthas, Khatris, Kashmiri Pandits, and Sindhi Amils adopted Muslim culture, cultivated Persian language and literature, and participated in the administration of Islamic states. They moulded their domestic life to the Muslim way of living, adopting partly Muslim names like Firuz Chand, Mahbub Karan, etc. In some Muslim cultural strongholds, they adopted literary forms such as the elegy (*marthiya*) on the martyrdom of Hazrat Husain. In the time of Sikandar Lodi, a Brahman is reported to have been so well-versed in Islamic learning that he taught Islamic precepts to Muslims.[2]

During the time of Sultan Zaynul Abedin, the Kashmiri Pandits, especially the Sapru clan took up the study of Persian. This was the only group of Brahmans who took to Muslim culture. The amils of Sindh were a hereditary caste of government servants. After the incorporation of Sindh in the Delhi sultanate they turned to the study of Persian. Their Sindhi literature remained fully integrated with Muslim traditions and they wrote Sindhi in the Arabic script.[3]

A similar response towards Hindi or rather Hindawi was made by Muslims. A number of Muslim scholars of Arabic and Persian adopted Hindawi as their language for prose and poetry, and even for daily conversations. Rizqullah Mushtaqi and Mian Toh were considered to be great scholars of Hindi.

The term 'Hindawi' was used by Persian-speaking people to denote all Indian regional dialects, and they had to use it for interaction with the local people. From the thirteenth century onwards the mystic poetry written in this language came to be recited in the Sufi *samas* musical gatherings, and gradually it became so popular that the Sufis believed that Hindi verses were more effective than Persian in arousing ecstasy.[4]

In the Chishti *khanqahs*, from the time of Shaikh Farid Hindawi came to be used. The Shaikh himself spoke the regional dialect, Saraiki, as the verses composed by him show. Since every Indian dialect was called Hindawi, Shaikh Farid's verses are also known as Hindawi poetry. A large number of Hindawi verses composed by Farid are included in the *Guru Granth* and in the *Panchavani* with some variations.[5] This practice was followed by Shaikh Hamiduddin Nagori (d. 1294) even more emphatically. Of three references (in his *Alakh Bani*), the third emphasizes that whereas idol worship was condemned, Hindi was freely used for spiritual matters.[6]

The Hindi poetry of Shaikh Sharafuddin of Panipat, famous as Abu Ali Qalandar (d. 1324), was filled with love of God and was popular in Sufi *samas*.[7] Shaikh Sharafuddin Yahya Muneri (d. 1380–81) of the Firdausi order was much attracted to Hindawi.[8] Shaikh Abdul Haq Muhaddis Dehlavi mentions that his uncle, Shaikh Rizqullah Mushtaqi (1491–1579), wrote many treatises in Hindi, of which the *Pamani* and *Jotniranjan* were famous.[9] His pen-name was 'Rajan'. From the late fifteenth to the sixteenth century, many of the Shattari mystic poets too expressed their spiritual ideals in Hindi; but most of their compositions are not now available.

Amir Khusrau (1254–1324) listed the major regional languages of India in his Persian *masnavi*. He gave a musical touch to Hindawi.[10] His knowledge of Indian and Persian music led to the creation of new melodies and tunes in which he blended Indian *ragas* and Persian *muqams*. He is said to have invented a new *shaili* (mode) of *chhand* or *geet*, termed *rekhta*, in which Persian and Hindi lines appear according to *tala* and *raga*. These innovations were made during Amir Khusrau's competition with Gopal Nayak and were popularized by his disciples, Samat and Nigar.[11]

The musical culture of India developed with substantial inputs from Persian and Arab music. In the sufi *khanqahs* the *samas* aimed to attain *hal* (ecstasy) which in a way was similar to Chaitanya's ecstasy at the time of performing the *kirtan*. For this purpose *padas* were equally popular among bhaktis and sufis. Yahya Kabuli, the author of a Persian musical treatise, *Lahjat-i Sikandarshahi*, defines the *pada* as a combination of poetry and the sweet and soft *kalmat* (phrases) of instruments, rendered in a pleasant voice.[12]

However, the popularity of Vaishnava themes in Sufi *samas* of Hindi-speaking regions was the most significant development of the time. As a result some very important Hindi works were translated into Arabic and Persian. In a letter of Shaikh Abdul Quddus Gangohi there is a reference to *Hauz-ul Hayat*, the thirteenth-century translation of *Amrit Kund*. This text which deals with the yogic system, was translated into Arabic and Persian.[13] It was re-translated into Persian by Shaikh Muhammad Ghaus (1500–63) with the title *Bahr-ul Hayat*. Shaikh Abdul Quddus Gangohi compiled *Rushd Nama* around 1480, containing verses of *sants*, Sufis and yogis. In explaining Islamic or Sufi views the shaikh has quoted Hindi verses together with Persian and Arabic verses. He finds the philosophy of Advaita identical with that of the Sufi *Wahdat-ul Wujud*. When Shaikh Ruknuddin, the son of Shaikh Abdul Quddus, and the commentator of the *Rushd Nama*, was asked to justify the contents of the work, he argued that since Indian religions were also founded on *Tawhid*, they must have contained the essence of reality.[14] In 1566, Mir Abdul Wahid of Bilgram (1510–1608) compiled a Persian dictionary of Vaishnava terms and symbols popular among the Sufis. This tract, entitled *Haqaiq-i Hindi*, is divided into three sections. The first gives a mystic explanation of Hindi words used in *Dhrupad* songs, the second section allegorically explains the words used in Vaishnava songs in Braj Bhasha, and the third gives the Sufi explanation of words used in Hindi mystic poetry.[15]

Besides, a number of versified love stories (*Premakhyan*) were composed in Awadhi by Sufi poets. Though modelled on Persian *mathnavis,* these deal with purely Indian themes rather than old Arabic and Persian legends. They include the *Chandayan* of Mulla Daud, AD 1379, the *Mrigavati* of Shaikh Qutban (1503), the *Padmavat* of Malik Muhammad Jaisi (1540), and the *Madhumalti* of Manjhan (1545).[16]

The *Premakhyan* literature is the byproduct of mutual influence between Hindus and Muslims. The speciality of such sources, particularly the *Chandayan* and the *Padmavat,* lies in their detailed description of the manifold aspects of Indian life—the socio-economic condition of the common people; their business centres, daily transactions, and means of conveyance; their customs and ceremonials, feasts and festivals, the various kinds of dishes ornaments, garments, and utensils. The most fascinating portions of *Chandayan* are the *nakh-sikh* (top-to-toe) descriptions of the heroine and in the *Padmavat* are detailed narrations of the various shops and markets of Chittor, one being the *sringar hat* or market cosmetics.

The *Chandayan* of Mulla Daud was not only popular among the Sufis but was also held in high regard by Muslim theologians.[17] The *Mrigavati* of Qutban describes the essence of God as 'Light' and, using Hindi terminology, the author calls Him *Niranjan, Kartar, Vidhata, Parmesh, Ek-Onkar,* and *Alakh.* Defining Muhammad as the cause of creation, he draws on the concept of Shiva and Shakti as the two bodies.[18] Similarly, in the theme of *Padmavat* there are a number of situations which the author describes in the light of the traditions and customs of the Nathpanthi yogis and the Sufis.[19]

The tradition of Hindi Sufi poetry continued in the seventeenth century. The eminent Hindu poet Shaikh Usman (son of Shaikh Husain) wrote the *Chitravali* in 1613 and Shaikh Nabi wrote *Gyandeep* in 1614.

The popularity of the Muslim mystics in India, especially the Chishtis, was due to their understanding of Hindu socio-religious systems, and to their efforts to interact with Hindus. The similarity of ideas brought the two groups closer to each other. For instance, the concept of *ahimsa* or non-violence which has been one of the essential features of Indian philosophy was adopted by the Sufis. Besides, many Sufis of different orders adopted Indian customs and practices, as we have discussed.[20] Apart from acknowledging the importance of breath control and the practice of *zikr*, some Sufis, especially of the Qadria order, recommended the seated posture of Yoga, and outlined several magical and mystical practices for the achievement of supernatural powers. In fact, there was a great impact on some of the Sufis of the Hath Yoga system as prescribed in the *Amrit Kund*.[21]

The cross-breeding of Sufi beliefs with those propounded by Lalded led to the foundation of the Rishi order of the Sufis in Kashmir. Its founder, Shaikh Nooruddin, popularly known as Nand Rishi, was Lalded's spiritual offspring. Some of the Shaikh's verses in Kashmiri appear to be almost identical to those composed by Lalded. It was, in fact, under Lalded's influence that Shaikh Nooruddin imbibed the spirit of folk Shaivism. His contemplative life was founded on the Sufi *pas-i anfas* similar to the *pranayama* of the Yogis. It is significant that the Shaikh and his disciples preferred to be called Rishis, not Sufis.[22]

Sufi and bhakti saints made a departure from orthodox Islam and Hinduism. Of course, while the Sufis essentially remained within the fold of Islam, the bhakti mystics, particularly those of the *Nirguna Marga*, challenged all religious norms including the religious scriptures, incarnation theory, and idol worship. All fought for an egalitarian society in which there should be respect, a sense of human dignity and fraternity for all without distinction.

The bhakti movement was led by the people of socially backward classes whose inner urge coincided with the liberal ideas of the Sufis. It was for this reason that both groups worked not for their personal ends but for the spiritual culture of all humanity. They played a vital role in bringing people closer to one other. There were many Sufi Shaikhs and Bhakti gurus who were equally popular among the Hindus and the Muslims, and there was an effective literary and cultural interaction between the two communities. The devotional form of bhakti literature, including the *Guru Granth*, the *Panchavani*, and the *Niranyanpanti* which include the sayings of a large number of religious thinkers are similar to the *Rushd Nama* of Abdul Quddus Gangohi and other *malfuz* compilations. All these contributed to the evolution of a common culture in India. They produced a new social and mystical terminology, and their ideas contained in them took an identical course. The mutual use of a large number of Hindi and Persian words, phrases, idioms, and similes in the Bhakti and Sufi literatures show the extent of social contact.

YOGIS AND SUFIS

There has been close contact, often cordial, between the Yogis and the Sufis in medieval northern India. Gorakh's cult was an attempt to reconcile Buddhism and Sufism. It adopted a way in between the two. In fact, the Yogis' monotheism to Param Shiva (as only invisible God) and radical opposition to Brahmanism brought them close to Muslim mystics, and both claim their converts from each other. If the Sufis made their first converts from among the Yogis, a number of Sufis became Yogis also. One such convert, was Jaipal or Ajaipal, Prithviraj's preceptor, converted to Islam by Khwaja Muinuddin Chishti.[23] Similarly, it is said that Gorakhnath converted Shah Madar, a contemporary of the Khwaja, to be a Yogi. Yogis had gone to the extent of declaring Prophet Muhammad a disciple of Gorakhnath.[24] Such impudent claims provoked resentment in Sufi circles, particularly among the orthodox, but on the whole, they co-existed, each taking the other as inferior and misguided. It is well known that respected yogis and *mahants* apart from being called Avadhu, Gosain, and *sadhu*, were also often called *pir* and *faqir*. This reflects confusion in the minds of people between the spiritual mystics and wonder-workers.

A typical Hindu-Muslim cult of *pirs* had also developed in northern and central India, generally taking over an old Buddhist shrine or the locus of some primitive cult: Thus Gugga Pir or Zahir Pir, Khwaja Khidar or Zinda Pir, and Ghazi Mian or Satya Pir.

Gugga Pir is supposed to have been converted to Islam by Khwaja Muinuddin Chishti. He was popular mostly in eastern Punjab as a protector against snake-bite. Khwaja Khidr or the 'Living Pir' seems to have been originally a divinity of the Indus River. He was honoured as a god of rain in Sindh and Punjab and in eastern Bengal, especially by fishermen and boatmen. Satya Pir enjoyed popularity in the eastern Doab and Bengal. He was sometimes represented as a Muslim *faqir* who cleared vast areas of land for tilling along the Hugli River, and sometimes as 'Satya Narayana', a popular form of the Vishnu. He is also supposed to be eternally alive, a distinction that he holds in common with the other divine *pirs* as well as with the celebrated Siddhas and Nath Yogis. A Bengali poem represents him as a Hindu saint, wearing the ochre robe, sandal-paste *tilak*, and the Brahman's thread over his shoulder. Like Krishna, he holds a flute in his left hand.[25]

Another half-yogic cult was that of Shah Madar, who is said to have come from Aleppo to India in the first half of the eleventh century and to have settled somewhere near Kanpur. Shah Madar mastered breath control. His followers, known as Madaris, closely resemble the Yogis in dress and behaviour as in their fondness for *bhang*. They claim to be true followers of the Prophet Muhammad. Yusuf Husain considers the hybrid cult of the *pirs* as 'the natural consequence of the convergent activity of Hindu and Muslim mystics'.[26] However, it seems that a Buddhist element also played a vital role in the development of such syncretic cults, though the kind of synthesis achieved in the cult of the *pirs* appear to be hardly 'mystical' in character.

Yogis and *pirs*, as wonder-workers and magicians, tended to replace the old minor cults of tutelary spirits, protectors of the people against evil spirits and dangers of all natural calamities. The tendency to replace the merciful local deities by different kinds of immortal human beings endowed with extraordinary magical powers is a characteristic feature of the Tantric tradition inherited from Mahayana Buddhism. Siddhas and the Yogis had acquired magical powers and physical immortality through hard esoteric Tantric practices. They also claimed to be the self-made gods.

Since such ideas and tendencies were not acceptable to Muslims, these cults took a Muslim garb and merged with the cult of *pirs*, more easily tolerated in Indo–Muslim society. On the other hand, the Muslim legends of the *pirs* were re-interpreted in familiar terms. In the process of intermingling of Hinduism and Islam at the general social level, yogis thus played an important role.

The Chishti Shaikhs held discourses with the Siddhas and Yogis who made frequent visits to the *jamaat khana* at Multan and Delhi.[27] We have already seen that some of the works of the Yogic cult like *Siddha Siddhanta Paddhati* provided common ground for the exchange of ideas with the Sufis. Discussions on different spiritual issues created a background for a better understanding between the Sufis and Yogis. The records of the conversations of the Yogis in the *khanqah* of Shaikh Farid show that amongst the subjects discussed were physical culture, Hindu alchemy, and the division of the body into the regions of Shiva and Shakti. Shaikh Nasiruddin Chiragh-i Dilli acknowledged the worth of the 'watching of breath' in the Sufi practice of *zikr*. Shaikh Bahauddin Shattari recommended the sitting posture of the Yogis, and outlined several magical and mystical practices for the achievement of supernatural powers. In fact, there was a great impact on some of the Sufis of the Hath Yoga system as prescribed in the *Amrit Kund*. Shaikh Abdul Haqq specified the Yogis who obtained supernatural powers by strict ascetic exercises and were able to perform miracles with divine favour.

The *Rushd Nama* of Shaikh Abdul Quddus Gangohi, written in mixed prose and poetry, is important not only for a comparative study of the Nathpanthi and Sufi ideologies but also for determing their influences on the medieval north Indian *sants*. Its distinct character lies in the profound use of Hindi verse composed by Shaikh Quddus and his teachers together with those of the Nath Yogis and Siddhas. The Naths called the supreme God *Alakh-Nath* or *Niranjan* (without apparent attributes), and the term used by the Shaikh in this context was *Alakh Niranjan*. In a verse of the *Rushd Nama* he identifies *Niranjan* with *Khuda* and calls him the creature of different worlds.[28]

The yogic practice of *ulti-sadhana* or regressive meditation was similar to the Sufi *salat-i makus*, or *namaz* performed by hanging with the legs suspended from a roof or tree-branch. In a Persian verse the Shaikh says: 'Unless the brain comes down to the foot, none can reach the doors of God.'[29] Using yogic terminology, Shaikh Quddus emphasizes that the control of vital breath should be the main object of Sufi practice. In fact, the Sufi *pas-i anfas* was founded on the *pranayama* of yoga and the Shaikh along with his Rudauli *pirs* were involved in this exercise.

Like the Yogis, Shaikh Quddus attaches importance to *onkar*. He suggests Sufis should be absorbed in *onkar* through *zikr*, leading to a void or *sunyata*.[30] He also explains the concept of *sahaj* in the yogic traditions in terms of union between Shakti and Shiva, the realization of which leads to achieving *jivan-mukti* similar to the Sufi *baqa*.

On the other hand, however, Baba's interest in mysticism induced him to visit Gorakhtari near Peshawar, just before his so-called meeting with Guru Nanak on 26 March 1519.[31] Akbar and Jahangir had assigned land grants to the Yogis of Jakhbar, the details of which are given by Goswami and Grewal.[32] Unique information is provided in the same work, a letter of Aurangzeb saying he had sent an offering to the *mahant* of a Yogi shrine and asked for a second dose of magically treated quicksilver.[33]

Describing in detail the influence of Indian religious thought and practice on Muslim mysticism, Tara Chand concludes that the 'conception of Nirvana, the discipline of the eightfold-path, the practice of yoga and the acquaintance of miraculous powers were appropriated in Sufism under the names of *Fana, Tariqa* or *Saluk, Maraqaba* and *Karamat* or *Mujiza*.'[34] But the comparison does not appear to be accurate. The doctrine of *fana* (annihilation), first introduced by *Bayazid Bistami* (d. 848), is not identical with *moksha* or *nirvana*, which means freedom from the bondage of rebirth. While both terms imply the passing away of individuality, *nirvana* denotes salvation for ever, but *fana* is accompanied by *baqa*, i.e. everlasting life in God.

The doctrine of Mansur al-Hillaj relating to *hulul* or the infusion of the divine into the human soul resembles the Hindu doctrine of the illumination of *buddhi* by *purusha*. Certain Sufi exercises such as *habs-i dam* (holding back the breath) seem to have been derived through Buddhist channels from the yogic *pranayam*.[35] The Sufi doctrine of *Wahdat-ul Wajud* is close to the Indian *Advaitvad* and the Sufi *Nafs-i Lawwama* is similar to the concept of *maya*.

The impact of the socio-cultural revolution brought about by the Sufis was nowhere so deep than in India. The reason was obvious. Indian society was divided into castes and creeds; and outcasts, who constituted the majority of the population, were not only deprived of all benefits of civic life but were also lived outside the cities. It is significant that many of the *khanqahs* of early Muslim mystics in India were developed outside the old cities, in the midst of settlements of the poor. The liberal and secular ideas of the Sufis, and their humanitarian attitude towards all, attracted particularly the depressed classes to the *khanqahs*. Besides, the two basic socio-religious ideals, the unity of God and the unity of human being taught by the Sufis determined the extent of discontent of the lower classes of people towards the established thought and practice in Hinduism. They were bound to gravitate towards this new social order, so different from their own.

CONVERSIONS

For the Muslim state, the apostasy of Muslims was not allowed; it was severely punished, and the punishment fell not so much on the person converted but on the proselytizers. A Brahman, accused of tempting a Muslim woman to the erotic Shakti cult was burnt alive by the order of Firoz Shah Tughluq.[36] The forcible conversion of the people of other communities to Islam was not state policy either. It was considered the duty of an Islamic state to give to non-Muslims protection and full freedom of worship.[37] Habibullah says that the Muslim rulers were not interested in conversion to Islam, as 'it would have resulted in an unwelcome falling off the revenues'.[38]

There is very little information in contemporary historical works about the conversion of the Hindus to Islam in medieval India. Stray references found in some works are insufficient to understand the processes and mechanism involved in it. The traditional assumption that Muslim mystics were responsible for a large number of conversions of Hindus, is based on the fabricated *Malfuz* or hagiographies of Sufis. According to Mohammad Habib, the popular *Malfuzat* attributed to Sheikh Muinuddin Ajmeri, to Shaikh Qutbuddin Bakhtiyar Kaki and to Shaikh Fariduddin were fabricated and have nothing to do with these men. However, he gives the names of three authentic and reliable texts of the Khalji and the Tughluq periods: the *Fawaid-ul Fuwad* compiled by Amir Hasan Sijzi, the *Khair-ul Majalis* by Hamid Qalandar, and the *Siyar-ul Auliya* by Amir Khurd. These give the impression that the Sufis were not interested in conversion.[39] For instance, it appears from the *Fawaid-ul Fuwad* that when a Muslim follower of Sheikh Nizamuddin Auliya brought to him his Hindu friend to conversion, the Shaikh took no interest as if it was not his mission, and answered 'In the early days of Islam conversion to Islam took place owing to the excellence of Muslim character. But where is that excellence now?'[40]

This does not mean that there were no conversion. Obviously the increase in the Muslim population of northern India was largely due to conversions. We need to investigate how these conversions took place and to what extent they represent a reaction against the socio-religious conditions of India. Jafar Makki, an important Sufi of the fifteenth century, writes that conversions took place under five circumstances: fear of death; fear of the enslavement of one's family; the preaching of Muslims; the desire for stipends and booty; and the bigotry of the ancestral religion.[41] After analysing circumstantial evidence, Mohammad Habib has come to the conclusion that 'the acceptance of Islam by the city-workers was a decision of local professional groups', and, for that, they were 'more concerned with . . . mundane affairs and their position in the social order than with abstract theological truths'.[42] But this is not sufficient, because the moral and spiritual roles played by the Muslim mystics cannot be ignored.

Many of the tribes of India, particularly those of Punjab, claim to have been converted to Islam by mystics like Sheikh Fariduddin of Ajodhan.[43] The great respect shown to the Chishtis by generations of these tribes proves the fact. Besides, some other tribes are said to have been converted to Islam by Shihabuddin and his Turkish slave officers. For instance, Minhaj Siraj refers to the conversion of a tribal chief at the hands of Muhammad Bakhtiyar Khalji.[44]

According to Dara Shukoh, Sheikh Abdul Qadir Sani converted a large number of Hindus to Islam.[45] Besides, though the number of Hindus mentioned by Badauni as converted by Sheikh Daud Qadiri was probably an exaggeration, it seems that the miracles attributed to him prompted many people of the newly settled towns of Shergarh to embrace Islam.[46]

It is significant that a few converts enjoyed a high position in Muslim society, and some of them made great contributions. Rinchana (d. 1323), a fugitive Buddhist prince from Ladakh and ruler of Kashmir, denied initiation to Shaivism by a Brahman priest on grounds of caste, embraced Islam at the behest of Syed Sharfuddin, popularly known as Bulbul Shah. Rinchana, who assumed the name Sadruddin and styled himself 'Sultan', founded a mosque, a *khanqah* and a *langar* for his spiritual mentor.[47] Besides, as reported in *Fawaid-ul Fuwad,* Faqih Shaikh Madho, disciple of Shaikh Husain Lahori of Qadiri order, was appointed Imam of the Jami mosque in Ajmer and Shaikh Ahmad was his disciple.[48] After the death of Shaikh Husain (in 1599) Shaikh Madho (d. 1646–7), a Brahman convert, became head of the *khanqah* in Lahore.[49] Similarly, Banwalidas Wali, a Hindu Munshi of Dara Shukoh, was a disciple of Mulla Shah.[50] After Aurangzeb's accession to the throne, however, Banwalidas withdrew to the wilderness where he died in 1674–5.

Hindus belonging to the lower strata of society were particularly influenced by the simple and straightforward religious and social precepts of Islam. Many weavers, oil-pressers, water-carriers, leather-workers and sweepers embraced Islam. This was the case particularly in Bengal, Uttar Pradesh, Panjab, and western India. In the later sixteenth century in north-eastern Bengal many regarded as outcastes, became Muslims.[51] But the hopes and aspirations of the lower-class converts for equality of status in Muslim society were not fulfilled. Muslim orthodoxy did not accord them this—they continued to remain in the same inferior status. Thus, they naturally were caught in a dilemma. But to say that in the medieval period there were attempts at reconversion[52] is a misconception: reconversion to Hinduism was not possible in the medieval period. Brahmanical orthodoxy and formalism could hardly meet such a challenge.[53] But in the course of Bhakti movement there was already a suggestion of the possibility of transcending the caste system.[54]

However, many converts retained 'their skilled or non-skilled ancestral professions and this brought into Islam some vague features of caste distinctions'.[55] In rural areas most of them continued to live with the Hindus of their caste and to observe Hindu rites and customs, as also to have Hindu wives. Nanak's remark in the *Guru Granth* is important: 'You wear a *dhoti* and a mark, and carry a rosary, yet you eat the bread of *mlechhas* (i.e. Muslims). You perform the Hindu ceremony at home, read the Koran in public and associate with (or act like) the Mohammedans.'[56] So in most of the cases converts were neither fully Hindu nor completely Muslim.

The Sufi attitude towards the Hindus and Hinduism was based on understanding and adjustment, because it was believed that all religions were different roads leading to the same destination. Believing in *ahimsa*, living as vegetarians, and giving equal status

Interaction between Sant and Sufi

to all, was bound to increase the scope of their contact with Hindus. Shaikh Muinuddin Chishti took two wives, and one of them was the daughter of a Hindu raja of Ajmer.[57] Shaikh Hamiduddin Nagori (d. 1276) was proud of being born in India.

Sufi poetry composed in Hindi added a new dimension to Sufism and the new lyrical and emotional expression made it possible to attain an ecstatic state. The subtle refinement of Hindi music, combined with Persian traditions and artistry, gave fresh meaning and depth to Sufi thought. Hindi offered the Sufis a spiritual satisfaction they could share with bhakti *sants*. Sufis and bhaktas rejected religious formalities and sought to create a universal religion and brotherhood. Unconcerned with the idea of union between two religions, they worked within their respective religious communities for an understanding of spiritual and social values.

The mutual use of a large number of Hindi and Persian words, phrases, idioms, and similes in the Sufi and Bhakti literatures shows the extent of social contact. Indian musical forms like Khayal and Thumri, and the recitation of Hindi verses have been very much in use in the *samas* of the *khanqahs*. Being a powerful means of spiritual satisfaction, the *sama* or *qawwali* became a popular institution of medieval mysticism, and attracted higher intellects as well as common people of both communities.

As discussed above, the various trends of spiritual thought that developed under the Bhakti and the Sufi movements drew much from each other, consciously and unconsciously. Yet the bhaktas and the Sufis remained essentially within the framework of their respective religious traditions. However liberal and secular the Sufis may have been, they remained bound to the basic tenets of Islam and *Sharia*.[58] For instance, though the Sufi doctrine of *Wahdat-ul Wajud* was very close to the Upanishadic Advaita, the quest of God the theory of incarnation was opposed to the Islamic and Sufi concept of strict monotheism. Similarly, the Sufis never subscribed to the Vaishnava faith of *avagaman* or transmigration of the soul. Besides, while the Sufis believed in *Wahdat-ul Adyan* or unity of religions, the Nirguna bhaktas challenged the institutional form of all religions. The essentials of the mystic thought of the *sants* were indigenous, and Sufism offered only an atmosphere of spiritual stimulus.

NOTES

1. Tara Chand, *Influence of Islam on Indian Culture,* Allahabad: Indian Press, 1963, p. 217.
2. K.A. Nizami, *Some Aspects of Religion and Politics During the Thirteenth Century,* rpt., Delhi: Idara-i Adabiyat-i Dehli, 1978, p. 237.
3. Aziz Ahmad, *Studies in Islamic Culture in the Indian Environment,* Oxford: Clarendon Press, 1964, pp. 105–7.
4. When someone enquired from Khwaja Mohammad Gesu Daraz (d. 1422), the chief disciple of Shaikh Nasiruddin Chiragh-i Dilli, the reason for the popularity of Hindawi in the sufi *sama,* the Khwaja emphasized that it was a soft and heart-touching language, and he was attracted to it. See *Jawaim-ul Kalam* of Syed Mohammad Gesu Daraz, ed. Mohd. Akbar Husain, Usmanganj, AH 1337–8, pp. 172–3.
5. In the *Guru Granth* there are 4 *pads* (in Raga Asa and Raga Suhi) and 130 *sloks* bearing the name Farid. See Macauliffe, *The Sikh Religion,* rpt., vol. VI, Delhi: Low Price Pubs., 1993, pp. 391–414. For his account in the *Panchavani* of the *Dadupanthis,* see *Basta* No. 12, compiled by Swamdas, 1636, part III, ff. 315b–316b, History Department, AMU.
6. For these references, *Siyar-ul Auliya,* compiled by Mir Khurd, Delhi, 1885, pp. 180–3; *Khair-ul Majalis,* compiled by Hamid Qalandar, ed. K.A. Nizami, Aligarh: AMU, 1959, pp. 19, 121.
7. *Akhbar-ul Akhyar* of Shaikh Abdul Haq Muhaddis Dehlavi, ed. Muhammad Abdul Ahad, Delhi: Mutabai Press, 1914, pp. 129–31.
8. The letters of his disciple, Shams Muzaffar Balkhi (found in the possession of Shah Taqi Hasan Balkhi of Alamganj, Patna), quote his many Hindi verses.
9. *Akhbar-ul Akhyar,* pp. 63–4.
10. Amir Khusrau belonged to a noble Turkish family, but he was born in India of an Indian mother. For this reason perhaps, his poetry is full of pride for his native land. Though his poetry was composed in Persian, he was well acquainted with Hindawi, the idiom spoken by common people in and around Delhi, and he experimented with it in some of his poems.
11. For further details of Amir Khusrau's contribution to Indian music, Madhu Trivedi, 'Sufi and Bhakti Saints in the Evolution of Hindustani Music', *Sufism and Bhakti Movement: Eternal Relevance,* ed. Hamid Hussain, Delhi: Manak Publication, 2007, pp. 266, 267.
12. Yahya Kabuli, *Lahjat-i-Sikandar Shah* or *Ghuniyet-ul Munya,* ed. Shahab Sarmadi, Delhi, 1999, pp. 479, 488, 492.
13. *Makhtubat-i Quddusiya,* Delhi, 1871, letter 119, p. 112. The manuscript copy of the *Hauz-ul Hayat* has been discovered in the Library of Anjuman-i-Taraqi-i-Urdu, Karachi. For details see A.A. Rizvi, *History of Sufism in India,* vol. I, Delhi: Munshiram Manoharlal, 1978, vol. 1, pp. 335–6.
14. The Hindi translation is entitled *Alakh Bani,* ed. A.A. Rizvi and S. Jafar

Raza Zaidi, Aligarh, 1971. For details about the Shaikh and his *Rushd Nama*, see *Alakh Bani*, pp. 66–148.
15. The dictionary was translated into Hindi and published by S. Athar Abbas Rizvi, Varanasi: Nagari Pracharini Sabha, 1957. For further details A.A. Rizvi, *History of Sufism in India*, vol. 1, pp. 359–62.
16. For details of the *Premakhyan* literature, see S. Iraqi, ed., *The Sarbangi of Rajabdas*, Aligarh: Granthayan, 1985, pp. 19–21, 79–83. Mulla Daud was a disciple of Shaikh Zainuddin, the Khalifa of Shaikh Nasiruddin Chiragh-i Dilli. Shaikh Qutub Ali or Qutban was a Suhrawardi *sant*. Malik Muhammad Jaisi was a disciple of Shaikh Burhan of Kalpi. Manjhan was a Suhrawardi *sant* and disciple of Shaikh Muhammad Ghaus.
17. The work was so popular among theologians that Mulla Abdul Qadir Badauni reports, 'Even Maulana Shaikh Taqi-uddin, a godly preacher (*Waiz-i Rabbani*), used to recite its verses from the pulpit'. *Muntakhab-ut Tawarikh*, part I, Calcutta, 1865–9, p. 250.
18. S.H. Askari, 'Qutban's Mrigavati', *Journal of the Bihar Research Society*, 1955, pp. 452–87.
19. A.A. Rizvi, *History of Sufism*, vol. 1, pp. 368–9.
20. See Chapter 2.
21. The treatise deals with the importance of the body. It prescribes exercises by which one may transform body into a state of *samadhi*. It emphasizes the discipline of the body, senses, and mind, and prescribes methods for the suppression of respiration, inhaling and exhaling in a specific manner. Rizvi, op. cit., vol. 1, pp. 335–6.
22. Rizvi, op. cit., vol. 1, pp. 350–1; Mohammad Ishaq Khan, 'The Rishi Movement as a Social Force in Medieval Kashmir', *The Making of Indo-Persian Culture: Indian and French Studies,* ed. Muzaffar Alam, Françoise 'Nalini' Delvoye and Marc Gaborieau, Delhi: Manohar, 2000, pp. 125-40.
23. M.T. Titus, *Indian Islam,* 2nd edn., Delhi: Oriental Books, 1979, p. 44; also T.W. Arnold, *The Preaching of Islam,* London, 1896, p. 281.
24. Baba Rayan Hajji was identified with Gorakhnath and it was asserted that the Prophet had learnt yoga through the Baba. Mobad, *Dabistan-i-Mazahib*, Kanpur: Munshi Newal Kishore, 1904, pp. 179–80.
25. *A Short Encyclopaedia of Islam*, ed. H.A.R. Gibb and J.H. Kramers, rpt., London, 1961, p. 235.
26. Yusuf Husain, *Indo-Muslim Polity,* cited by Ch. Vaudeville, *Kabir*, vol. 1, Delhi: Oxford University Press, 1974, p. 96.
27. *Fuwaid-ul-Fawad*, compiled by Amir Hasan Sijzi, Lucknow: Newal Kishore Press, 1894, pp. 59–60, 404–5, 417–18.
28. The verse is quoted by Rizvi, op. cit., vol. 1, p. 337.
29. Ibid., p. 337.
30. Like the yogis, the Shaikh too advocated the need to experience the whole cosmic system within the individual body (*panda*). He also held that 'gnosis' should be achieved only by true guide or preceptor and the

imperfect teacher was the cause of the destruction of both. The Sufis should retire into forest and meditate in seclusion.
31. *Baburnama,* as cited by A.A. Rizvi, *Mughal Kalin Bharat: Babur,* Aligarh, 1960, pp. 109–10.
32. R.N. Goswami and J.S. Grewal, *The Mughals and the Jogis of Jakhbar* Simla: Indian Institute of Advanced Study, 1967.
33. Ibid., document VIII, pp. 120–1.
34. Tara Chand, op. cit., pp. 64–7.
35. Aziz Ahmad, op. cit, pp. 125–6.
36. *Tarikh-i-Firoz Shahi,* ed. Molvi Vilayat Husain, Calcutta, 1890, pp. 380–1.
37. K.A. Hakim, *Islamic Ideology,* Lahore, 1961, p. 183.
38. A.B.M. Habibullah, *The Foundation of Muslim Rule in India,* Allahabad, 1989, p. 326.
39. Mohammad Habib, *Politics and Society During the Early Medieval Period (Collected Works of M. Habib),* ed. K.A. Nizami, vol. 1, Delhi: Peoples' Publishing House, 1974, pp. 76–7; K.A. Nizami, *On History and Historians of Medieval India,* Delhi: Munshiram Manoharlal, 1983, pp. 163–80; K.A. Nizami, 'Chishti Mystic Records of the Sultanate Period', *Medieval India Quarterly,* no. 2, 1950, pp. 1–42.
40. *Fawaid-ul Fuwad* as cited by Mohammad Habib, op. cit., p. 77.
41. Jafar Makki Husaini, *Bahrul Ma'an-i, Ethe,* 1867, ff. 162b-163a.
42. See Mohammad Habib, op. cit., p. 77. That the new converts maintained their Hindu traditions but gradually absorbed Muslim ways is apparent from a remark of Shaikh Nasiruddin Chiragh-i Dilli in earlier days, Musalmans of different professions in Delhi had separate graveyards. But in his own day (AD 1354), this curious anomaly had disappeared.
43. Nizami gives a list of eleven such tribes converted to Islam by Shaikh Farid. *Some Aspects of Religion and Politics Druing the Thirteenth Century,* p. 321.
44. Minhaj says, '. . . one of the chiefs of the tribes of Kunch and Mej (Meg), whom they were wont to call Ali, fell into the hands of Muhammad-i-Bakhtiyar, the Khalji, and, at his hand also, the former adopted the Muhammadan faith'. *Tabaqat-i-Nasiri* of Minhaj Siraj, ed. Abdul Hai Habibi, Kabul, AH 1344, p. 152.
45. *Safinat-ul Auliya,* Lucknow, 1872, p. 69.
46. A.A. Rizvi, op. cit., vol. II, p. 63.
47. Mohammad Ishaq Khan, 'The Rishi Movement', p. 133.
48. *Fawaid-ul Fuwad* as cited by A.A. Rizvi, op. cit., vol. I, p. 326.
49. Shaikh Husain's association with Madho prompted him to enjoy Hindu festivals like Holi and Basant, when he danced and sang, joining in the throwing of coloured powder. For centuries afterwards an orgy of colour on the days of Holi was the main feature of the Urs celebrations at the tomb of Shaikh Husain in Lahore. See Rizvi, op. cit., vol. II, p. 65.

Interaction between Sant and Sufi

50. Banwalidas established himself as a scholar and poet. He translated the Sanskrit drama, *Probodha Chandraodya* into Persian, naming it *Gulzar-i Hal*. His *Diwan* of *ghazals* and *mansnavis* were very popular. In his *masnawis* he composed a heart-touching elegy of his *pir* and the Qadiri *silsilah*. Ibid., p. 125.
51. E.T. Dalton, *Descriptive Ethnology of Bengal*, Calcutta, 1872, p. 89.
52. Srivastava, op. cit., p. 131. The author has also cited some such cases. See ibid., p. 132.
53. In the case of Harihara and Bukka, neo-Muslim governors of Mohammad bin Tughluq, who reverted to Hinduism and founded the kingdom of Vijayanagara, a special effort had to be made by a political minded Brahman sage Vidyaranya and his preceptor Vidyatirath to facilitate their conversion. R.C. Majumdar, *The Delhi Sultanate*, Bombay: Bharatiya Vidya Bhawan, 1960, pp. 271–2.
54. According to the *Bhagavat Gita* (IX.32), 'in the sight of God all devotees are equal whether they are born in sin or not, and to whatever caste or sect they may belong'. Alberuni quotes Vasudev on the question of *mukti* 'in the judgement of the intelligent man, the Brahman and Chandala are equal. . . . If to the eyes of intelligence all things are equal, to ignorance they appear separate and different.' *Kitab-ul Hind*, Edward C. Sachau, rpt., Delhi: S. Chand, 1964, vol. II, pp. 137–8.
55. Aziz Ahmad, op. cit., pp. 84–5.
56. Macauliffe, *The Sikh Religion*, vol. 1, p. 239.
57. *Akhbar-ul Akhya*, op. cit., pp. 112–13.
58. According to Shaikh Muinuddin Chishti (1142–93), Sufism is neither a knowledge nor a custom (*rasm*) but an ethical discipline (*akhlaq*). Its first stage is strict conformity to the *sharia*, leading to the second state of *Tariqa* (or Sufism). The third stage is *Marifa* (gnosis), finally leading to the fourth stage of *Haqiqa* (truth). Qutbuddin Bakhtiyar Kaki, *Dalil-i Arifin*, Delhi, n.d., pp. 47ff.

Conclusion

The Bhakti movement in medieval northern India started as a protest against orthodoxy. The nature and scope of the movement was almost the same as that of Sufism. But, whereas the Sufis did not go against Islam, Quran or Prophet, the bhakti as particularly those of *Nirguna* school, emerged as a reaction against Hinduism or Brahmanism. It was, in fact, due to the long term socio-religious bias and humiliation faced by the people of lower strata that spiritual leaders of this class not only challenged the religious system of traditional Hinduism but also took over the leadership in their own hands and broke the religious monopoly of the Brahmans. So to believe that all the leaders of the Bhakti movement were peaceful socio-religious reformers seems inappropriate. In fact, the idea of reform formed their ethical and ideological base, while their mission was to deal with practical aspect of life, having certain aims and objectives in mind. Some turned to political and even militant action for the attainment of their objectives.

As we have discussed in Chapter 3, from the fifteenth century onwards there appear a number of bhakti saints in northern India, both of *Nirguna* as well as of *Saguna Marga*. Figures of *Nirguna* school, Kabir, Nanak, Dadu, were generally non-sectarian and secular. They did not follow any *parampara* as such, but formed a spiritual lineage, and remained independent teachers throughout. Their philosophical base was founded on the Vedantic *Advaitvad* as propounded by Shankaracharya and Ramanuja, yet they were not the *smartta* Hindus. They were not bound to any of the four popular Vaishnava sects, nor were they systematic philosophers. These mystic men were not systematically educated, even though their ideas took an identical course, and there was also a good deal of mutual understanding among them. Thus, it was not by chance that all the radical religious figures denied an identity either as Hindu or as Muslim.[1] Their religious ideas conformed neither to Hinduism nor to Islam but simply gave expression of universal religion with unity of divinity. Dadu specifically says: 'No Hindu am I, nor yet a Musalman. I follow none of the six systems. I am a devotee of the Merciful.'[2]

There was deep concern with religious differences between Hinduism and Islam, founded on false notions of religious superiority and, therefore, the leaders wanted to bring the people out of the narrow limitations of religious beliefs and practices. But this idea was not appreciated and for this concept of Dadu, for instance, according to Dadu himself, 'fierce and terrible have the people become, when they saw I was of neither faction'.[3] It is significant that the complaint against Kabir to Sikandar Lodi was lodged by the religious leaders of both the communities, which reads thus: 'Those who paid heed to what Kabir said remained neither Hindus nor Musalmans.'[4]

In fact, the radical saints were particularly against the institutional structure and practices of Hinduism and Islam both and, therefore, they challenged even the infallibility of the religious scriptures of both the communities, which provided base and a separate identity to them in the society. Kabir says, 'The Musalmans accept the *Tariqat*; the Hindus, the Vedas and Purans; but for me the books of both the religions are useless.'[5] Dadu says, 'I have diligently searched the Vedas and Quran. But the dwelling-place of Niranjan is not here but far off. . . . How many have wasted a lifetime blackening paper, producing Vedas and Puranas. . .'.[6] Repeating the same thing once again he concludes, 'but what profits it, without love, to have read the Vedas and the Puranas and other scriptures'.[7]

Thus, the saints took the scriptures as biased sources of religious knowledge leading to conflicts among different religionists and, therefore, they emphasized the need of *anubhava jnana*, i.e. direct knowledge from personal experiences. This reminds the famous statement of Imam Ghazali that the true knowledge could be achieved only through personal experiences, and that the theological doctrines could not be proved by speculative methods but by direct knowledge.[8] For the same reason the radical saints and their followers developed their own scriptures in the form of compilations like Kabir's *Bijak* known as *Khas Granth*, *Guru Granth* of the Sikhs and the *Panchavani* of the Dadupanthis, which were and are still followed and usually recited in their respective sectarian centres as basic part of their spiritual obligation. It is significant that though most of the sectarian centres are constructed on the model of ordinary Vaishnava temples, their own compilations take the place of the customary scriptures in the inner shrine.[9] But this system was taken up only by the non-conformist saints of *Nirguna Marga* and their followers. There were the Krishnite saints like Vallabhacharya, Chaitanya, Surdas, and the most important Saguna Ramaite saint, Tulsidas who also emphasized personal devotion to God but they did not consider the scriptures as irrelevant or hurdle for true devotion. Their works do not replace the early scriptures at their sectarian centres.

Not only this but the non-conformist radicals also discarded the Sanskrit of the scriptures for the language of everyday use, as we have seen. *Bhasha* was a mixed form of the vernacular dialects and was called *sadhukkari*. It was the language of common people. Kabir is said to have declared: 'Sanskrit is like water of a well, whereas *Bhasa* is flowing water.'[10]

On the other hand, by rejecting the concept of more than one God, these men tried to establish a strict monotheism and monism. They discarded not only idol worship and the rituals related to it, but also the idea of incarnation. Kabir declared that the incarnations of God did not concern him, because his Master was such a Lord as had 'neither father nor mother'.[11] The bhakti as used popular Vaishnava names such as Ram and Hari to denote God, but did not believe in them as such and they were not Vaishnavites. (They have used Islamic names of God, such as Rahim also.)

The emphatic denial by these radical figures of ritual in the realization of God was because they considered these useless and a basic cause of conflict. For the same reason they discredited the role of priests, both Brahman and mullah, as professional mediators between God and man. These people kept alive the issue of socio-religious and cultural difference in order to maintain a hold over the people. There was no place for human gurus. Such teachers were condemned[12] and God Himself was the Guru. It is significant that the concept of divine teacher was already prevalent among the Siddhas and some Yogis who had emerged as independent teachers. It is thus quite possible that the radical teachers adopted this concept under Tantric influence, which had been deliberately ignored by the orthodoxy.

In fact, the integration of beliefs and superstitions of Hinduism, the yogic cults and the radical form of Muslim syncretic cults had advanced greatly. It seems that not the popular rituals of Hinduism or of Islam but the basic ideals of the *pirs* and Yogis were acceptable to them. The *sants* rejected false belief and superstition, but kept exalting the Satguru and the *sant* as the true conqueror of the soul within the body. In their verses the yogic ideal of salvation prevails over the Hindu concept of salvation; and in this aspect particularly, they seem to have been directly influenced by the yogic tradition, which established the superiority of the perfect Yogi over the ancient deities of Puranic lore and local traditions. Only such gods or deities were acceptable who somehow qualified as perfect Yogis—be they guru or *pir*.[13] But the point cannot be ignored that whereas in these beliefs a particular human being is exalted as guru to the position of divinity, the *Nirguna* school take an altogether different position by holding god in the position of guru or Satguru.

The radical or non-conformist saints revolted against the entire system and all norms of institutionalized religion. The kind of religion that they emphasized in their accounts appears to be based on inherent divinity of human soul and not as weakness that man is a born sinner and he has to spend his whole life in repentance, an idea elaborated by great modern thinkers like Tagore. Caste discrimination was a serious problem. It was not only a socioreligious matter but was also related to trade and to the exploitation of the labour of many people. The *sants* denounced caste exploitation. In this respect, therefore, they influenced social attitudes and perceptions of the time. The idea that the individual apprehension of God formed the basis of true religion amounted to dissent and protest against the Brahmanical theory of social hierarchy.

The charismatic religious leaders addressed Hindus and Muslims of all classes. Strictly against the caste system by ideology, they themselves seem to have formed a separate class or community of their own. This is evident from the fact that Dadu places Namdev, Kabir, and Raidas in one category, and says, 'Those who have attained (salvation) have left their message . . . (that all of them) are of one faith, all are of one caste'.[14] He includes himself also in the same category, saying that the 'Lord of Kabir is my soul wedded'.[15] This kind of group consciousness was perhaps necessary for an organized fight against the existing system.

In the way of bhakti, religious teachers led a family life and earned their livelihood without begging or accepting charity. They upheld the dignity of labour. They tend to be generally suspicious of the rulers and the ruling class and, therefore, they kept their distance from the state. They asked their followers not associate with governments or with the rich. The voice of protest was thus not confined to religious issues: it extended to existing socio-economic and even political and administrative systems, for which some of the leaders turned to politics.

We have already discussed that Dadu's political approach was quite different than other Bhakti saints of *Nirguna* school. He did not hesitate to have ties with the rulers and the nobles. While within Rajasthan, Dadu enjoyed the patronage of local rulers like Raja Bhagwandas at Amber, he was extended due respect at the Mughal court. There are certain references and symbolic expressions in Dadu's account which indicate that he was in favour of the institutions of the government. The Dadupanthi Nagas were employed by Rajput chiefs to fight for them.

The men of the Pushti Marga and of the Radha-Vallabha Sect were formally associated with the Mughal government under Akbar. Yet there were others who expressed disgust and anxiety when persuaded to visit the royal court. For instance, Kumbhandas, declined to accept the gift of a hundred gold coins and a portion of land offered by Akbar. Surdas also had to meet Akbar against his own wishes at Braj in Mathura. He too declined the Emperor's offer of a village and some cash and requested no further meetings.

Sikhism, Maharashtra Dharma, and the Pranami and Satnami sects initially emerged as movements of protest against Hinduism, but later turned political. The Sikhs called it *dharamyuddh* (religious crusade). Such war was religious and yet not communal at all. It was directed against the Mughals. In the same way, the imprisonment or execution of Sikh gurus by the Mughals should also be characterized not as religious persecution but as political reaction.

The Satnamis disapproved of communal differences and talked about Hindu-Muslim unity, maintained a curious distinction between the conduct within the sect and outside under the commandment that 'one may create whatever disturbance (*udham*) one liked but not where one lived'. Being always armed, they did not tolerate oppression and fought against the Mughals with valour.

It is really very significant that while in spiritual capacity both Guru Ramdas in Maharashtra and Prannath in Bundelkhand talked of communal harmony by emphasizing the unity of religions and unity of human beings, in political matters they adopted a different attitude and exploited religious prejudices. They spoke of politics in terms of religion and called upon the Hindu rajas to unite and organize under their respective political heads for *dharamyuddh* against the Mughals. Their call for Hindu Rashtra or Hindawi Swaraj was to infuse a strong current of militant Hindu revivalism in the mind of the people, as is evident from Ramdas's *Anandvanabhuvana* and Prannath's *Qayamatnama*. Guru Ramdas specifically called for *jaishnu* or aggressive Hinduism (as against *sahishnu* or tolerant Hinduism) in order to provide a communal base and moral strength to Shivaji. Yet both failed to create communal hatred, and social relations between Hindus and Muslims remained cordial in both areas. Even the followers of Ramdas and Prannath, who hailed from both the communities, remained intact in their sects.

In the same manner, though the ulama and the Sufis in general were not biased against the Hindus, there were some religious fanatics who from the beginning have been insisting Muslim rulers adopt discriminatory policies. For instance, some fanatic ulama in the time of Iltutmish insisted that the sultan reduce the Hindus' position by giving them the alternative of death or Islam, or at least by maintaining discriminatory attitude with them in all spheres of life. But their demand was turned down by the sultan on political grounds.[16] Balban also rejected the suggestion of some of the nobles to wipe out idolatry from the state and take steps for forcible conversions to Islam.[17] The assertion of *shariat* law in state policies by Qazi Mughisuddin was rejected by Alauddin Khalji: 'I do not know whether the order is in conformity with the *shariah* or contrary to it. Whatever I consider to be for the good of the people, and expedient, that I decree.'[18]

During the Mughal period the ulama were not allowed to assert the *sharia* law in state policies. The prejudiced ideas and suggestions extended by some of the Sufis like Abdul Quddus Gangohi, Abdul Haq Mohaddis Dehlavi, Shaikh Ahmad Sirhindi, and Shah Waliullah were not conceded by Mughal rulers. Jahangir's attitude to Shaikh Ahmad of Sirhind is a glaring example of it. Even under Aurangzeb, when *Maktubat-i Imam Rabbani* were included in the syllabus of the *madrasas* of Aurangabad, the Emperor ordered this to stop.[19]

Hence, bias towards Hindus was the product of the mind of some fanatic elements of Muslim society. Whereas this communal attitude adopted by some of the ulama and Sufis it was rejected by the rulers. The hostile attitude of some of the bhaktas towards the Mughals was based on political grounds, and it was not only supported but also exploited by Hindu rulers. However, since the general religious and spiritual leaders and the common people of both communities remained cordial, the rigid elements, whether Hindu or Muslim, could never succeed in dividing the Indian society on a communal basis.

As discussed earlier, there were two distinct facets of the bhakti movement—*nirguna* and the *saguna*, also known as 'non-conformist' and 'conformist'. The most important saints of the *Saguna* school were Tulsidas and Chaitanya. Both schools were generally reformist but those of the first school were quite uncompromising in all matters, while those of the second school compromised and were accommodating on some basic issues. But the saints of both categories, irrespective of their different forms of bhakti, attacked the degenerate varna system and the exploitation of the common people in the name of religion.

Tulsidas was not against liberal ideas, but opposed the radical trend of uprooting altogether the Vaishnava traditions and criticising the Vedic authority. He says, 'Neither four varnas nor four asharams are followed; All men and women are engaged in opposing the Vedas.'[20]

Tulsidas believed that the varna system was fundamentally based on a social division of labour. He emphasized its utility by pointing out that the existing social disorder was caused by the breakdown of the essence of this system. In fact, Tulsidas was also a social reformer but not revolutionary. He tried to build up an ideal society on a solid base of moral and ethical values in family life. Every father, mother, son, brother, wife and husband had specific duties to the family and to society as a whole. He was not against the concept of equality but was more concerned with the social disorder, which was due to the encroachment of the members of one caste on the functions of the other. So, for a stable society it was necessary for all the four varnas to perform their own respective duties without interfering in the other's defined area.

Tulsi has defined a stable social and political structure in his work. He gives an ideal social order functioning on the basis of a sound political system, i.e. *Ramrajya*. His *Ramcharitmanas* clearly speaks of the duties of the ruler, the relations between the ruler and the ruled, the duties and relationships among the members within the family and outside, and the conduct of men and women in different capacities. Tulsidas puts moral duties above all sentiments. His *Ramcharitmanas* thus symbolizes an ideal form of social interaction. Never aiming at founding a new religious order or going out of the *varnashram dharma*, Tulsidas tried to eliminate the evils of superstitions and formalism. For this reason, he denounced the religious monopoly of the brahmans by referring to them contemptuously as 'Bhudevas' and 'Bhusuras'.

Like Tulsidas, Chaitanya was also basically a religious philosopher. It was due to his religious experiment that he came into conflict with the prevalent social system. He advocated religious freedom for all and bhakti to be open to the lowest class of people. So, Chaitanya may also be called a social reformer but his reformation was 'only a by-product of his bhakti'.[21] Once Chaitanya declares in a very revolutionary manner, 'God is wholly independent; His grace does not follow the lines of the Vedas. God's grace does not care for caste and family', and that 'there is no consideration of caste or family in the worship of Krishna'.[22]

Chaitanya's flouting of caste rules is also evident from the fact that he, himself a brahman, maintained social contacts with people of lower castes and with Muslims. 'The maintenance of dignity is the ornament of a sadhu. . . . My mind is pleased when propriety of conduct is maintained.'[23]

Chaitanya's Krishna bhakti, based on purity and simplicity, was a contrast to the prevalent formal and ritualistic religious systems of Vaishnavism. His spiritual simplicity posed a threat to the priestly class and liberated the common people from ecclesiastical tyranny, as is gleaned from the following passage: 'Krishna's name alone removes all sins. . . . It does not depend upon initiation or priestly ceremonies. A mere utterance of the name saves everybody down to the Chandal.'[24]

Such thought led to the emergence of an enlightened Vaishnava community distinct from the traditional one. Chaitanya also tried to improve the position of women in the society and encouraged their initiation in the Gaudiya sect. Widow remarriage came to be practised among the lay Vaishnavas without caste barriers. The most important feature of his bhakti was the organization of *kirtan* or *sankirtan*, in which his followers, divided into several groups, went from door to door beating drums and chanting the name of Krishna and inviting people without to join the cult. This was done at city level and, therefore, it was also called *Nagar Kirtan*. This socio-religious character of Chaitanya's bhakti took the shape of a mass movement.

The attitude of Tulsidas and Chaitanya regarding the institution of caste should be viewed in terms of their Saguna bhakti. Both stressed the importance of the essence of varna system for social stability. The ideal of their bhakti, however, gave a broadness and catholicity to their ideas and both placed bhakti above the rules of caste.

Tulsidas and Chaitanya believed in Ram and Sri Krishna as embodiments of God, and in idol worship, but were not ready to accept useless rituals and formalities. For both, bhakti was supreme and did not include abstract meditation, sacrifice, penance or fasting. They helped people to differentiate between true religion and superstition. They also took up not only the socio-religious matters but also the political, administrative and economic aspects and the material condition and hardships faced by the common people.

However, the greatest contribution of the radical bhakti saints was that they broke the religious monopoly of the Brahmans and brought religious leadership to the lower classes. They simplified the religion, substituted the Vedas by their own compilations and adopted the language of the masses in lieu of Sanskrit as a medium of instruction. It is also significant that during the time of such a rigid socio-religious systems, the saints cultivated rational thought and practices and adopted freedom of speech without fear. They injected into society the ideal of ethical values, rationalism, and humanism, and were successful in awakening mass consciousness of these values. The philosophical base was founded on Islamic monotheism and later Vedic monism and, there was a very deep mutual understanding and interaction among them. If Kabir and Dadu were Muslims by birth, Banwaridas Wali and Shaikh Madho, both Hindus, became disciples of Mulla Shah and Shaikh Husain, repectively. Shaikh Madho even succeeded his master as his *khalifa* at Lahore in 1599. An interesting reference comes from the *Akhbarul Akhyar* of Shaikh Abdul Haq Dehlavi, according to which theologians were not sure whether Kabir was to be reckoned as Muslim or *kafir*, but his verses were read and quoted in Sufi centres in Delhi and Agra from the beginning of the sixteenth century.[25]

It is a fact that the followers of the radical movements have violated some of the basic ideals of their leaders. For instance, all (with the only exception of Nanak) disapproved, even fought, throughout, institutional organization of any kind, but their followers founded separate sects in their names. Not only this, they ascribed to their masters divine qualities and even attributed miracles to them. Thus, the saints themselves were held divine, which they would have never expected. None of the followers of these saints except the Sikh gurus ever thought of taking the place or position of his guru.

A subtle change took place in the inner character of the Bhakti movement after the demise of the teachers. These men, along with their contemporary followers, rejected formal doctrines, distinctive marks, initiatory rites, and prescribed modes of worship. Their doors were open to all without distinction of caste or community. But, after them particular rituals were adopted by particular groups. The divine position that was later given to them created a suitable background for their own worship in all the cults formed in their names. The *Bijak* for the Kabirpanthis, the *Guru Granth* for the Sikhs and the *Panchavani* for the Dadupanthis occupied not only the position of scriptural authority but also became objects of formal worship. *Arti* was adopted by Hindu devotees who were familiar with the temple service. This led to the growing approximation of the cult to traditional Hinduism, in a different form.

NOTES

1. Kabir refers to himself in his verses as Kori and Julaha, and calls God Rama and Rahim. Nanak characterizes himself as neither Hindu nor Musalman but a worshipper of the Formless. Similarly, Dadu advocated the concept of *nipakh* (i.e. non-attachment to any religious or sectarian order) and declare he was neither a Hindu nor a Musalman but a human being.
2. *Mahdi*, 46, 48, as cited by W.G. Orr, *A Sixteenth Century Indian Mystic: Dadu and His Followers*, London: Latterworth Press, 1947, p. 62.
3. *Mahdi*, 56, cited in ibid., p. 63.
4. M.A. Macauliffe, *The Sikh Religion*, vol. VI, rpt., Delhi: Low Price Pubs., 1993, p. 132.
5. See Kabir's Acrostic no. 5 in ibid., p. 182.
6. *Sach, Sakhis* 98, 100, as cited by Orr, op. cit., p. 62.
7. *Sach, Sakhis* 102-4, as cited in ibid., p. 166.
8. D.B. Mac Donald, 'The Life of Al-Ghazali', *Journal of the American Oriental Society*, vol. XX, 1899.
9. The *Guru Granth* was first enshrined by Guru Arjan in the Har Mandir in Mukhud. Guru Gobind Singh declared the *Granth* as the ultimate authoritative Guru (spiritual teacher) for all matters after him. Henceforth, it had to be regarded forever as 'the body of eleventh incarnated Guru', a living testament to the *bani* of the gurus. It is now kept on a raised platform under a canopy, covered with richly embroidered cloths in the gurdwara. The *Angabandha* comprising Dadu's sayings in the Naraina Dadudwara is an early manuscript wrapped in red and gold cloth with a coloured rosary laid across it. The *Bijak* or the *Khas Granth* of Kabir has also been placed almost in the same glorious position at Kabir Chaura in Varanasi. The texts, placed on their *gaddis* or cushions, almost take the place of the scriptures of the orthodox. The essential feature is recital from the text.
10. The line is often quoted but is not found in any of the authentic sources on Kabir.
11. See Kabir's *Gauri* LXX, Macauliffe, op. cit., vol. VI, p. 179. The way Kabir has repeatedly emphasized the oneness of God is important and reminds us of the strict monotheism of Islam: 'There is no God but Him, the One Creator'. 'Dadu too took up this issue, almost in the same spirit as Kabir. He says, 'Call Him Rama, Call Him Allah: It is all one'. Further 'All are mortal, even Brahma, Vishnu, and Mahesh, but there is one immortal, who is without a second.' For these and other such references, see Orr, op. cit., pp. 134-5.
12. Kabir says that those 'carrying rosaries on their necks and glittering brass utensils in their hand should not be called saints of God but the cheats of Banaras'. Kabir, *Asa* II, Macauliffe, op. cit., vol. VI, p. 196. Nanak

Conclusion

remarked that the Brahmans had become very rich. See Macauliffe, op. cit., vol. 1, p. 49, Dadu too condemned gurus by saying that 'the disciple is the cow, the guru is the milkman'. *Anga Gurudev, Sakhis* 123, 124, cited by Orr, op. cit., p. 63.

13. Ch. Vaudeville, *Kabir*, vol.1, Oxford: Clarendon Press, 1974, p. 97.
14. *Pad* 296: 3 and *Sach, Sakhi* 189, as cited by Orr, op. cit., pp. 74–5.
15. *Piw Pichhan*, II, as cited in ibid., p. 74.
16. S. Nurul Hasan, 'Sahifa-i Nat-i Muhammadi of Ziauddin Barani', *Medieval India Quarterly*, vol. 1, no. 3, 1950, p. 103. A similar idea was also extended to Iltutmish by Syed Nuruddin Mubarak who asked the Sultan that if the polytheists were so numerous that Muslim ruler could not possibly eradicate them, at least he should strive to insult them and bring disgrace, dishonour, and ignominy upon them. *Tarikh-i-Firoz Shahi*, ed. Sir Syed Ahmad Khan, Calcutta, 1862, pp. 41–2.
17. Ibid., pp. 72, 74, 75.
18. For details about Alauddin's conversation with Qazi Mughisuddin, ibid., pp. 290–1, 296.
19. Shaikh Muhammad Ikram, *Raud-i Kausar*, Lahore, 1966, p. 450.
20. Tulsidas, *Ramcharitamanas*, ed. M.P. Gupta, Allahabad: Hindustani Academy, n.d., *Uttarkand, Chaupai* 97.1.
21. M.T. Kennedy, *The Chaitanya Movement*, London: Oxford University Press, 1925, p. 57.
22. *Chaitanya Charitamrit*, as cited in ibid., p. 119.
23. Ibid.
24. Ibid., p. 121.
25. Abdul Haq Mohaddis Dehlavi, *Akhbar-ul Akhyar*, ed. Muhammad Abdul Ahad, Delhi: Muitabai Press, 1914, p. 300; also Ch. Vaudeville, op. cit., p. 34.

Bibliography

PRIMARY SOURCES

Abdullah, *Tarikh-i Daudi*, ed. Shaikh Abdur Rashid, Aligarh: Department of History, Aligarh Muslim University (AMU) AMU, 1954.
Abul Fazl, *Ain-i-Akbari*, Delhi: Oriental Books, 3 vols., 1977–8.
———, *Akbarnama*, ed. Molvi Abdur Rahim, Calcutta: Asiatic Society, 1877.
Afifi, Shams Siraj, *Tarikh-i Firoz Shahi*, ed. Molvi Wilayat Husain, Calcutta, 1890.
Ahmad, Yadgar, *Tarikh-i Shahi*, ed. Muhammad Hidayat Husain, Calcutta: Bibliotheca Indica, 1939.
Ain-ul Mulk, *Insha-i Mahru*, ed. S.A. Rashid, Lahore: Idara-i Tahqiqat-i Pakistan, 1965
Alberuni, *Kitab-ul Hind*, tr. Edward C. Sachau, Delhi: S. Chand, 1964.
Ali Bin Hamid bin Abu Bakr, *Chachnama (Fathnamah-i Sindh)*, ed. N.A. Baloch, Islamabad, 1982, tr. Elliot and Dowson, *History of India*, vol. I, Delhi: Low Price Publication, 2001.
Ali Bin Usman AL-Hujwiri, *Kashaf-ul Mahjub*, tr. Reynold Nicolson, Delhi: Taj Company, 1982.
Amir Hasan Sijzi, *Fawaid-ul Fuwad*, Lucknow: Newal Kishore Press, 1312 AH.
Amir Khusrau, *Aijaz-i Khusravi*, Lucknow: Newal Kishore Press, 1876.
———, *Tughlaqnamah*, ed. Syed Hashmi Faridabadi, Aurangabad, 1933.
Anonymous *Surur-us Sudur*, MS, Habib Ganj Collection, Maulana Azad Library, AMU.
———, *Sirat-i-Firoz Shahi*, compiled 1370 at the instance of Firoz Shah, Rotograph, Aligarh: AMU.
Babur, *Baburnama*, tr. in 2 vols., Mrs. Beveridge, Delhi: Oriental Books, 1979.
Badauni, Abdul Qadir, *Muntakhab-ut Tawarikh*, ed. Molvi Ahmad Ali, Calcutta: Asiatic Society, 1865.
Bakhshi, Nizamuddin Ahmad, *Tabaqat-i Akbari*, ed. B. De and Molvi Hidayat Husain, Lucknow: Newal Kishore Press, 1875.
Barani, Ziauddin, *Fatawa-i Jahandari*, Rotograph, Aligarh: AMU, tr. with annotation and introduction by Muhammad Habib and Mrs. Afsar

Khan, *The Political Theory of the Delhi Sultanate*, Allahabad: Kitab Mahal (n.d.).

———, *Tarikh-i-Firoz Shahi*, ed. Sir Syed Ahmad Khan, Calcutta: Bib. Indica, 1862.

Bhandari, Sujan Rai, *Khulasat-ut Tawarikh* (compiled in 1696), ed. Zafar Hasan, Delhi: G. & Sons, 1918.

Bitthalnath, *Do Sau Bawan Vaishnavon ki Varta*, ed. Dwarkadas Parikh, in 3 parts, Kankraul: Sudhadvait Academy, 1953.

The Bitak of Braj Bhushan, ed. K.D. Sharma, Jamnagar: Pranami Dharm Sabha, 1931.

The Bitak of Laldas, ed. Matabadal Jaiswal, Bankura, 1966.

Dadu Dayal, *Shri Daduvani*, ed. Narayandas, 2nd edn., Jaipur, 1969.

Dehlavi, Shaikh Abdul Haq Muhaddis, *Akhbar-ul-Akhyar*, compiled 1590–1, ed. Muhammad Abdul Ahad, Delhi: Muitabai Press; Urdu tr. Subhan Mahmood, Delhi: Noor Publishing House, 1990.

Dehlavi, Shaikh Noorul Haq, *Zibdat-ut Tawarikh*, Rotograph, Aligarh: AMU.

Dharamdas, *Dharamdas Ki Shabdawali*, Prayag: Velvedier Press, 1887.

Fakhr-i Mudabbir, *Tarikh-i-Fakhr-i Mudabbir*, ed. E. Dension Ross, London, 1927.

Firishta, Muhammad Qasim, *Tarikh-i Firishta*, Lucknow: Newal Kishore Press, 1323 AH, tr. John Briggs, *History of the Rise of the Mohamedan Power in India*, rpt., Calcutta, 1911.

Gangohi, Abdul Quddus, *Maktubat-i Quddusia*, Delhi: Matba-i Ahmadi, 1871.

———, *Rushd Nama* (a compilation of Persian and Hindi verses of different Sufis, saints and yogis), Hindi tr. as Alakh Bani with introduction by A.A. Rizvi and Jafar Raza Zaidi, Aligarh: Bharat Prakashan Mandir, 1971.

Gokul, *Bhao Sindhu ki Varta*, ed. Dwarkadas Parikh, Saurashtra: Star Printing Press, 1965/1908.

Gorakhnath, *Gorakh Bani*, ed. P.D. Barthwal, Prayag: Hindi Sahitya Sammelan, 1999/1942.

Guru Govind Singh, *Sri Dasam Granth Sahabji*, compiled by Bhai Mani in 1716, 1st approved edn., Amritsar: Sikh Singh Sabha, 1925.

Gyandev, *The Gyaneshwari*, tr. V.K. Rajvade, Bombay, 1990.

Husain, Mohammad Murtaza, *Hidiqat-ul Akalim*, Lucknow: Matba-i Nami, 1879.

Ibn-i Battuta, *The Travels of Ibn-i Battuta*, tr. Sir Hamilton Gibb, Delhi: Munshiram Manoharlal, 1993.

Ijad, Muhammad Ahsan, *Tashrih-al Aqwam*, Rotograph, Aligarh: AMU.

Imperial Farmans (1577–1605), tr. K.M. Jhaveri, Rotograph, Aligarh: AMU.

Bibliography

Isami, *Futuh-us Salatin*, ed. A.S. Usha, Madras, 1948.
Jahangir, *Tuzuk-i Jahangir*, ed. Sir Syed Ahmad Khan, Aligarh, 1864.
Jan Gopal, *Dadu Janma Lila Parichaya*, Jaipur: Mangal Press, 1949.
Kabir, Muhammad, *Afsana-i Shahan*, Rotograph, Aligarh: AMU.
Kabirdas, *Kabir Bijak*, ed. Sukdev Singh, Allahabad: Nilam Prakashan, 1972.
Kazim, Muhammad, *Alamgirnama*, Calcutta: Asiatic Society of Bengal, 1868.
Khan, Khafi, *Muntakhab-ul Lubat*, vol. 1, ed. Hashim Khan, Calcutta: College Press, 1870, vol. II, ed. Kabiruddin Ahmad and Ghulam Qadir, Calcutta: Urdu Guide Press, 1874.
Khan, Sadiq, *Tawarikh-i Shahjahani*, copy no. 9, Aligarh: AMU.
Khan, Shah Nawaz, *Maasir-ul Umara*, Calcutta: Asiatic Society of Bengal, 1891.
Krishnadas Kaviraj, *Shri Chaitanya Charitamrita* (Bengali Biography of Chaitanya), tr. Jadunath Sarkar as *Chaitanya's Life and Teachings*, Calcutta, 1932.
Kumbhandas, *Kumbhandas ki Bani*, ed. Braj Bhushan Sharma, Kankroli: Vidya Vibhag, 1954.
Lahori, Ghulam Sarwar, *Khazinat-ul Asfia*, Urdu tr., Lahore: Maktaba Nabvia, 1983.
Lalded, *Lalla Vakyani*, tr. as *Wise Sayings of Lalded: A Mystic Poetess of Ancient Kashmir*, G. Grierson and Dr. Bainett, London, 1920.
Manusmriti, tr. G. Buhler, *The Laws of Manu*, Delhi, 1975.
Minhaj Siraj, *Tabaqat-i Nasiri*, ed. Abdul Hai Habibi, Kabul, 1964.
Mir Khurd, *Siyar-ul Aulia*, Delhi: Muhib Hind, 1302 AH/AD 1885.
Mobad, *Dabistan-i Mazahib*, Kanpur: Newal Kishore Press, 1904; tr. Shea and Troyer, Lahore: Khalil and Co., 1973.
Mudit, Bhagwat, *Sri Rasik Ananyamal*, ed. Lalita Prasad, Vrindaban: Venu Prakashan, 1960.
Nabhadas, *Bhaktmala*, ed. S.R. Bhagwandas, Lucknow: Newal Kishore Press, 1913.
Nagar, Ishwaridas, *Futuhat-i Alamgiri*, Rotograph, Aligarh: AMU.
Panchavani (Dadupanthi compilations), MS copies, *Basta* No. 12, compiled by Swamdas, 1693/1636; and *Basta* No. 2, compiled by Narharidas 1733/1676, brought by the author from Dadu Mahavidyalaya, Jaipur, are available in our Seminar Library, Aligarh: AMU.
Pramit, Hari Rai, *Chaurasi Vaishnavon ki Varta*, ed. Dwarkadas Parikh, Mathura: Agrawal Press, 3rd edn., 2017/1960.
Prannath, *Kulzum Swaroop*, ed. Matabadal Jaiswal, Bankura, 1965.
Qalandar, Hamid, *Khair-ul-Majalis*, compiled 1354, ed. K.A. Nizami, Aligarh, 1959.

Rajjabdas, *The Sarbangi of Rajjabdas,* ed. Shahabuddin Iraqi, Aligarh: Granthayan Publication, 1985.
Saqi, Mustaid Khan, *Ma'asir-i Alamgiri,* Karachi: Nafees Academy, 1962.
Satnami, Bhawanidas, *Pothi Gyan Bani,* MS, in Royal Asiatic Society Library, London (Hindi-1) (Abstracts from the manuscript were provided to the author by Prof. Irfan Habib).
Shaikh Jamali Dehlavi bin Fazl-ullah, *Siyar-ul Arifin,* Rotograph, Aligarh: AMU.
Shaikh Rizqullah Mushtaqi, *Waqiat-i Mushtaqi,* Rotograph, Aligarh: AMU.
Shaikh Shihabuddin al-Umar, *Masalik-ul Absar fimumalik-i Amsar,* tr. Iqtidar H. Siddiqui, Aligarh, 1971.
Shattari, Muhammad Ghausi *Gulzar-i Abrar,* Rotograph, Aligarh: AMU; Urdu tr. Molvi Fazl Ahmad, Agra, 1326 AH.
Sherwani, Abbas Khan, *Tarikh-i Shahi,* Eng. tr. *The History of India As Told by its own Historians* by H.M. Elliot and John Dowson, vol. IV; rpt. Delhi: Low Price, 2001.
Shri Guru Granth Sahab (both in Gurmukhi and Nagari scripts), Amritsar: Shiromani Gurdwara Prabandhak Committee, 1952.
Sirhindi, Shaikh Ahmad, *Muktubat-i Imam Rabbani* (collection of his letters in Persian) in 3 vols., ed. Ghulam Mustafa Khan, Istanbul, 1977.
Surdas, *Sursagar,* Kashi: Nagari Pracharini Sabha, in 2 vols, 4th edn., 1969.
Swami Mangaldas (ed.), *Panchavani* (a Dadupanthi compilation), Jaipur: Dadu Mahavidyalaya, 1948.
Tegh Bahadur, *Hukmname* (a collection of his 22 orders), pub. with Eng. tr. by Ganda Singh, Patiala: Punjabi University, 1967.
Tughluk, Firoz Shah, *Futuhat-i Firoz Shahi,* ed. Shaikh Abdur Rashid, Aligarh: AMU, 1954.
Tulsidas, *Sri Ramcharitmanas,* ed. M.P. Gupta, Allahabad: Hindustani Academy, n.d.
———, *Tulsi Granthawali,* ed. R.C. Shukla et al., Kashi: Nagari Pracharini Sabha, 3rd edn., 2004/1947.
Yahya Sirhindi, *Tarikh-i Mubarak Shahi,* ed. M. Hidayat Hussain, Calcutta, 1931.

SECONDARY SOURCES

Abdul Halim, *History of the Lodi Sultans of Delhi and Agra,* Delhi: Idara-i Adabiyat-i Dehli, 1974.
Agrawal, Sarju Prasad, *Akbari Darbar ke Hindi Kavi,* Lucknow: Lucknow University Publications, 1950.

Bibliography 275

Ahmad, Aziz, *Studies in Islamic Culture in the Indian Environment*, Oxford: Clarendon Press, 1964.

Ahmad, Nazir and I.H. Sidiqui, eds, *Islamic Heritage in South Asian Subcontinent,* vol. 11, Jaipur: Publication Scheme, 2000.

Ahmad, M. Basheer, *The Administration of Justice* in Medieval India, Karachi: Manager of Publication, 1951.

Alam, Muzaffar, Françoise 'Nalini' Delvoye and Marc Gaborieau, eds., *The Making of Indo-Persian Culture, Indian and French Studies*, Delhi: Manohar, 2000.

Ameer Ali, *A Short History of the Saracens*, Delhi: Kitab Bhawan, 1977.

Anonymous, *Saints of Northern India (from Ramanand to Ram Trath)*, one of the Series of the World Teachers, Madras: G.A. Natesan & Co., n.d.

———, *Three Great Acharyas (Shankara, Ramanuja and Madhva)* 2nd edn., Madras: G.A. Natesan & Co., n.d.

Arberry, A.J., *Sufism: An Account of the Mystics of Islam*, London: Unwin, 1979.

Arnold, Sir Thomas and Alfred Guillaume, eds., *The Legacy of Islam*, London: Oxford University Press, 1931.

Ashraf, K.M., *Life and Condition of the People of Hindustan*, Delhi: Jiwan Prakashan, 1959.

Baillie, N., *Digest of Muhammadan Law*, London, 1975.

Banerjee, Indu Bhushan, *Evolution of the Khalsa*, in 2 vols., Calcutta: A. Mukherjee, 1947.

Barthwal, P.D., *The Nirgun School of Hindi Poetry*, Banaras: Indian Book Shop, 1936.

Behere, N.K., *The Background of Maratha Renaissance in the 17th Century*, Bangalore, 1946.

Bhandarkar, R.G., *Vaishnavism, Shaivism and Minor Religious Systems*, Delhi: Skylark Printers, 1965.

Bhatnagar, Ram Ratan, *Kabir Sahitya ki Bhumika*, Allahabad, 1950.

Bhattacharya, Haridas, ed., *The Cultural Heritage of India,* vol. IV, Calcutta: Calcutta Institute of Culture, 1956.

Bhattacharya, Siddheshwar, *The Philosophy of Sirimadd Bhagavat*, Santiniketan: Vishwabharti, 1960.

Briggs, G.W., *Gorakhnath and the Kanpatha Yogis*, Calcutta, 1938.

Chandra, Satish, *Medieval India from Sultanate to the Mughals (1206-1748)*, Delhi: Har-Anand, 1997, 1999.

———, *Mughal Religious Policies: The Rajput and Deccan*, Delhi: Vikas, 1983.

———, *Parties and Politics at the Mughal Court (1707-1740)*, 4th edn., Delhi: Peoples' Publishing House, 2002.

Chaturvedi, P.R., ed., *Dadu Granthawali* (based on a MS., dated 1710/ 1653) Varanasi: Kashi Nagari Pracharini Sabha, 1966.

Chaturvedi, P.R., *Uttari Bharat ki Sant Prampara*, 2nd edn., Allahabad: Bharati Bhandar, 1964.

Chawla, Govind Lal, *Krantikari Kabir*, Delhi: Ranjit Printers, 1971.

Cunningham, J.D., *A History of the Sikhs*, ed. N.L.O. Garrett, Delhi: S. Chand, 1955.

Darshan Singh, *Indian Bhakti Tradition and the Sikh Gurus*, Jalandar: New Age Publication, 1979.

Dasgupta, S.B., *Obscure Religious Cults*, Calcutta: Calcutta University Press, 2nd edn., 1962.

Dasgupta, S.N., *A History of Indian Philosophy*, rpt., Delhi: Motilal Banarsidass, 1975.

Dikshit, P.N., *Nabhadas Krit Bhaktmal: Ek Adhyayan*, Allahabad: Sahitya Bhawan, 1961.

Dwivedi, Hazari Prasad, *Hindi Sahitya ki Bhumika*, Delhi, 1969.

———, *Kabir*, Bombay: Hindi Granth Ratnakar, 2nd edn., 1947.

———, *Nath Sampradaya*, Allahabad: Hinduatani Acadamy, 1950.

Dube, Kedarnath, *Kabir aur Kabir-Panth*, Prayag: Hindi Sahitya Sammelan, 1965.

Engineer, Asghar Ali, *Theory and Practice of Islamic State*, London, 1985.

Farquhar, J.N., *An Outline of the Religious Literature of India*, rpt., Delhi: Motilal Banarsidass, 1984.

Fuhrer, A., *The Monumental Antiquities and Inscriptions in the N.W., Provinces and Oudh*, rpt., Delhi, 1969.

Ghurye, G.S., *Indian Sadhus*, 2nd edn., Bombay, 1964.

Gopal Singh, *Guru Nanak*, Delhi, 1992.

Goswami, Lalita Charan, *Shri Hita Harivansh Goswami: Sampradaya aur Sahitya*, Vrindaban: Venu Prakashan, 1957.

Grewal, J.S., *From Guru Nanak to Maharaja Ranjit Singh*, Amritsar, 1972.

———, *Guru Nanak in History*, Chandigarh: Punjab University, 1969.

———, *The Sikhs of the Punjab*, Cambridge: Cambridge University Press, 1994.

Grower, F.S., *Mathura: A District Memoir*, Delhi, 1979.

Gupta, Bhagwandas, *Maharaja Chhatrasal Bundela*, Agra, 1958.

Habib, Irfan, *The Agrarian System of Mughal India*, Delhi: Asia Publishing House, 1963.

Habib, Mohammad and K.A. Nizami, eds., *A Comprehensive History of India*, vol. V, *The Delhi Sultanate*, Delhi: Peoples' Publishing House, 1970.

Habib, Mohammad, *The Political Theory of the Delhi Sultanate*, Allahabad: Kitab Mahal (n.d.).

Habibullah, A.B.M., *The Foundation of Muslim Rule in India*, Allahabad, 1989.
Handoo, C.K., *Tulsidas: Poet, Saint and Philosopher of the Sixteenth Century*, Bombay: Orient Longman, 1964.
Hastings, James, ed., *Encyclopaedia of Religion and Ethics*, Edinburgh, 1914.
Hedayetullah, Mohd. Kabir, *The Apostle of Hindu-Muslim Unity, Interaction of Hindu-Muslim Ideas in the Formation of the Bhakti Movement with Special Reference to Kabir, the Bhakta*, Delhi: Motilal Banarsidass, 1977.
Husain, Mahdi, *The Tughlaq Dynasty* (revd. and enlarged edn. of *The Rise and Fall of Muhammad bin Tughlaq*), Calcutta: Thacker, 1963.
Husain, Waheed, *Administration of Justice During the Muslim Rule in India*, Calcutta: Calcutta University Press, 1934.
Husain, Yusuf, *Glimpses of Medieval Indian Culture*, Bombay: Asia Publishing House, 1962.
Ibbeston, *A Glossary of the Tribes and Castes of Punjab*, Lahore: Punjab Government Press, 1936.
Islam, Riazul, *Sufism in South Asia*, rpt., Karachi: Oxford University Press, 2002.
Jaiswal, Suvira, *The Origin and Development of Vaishnavism*, Delhi: Munshiram Manoharlal, 1967.
Jauhari, R.C., *Firoz Tughlaq (1351-1388)*, Agra: Shivlal Agrawala, 1968.
Jha, D.N., ed., *The Feudal Order: State, Society and Ideology in Early Medieval India*, Delhi: Manohar, 2000.
Jutsi, P. Manohar Lal, *Kabir Saheb*, Prayag: Hindustani Academy, 1930.
Keay, F.E., *Kabir and His Followers*, rpt., Delhi: Mittal Publication, 1967.
Kennedy, M.T., *The Chaitanya Movement: A Study of the Vaishnavism of Bengal*, London: Oxford University Press, 1925.
Kosambi, D.D., *The Culture and Civilization of Ancient India in Historical Outline*, 2nd rpt., Delhi: Vikas, 1975.
Kulkarni, A.R., *Maharashtra in the Age of Shivaji*, Poona: Deshmukh Prakashan, 1969.
Lal, K.S., *Studies in Medieval Indian History*, Delhi: Ranjit, 1966.
———, *Twilight of the Delhi Sultanate*, Delhi: Asia Publishing House, 1963.
Levy, Reuben, *The Social Structure of Islam*, 2nd edn., Cambridge: Cambridge University Press, 1957.
M. Hasan, *Kashmir Under the Sultanate,* Calcutta: Iran Society, 1959.
Mac Leod, Hew, *Life of Guru Nanak*, London: Oxford University Press, 1968.
Macauliffe, M.A., *The Sikh Religion*, rpt., Delhi: Low Price Pubs., 1993.

Macdonald, D.B., *Development of Muslim Theology, Jurisprudence and Constitutional Theory*, Beirut: Khayat, 1965.

Majumdar, ed., *The Delhi Sultanate*, Bombay: Bharatiya Vidya Bhawan, 1960.

Max Müller, *Six Systems of Indian Philosophy*, London: Longmans Green and Co., 1919.

Menaria, Motilal, *Rajasthan Mein Hindi Hast Likhit Granthon ki Khoj*, Udaipur: Rajasthan Vidyapith, n.d.

Misra, S.C., *The Rise of Muslim Power in Gujrat*, 2nd. edn., Delhi: Munshiram Manoharlal, 1982.

Mohan Singh, *Gorakhnath and Medieval Hindu Mysticism*, Lahore, 1937.

———, *Kabir, His Biography*, Lahore, 1934.

Mukharyar, P.S., *Mahamati Prannath and the Synthesis of All Religions*, Jamnagar: Navatanpuri Dham, 2003.

Nandinath, S.C., *A Hand Book of Vira Saivaism*, Dharwar, 1952.

Narayandas, *Shri Dadupanth Prarichaya*, Jaipur: Dadu Mahasabha, 3 vols, 1978–9.

Nicholson, R.A., *Studies in Islamic Mysticism*, New York: Cambridge University Press, 1989.

Nizami K.A., ed., *Politics and Society During the Early Medieval Period (Collected Works of Mohammad Habib)*, Delhi: Peoples' Publishing House, 1974.

———, *On History and Historians of Medieval India*, Delhi: Munshiram Manoharlal, 1983.

———, *Studies in Medieval Indian History*, Aligarh: Cosmopolitan Publishers, 1956.

———, *Some Aspects of Religion and Politics in India during the Thirteenth Century*, rpt., Delhi: Idara-i Adabiyat-i Dehli, 1978.

———, *Akbar and Religion*, Delhi: Idara-i Adabiyat-i-Dehli, 1989.

———, *Hayat-i Shaikh Abdul Haq Muhaddis Dehlavi*, Delhi, 1964.

———, *Salatin-i Dehli Ke Mazhabi Rujhanat*, Delhi, 1958.

———, *State and Culture in Medieval India*, Delhi: Adam Pubs, 1985.

———, *The Life and Times of Shaikh Fariduddin Ganj Shakar*, Aligarh, 1955.

Nurul Hasan, S., *Thoughts on Agrarian Relations in Mughal India*, 2nd rpt., Delhi: Peoples' Publishing House, 1990.

Orr, W.G., *A Sixteenth Century Indian Mystic: Dadu and His Followers*, London: Latterworth Press, 1947.

Pandey, Susmita, *Birth of Bhakti in Indian Religions and Art*, Delhi, 1982.

Pannikar, K.M., *A Survey of Indian History*, Bombay: Asia Publishing House, 1956.

Bibliography

Prasad, Ishwari, *A Short History of Muslim Rule in India*, revd. edn., Allahabad: Indian Press, 1965.
Qureshi, I.H., *The Administration of the Sultanate of Delhi*, Lahore: S.H. Muhammad Ashraf, 1942.
———, *The Muslim Community of the Indo-Pakistan Sub-Continent*, Gravenhage: Mouton, 1962.
Radhakrishnan, S., *Indian Philosophy*, Indian Edition, Delhi, 1940.
Ranade, M.G., *Rise of the Maratha Power*, Bombay: Bombay University, 1961.
Ranade, R.D., *Pathway to God in Marathi Literature*, Bombay: Bharatiya Vidya Bhawan, 1961.
Rashid, A., *Society and Culture in Medieval India (1206-1556)*, Calcutta: Firma, 1969.
Rizvi, S.A.A., *A History of Sufism in India*, Delhi: Munshiram Manoharlal, 1978, 1983.
———, *Muslim Revivalist Movements in Northern India in the 16th and 17th Centuries*, Agra: Agra University Press, 1965.
Saran, P., *A Descriptive Catalogue of Non-Persian Sources of Medieval India*, Bombay: Asia Publishing House, 1965.
Sardesai, G.S., *The Main Currents of Maratha History*, revd. edn., Bombay: Phoenix Publications, 1949.
Sarkar, J.N., *History of Aurangzeb*, Calcutta: Sarkar, 1912.
Sen, D.C., *Chaitanya and His Age*, Calcutta: Calcutta University Press, 1922.
Sharma, Divendranath, ed., *Hindi Sahitya ka Vrihat Itihas*, part 5, Varanasi: Kashi Nagari Pracharini Sabha, 2031/1974.
Sharma, Krishna, *Bhakti and the Bhakti Movement: A New Perspective*, Delhi: Munshiram Manoharlal, 1987.
Sharma, R.S., *Material Culture and Social Formations in India*, Delhi: MacMillan, 1983.
Sharma, S.R., *The Religious Policy of the Mughal Emperors*, 3rd edn., Delhi: Munshiram Manoharlal, 1988.
Sharma, Vasudev, *Sant Kavi Dadu aur Unka Panth*, Delhi, 1969.
Shibli Nomani, *Al-Farooq*, Azamgarh: Darul Musannafin, 1956.
———, *Al-Ghazali*, Delhi: Helal Press, 1914.
———, *Maqalat-i Shibli*, Azamgarh: Darul Musanafin, 1955.
'Shobha', Savitri Chandra, ed., *Medieval India and Hindi Bhakti Poetry: A Socio-Cultural Study* (collection of her articles), Delhi: Har-Anand, 1996.
Shrivastava, Purushottamlal, *Kabir Sahitya Ka Adhyayan*, Banaras: Sahitya Ratn Mala Karyalaya, 2008/1951.

Shukl, Ram Chandra, *Hindi Sahitya ka Itihas,* 2nd edn., Varanasi: Kashi Nagari Pracharini Sabha, 2025/1968.

Shushtery, A.M.A., *Outlines of Islamic Culture (Historical and Cultural Aspects),* 2nd edn., Banglore, 1954.

Siddiqui, I.H., *Authority and Kingship Under the Sultans of Delhi,* Delhi: Manohar, 2006.

———, *Islam and Muslims in South Asia: Historical Perspective,* Delhi: Adam Publishers, 1987.

———, *Some Aspects of Afghan Despotism in India,* Aligarh: Three Men Publishers, 1969.

Singh, Khushwant, *A History of the Sikhs,* London: Princeton University Press, 1963.

Singh, Rajdev, *Shabad Aur Arth Sant Sahitya Ke Sandarbh Mein,* Varanasi: Nand Kishore, 1968.

Singh, Sher, *Philosophy of Sikkhism,* 2nd edn., Jalandhar, Sterling, 1944.

Smith, V.A., *Akbar The Great Mughal (1542-1605),* Delhi: S. Chand, 1958.

Srivastava, K.L., *The Position of Hindus under the Delhi Sultanate (1206-1526),* Delhi: Munshiram Manoharlal, 1980.

Sundardas, Shyam, *Hindi Sahitya,* Prayag: Indian Press, 1956.

———, ed., *Kabir Granthawali,* Varanasi: Kashi Nagari Pracharini Sabha 13th edn., 2032/1975.

Swami Mangaldas, ed., *Dadu Sampradaya ka Sankshipt Parichaya,* Jaipur: Dadu Mahavidyalaya, 2009/1952.

Swami Narottamdas, *Kabirdas,* Lahore: Hindi Bhawan, 1997/1940.

Tara Chand, *Influence of Islam on Indian Culture,* Allahabad: Indian Press, 1963.

Temple, R.C., *The Words of Lalla,* Cambridge: Cambridge University Press, 1924.

Thipperudra Swamy, H., *The Vir Saiva Saints: A Study,* Mysore, 1968.

Thomas, E., *The Chronicles of the Pathan Kings of Delhi,* Delhi: Munshiram Manoharlal, 1967.

Titus, M.T., *Indian Islam,* 2nd edn., Delhi: Oriental Books, 1979.

Tiwari, P.N., ed., *Kabir Granthawali,* Prayag: Hindi Parishad, 1961.

Trigurayat, Govind, *Kabir ki Vichardhara,* Kanpur: Sahitya Niketan, 2009/1952.

Vaudeville, Ch., *Kabir,* vol. I, Oxford: Clarendon Press, 1974.

Verma, Ram Kumar, *Hindi Sahitya ka Alochnatmak Itihas (Samwat 750–1750),* Allahabad: Ram Narayan Publisher, 1958.

———, *Kabir ka Rahasyavad,* 9th edn., Allahabad: Sahitya Bhawan, 1961.

———, *Sant Kabir,* Allahabad: Sahitya Bhawan, 1948.

Westcott, G.H., *Kabir and the Kabirpanth,* Calcutta: Susil Gupta, 1953.

Wilson, H.H., *Sketch of the Religious Sects of the Hindus*, Calcutta: Susil Gupta, 1958.

ARTICLES

Ahmad, Aziz, 'Theocracy Versus Autocracy', *Journal of Indian History*, vol. XVII, part III, December 1939.
Ahluwalia, M.S., 'Reflections on Bhakti Movement in Tamil Nadu and Punjab', *Journal of Sikh Studies*, vol. XXIX, no. 1, 2005.
Askari, S.H., 'Qutban's Mrigavati', *Journal of the Bihar Research Society*, 1955.
———, 'The Correspondence of the Fourteenth Century Sufi Saints of Bihar With the Contemporary Sovereigns of Delhi and Bengal', *Journal of the Bihar Research Society*, March 1956.
Digby, Simon, 'Add Al-Quddus Gangohi (1456–1537 A.D.): The Personality and Attitude of a Medieval Indian Sufi', *Medieval India: A Miscellany*, vol. 3, Aligarh: AMU, 1975.
Dikshit, P.N., 'Gleanings on the Bhaktmala', *JRAS*, 1909, 1910.
Habib, Irfan, 'The Political Role of Shaikh Ahmad Sirhindi and Shah Waliullah', Proceedings of Indian History Congress (23rd Session, Aligarh, 1960), part I, Calcutta, 1961.
Habib, Mohammad, 'Chishti Mystic Records of the Sultanate Period', *Medieval India Quarterly*, no. 2, Aligarh, October 1950.
Hasan, S. Nurul, '*Sahifa-i Nat-i Muhammadi* of Zia-uddin Barani', *Medieval India Quarterly*, vol. 1, no. 3, Aligarh, 1950.
Iraqi, Shahabuddin 'Historical and Religious Dimensions of Dadupanthi Sources', *Islamic Culture*, Hyderabad, vol. LXX, no. 3, July 1977.
———, 'Historical Importance of the Literature of Prannami Sect', *Islamic Culture*, vol. LXXV, no. 4, October 2001.
———, 'Dadu's Relations with the Rulers of His Time', *Medieval India 2*, Delhi: Manohar, 2008.
———, The Rise of Politics and Armed Resistance in Sikkhism', *Islamic Culture*, Hyderabad, vol. LXXVII, no. 4, October 2004.
———, 'The Satnami Sect of Narnaul', *U.P. Historical Review*, Allahabad, vol. 1, no. 1, 1982.
Lal, K.S., 'Nasiruddin Khusrau Shah', *Journal of Indian History*, vol. XXIII, part 3, December 1944.
Mac Donald, D.B., 'The Life of Al-Gazzali', *JAOS*.
Monier-Williams, Monier, 'Indian Theistic Reformers', *Journal of Asiatic Society*, London, 1881.

Nizami, K.A., 'Naqshbandi Influence on Mughal Rulers and Politics', *Islamic Culture*, Hyderabad, Jubilee Number, vol. XXV/1, 1951.

———, 'The Shattari Saints and their Attitude Towards the State', in *Medieval India Quarterly*, October 1950.

———, 'The Suhrawardi Silsilah and its Influences on Medieval Indian Politics', *Medieval India Quarterly*, July–October 1957, vol. III, nos. 1 & 2.

———, 'Attitude of Muslim Mystics Towards Society and State during the Sultanate Period', *Sanskrite*, Delhi, 1996.

Ranade, P.V., 'Feudal Content of Maharashtra Dharma', *Indian Historical Review*, New Delhi: ICHR, 1974.

Sharma, R.S., 'Problem of Transition from Ancient to Medieval in Indian History', *Indian Historical Review*, New Delhi: ICHR, 1974.

Siddiqui, I.H., 'The Composition of Nobility under the Lodi Sultans', *Medieval India—A Miscellany*, vol. IV, Aligarh, 1977.

———, 'The Pir and Murid: A Case Study of the Sufis of Suhrawardi Silsilah in India during the Thirteenth and Fourteenth Centuries', *Hamdard Islamicus*, vol. XXI, no. 3. July–September 1998.

———, 'Social Mobility in the Delhi Sultanate', *Medieval·India*, vol. I, Aligarh, 1992.

Singh, Fauja, 'Foundation of the *Khalsa* Commonwealth, Ideological Aspects', *Punjab Past and Present*, vol. V, part 1, Patiala, April 1971.

Singh, Ganda, 'Development of Sikh Though', *Punjab Past and Present*, vol. II, part 1, Patiala, April 1968.

Verma, Dhirendra, 'Kya Do Sau Bawan Vaishnavon Ki Varta Gokulnath Krit Hai', *Hindustani*, 1932.

Zilli, I.A., 'Early Chishtis and the State', *Sufi Cults and the Evolution of Medieval Indian Culture*, ed. Anup Taneja, New Delhi: ICHR, 2003.

Index

Abdullah, Shah 85
Adi Granth and Gurmukhi script by Guru Angad 124, *see also Guru Granth Sahib*
Akbar 43–4, 110, 118; accession to throne 77; and land for Sikhs 172; his liberal policy 44–5; meeting Surdas 238–9; and Sufis 74–5
Alberuni 84; on social conditions 35
Alvar saints 103–4
Amardas, Guru 172
Amolakdas 206
Anbhai Sargarh 128
Angad, Guru 134
Arjan, Guru 124, 172, 180; fiscal policy of 174–5; on idea of equality 184–5; Jahangir's impression of 173
Arti 267
Auliya, Shaikh Nizamuddin 56, 61–2
Aurangzeb 76

Babur 42–3; on religious tolerance 44; to widow of Rana Sanga 44
Badauni 44
Badshah-i Islam 30
Bahlul, Shaikh 77
Baillie on Islamic law 34
Bakharzi, Shaikh Saifuddin 73
Balban 38
Barani, Ziauddin 29–30, 65; on Islamic law 34; on Rai Bhiru Bhatti, 41; on spirituality 60; works of 29, 32–3

Barwaris 38
Bauls 105
Bhagavat Purana 102–3
Bhagvatism 103
Bhakti movement 258; facets of 264; for liberal ideas 245; in northern india 107–11
bhakti saints and concepts of Islam 109
bhakti, hymns 103; literature 115, 245
Bhaktmala of Nabhadas 111, 116, 145
Bhaktmala of Raghavadas 116
Bhaktnamavali of Dhrudas 116
Bhao Sindhu ki Varta of Gokul 119
Bhasha as Sadhukkari 260
Bhim 42
Bhushan, Braj 121
Bibi, Madhava 105
Bihari, Ahmad 42–3, 105
Bijak for Kabirpanthis 267
Billah, Khwaja Baqi 80
Birbhadara 105
Bitaks 121–2
Brahman 35, 159, 265; to realize *jizyah* from Hindus 37; and tax exemption 31
Bukhari, Sayyed, as Makhdum-i Jahanian 69

caste discrimination, Kabir and Raidas on 261–2
Chaitanya 134, 265–6; Krishna bhakti of 265–6
Chaitanya Sect 122

Index

Chand, Prithi 180
Chand, Tara 109, 152; on conception of Nirvana 249; on Qutbuddin Aibak 39–40
Chandayan of Mulla Daud 244
Chandragupta II 103
Chaturvedi, P.R. 105
Chishti *khanqahs* 242
Chishti mystic centres 56
Chishti saints 55–6; and *jagirs* 62
Chishti, Khwaja Muinuddin 61, 85
Chishtia *silsilah* 61–4; of Khwaja Abu Ishaq Shami 56
conversions 250–3; and Sikh gurus 183–4

Dadu 110, 116, 134, 135, 189–91, 258, 267; and Akbar 195–6; his bhakti 192; and caste system 191–2; on celibacy 200; Dadu Dwar at Naraina 199; disciples of 201; disputes among followers of 198; followers of 194–5; and Hindu element 200; Jan Gopal on 196–7; on living and doing good deeds 193–4; and Man Singh 197; Narayandas on 196; a Nirguna Bhakt 195; his political ideology 196; and salvation 192; and sectarian consciousness 200; on self-control 194; on self-restraint 196; on spirituality 193; teachings of 194; temple of white marble 207
Dadu Janma Lila Parichaya by Jan Gopal 116, 195
Dadu Mahavidyalaya 126–9
Dadupanth 124; sources of 135
Dadupanthi Nagas 197, 202–8; and Khalsa 205; under Santokhdas 204
Dalail-i Firuzshahi 42

Dasbodh of Ramdas 216–17
Dehlavi, Shaikh Abdul Haq Muhaddis 30, 80, 242, 267; and his *Akhbar-ul-Akhyar* 144
Desika, Vedanta 104
Dev, Kishan 201
Dhanna 110
Dharkari 214

Eknath 214

Fakhri-i-Mudabbir and Sultan Qutbuddin Aibak 38
Farid, Baba 135
Farr-i Izadi concept of and kingship 29
Fazl, Abul 238; his *Ain-i-Akbari* 144; on Shaikh Muhammad Ghaus 78
festivals, Hindu and Muslim 41
Firdausis *silsilah* 73–4

Gangohi, Shaikh Abdul Quddus 64, 243
Ganj-i Shakar, Shaikh Fariduddin 56, 61
Gazruni, Shaikh Safiuddin 55–6
Gharibdas 124
Ghaus, Shaikh Muhammad 243; as Shattari saint 86
Ghazali, Imam 55–6; 61; on achieving true knowledge 259
Ghaznavi, Sayyed Nooruddin Mubarak 65
Ghiyasuddin, Sultan 77; death of 63
Grierson, George 102
Gugga Pir 246
Gunganja-namah by Jagannathdas 130
Guru Granth Sahib 124–6, 134–6, 259, 267
Gwaliori, Syed Muhammad Ghaus 77
Gyandev or Gyaneshwar 213

Habib, Mohammad 30, 36–7; on Alauddin 39; on popular *Malfuzat* 250–1
Habibullah, Shah 74
Haq, Shaikh Abdul 75
Hargobind, Guru 173–4
Haridas, Guru 134
Hindawi, Shaikh Farid 242
Hindi Sahitya Sammelan 128
Hindu artisans 36–7; as Multani traders 39; as Sultans mercenaries 40
Hindu–Muslim, cult of *pirs* 246; reconciliation 108–10; unity 43, 184
Hindus 252; Alauddin Khalji employed 40; in Ghiyasuddin Tughluq's army 40; and Muhammad bin Tughluq 40; joining Jalaluddin Khalji 38; and Islamic canon law 34; and Muslims in Khusrau Shah's army 38; rebuilding temples 37; Sufi attitude towards 252–3; in Sultans administration 39; Waheed Husain on 34
Hujwiri, Shaikh Ali of Ghazna 55
human gurus 260
Humayun 44
Humayun, Sultan Alauddin 74

Ibn-i Arabi, Shaikh Muhiuddin 55–6; his *Awarif-ul Ma'arif* 55; works of 55
India(n), Arabs establishing *junus* (armies) and *amsar* (cities) in 37; merchants 39; Turkish conquest as *jihad* 29; Ghorian conquest of 29; Ghuri conquest 34–5; invasion and rulers of 45
Isami on Sultans 40, 42

Jagan 116
Jagannathdas 127
Jahangir, death of 174
Jain images in Etah 41
Jaipur, battles of 203–4
Jait Sahib 202–3
Jalaluddin, Sayyed 69
Jamali 71
jatis 214–15
Jawahir-i Khamsa by Syed Muhammad Ghaus 87
jihad, and Akbar 43; and Babur's war on Hindu rulers 43–4; Ghazi Malik declares 38
Jinprabha 42
jizyah 30–1; abolition of 45; on Christians 31; and Delhi Sultans 32

Kabir 110, 116, 144, 258–9, 267; against reciting *mantras* 160; his belief in *anubhava jnana* 148–9; his *Bijak as Khas Granth* 259; concept of *maya* 148; on contentment 157; on corruption 155; on disciples 157–8; on governments 157; incarnations 260; on *munsif* 155; his *Parchai* 116; on political authorities 156; on scriptures 259; on elite 157; on wealth accumulation 156; on zamindar (Thakur) 155
Kabir Chaura section 161
Kabirpanth, formation of 158–9; sources of 124
Kabirpanthis 232–3; wear *dwadash tilak* 160
Kabuli, Yahya 243
Kaki, Shaikh Qutbuddin Bakhtiyar 56; visits Iltutmish's court 61
Kalidas Harzara by Kalidas Trivedi 116
Kalimullah, Shah 74
karkhanas 36
Kavi Mala by Tursidas Nranjani 116

Kevaldas of Udehi 203
Khalji, Alauddin 33, 62, 83; and Hindus 40; marries Hindu Kamla Devi 41; and Qazi Mughisuddin 263
Khalji, Jalaluddin 33
Khalji, Qutbuddin Mubarak 38
Khalji, Sultan Mahmud Shah 76–7
Khalsa 177–8, 201
Khan, Akat 38
Khan, Khizr 39
Khan, Qutbuddin 121
Khan-i Khana, Abdur Rahim 80
khanqah of Shaikh Wajihuddin 78
Khatris of Punjab 39
Khilafat-i Rashida, fall of 65
Khusrau, Amir 242–3
Kirti, Bhallarka Sinha 42
Krishna bhakti 107–8
Kumbhandas 238

Lal, K.S. 38
Laldas, Swami 121
Lalla or Lalded 106
Lallu Maharaj 121
Lodi Sultans 154; religious policy of 43
Lodi, Bahlul 70
Lodi, Sikandar 71; K.S. Lal on 43
Lokacharya, Pillali 104

Madar, Shah 247
Madho, Faqih Shaikh 251–2, 267
Maharashtra Dharma 213, 262; as cult of Vitthal 213
Mahdavi movement 111
Mal, Dhir 180
Maneri, Shaikh Sharfuddin Yahya 60
Mansur al-Hillaj, doctrine of 249
Maratha uprising 215
Maratha *watandars* 221–2
Mardan, Shaikh Ali 75
Maths 158–9

maya, concept of 249
militant on *dharma* of Ramdas 221
Minhaj Siraj on Qutlugh Khan 38
Mira Bai 134
Mirza, Umar Shaikh 79
Mohammad, Syed 111
Mohanji 'Daftari' 135
Mubarak, Syed Nuruddin 65
Mughal conquest of Ahmadnagar 215
Muhibullah, Shah 74
Multani, Shaikh Ruknuddin 67
Muneri, Shaikh Sharafuddin Yahya 73, 242
Musa, Shaikh 75
Mushtaqi, Shaikh Rizqullah 242
Muslim(s), and Hindus, discrimination among 32–3; invasion 117; rulers appointment of pandits 34; unity among 36; slavery in 36
Muzaffar, Shaikh 73

Nabhadas' *Bhaktmala* 111, 116, 145
Nagari Pracharini Sabha at Varanasi 129, 133
Nagas as militant force 201; and revolt of 1857 205–6; under Ram Krishandas 203
Nagauri, Shaikh Hamiduddin 62
Nahta, Agarchand, Bikaner 129
Naik, Malik 38
Nakhshabi, Ziauddin's *Tutinama* 42
Namdev or Nama 213–14
Nanak, Guru 110, 116, 134, 258, 168; and *avatar* theory 181; on Brahmans and Kshatriyas 182, 183; his followers 181; on impurity 182; on Muslim rulers 170; on political power 170; political views of 168; on religious authorities 183; on salvation 182; on *sangat* and *pangat* 182; and scriptural

Index

authority 182; on wealth accumulation 181–2
Naqshbandi *silsilah* 79–82
Naqshbandi, Khwaja Bahauddin 79
Naqshbandi, Khwaja Muinuddin 85–6
Naraindas 117, 127
Nawahun 195
Nayanar or Nayanmar saints 103
Nimbarka Sect 122
Niranjanpanth 116
Niranjanpanthi compilations 133
Niranjanpanthi literature 124
Nirguna 258
Nirguna Bhakti 150
Nizami, K.A. 110, 134–5
Nizamuddin, Shaikh 62–4
Nooruddin, Shaikh 106; his Rishi order of Sufis 245
Nuruddin, Syed 65–6

Panchavani 129, 259, 267; collections 131–2
Panchayatan 124
Panchvani of Dadupanthis 126
Pipa 110
Pothi Gyan Bani of Satnami Sect of Narnaul 123
Pranami or Prannathi Sect 225, 262
Prannath 121; against Aurangzeb 226–7; in favour of Chhatrasal 227; his *Kayamat Nama* 228; his *Kulzum Sharif* 119, 225; as political figure 226–8; his *Qayamatnama* 263; on unity of religions 225–6; works of 225
Premakhyan literature 244
Punch Sakha 105
Pushti Marga 237; literature of 117

Qadiri *silsilah* 74–6
Qadiri, Mir Muhammad Ali 75
Qadiri, Shaikh Abdur Rahman 86
Qahir, Shaikh Najibuddin Abdul 65

Qasim, Mohammad bin 31
Quddus, Shaikh 248
Qulzum Sharif of Prannath 119, 225
Qureshi, I.H. on Sultan 30

Radha–Vallabha Sect 237
Raghavadas's *Bhaktamala* 116
Rai, Har 175
Raidas, Guru 110
Rajabdas 135
Rajwade, V.K. 216
Ram bhakti 107–8
Ram, Hirdaya 203
Ram, Mahant Dalai 207
Ramanand, Cunningham on 109
Ramananda, works of 108–9
Ramanuja 103–4; Vishishta Advaitavad by 104
Ramdas, Guru 172, 214, 216; his *Anandvanabhuvana* 221, 263; on Aurangzeb 219; on communal harmony 263; on cultural unity and identity 220–1; on destiny 218; establish *maths* 217–18; and Marathas 219–20; poetic work 217; on politics 219; relationship between Shivaji 222; on Shivaji 219–20
Rathor, Maharaja Yashwant (Jaswant) Singh 116
religious tolerance 41
revolutionary saints 111
Rishi, Ganga 238
Rishi, Nand 106, *see also* Nooruddin, Shaikh
Ruknuddin, Shaikh 243
Rumi, Maulana Jalaluddin 55
Rushd Nama of Shaikh Abdul Quddus Gangohi 248

Sadh Sect founded by Bir Bhan 229
Sadruddin, Sayyed, as Raju Qattal 69–70

288 Index

Saguna Marga 258
sahaja, state of 105
Sahib, Jait 200–1
Sam, Sultan Muizuddin bin 37
samas, sufi *khanqahs* 243
Samauddin, Shaikh 71
Sani, Shaikh Abdul Qadir 74
Santokhdas, death of 206
sants, false belief and superstitions 261
Sant-sahitya 115
Sapru clan 241
Sarbangi Chintamani by Gopaldas 129
Sarbangi or *Sarvanga-yoga* of Rajabdas 129–31
Sarkar, Jadunath 122
Satnami Panth 230
Satnami Sect of Narnaul 229, 262–3; code of conduct 231–2; on communal differences 230–1; on false practices 233; on Hindu–Muslim unity 234; identity of 231; and Kabir 232–3; on other communities 233–4; on pandit and qazi 233; on poor 231; *Pothi Gyan Bani* 229; revolted against Aurangzeb 229; on women 231
sattada mudlias 104
sectarian hagiolographies 115
Shah Pir 78
Shah, Ahmad 82
Shah, Firoz, his state policy and *sharia* 41; appointed Rajputs 41
Shah, Husain of Ghaur 122
Shah, Launka 106
Shah, Mulla 75
Shah, Nasiruddin Khusrau 38
Shahjahan 174
Shaikhs, Chishti 62–3, 247–8
Shaivism and Vaishnavism 103

Sharafuddin, Shaikh, Hindi poetry of 242
sharia 30, 34, 263; Hindu and Muslim 37
Sharma, Krishna 106
Sharma, Purohit Hari Narayan 129
Shattari, Shaikh Bahauddin 86
Shattaris silsilah by Shaikh Bayazid Bistami 76–9
Shekhara, Raj 42
Shri Dasam Guru Granth Sahebji by Guru Gobind Singh 126
Sijzi, Khwaja Muinuddin 56
Sikh movement 180
Sikhism 262; *varnas* and women 184
Singh, Guru Gobind 124, 175–7, on idea of equality 184–5; military measures by 177; met Bahadur Shah 179; *Zafarnama* to Aurangzeb 179
Singh, Jagat, death of 205
Singh, Jaswant 121
Singh, Maharaja Ram 205
Singh, Raja Bhagwat 117
Singh, Raja Sawai Jai 203
Sirhindi, Shaikh Ahmad, known as Mujaddid-i-Alf Sani 80–1
Srivastava, K.L. 36
Sufi(s) beliefs, cross-breeding of 245; in Indian society 82–7; *pas-i anfas* 106; poetry 244, 253
Sufism, institutional structure of 56–60; and state 60–1
Suhrawardi *silsilah* 64–72
Suhrawardi, Shaikh Shihabuddin 45
Sundardas, Shyam, his *Kabir-Granthawali* 128
Surdas 134
Suri, Gunabhadra 42
Suri, Jinprabha 42
Suri, Mahendra 42

Index 289

Suri, Munibhadra 42
Suri, Puran Chandra 41
Suri, Sena 42
Suri, Somaprabha 42
Suri, Somatika 42
Swamdas 127
Swami, Bahurang 121
Swami, Hansraj 121
Swami, Mukund 121
Swami, Taran 106

Tahmasp, Shah 44
Tegh Bahadur, Guru 175
temples as Mahoba and Khajuraho 41
Tenkalai and the Vadagali 104
Tibbi-i Sikandarshahi 43
Tonga, battle of 204
Tughluq, Muhammad bin 38–9, 63, 73; in Hindu festivals 41–2
Tughluq, Sultan Firoz Shah 69
Tukaram 214, 216
Tulsidas 111, 134, 171, 237–8, 264–6; writings of 123
Turkish Sultans 40–1

Ulama and Sufis 263–4
Uttarardha 201

Vaishnava sects 104
'Vaishnava–Sahajiyas' group 105
Varkari 214; on devotees of Vithoba 219
varnas 35–6; outcastes *antyaja* 35
Vedas 104
Vrishni as Vasudev 102

Wahdat-ul Wajud, doctrine of 249
Wahid, Mir Abdul's *Haqaiq-i Hindi* 243
Wali, Banwaridas 267
Waliullah, Shah 82
Wilson, H.H. 102

yavanis 29
yogic practice of *ulti-sadhana* 248
Yogis and *pirs*, as wonder-workers 247; and Sufis 246–50
Yusuf, Shaikh 70

Zakariya, Shaikh Bahauddin 56, 65–7, 71
Zakariya, Shaikh Yusuf 70
zawabit 29
Zilli, I.A. 62
zimmi to non-Muslims 31